fishes of
lake tanganyika

pierre brichard

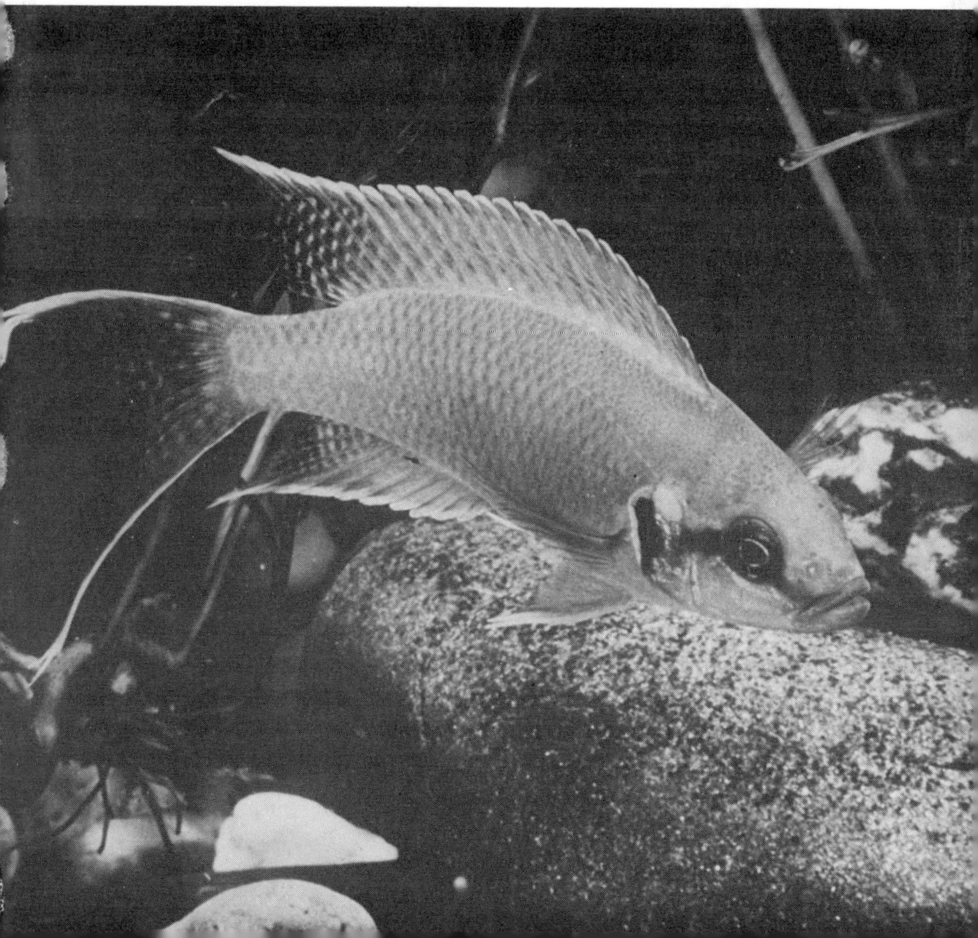

Front Cover: *Lamprologus leleupi.* Photo by Hans J. Richter.

Frontispiece: *Lamprologus brichardi.* Photo by Hans J. Richter.

ISBN 0-87666-464-8

Copyright © 1978 by T.F.H. Publications, Inc.

Distributed in the U.S.A. by T.F.H. Publications, Inc., 211 West Sylvania Avenue, P.O. Box 27, Neptune City, N.J. 07753; in England by T.F.H. (Gt. Britain) Ltd., 13 Nutley Lane, Reigate, Surrey; in Canada to the book store and library trade by Clarke, Irwin & Company, Clarwin House, 791 St. Clair Avenue West, Toronto 10, Ontario; in Canada to the pet trade by Rolf C. Hagen Ltd., 3225 Sartelon Street, Montreal 382, Quebec; in Southeast Asia by Y.W. Ong, 9 Lorong 36 Geylang, Singapore 14; in Australia and the south Pacific by Pet Imports Pty. Ltd., P.O. Box 149, Brookvale 2100, N.S.W., Australia. Published by T.F.H. Publications Inc. Ltd., The British Crown Colony of Hong Kong.

CONTENTS

FOREWORD..........................5
INTRODUCTION by Prof. Max Poll..............7
1. GEOGRAPHY AND GEOLOGICAL HISTORY
  11
2. LIFE IN THE LAKE OTHER THAN FISHES
  21
3. ECOLOGY OF THE LAKE FISHES............34
4. SURVEY OF LAKE TANGANYIKA AND THEIR
   ENDEMISM.............................67
5. BRIDGES AND FORDS....................83
6. GENETIC DYNAMISM.....................87
7. REPRODUCTIVE MODES OF LAKE FISHES...105
DESCRIPTIONS OF THE FISHES OF LAKE
   TANGANYIKA..........................143
    Cichlids............................143
    Non-Cichlids........................396
        Polypteridae.......................397
        Lepidosirenidae....................396
        Clupeidae..........................398
        Mormyridae.........................400
        Kneriidae..........................401
        Characidae.........................402
        Citharinidae.......................405
        Cyprinidae.........................407
        Bagridae...........................416
        Mochokidae.........................421
        Amphiliidae........................425
        Clariidae..........................407

  Malapteruriidae 429
  Cyprinodontidae 430
  Centropomidae 434
  Anabantidae 436
  Mastacembelidae 437
  Tetraodontidae 440
BIBLIOGRAPHY 442
INDEX 445

Foreword

When I am meeting people for the first time and they ask me about my job, I answer "I am an aquarium fish collector." Most of the time I have to explain what that means because not many people know much about this activity. And then they say: "You are really a lucky man to be in contact with nature all the time, far away from the civilized world, its problems and its mess." And indeed I am a very lucky man, especially since I started—in my late forties—to dive with SCUBA gear in the underwater world of Lake Tanganyika.

After many years of collecting tropical fishes in the murky shallows of the rivers of Central Africa without ever having a chance to watch them in their natural habitat and understand some of the riddles which kept popping up from a blind collecting method, I could at last, in the clear waters of Lake Tanganyika, see the fishes in their natural surroundings. Moreover, thanks to the compressed air tanks I carried on my back (SCUBA), I could spend as many hours as I wanted to studying the habitats, the fish populations which live there and their behavior.

Although these explorations were the first of such intensity to have been made in the lake and were made repeatedly over a period of five years on a stretch of coast not longer than 150 km, they have left more problems unsolved and more riddles open to question than they have helped to explain some of the major phenomena related to freshwater ichthyology.

Lake Tanganyika is a fantastically rich, infinitely complex biosystem, and it is beyond my powers and poor practical knowledge to tell everything about the lake and to give answers to all the riddles. The purpose of this book is thus to tell what I and the people I work with have seen, outline some of the phenomena and suggest, very cautiously and with the risk of error, explanations—even when going against established and accepted theories! For more than 15 years all systematic research on the lake fauna has been, for all practical purposes, abandoned. Some of the ideas outlined in this book are perhaps too controversial and might not be borne out by further study. My objective would be reached, however, if field studies might be given a new impetus.

To all those who during these many years have helped me gather the data and discussed them with me, to Mireille, my daughter, to Jacques and Andre Schreyen, to Thierry, my son, my thanks and love.

Pierre Brichard

About the Author

Pierre Brichard was born in Belgium in 1921. His involvement with fish started, rather reluctantly, when he as a teenager helped his father in his fish-farming experiments before World War II. He started collecting fishes, as a hobby, in the Congo River in 1949 and became a professional fish collector and exporter in 1955. As such Pierre was the first in the Congo to export tropical aquarium fishes to the United States.

From the start Pierre Brichard was helped by his daughter Mireille (who was only 11 years old at the time). After having built collecting stations for the Stanley Pool and Regina Rapids species, he started other stations for estuarine fishes and virgin forest specimens. He left Zaire in 1971 to start the "Fishes of Burundi" collecting station in Bujumbura, Burundi on Lake Tanganyika. This operation was handed over to his daughter (who had in the meantime received a master's degree in biology from the University of Kinshasa).

Along with the members of the "Fishes of Burundi" team (composed of Pierre's son Thierry, Jacques Schreyen and Andre Schreyen), Pierre and his daughter explored the underwater slopes during more than 1,000 individual dives, lasting in excess of 1,500 hours, between 1971 and the time of the writing of this book. This intensive exploration by SCUBA (dives were made repeatedly along the same coastlines month after month) uncovered many data on the fish populations, their behavior and their relationships to their habitat.

Having freed himself from many chores, Pierre Brichard is now able to concentrate on research along the southern coast of Lake Tanganyika.

Introduction

There are many reasons for the attraction which hobbyists and naturalists alike feel for the Lake Tanganyika fish fauna. First of all, as a natural laboratory the lake is quite exceptional. There life forms, and especially fishes, have been placed in unusual surroundings, and the prevailing conditions of this ecosystem have apparently been very propitious to their speciation.

With a maximum depth of 1,470 meters, Tanganyika is the second deepest lake on our planet, second only to Lake Baikal, which is 1,740 meters deep. But the location of Lake Tanganyika within the tropical zone has resulted in an exceptional set of conditions. Lake Baikal has been colonized by life forms down to the deepest water layer because oxygen is present throughout the lake in sufficient quantities, and these forms include a rich cold and temperate water fish fauna.

In strong contrast to this cold lake, Tanganyika harbors life only in its upper layers, as only those layers with the indispensable oxygen can sustain life. Deeper down, around the 200 meter level, the lake waters, laden with hydrogen sulphide and depleted of oxygen, are dead and void of life. Under such conditions only coastal waters less than 200 meters deep and superficial open waters have been colonized.

The exceptional length of the sinuous coastline, with its alternating steep rocky slopes and sand beaches, interrupted also by torrents, slow-moving river estuaries, or even swamps, has created a wide variety of peripheral habitats. Sometimes very shallow—and then with sand or mud floors—at other times steep and composed of rock, all these habitats are spread unevenly around the lake coasts and have formed for the littoral fauna many isolated ecological niches.

Aside from these shores, one has to keep in mind that the surface of the lake (rippled by daily winds and thus with a high oxygen content) and the underlying layers (when deeper than 100 meters) are separate and entirely different habitats. The deep layers of the oxygen-bearing belt, because of the dwindling supply of oxygen, the dim light, if any, and the pressure involved, especially add to the variety of the very peculiar natural conditions prevailing in the lake and to which the fish fauna had to adapt.

The African fish fauna is especially rich in species belonging to the tropical cyprinids, silurids, mormyrids, characids and cichlids, to name only the families playing a leading role. But in the Great African lakes, and mainly in Lake Tanganyika, the first four groups are relegated to a very secondary place if we disregard the affluent rivers of the respective lake basins.

In strong opposition to this trend are the cichlids, which have assumed a very dominant position. This is also the case in Lakes Malawi and Victoria, which have been populated by even more cichlid species than Lake Tanganyika. But in the first two lakes, though they have specialized and developed as much endemicity as they did in Lake Tanganyika, the cichlids are of less interest because they formed "species flocks" originating from a few ancestors, all of which belonged to the genus *Haplochromis*. In Lake Tanganyika the systematic differentiation of the cichlids has reached much greater levels; there are more than 35 genera in this lake, and some of them are very differentiated. These genera are represented by a variable number of species, which can be quite high.

Why did the cichlids alone really succeed in colonizing the lake and then start to divide into so many distinct forms? It is very hard to tell why a given group of fish becomes dominant, but it appears highly probable that the special ecological conditions of the lake are responsible for the speciation process of the cichlids. Outstanding among these conditions is probably the ionic qualities of the water (alkaline with a high pH), which is much to the liking of the cichlids.

As for the exceptional multiplication of the many "species flocks" among the cichlids in the lake, the physical isolation of the lake—without any outlet for most of its long geological history—and its ecological isolation—due to its special marine-like life conditions—have allowed one group of fish to proliferate without outside influences. This group was protected from competition, living in a wide range of habitats and ecological niches. With time this led to the birth of some most remarkable adaptations to the various surroundings. There is thus a direct relationship between the many ecological niches and their respective fish populations, in species as well as genera.

Lake Tanganyika in the middle of Africa is as much isolated as a volcanic island in the middle of the ocean and, as with islands, local fauna populations have grown from the only faunistic stock which succeeded in reaching the isolated habitat. They then differentiated to become adapted to the many available ecological niches.

Ichthyologists were impressed from the days of the lake's discovery at the end of the last century by the unusual features of its fish and their similarities to marine species. Discoveries started to pile up, but one had to wait until the Belgian exploration by the Hydrobiological Mission to the lake in 1946 (in which I took part as ichthyologist) before it was possible to realize and understand the importance of the lake fish fauna.

Because of this long exploration I was fortunate to be able to increase by one-third the number of identified species, to understand that there were several biocoenoses (specific associations), each typical of one of the various lacustrine habitats, and to identify the associations.

For the first time marine-type fishing gear—such as trawl nets—was used in the lake and allowed more extensive fishing than the traditional coastal fishing methods would permit. These trawl nets were dragged on shallow mud flats in front of some river estuaries, sand plains near the shores and progressively deeper bottoms. This method enabled us to discover that fauna disappeared along with oxygen and the appearance of hydrogen sulphide long before our nets reached the deep lifeless bottom.

This exploration increased to no small extent our knowledge of the phenomena involved. Not only was the lake covered as an ecological system, but also its fauna and flora in relation to the various habitats. The scientific results were published by the Belgian Institute for Natural Sciences in Brussels.

Unfortunately, back in 1946 it was still too early to have included underwater diving in our exploration, as this technique was then just being developed. Needless to say, the beautiful crystal clear and blue waters of the lake offer excellent opportunities for underwater exploration on many stretches of the shore, and Pierre Brichard showed that it was the best way to collect fishes in holes and recesses and to secure rare or even unknown specimens, as well as to get close for direct observations. Pierre Brichard's book shows that this technique, when backed by a curious and searching mind, can secure many scientific observations in the fields of ecology and behavior.

By no means has the full inventory of the lake fish fauna been completed as yet. In spite of the many discoveries in recent years, Brichard has demonstrated that many more species remain to be discovered—and not the least important ones—with intense searching and even without fishing all around the lake shores. That many more riches in the lake remain untapped as yet is proved by the fact that several species found years ago have yet to be rediscovered in spite of the many explorations made since their first capture.

Pierre Brichard, with more luck perhaps than any other, succeeded in discovering several new interesting species which I have had the privilege to describe. Endowed with a keen mind and being an excellent naturalist, Pierre Brichard, during his many dives in the lake, has accumulated many very good observations on the habitat and behavior of the species. His on-the-spot notes are of exceptional interest and fill a very important gap in our knowledge of the lake; they demonstrate the very long experience of the author with the underwater exploration of the lake. His comments on the reproduction of some species are to be put among the best to come from Africa in recent years.

Cichlids have a most interesting behavior in a tank, and many of the Lake Tanganyika species are among the most beautiful I know of. Pierre Brichard's book will arouse the enthusiasm of the increasing numbers of those who share his interest in the Lake Tanganyika fishes.

Prof. Max Poll

1. Geography and Geological History

Lake Tanganyika spreads its turquoise waters between 3°20'S and 8°45'S latitude and between 29°E and 31°E longitude, thus roughly on a north-south bearing just south of the Equator. It fills most of a deeply cut rift, part of the Great African Rift Valley, which extends from the Danakil Coast on the Red Sea to Mozambique, a distance well over 4,000 km. The lake valley extends for more than 450 miles (nearly 700 km). The width of the lake averages about 40 km, but the maximum of 80 km is reached in the central part of the lake. To illustrate these abstract figures, let us say that the length of Lake Tanganyika equals the distance between Brussels and Berlin, between Paris and Marseilles or between New York and Cleveland.

To the north the lake borders on a huge alluvial plain filled by the Ruzizi River flowing down from Lake Kivu. The coast is made up entirely of sand beaches and estuary swamps. The western shores are mostly precipitous, as mountains with an average altitude of 3 km plunge directly into the lake at a 30% to 45% gradient. Depths of 1,000 meters have been discovered 3 km off shore.

The northeastern shores line the Congo-Nile Divide, with altitudes to 2.5 km. The mountains then slope down toward the Malagarazi delta. South of the river estuary the slopes rise again to 2.1 km at the Kungwe range. The southeast and southern coastlines are composed of gently rolling hills averaging about 1.5 km.

The underwater profile is a broad "U" with two main basins, the southern with a depth in excess of 1.4 km and the central, reaching 1.3 km, separated by an underwater mount about 600 meters high. The floor of these two basins is formed by a vast plain, gently rolling hills extending from the foot of the western and eastern coastal walls. The central basin is limited to the north by a precipitous wall about 700 meters high extending between the Ubwari Peninsula and the east coast, opening toward the nor-

A view of the lake from the vicinity of Burundi. The total surface of Lake Tanganyika is about 34,000 square kilometers. Photo by Dr. Herbert R. Axelrod.

thernmost section of the lake. This part of the lake, with a depth of about 250 meters, is thus the latest addition to the lake and was flooded only when the lake waters rose over the top of the cliff.

The total surface of the lake is now 34,000 square km or more than the area of Belgium. The volume of water is about 35,000 cubic km (or about half the North Sea). The hydrographic basin covers about 250,000 square km, about the same as the whole of Great Britain.

GEOLOGICAL HISTORY

This lake is probably the oldest of the Rift Valley lakes, and by every available evidence is several million years old. Its birthdate? Near the middle of the Pliocene period, something like 3 to 6 million years ago.

The rift was not cut, as one could imagine, by one gigantic cataclysm, but progressively by the slow sinking of the ground. Counterpressure pushed the adjacent areas upward and slowly built the present mountain ranges lining the lake.

The rift cut across river beds, one of which was the Malagarazi. The river most probably flowed initially into the Congo River (several Congo River fishes still live in its estuary) before it started to empty into the newly caved-in depression.

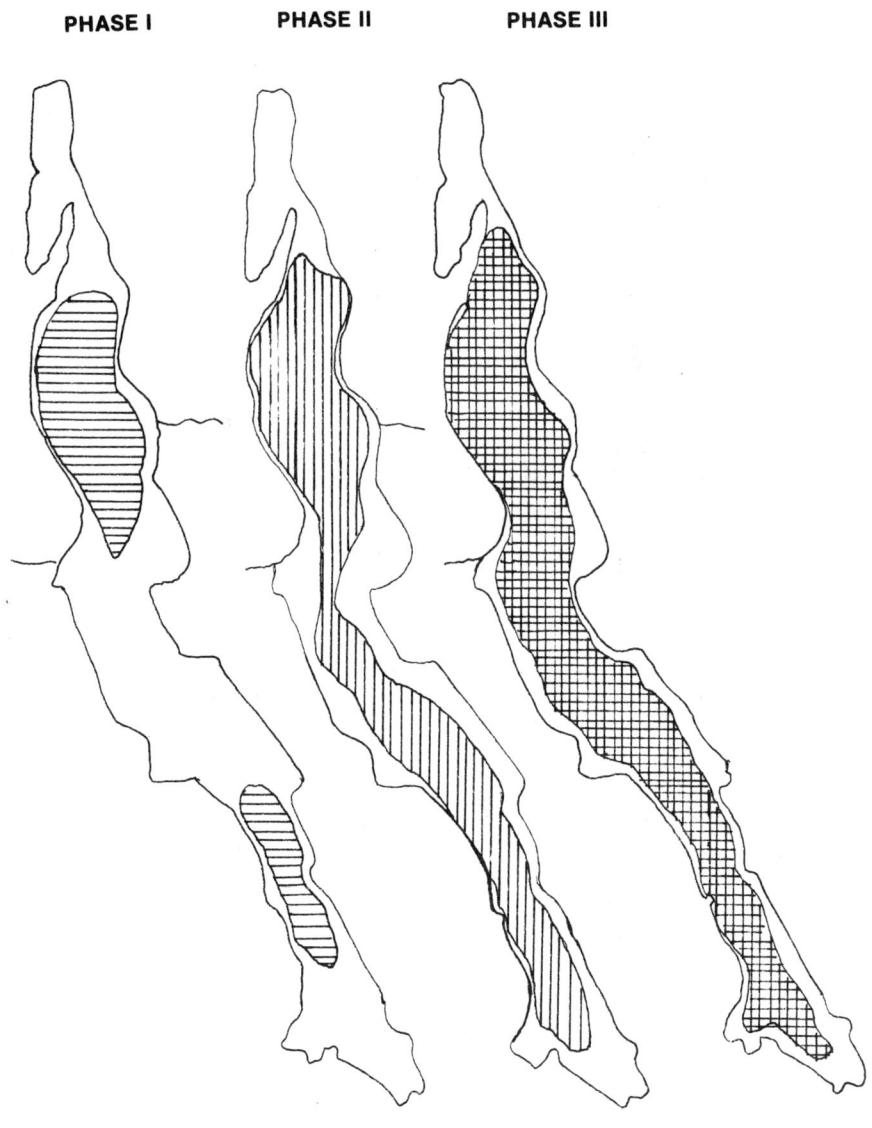

Three phases in the probable evolution of Lake Tanganyika since its birth: Phase I. Two separate lakes with a central mound 500 to 600 meters high. Phase II. The depth of the lake has increased to about 700 meters and the two separate lakes have joined. Phase III. The maximum depth has increased again to 900 meters, 550 meters below the present level. This condition remained for what is believed to be a long period of time. The northern basin is still separate and probably dry.

Heavy cloud cover and heavy rains brought by the clouds contribute to some of the fluctuations of the lake level. Photo by Dr. Herbert R. Axelrod.

Two separate lakes filled the south and central basins, and as the area went through alternate periods of drought or abundant rains, semi-desert or very wet climates, they grew or shrank accordingly. The salinity of the water in the two lakes should thus have varied considerably as water evaporated when the input was small or was much diluted by regular rainfall.

Finally, the two lakes mixed when they bridged the central mound. This process was undoubtedly slow and perhaps was even reversed at times.

The lake level finally reached what it is now, but only after it had been stabilized for a very long time at a level about 550 meters below the present one. The discovery of deeply cut underwater gullies in front of present rivers seems to bear out this theory. These gullies all disappear at 550 meters depth, and they were presumably cut by the cascading torrents on slopes now deeply submerged.

At what time the lake reached its present level, after flooding of the northern mid-cliff valley, is not known. When the lake was discovered by European explorers, it was as it is today.

If, with heavy rains and the accidental obstruction of the Lukuga River outlet, the lake exceeds its present 773 meters altitude, it is not by very much. The last rise was in 1962-63, to 778 meters, and the lake now has been going down ever since at an annual rate of 50 cm.

A semi-arid climate could well drop the level of the lake lower than the Lukuga outlet which, anyhow, doesn't account for more than a few percent of the total water loss. Of the 1.5-meter layer of water brought by rains annually to the lake volume, about 90% is lost again by evaporation alone. Heavy cloud cover restricting evaporation and heavy rains brought by the clouds contribute to some of the level fluctuations.

The Ruzizi and Malagarazi Rivers are the two most important affluents, but countless mountain brooks and torrents add their share of the water input and minerals.

The lake is thus a closed basin, totally dependent on the climatic conditions prevailing in the area. During its long history, it has persisted through many different climates. What we see now is the result of countless momentous evolutions, a fleeting second in the life of the lake.

PHYSICAL PROPERTIES

The lake is the prototype of deep tropical lakes, with little stratification in decreasing temperature layers. In fact, Lake Tanganyika can be said to be remarkably isothermic. In open waters far from shore the temperature at a depth of 10 meters is about 26.5°C, at 1,000 meters it is still 23.3°C, and at 1,400 meters (on the floor) it is even a bit warmer than at 1,000 meters. This means that from the surface to the floor there is only a 3°C drop. This exceptional phenomenon is as yet not very well understood, but the most common explanation is that a slow turnover mixes the water in such a way that it prevents the formation of temperature layers. The turnover could be caused by the daily winds and resulting wave action.

We have personally noted, during many SCUBA dives, strong surface currents sweeping promontories and shallows. No doubt such strong currents could create powerful disturbances deeper down before petering out in the deepest reaches of the lake.

A second point of interest is the slight but noticeable temperature rise close to the bottom. One should remember that the lake is in a tectonic rift with strong volcanic activity and that geothermal radiation through the lake floor is not to be ignored. Also, the presence of thermal springs at the tip of the Ubwari Peninsula (Cape Banza) is well documented. Our team recently discovered underwater springs on the northwestern coast. Of course shallows in well protected bays or the shoreline waters present wider temperature ranges either daily or seasonally.

The *density* of the lake water is also rather constant down to the bottom, and although the rain of settling sedimentary particles has created over millennia a layer on the lake floor sometimes several hundred meters thick, the ion content of the water is very similar throughout all the water layers. This again seems due to a slow turnover, an "updrift" of life-sustaining matter to feed plankton.

Another character of Lake Tanganyika is the relatively shallow layer in which oxygen dissolved in the water can sustain life. In the south this layer might extend 250 meters from the surface. In the north the layer is seldom more than 100 meters thick, with an occasional thinning to 40 or 50 meters. Underneath this no life is possible; the deepest fish catch has been made at a depth of 250 meters in the south.

When an accidental powerful updrift brings "dead" water from the deeper reaches toward shallow slopes, mass killing might occur among the fish population. A whole stretch of coast can thus be devastated in a matter of hours.

In the northern part of the lake at least, the 24°C thermocline and the limits of livable oxygen content are very close to each other, so that most fish never get to live in water cooler than 24°C. This is one of the reasons why the lake fishes are so sensitive to a cold spell.

CHEMISTRY AND TURBIDITY

There is a relatively high quantity of minerals in solution in the lake water (approximately 400 mg per liter), much more than in most African rivers and lakes.

As the lake water is also much warmer than the rivers and mountain torrents flowing into the lake, the colder, denser river water, instead of mixing at once with the lake water, just falls straight toward the bottom along the underwater slopes. In front of river estuaries the surface water is usually crystal clear, but the deep waters are murky. This is especially visible in front of kaolin clay-laden torrents. The whitish water runs straight down the slopes, bathing rocks, rubble and boulders in a ghostly fog only a few inches thick.

Few fish stay for long in such a cool and chemically different habitat. If the river flow is narrow, they cross it quickly; if too broad for them, it is a barrier.

One noteworthy exception to the plunge of river water underneath the lake water is the Malagarazi, whose long delta and meandering bed have given its water time to warm up. When it reaches the lake the river water glides over the surface, spreading out for miles from the confluent and turning the lake a dirty brown up to 10 miles offshore.

The thermal stability of the lake can also be locally affected by tropical downpours and storms. The rain sinks into the lake much faster than one would imagine and might thus also create a slow turnover from the depths.

Over shallows the water is often murky, with visibility eventually cut to a few centimeters; over deep floors far from river estuaries it is usually crystal-clear and totally free from green algae. In the central part of the lake visibility in the rainy season might reach 20 meters vertically and 10 meters laterally. In the northern part of the lake visibility is, at best, cut by half.

CHEMICAL ANALYSIS OF LAKE TANGANYIKA WATER

(Through the courtesy of Dr. Kuferath, member of the 1946–1947 Belgian Hydrobiological Mission.)

Salt	*Mg/l*
Na_2CO_3, anhydrous	125
KCl	59
KNO_3	0.5
Li_2CO_3	4
$CaCO_3$	30
$MgCO_3$	144
$Al_2(SO_4)_3 \cdot 18H_2O$	5
K_2SO_4	4
Na_2SO_4	1
$FeCl_3 \cdot 6H_2O$	0.5
$Na_3PO_4 \cdot 12H_2O$	0.4
Na_2SiO_3	13.5

Several salts in solution in the lake water seem to have a very inhibiting effect on algal growth. . . as they also do, unfortunately, on the effects of several remedies against fish diseases. This has led us to have to sometimes use doses ten times more potent than the dosage we used in the Congo to cure river fishes. On the plus side, we must say that the same lake water prevents the spread or cures the dreadful African "ich." Fishes received from the Congo River and put into our tanks filled with lake water were cured and rid of the parasites in a matter of days.

The pH of Lake Tanganyika is in excess of 9.0, the DH 10° (German) and the conductivity between 550-600° Siemens Hardte. Carbonates account for more than 300 milligrams of the 400 mg per liter total salt content of the water. The other salts are compounds of aluminum, lithium, silica, sodium, etc.

Calcium carbonate, from a depth of 6 meters down, settles on all rocks, embedding them in a crust of calcite, welding all pebbles together until it becomes impossible to lift the smallest stone from the lake floor. This phenomenon is very important as far as ecology is concerned because it builds from rubble a second floor on top of the original one, assembles loose pebbles in caves, labyrinths, holes and all over the slopes and in some cases even keeps overhanging cliffs over steep sand slopes bonded and fast. Innumerable microhabitats are thus created on rock slopes by the carbonate sedimentation. This encrusting process has, to our knowledge, never been studied.

The rocky shores are strewn with big boulders which become broken down into smaller stones, rubble, pebbles, and finally course gravel. Photo by Dr. Herbert R. Axelrod.

SHORES AND FLOORS

Except where coastal plains line the lake shores, the underwater slopes are rather steep. The Malagarazi and Ruzizi deltas are no exceptions. The alluvial cone of the Malagarazi reaches well into the lake, nearly to its middle. It probably has been building up since the early days of the lake. The silt output of the Ruzizi is slowly filling in the northern end of the lake, although the base of the alluvial cone is at 100 meters depth.

The deep floors are usually covered by a fine gray-green mud, as are the shallow floors in wave-protected bays. The shallow floors in unprotected areas, usually lining sand beaches (and some are several miles long), are composed of sand, as the waves make their action felt down to 7 or 8 meters. Because of the waves, sand bars are frequently erected along beaches and shallow bays, leading to the building of lagoons cut off from the lake.

The rocky shores (constantly battered by waves) are strewn with big boulders which in turn are broken into stones, rubble, pebbles and finally coarse gravel. As we will see, this is what will bring the immense variety of fishes to the rock shore populations.

Storms over the lake are a daily occurrence during the rainy season, with the resulting waves reaching 6 meters in height. They are often very dangerous for small or medium sized craft. Water spouts are not uncommon.

HISTORY OF THE FAUNA

From a biological point of view, what are the facts and guidelines which we can derive from the lake's million-year history? Perhaps most important is the long isolation of the lake basin, entirely dependent on the local area for the supply of initial life forms. The second most important fact is that the lake during its long life has been subjected to drastically different climatic conditions, from arid to very wet, with correlated drastic changes in the mineralization of its water. This should have led to successive orientations in the original living organisms.

The relationship of the endemic lake populations, mainly fishes, to those in the rivers nearby is undoubtedly hard to assess. No fossils older than ten or twenty thousand years have been discovered in the area. This is really very young when you keep in mind how long the lake has been there.

The endemicity of the lake fauna is extremely high. The fishes in particular have not settled abroad, nor have many fishes from outside basins reached the lake, even when they could swim upstream from the Congo—up the Lukuga—and settle in the lake. Few have done so, but the presence in the Malagarazi River of Congo River species, and in the lake of a few of these species, might perhaps show that they were in the lake very early.

It is entirely possible that the salinity of the lake, which is said to have been increasing for a long time, has permitted river species in the past to settle and colonize the lake. The present salinity might prevent river species from doing so now.

It is a fact that planorbis snails, abundant in the Ruzizi delta and swamps, die off in the lake. It is also a fact that the endemic fishes from the lake haven't traveled down the Lukuga and settled in the Congo River, and that most of them die in a matter of days when put into water from the torrents flowing into the lake.

The last, and also very important, fact to remember is the shallowness of the life-bearing layer, restricted in fact for most species to the first 50 to 70 meters below the surface. It means that since the lake has started to support life, this layer, rising slowly along the lake slopes, has opened or closed migration routes, isolated or put into contact different local fauna populations, permitted crossbreeding or, on the contrary, forced inbreeding.

The immense variety of the lake fauna there has its explanation, and also its challenge.

Snails of the genus *Planorbis* do not survive in the waters of the lake. Photo by Milan Chvojka.

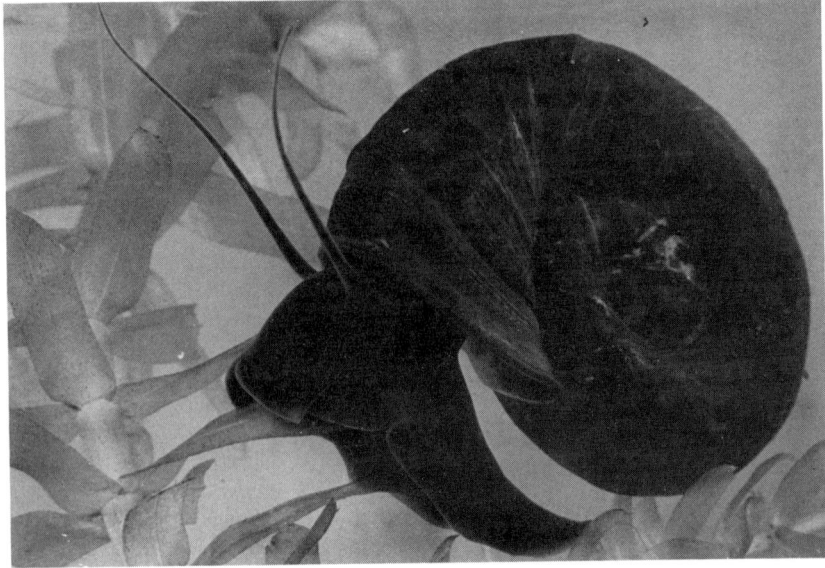

2. Life in the Lake Other Than Fishes

Lake Tanganyika is an unbelievably rich reservoir of endemic plant and animal life, without parallel in the world except for Lake Baikal in Siberia. To describe this life in detail is beyond the scope of this book. But, even if the intricate relationships between the Tanganyika life forms are still unknown territory, after many decades of research we know that they are responsible for and essential to the well-being of the fish populations. As such, they deserve a brief survey in this book so that the reader might gain an idea of the ecosystem the lake fish are part of.

PLANKTON

The lake contains one of the richest assortments of freshwater plankton, both phytoplankton (plants) and zooplankton (animals). The phytoplankton alone includes more than 300 species, with the zooplankton, especially rich in copepods, not far behind. Noteworthy is the absence in the lake proper of *cladocerans* (daphnia), which are found only in the lagoons fringing the beaches or in swamps.

The plankton is concentrated in layers, by day ranging from 50 to 125 meters deep, rising by night toward the surface to a depth of about 10 meters. This daily nyctemeral cycle is followed by identical migrations of clupeids (*Limnothrissa, Stolothrissa,* etc.) whose schools prey on the plankton. At the same time, these clupeids are being preyed upon by predatory fish such as the Tanganyika perch (*Lates angustifrons* or *L. mariae*), species of *Bathybates, Luciolates* and the biggest cichlid in the world, *Boulengerochromis microlepis*.

These clupeid schools, although individual fishes may measure little more than 75 mm (and often less), are incredibly dense. They are the staple food of hundreds of thousands of people, not only around the lake shores but even far away, where they provide essential, and often the sole, supply of animal proteins.

To provide one of the few pieces of information available from official statistics (and only a small one at that) of their economic importance, in Bujumbura, Burundi, their catch, amounting to 90 % of all fishes caught, totalled more than 12,000 tons in 1972. This figure refers to the official catch by commercial trawlers, without any captures by individual fishermen, and thus is only part of the total catch in the northern basin. The center of the lake is known to be richer. Schools of clupeid fishes estimated at 50 tons have been located by echo-soundings. As the clupeids rely entirely on the plankton of the lake for food, it would be very hard to imagine the tremendous weight of the lake plankton.

Of course, the plankton density varies according to the season, and underwater observations by our team have shown that definite patterns do exist in the overall abundance with peaks—one might even say "blooms"—and periodical scarcity. The peaks seem, according to our team, to be related to the mineral input by countless brooks and mountain torrents after the rainy season has started. But no long-term research has been conducted as yet on the plankton in the lake to yield enough light to understand fully the what, why and how of what is happening, nor of the differences which might exist between the "fixed" plankton having taken a permanent hold on the substrate and the floating or "pelagic" forms. This is an essential study to be undertaken, in direct connection with the respective littoral and pelagic fish populations.

AQUATIC PLANTS

Unfortunately for the aquarist, the lake, although in some places very rich in plant clusters, is rather poor in plant variety.

The depths of the lake (with poor light or no light at all) and the steep rocky slopes are unfavorable for heavy plant growth. Shallows, with their strong sunlight, and lagoons harbor dense fields of aquatic plants. The huge cichlid populations, many of them being plant eaters like the *Tilapia*, wreak havoc on the *Vallisneria* beds, which are often grazed to the ground.

The plant inventory of the lake includes species belonging to the following genera: *Ceratophyllum, Myriophyllum, Nymphaea, Utricularia, Najas, Potamogeton, Vallisneria, Azolla, Chara* and *Ceratopteris*. As expected, most of them do not grow well in neutral or acid water.

The large cichlid population often graze the *Vallisneria* beds to the ground. Such plants should not be included in a lake cichlid aquarium. Photo of *Vallisneria* by Dr. D. Sculthorpe.

JELLYFISH

The author had the privilege back in the 50's to discover a small jellyfish in the Congo River, *Limnocnida congoensis*. Lake Tanganyika has the second known jellyfish from the freshwaters of Africa, *Limnocnida tanganycanae*. But if the Congo River jellyfish is rather rare, its lake cousin, not exceeding 2 cm in diameter and a transparent white in color, might travel with wind and current in lethally dense clouds. So dense in fact are the swarms that underwater it looks as if it were snowing. At various times during the year (now unpredictable) the beautiful umbrella-shaped mantles will drift, pulsating over wide areas. When you see them, so tiny, slow and beautiful, it gives you no hint of the deadly menace they represent for the young fish.

During our early exploration work over vast shallow areas, we towed one of our group at the end of a long line behind our boat. By this simple method we could quickly, without undue exhaustion, explore large areas. I remember several such explorations during which we encountered huge clouds of *Limnocnida* so dense that visibility was cut to a few centimeters. They stuck to everything, festooned the towing rope and even clung to our lips, although without harm. When the clouds drifted along rock beds, usually the scene of much fish activity, everything looked dead. The fish were under the rock ledges and in the crevices, as much out of reach of the insidious menace as they could. It brought back to my mind, irresistibly, personal memories of my native town in Europe being bombed during WW II, with everybody underground in shelters. All fish in the open flee. The young fry, when hit by a single jellyfish, dies in a few seconds.

Collecting at such a time is useless as all fish caught in a hand net are dying, coated in the slime of countless jellyfish and stung by the tentacles a hundred times. Professional trawler fishermen with whom we investigated the matter told us the same story. When they fish at night for clupeids and see the jellyfish around, they haul their nets in and head back home. They know the fishes are gone.

It is our feeling after these experiments that the jellyfish clouds are potentially one of the main causes of mass mortality among fish fry unable to escape the drifting menace, and that occasionally whole populations of the younger generations might be totally wiped out.

The regular diet of the jellyfish is not known. It is certainly not fish and most probably is zooplankton. Whether the jellyfish themselves fall prey to a fish has never been discovered. Very little, in fact, is known about them.

One would gather from what I have said that *Limnocnida* would not make a valuable aquarium addition. In fact, alone or only a few together, they represent no danger at all for aquarium fishes, even the very young. The danger lies with their dense clouds. Any fish is capable of avoiding their eerie and beautiful umbrella. Freshwater invertebrates from the lake are so few that *Limnocnida* might well be worth a try. If *Cyclops* or *Daphnia* are available, feeding should not be difficult.

SPONGES

If the shores are not too battered by waves and if light is available, many rocks in the lake are coated with several species of many-hued sponges. Their soft white, pink or light or dark green patches enhance the rather dull grey-green underwater landscape. Some overhanging sandstone slabs even shelter bright crimson sponges which later on turn a rich brown. Unfortunately they are too thin to successfully pry loose.

Where food and light are abundant, the sponges grow fat and sometimes several inches high, building beautiful towers and arches. They might also encrust upon driftwood and aquatic plant stems.

Seven species of sponges have been reported from the lake at the time of writing this book, but little or nothing is known about their life cycles, which seem to have seasonal peaks and reproductive periods, most probably related to the abundance of food.

It is the author's personal opinion, an opinion which is not shared by the other members of the team, that areas with a high percentage of sponge coating have smaller fish populations. It is possible that the sponges exude a kind of toxic repellent. Unusually high mortalities of fishes carried along with sponges in a pail might perhaps have been caused by the presence of the sponges. This phenomenon might have been seasonal and related to sexual activity. It is a fact that we never have seen sponges eaten by a fish nor showing traces of having been preyed upon.

If the lake sponges could be proven compatible with aquarium fishes in a tank and able to adapt to other water conditions, they would, without any doubt, be one of the most val-

Many rocks in the lake are covered with several species of sponges. This green sponge was collected and photographed by Dr. Herbert R. Axelrod.

uable additions to the hobby and bring to the aquarium a wholly new possibility of landscaping.

LEECHES

Freshwater fish collectors everywhere in the tropical world have had problems with these obnoxious animals. We encountered them in the Congo basin, often wondering what attracted them to us so quickly, sometimes spending more time to get rid of them than to put the fish in pails. We have them in the lake too, but fortunately they are rare. One unidentified species hides in rock crevices in shallow water, but we have never seen one on a fish. This rare species, about 5 cm long, is a rich brown with darker longitudinal stripes. The estuary swamps are the habitat of the common African black leech, sometimes found in very large numbers.

MOLLUSKS

The lake has been endowed with one of the largest collections of freshwater snails, some of them looking so much like marine shells that at the turn of the century a zoologist came up with a theory—since dismissed—that the lake at one time or another in its long history had been linked to the Indian Ocean and filled with seawater and marine life. As a matter of fact, if some lake shells

Of the seven species of crab reported from the lake (all endemic) six belong to the genus *Platythelphusa* an example of which is shown here. Photo by Dr. Herbert R. Axelrod.

look like their marine counterparts, it is a matter of convergence rather than kinship.

The lake shells show a remarkable degree of adaptation to various ecological conditions. The snails living on wave-battered shores are heavy, rugged, and compact; those creeping on the fluid mud floors have shells of little weight with a wide surface to keep them on top of the mud. Their shells often have long spikes and ridges. Two of the most abundant shells among the more than 100 species which have been discovered are *Iridina*, a 15-centimeter long mussel with a very gorgeous mother-of-pearl inner lining, and *Neothauma*, a 3 to 4 cm in diameter snail, the favorite diet of the beautiful and very common *Synodontis multipunctatus*. One might say it is the only normal constituent of the diet of this catfish, and it is very difficult to acclimatize it to another type of food.

A curious feature of the lake shells is due to the high calcium carbonate concentration and high pH of the water. The shells do not dissolve slowly after the death of the snail as they would in acid waters, but become embedded in calcite. The old shells roll about in the lake until they fall into a depression, where they pile up and are put to use by some tiny species of fish as shelters for their broods. One of these shell dwellers is *Lamprologus ocellatus*, which seldom reach more than 5 cm when adult.

CRUSTACEA

The multitude of copepods in the plankton layers are not the only representatives of the crustaceans. Many endemic shrimps and crabs take shelter in the rocks and swamps of the lake shores, some of them in large concentrations, such as 5 mm long bright red shrimp. This shrimp at some periods of the year can be collected in incredibly large numbers and is sold in the local markets as a delicacy.

Seven species of crabs have been reported from the lake, all endemic, six of them belonging to the genus *Platythelphusa*, the other one to *Potamon*. They live mainly on the rocky substrate, where they hide in crevices and caves. They are scavengers and fish-eaters. In some isolated rock outcrops in the middle of huge sand plains they have multiplied to such a degree that every nook and cranny shelters several specimens. In their breeding season they lay their eggs, apparently unprotected, on a slab in the open, which may indicate that the eggs are probably not edible for the fish living close by. But the crabs themselves are by no means free of predation by fish. They are sucked out and crushed between the powerful jaws of the big catfishes, like the *Chrysichthys* and

Bagrus, the giants of the fish populations in Africa. In the pebble and rubble shores the crabs seem to be fewer and usually smaller.

Parasitic crustaceans, like the horrible *Lernaea*, have often been reported on lake fishes. Yet we discovered only one *Tropheus* which was infected by *Lernaea* in all our fishing trips among the several hundred thousand fishes we have collected from the lake in four year's time.

One *Chrysichthys* catfish which happened to get caught in our nets was covered with hundreds of small *Argulus*, though all catfishes do not seem to be susceptible to the parasites—even among the same species. Perhaps some areas are favored by the parasites; perhaps some catfishes are immune. The same is true with *Malapterurus electricus*, the electric catfish, which we had the displeasure of meeting, or touching, underwater in many a shocking encounter. These fish never had any parasites, even at the same spot as we collected the other catfish which were *Argulus*-covered. Little wonder if they shrug them off as they do us!

A detailed study of lake crustaceans and the impact on fish populations of their parasitic forms has still to be undertaken. Although the parasitic forms do not seem to have many harmful

This parasitic crustacean *Lernaea* was seen by the author only in one instance, although it has been reported often on the fishes of the lake. Photo by Dr. R. Geisler.

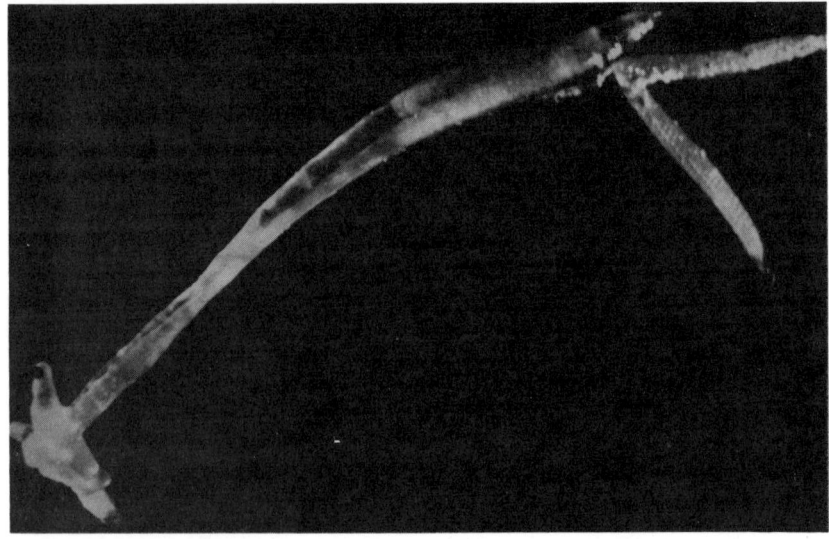

effects on the aquarium-type fishes from the lake, it is standard practice in our fish compound to treat them at once, along with the other standard treatments, against this harmful potential.

WATER SNAKES

Climbing the ladder of aquatic life in the lake from the simplest forms to the more sophisticated, we unavoidably reach a point where the animals we deal with are getting a bit more worrisome as an occupational hazard for the fish collector.

Reptiles, mainly crocodiles and water snakes, are one of these groups, and no account of collecting fish in the lake can overlook them.

The most common encounters (if by principle crocodile-infested waters are avoided) are with snakes, and the archetype of African water snakes is *Boulengerina annulata* variety *stormsi*. We have met all sizes of this deadly cobra, from small specimens less than a meter long to the really big ones from 2.50 m to 3 meters long, swimming on the surface, creeping among rocks, squeezing into underwater caves or labyrinths or suddenly thrusting their head out of a hole we planned to explore and frightening us to death before, very slowly and with utmost precaution, we paddled backward out of reach. Although at least once I faced a *Boulengerina*, about 2 meters long, less than a foot away from my face, it has never happened that they attacked any of us. In fact, on the ground where they spend most of their days (they go into the lake only to feed, mainly on fish) they would never tolerate as close a contact as we had without striking at once.

It is apparent from our many encounters that the snake is ill at ease in water and knows as well as we do that it has to go back to the surface for air, even if it is only every 15 minutes, and that its enemies are many. It will flee unless really cornered. Its behavior also suggests that its vision is impaired. We always saw the snake first, even at close quarters.

We have met cobras coming up from deep water at 12 meters, and I have been told by a SCUBA-diving scientist that he once encountered *Boulengerina* at 40 meters depth.

Some rock shores really harbor many water cobras, to such a degree that one should expect them during every dive, but from our experience the hazard should be considered light.

CROCODILES

Several zones in the lake are known to be infested with the worst of the African saurians, *Crocodilus niloticus*, the man-eater.

It is reasonable to fear the Nile crocodile which lives in the lake. Many persons are eaten during the year in some areas of the lake. Photo of a young specimen by L.E. Perkins.

It is a fact that in the Ruzizi estuary there are many people who are seized, crushed and eaten every year by crocodiles, to such a point where half of the crocodiles killed by hunters have human remains or artifacts in them.

Rumonge Bay, south of Bujumbura, is another such place, as are the flooded forest swamps 80 km to the south and the Nyanza-Lac sand beaches where at night at least a dozen of the huge beasts can be spotted in the searchlights.

Little is known about their reactions toward a SCUBA-diver. It has been said that they are rather timid when they meet the unknown. Recent surveys and television films tend to show them as fleeing in the face of a threatening posture by a diver. Well, it might be! But the case of a diver who is busy with collecting, his nose in the rocks and his mind on the fish he wants to get, is a bit different. Sometimes, when I know there might be a crocodile around and I am underwater with my back to the "open" water, I feel ill at ease and I wonder. . . . Incidentally, a friend of mine in 1958 killed a crocodile in Matadi, Zaire, 5.55 m long and weighing a bit over 800 kg.

HIPPOS

Provided one doesn't get really too close, hippos are peaceful animals. The best protection in case of a sudden encounter is to head for the deep water fast! It is highly unlikely that a hippo could physically go very deep, especially with bad footing on steep slopes.

They walk along the bottom in the water and usually don't swim much, but don't be misled by their bulk! They can travel fast, faster than a fin-equipped diver. The best thing to do is to leave these herbivores alone, more so when there are young babies around, and never try to reach the surface where they would recognize you at once for what you are in their mind—an enemy.

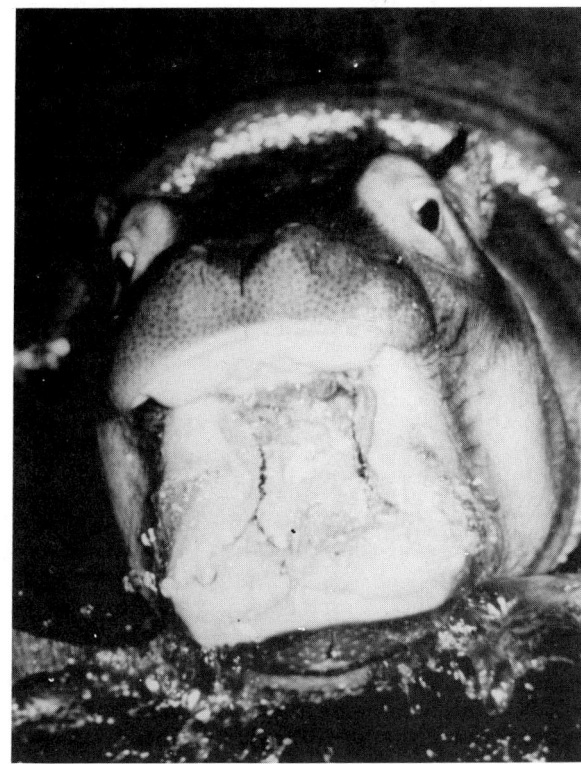

In spite of the great bulk of hippos, these docile animals can move fast underwater and harm a diver unintentionally. It would be wise to stay away from them altogether. Photo by Muller-Schmida.

OTHER ANIMALS

Monitor lizards, *Varanus niloticus*, are a common sight along the lake shores. They also prey on fish, as do the rarer lake otters, which we were fortunate to see on several occasions during their gracious aquatic ballets.

The aquatic birds as a rule do not populate the lake as they do famous East African bird sanctuaries. Occasional pink flamingos, black ibises, storks, pelicans, crowned cranes and a multitude of fishing eagles, falcons and the black and white kingfisher make up most of the flock. Very unexpectedly seagulls are a common sight on the lake. One wonders how they got 1,000 km inland, crossing wide expanses of savannah to settle there.

As one can realize from this fast survey of the aquatic life in the lake, much remains to be done before an accurate picture of this tremendously complex ecosystem can be sorted out. Fortunately for science the remoteness of the lake from all main sources of pollution and the absence of significant industries in its basin should leave its serene beauty unspoiled for future generations.

An example of an underwater scene in Lake Tanganyika, near Burundi. Photo by Dr. Herbert R. Axelrod.

An aerial view of a part of the Great Rift Valley west of Nairobi, east of Lake Victoria, showing the crevices of the earth's surface. In the distance the craters of extinct volcanoes pock the valleys. This area may some day develop into another rift lake.

3. Ecology of the Lake Fishes

Three main investigations of the fish populations in Lake Tanganyika have successively brought to us what is known today of their variety and distribution.

The first (by Boulenger) was the result of several collections made before World War I and was published in his famous *Catalogue of the Fresh-Water Fishes of Africa*. For the first time more than a hundred species were identified from the lake, which had been described by the first explorers as "practically void of any fish"!

The second and most important investigation was by Professor Max Poll, who reported on the huge collection assembled during the 1946-1947 Belgian Hydrobiological Mission on Lake Tanganyika, a model of concerted and sustained effort in many hydrobiological disciplines. Prof. Poll's work called to the attention of biologists for the first time the segregation by type of habitat of the various fish populations in the lake.

The third investigation, again made by a full team of scientists and this time covering more than a decade of work, was conducted by the Institut de Recherches Scientifiques en Afrique Centrale (in short IRSAC) at their station in Uvira (northwest coast of the lake). This research center was abandoned and practically destroyed after the unfortunate events which followed independence in the Congo (now Zaire).

The IRSAC scientists, led by Professor Marlier, were the first to discover the effects of isolation on fish speciation in the lake. The report of this discovery has become the basic reference for all further studies on this phenomenon around the world. One regrets that since the IRSAC station was closed down no systematic or concerted research has been conducted on the lake populations and that only heterogeneous and short-term studies have been started lately.

As it is, what do we know about the spread and distribution of the fishes in the lake?

M. Poll divided the fish into three main populations:
1. The open water or pelagic species living far from the shores, or better yet, independently of them.
2. The deep-water or *benthic* species living in the deepest available reaches of the lake, sometimes in open water, but perhaps more often near the bottom or on the slopes.
3. The *littoral* populations living near the shores or in shallow water.

Of the three populations, the littoral fishes attracted attention because of the ease of their capture and their wide diversification. So did the pelagic species because of their economic value as a seemingly inexhaustible supply of animal proteins for local human concentrations. These pelagic species are the plankton-eaters and their predators.

To give an estimate of this fishery potential based on the latest data available, the total weight of the pelagic species living at any one time in the lake could reach from 2.8 to 4 million tons. Their density is about 23-30 kilograms per hectare (10,000 square meters or 2.5 acres). The catch could well be increased without depleting the stock to about 200,000 tons a year!

The benthic fishes, because of the problems involved in their capture and observation, have been very poorly investigated as they live by day at depths between 60 and 200 meters.

Needless to say, the frontiers between these three populations are, in fact, difficult to trace. There are no clear-cut boundaries between them. Pelagic and benthic species must mix to some degree during their nyctemeral vertical migrations. And the same mixing must occur between these two populations and the littoral fishes when they follow their horizontal migrations, eventually coming into contact with the lake shores for breeding purposes. But one might say that as a whole, and more often than not, these fish live in different worlds.

Aside from the pelagic fishes (which include species less interesting to the aquarium world and which are now subject to long-term studies by international organizations) and the benthic species (as so little is known about these unusual fishes), we will concentrate on the littoral species of Lake Tanganyika and their various habitats.

Prof. Poll discovered that they should be divided into three main populations according to the type of substratum they were living on:

Twenty-five miles across the lake, as seen from the Congo-Nile Rivers divide, the 10,000 feet-high ridge of the western wall rises.

Below:
A very seldom seen old-fashioned sail-rigged dugout drifts slowly by the rock-strewn base of the cliffs.

A view of the Ruzizi River estuary and alluvial plain as seen from the Burundi hills.

The northern beaches near the Ruzizi delta. In the background is the western ridge.

1. Fishes living near river estuaries, mud floors and mud swamps. Most of these are endemic to the lake, although this group has the highest number of non-endemic fishes and has felt the influence of nearby rivers more than any other group of fishes in the lake.
2. Fishes living exclusively in the lake, mostly over sand floors (sometimes mud). These fishes exhibit a very high proportion of endemic species even though some are related to families and genera living in African rivers. Typical of this group of fishes and closely related to other African species are *Sarotherodon tanganicae*, several species of *Mastacembelus*, several genera of catfishes and other fishes, among which the most remarkable are the cyprinids—*Labeo, Barbus* and *Varicorhinus*.
3. Fish living on rocks to which they are more or less bonded. Typical of this group are the various geographical races, subspecies and species of *Tropheus*. All the rock-dwelling cichlids in the lake are endemic, and most of the non-cichlids as well, although there are several catfishes (*Malapterurus, Heterobranchus*, etc.) which might have reached the lake from the Congo basin.

Small crustaceans and invertebrates living on the surface of the rocks comprise the main food of *Lamprologus brichardi*. This school of feeding *L. brichardi* was taken by Dr. H.R. Axelrod.

An area of Lake Tanganyika which can serve as habitat for both rock- as well as sand-dwelling species. Photo by Dr. H.R. Axelrod.

Twenty-five years later this classification of the littoral fishes still holds basically true. It is remarkable, in the context of the traditional collecting equipment then available, that underwater exploration has corroborated so much of the initial data.

It was found that the three main littoral fish populations had evolved in different directions and were morphologically very well adapted to their various environments. Fishes living over open ground often have streamlined bodies built for speed, have teeth shaped for shoveling sand from the floor and form schools more than those living in shelters. On the other hand, rock-dwellers often have very short, muscular bodies to enable them to live on the surf-washed shores amid the breakers. Their teeth are shaped to cut, graze on or pick food from the rock biocover.

Again, needless to say, there are not always clear-cut boundaries between the littoral habitats. There are zones where patches of mud lie in the middle of huge sand plains, there are sand patches or slopes on rocky shores and there are rocky outcrops on mud or sand floors, even in muddy water near river estuaries. In these areas two different littoral fish populations come into contact with each other, and the respective density ratios (the presence of some species in abundance while others have become rare or dis-

Daily afternoon storms break over the lake during the rainy season, but the rainfall, due to heated uplifts, is only ⅓ of that on the shores.

An exceptional view taken during a storm on top of the Congo-Nile Rivers divide at 8,000 feet. The glittering surface of the lake is 5,000 feet below and the western wall of the Rift Valley is 60 miles away.

Mountain slopes continue straight into the lake keeping the same slope angle.

This coastline, about a mile from the southern escarpment, offers no shelter to the unwary should he be surprised by one of the daily storms or high winds.

500 meters from these hills marking the southern end, the lake is already 300 meters deep or deeper. The underwater slopes are thus more steep than the hills.

appeared) in these "no-man's-lands" would probably reveal much about the ethology of these species.

Needless to say, there are many species which cannot be categorized into any of the three littoral populations because they may be found everywhere—on sand, mud and rock. They are the "ubiquitous" species, but most of these fishes show in one way or another and to various degrees a preference for a given habitat.

SCUBA diving was used for the first time by Dr. Marlier and his team from IRSAC in Uvira to explore the northwestern coast. This led to the discovery that along this coast the succession of sandy and rocky shores resulted in the "de facto" isolation of the fishes living among or on the rocks. The very sedentary habits of these fishes that are bound to their habitat and the seclusion in which they live (without any contact with the same type fish living on another stretch of coast) have triggered in each local population a slow process of specific, morphological diversification.

Dr. Marlier, in a very well documented case, showed that the original species of *Tropheus* on a 60 km coast with successive sandy beaches and rocky habitats had differentiated into three color morphs or races and one other species. Since then, several other local races have been discovered which might eventually reach specific or subspecific status. This genetic "dynamism" is called "speciation," and the discoveries in the case of *Tropheus* started the study of this phenomenon in many other species in other parts of the world, but mainly in the Lake Malawi (Nyassa) cichlids.

When he was working on speciation in *Tropheus*, Dr. Marlier also described the habitat of this fish, noting that it was slightly different for each of the two species known at that time (*T. moorii*, *T. duboisi*). *Tropheus*, according to Marlier, lives on well-established rocky coasts with heavy biocover (not on bare rock where it cannot feed) and rather close to the surface (down to about 10 meters for *T. moorei* and to 15 meters for *T. duboisi*). He also stated that *Tropheus* are only found on rocks from which they never wander more than 2 to 3 meters.

The fishes thus could not wander from one rock slope to the next by crossing sand floors between the rocks. Isolation of a population in the case of this genus was then possible by the specialized ethology of the fish—being bound *strictly* to its habitat, which is suitable rocks in shallow water covered with biocover. It was until recently the only fish in the lake for which the ethology and the ecology, the "ecological niche," had been simultaneously documented in relationship with its genetic radiation potential.

Rock rubble sites are used as communal nurseries by species like *Lamprologus brichardi*. Adults guard the fry resulting from different spawns. Photo by Dr. H.R. Axelrod.

Encrusting algae have covered the vertical sides of the rocks with coral-like calcite formations; horizontal surfaces are smooth. This as yet unstudied phenomenon occurs in about 5 m depth. The picture was taken at about 12 m.

Chalinochromis brichardi swimming over large boulders with recognizable biocover. Photo by Glen S. Axelrod.

Underwater macrophotograph of brown algal growth. This particular biocover is very thin and poor in variety. Other rocks with denser biocover can offer a wider selection of food to the fish.

Encrusted algae on calcite-welded rocks at 5 meters depth. The biocover includes crustaceans and insect larvae brought in by the currents.

More problems connected with the phenomenon have been uncovered since 1958 when Marlier made his discovery. The most important is related to the ecology of the rock shores (one might say of *each* rock shore, as none is exactly the same as the next). Rocky shores along the entire lake coast are not endless repetitions of a typical slope facies made up of geologically identical rock substrata, nor is the influx of life-bearing currents everywhere the same. Most probably local variations in the water chemistry due to the output of underwater thermal springs, some of which have been discovered, might also account for the immense variety of rock-dwelling fishes in the lake and trigger some speciation.

Underwater rocky slopes can be strewn with sandstone slabs, quartz, gneiss, micashists, etc., and we have noted remarkable differences in the biocover growths according to the nature of the rocks. Monolithic boulders jutting out from the floor close to the surface are totally devoid of biocover, and the area is practically deserted by fishes. At the same time, a few hundred meters away rock slopes of a different geologic nature team with fish.

Rock formations go all the way in size from coarse sand, gravel, pebbles, rubble, slabs or blocks to gigantic boulders or precipitous cliffs. The accumulation of these shapes on a slope in dif-

The large masses of sponge are easily identified in this photograph by their siphons or oscula. Photo by Dr. H.R. Axelrod.

ferent outcrops is what will determine, along with the depth at which they are found, the density and variety of the fish populations. There are thus many different rocky slopes on a single coastline, several rocky shores along a coast within a given zone, and several zones all around the lake.

In the northernmost part of the lake, extending from the Ubwari peninsula toward the Ruzizi estuary and from there to the north bank of the Malagarazi River in Tanzania, three main zones have so far been explored. The first is from Uvira to the sand plains of Burton Bay, the second from Bujumbura to Rumonge in Burundi and the third from Nyanza-Lac near the Tanzania border to the Malagarazi River. Each one of these three zones has different fish populations in addition to different races within several species. The southernmost coast of the lake, in Zambia, has yielded a whole new set of species and geographical races and apparently should be considered as another coastal zone of its own.

But although these discoveries are spectacular and the systematic exploration of all the lake coasts seems to be, from the aquarist's point of view, long overdue, we feel that the first order in research should be to determine the ethology of the fishes in each case and, more importantly, the ecology of each coast. We must attempt to understand what factors in the water chemistry or the nature of the rocks and the biocover on them are behind the wide variations in the rock-dweller's populations. The fish populations depend, within each zone and within each slope, on the presence of specific "ecological niches" or "micro-habitats" inside of the rocky habitat.

There is a definite, often very apparent, relationship between the fishes and some types of rock shapes at a suitable depth. Some fishes swim in the open off the slopes; many others dwell on the floor or even inside the substratum in caves, labyrinths, slits, crevices, piles of rubble, etc. If these shelters are not available where the fish is forced to live, for example by its oxygen requirements, the fish will not be present. Each species has its own sets of bonds toward its ecological niche. If the particular ecological niche isn't one of the many on the rocky slopes, the fish related to it will not be present in the area.

It is thus not enough to divide the littoral species among sandy, muddy or rocky shores; one has to study the intricate relationship between the fishes and their surroundings in each zone. What is in order now is the systematic study of each identified ecological zone in the lake. Such a study should include crystallogra-

An inch-thick sponge has grown on a sandstone slab in an area 5 meters deep and with a very strong inflow of suspended particles.

The most sacred mountain around the lake is this impressive "mesa." A few decades ago humans were thrown from the cliffs once a year as an offering to the mountain god.

Two different sponges growing on the same rock slab.

A red plankton tide turned the usually blue lake water to a deep rusty red. The phenomenon happened in the South at the end of the rainy season instead of at the start of the rains as it is with the green plankton. This red bloom of a still unidentified plankter lasted several days and covered a wide area.

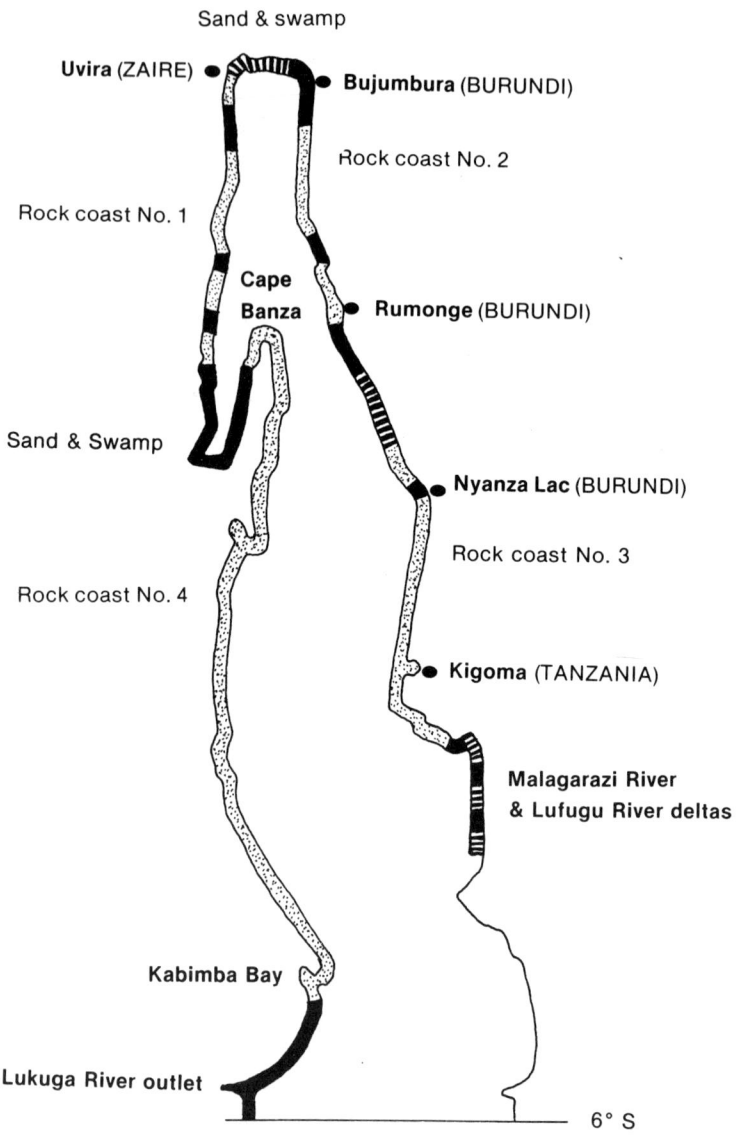

Three main coastal rock habitat identified in the northern section of Lake Tanganyika.

phy and geological composition of the rock substratum, thorough study of samples from the biocover periodically and in relationship to incoming currents with their plankton, stomach contents inventories of the related fish populations and quantitative inventories of the fishes. When all the data have been collected, perhaps then it will be possible to understand the wide discrepancies in fish populations between the many coastal areas of the lake.

What is in order now is the understanding of the bonds between the fishes and their habitat. Let us return to a quick survey of the three main littoral fish flocks.

FISHES IN RIVER ESTUARIES AND SWAMPS

This habitat is the most difficult to explore underwater since sediment and silt prevent good and accurate direct observations beyond at best a few feet (more often a few inches). One literally gropes his way through these areas, and it is only on the fringe of river estuaries that it is possible to see the fish, identify them and note their approximate density.

In the Ruzizi River estuary, for example, the following species have been identified: *Haplochromis burtoni, Astatoreochromis straeleni, Sarotherodon nilotica, Tilapia rendalli, Protopterus aethiopicus*, two species of *Polypterus*, several mormyrids and cyprinids (*Labeo*). None of these species seem to wander much into the lake. *Haplochromis burtoni* is collected in the lake, on both sides of the estuary and shoreline mud flats, and then it disappears altogether.

It is remarkable to note that although the lake is so rich in cichlids, very few live in the river and mountain torrents of the lake basin. Moreover, none of the other river fishes, like the typical East African Kneriidae or catfishes, have been able to settle in the lake. There is thus a marked reluctance on the part of the river flock to leave their habitat and colonize the lake. Let us say this is true of at least the *present-day* flock.

Noteworthy perhaps is the fact that a ubiquitous and very harmful river and swamp snail, *Planorbis*, vector of the dreaded African disease bilharzia, has been unable to settle in the lake proper and seems to die quickly as soon as it comes into contact with the lake water. As a result all areas remote from the estuaries are free of the parasite.

Several lake fishes have been collected near the river estuaries. They either belong to the rock-dwellers (*Simochromis, Petrochromis, Telmatochromis*) when rocks are available, to the sand-

A *Julidochromis marlieri* photographed near its hiding place. This species swims into open water but stays close to the rock cover. Photo by Glen S. Axelrod.

Small pebbles line a narrow beach squeezed between the water and the edge of luxuriant bushes. This type of habitat is the domain of *Eretmodus*.

A young crocodile, caught by fishermen in a seine, has been killed and will be sold at the local market. The big ones tear the nets and escape.

Below: Surprised by the flash, a three-inch crab is discovered at the mouth of a small cave at 15 meters depth. Calcite deposits are clearly visible on both sides of the hole.

Polypterus ornatipinnis. Photo by H. Hansen.

dwellers (*Callochromis, Xenotilapia*) or to the mud-dwellers (*Limnochromis auritus, Sarotherodon tanganicae*). To what extent these endemic lake species are capable of living in high concentrations of river water has not been established due to the murkiness of water in front of the estuaries, but the fact remains that these fishes do not live *in* the rivers.

SAND FLOORS AND SLOPES

The first feeling a diver has when swimming over the vast expanses of the open sand floors is one of nearly total void. Seldom, even over long distances, does one see a fish. Here and there a pair of *Lamprologus tetracanthus, L. pleuromaculatus* or *L. attenuatus* busy themselves around their huge crater-like nest. Funnel-shaped depressions, often half-filled with empty *Neothauma* snail shells, show the site of an abandoned *Boulengerochromis* nest. An occasional school of about a dozen *Lamprologus callipterus* may gather behind you like a pack of wolves. They rush into the sand cloud billowing behind your fins and voraciously swallow whole mouthfuls of particles.

A big hole in front of you may challenge your imagination. It is three to four meters across and nearly one meter deep, with tons of sand removed! What can it be? Then you see the hazy shape of a huge fish in front of you. No—two shapes circling slowly! You stay quiet and hold your breath. . . there they come, male and female *Boulengerochromis microlepis!* In the middle of the crater, forming a small patch of about 25 to 30 cm diameter, perhaps 12,000 to 15,000 freshly hatched fry vibrate under the effective protection of their huge parents. The female is perhaps 80 cm long and weighs close to 4.5 kg (10 pounds). As you lie prone at the crater's edge she comes closer and starts to be really bothersome. Nibbling at your fins is nothing; she soon starts ramming your face mask and tearing at your hair.

These huge beasts really have little to fear in the lake. Crocodiles don't venture far from shore nor very deep; the Nile perches aren't very abundant; and the big catfishes hide in their caves. So *Boulengerochromis*, although a bit nervous about your size and the noise from the air regulator, doesn't hesitate to attack. Moments like these are a reward for other less fascinating or perhaps even dangerous hours spent underwater.

Lamprologus modestus also wanders into the area. It is much less prepossessing because of its small size and doesn't seem as much at ease here as it is over rocks. To build a shaft for its tunnel nest,

Boulengerochromis microlepis, juvenile. Photo by P.V. Loiselle.

A typical rubble floor with a good biocover will harbor many different rock-dwellers, such as the flock of *Lamprologus brichardi* seen here.

A school of adult *Lamprologus brichardi* hovers over the rubble in which breeding adults have teamed together to raise the fry. It is the only known examples in cichlids of "nursery" breeding; even the eldest fry help ward off potential predators.

A *Lamprologus elongatus* swimming along a steep drop-off or cliff-like edge of the lake. Photo by Glen S. Axelrod.

A sandy habitat in the lake in which a species of *Lamprologus* with light coloration can be seen. Photo by Glen S. Axelrod.

the fish needs some props—a shell of the large lake mussel, *Iridina*, a stone, anything. The fish, with its maximum size of 15 cm, is too small to build an open nest and protect the brood.

So is *Lamprologus ocellatus*, with its maximum length of 5 cm. This species lives on this open floor and nests in empty *Neothauma* snail shells. Its color, pale beige with deep mauve stripes on the jaws and opercles, is excellent camouflage.

The typical sand-dwellers are not the solitary species, but the gregarious *Callochromis*, *Xenotilapia* and *Cardiopharynx*, whose flocks usually number several hundreds. These sand-dwellers have become well adapted to their habitat. They are pale yellow or greenish in color with patches of blue dots or mauve areas on their body. They have developed their gregarious instincts to an extreme degree, having group stimuli for danger, feeding and even breeding. They feed on particles sifted from the sand with their shovel-like teeth. Their dentition would be useless if they had to pry or pick microorganisms from a rock. Some of these species have developed original ways to escape danger. *Callochromis pleurospilus* is the only cichlid we know of that buries itself in the sand in a lightning-quick motion as soon as it is threatened.

It is perhaps difficult to talk about speciation when dealing with free-roaming cichlids. The fact remains that there seems to be several local races and subspecies among the sand-dwellers. There are two subspecies of *Callochromis macrops* and several of *Ophthalmochromis ventralis*. All these local subspecies have well defined grounds in the lake.

Some mud flats do exist in sheltered areas in the lake, like the huge mud floor of Burton's Bay. This is protected by the Ubwari peninsula. Near the shore, over shallows and mud, *Sarotherodon tanganicae*, *Triglachromis otostigma* and *Limnochromis auritus* might shelter. In deeper water the other species of *Limnochromis*, except *L. nigripinnis* and *L. microlepidotus* (which appear to be bound to rock floors), seem also to be associated with mud plains. Most of the time mud flats, when not in shallows, are in rather still water. Emanations of toxic gases usually prevent fishes from staying in such areas.

Pelagic fishes often cross the shallow sand plains in their wanderings, and it is not exceptional to see big flocks of *Plecodus paradoxus*, a scale-eating species, speeding over such shallows in apparently aimless pursuit. They blend wonderfully well with the color of the water and are visible only at short distances because of the black spot on their caudal peduncle. One should remember that this fish has been collected at depths of nearly 250 meters, one of the deepest captures ever recorded in the lake. We have seen countless schools in very shallow water near rocky shores. This shows very well that there are no well differentiated limits between the pelagic, benthic and littoral species.

ROCKY SHORES AND THEIR INHABITANTS

As we have seen, this habitat is made up of a wide variety of rock formations sloping down at various angles toward the deep reaches of the lake. Depending on the influx of life and food-bearing currents, on the oxygen levels at various depths (which depend on wave action and also the currents), on the mineralogical structure and on the shape and size of the rocks, each slope is a different biotope. The relationship between this biotope and the fish is a very challenging problem to study and even, at first, to visualize.

What are these fishes? They are gregarious or individualistic; some build nests, others build nests but are still mouthbrooders. As for feeding, some live off the rock biocover, scraping, grazing or picking their food loose; some feed on particles in suspension in the water; some are carnivorous; and, in a few cases, some live exclusively on scales which they tear off the other fishes' bodies. Some species are restricted to the shallowest surf-washed shores, while others are found only in deep water. A few live all the way from the surface down to 60 meters or more.

The following list is in no way exhaustive, as only 10% of the lake coasts have been systematically explored at this time, but it gives a fair idea of the variety of rock-dwellers.

Non-cichlids: The only cyprinodont of the lake, *Lamprichthys tanganicus* (which is also the largest of all the known killifishes) might be related to the rock-dwellers (although ubiquitous in coastal waters) because it spawns on rock shelves.

The mastacembelid eels live in rock furrows and under pebbles and are found only on the rocky shores or outcrops where their ethology is similar to that of the marine moray eels. Some of the species seem to be very restricted in their distribution.

The catfishes are very varied on the rocky slopes, ranging from the tiny species of *Phyllonemus* and *Lophiobagrus*, the species of both genera hiding in deep crevices in the dark, to big species like those in the genera *Chrysichthys, Bagrus, Heterobranchus* and the electric catfish, *Malapterurus electricus*.

There is a total of about ten species of *Synodontis*, most of them sharing the same type of deep, dark habitats in the under-

An "explosive" panic in a school of *Limnochromis nigricans*. This behavior is typical in schooling fish. The school will re-assemble afterwards.

A school of *Lamprologus brichardi*, numbering several hundreds, enters a net. Distributed in the upper 40 meters, schools of *L. brichardi* number in excess of 50,000 fish. But the species seems to be restricted to the northeastern coasts of the lake.

On a sand flat near sandstone slabs at 4 meters depth, a *Boulengerochromis* pair has built a wide but shallow nest pocketed with small craters in one of which the eggs have been laid. Here the male keeps close watch while the female circles the area.

Checking the sandstone slabs nearby for posssible predators, a pair of *Boulengerochromis* (the female larger but with drabber body pattern) start circling in opposite directions. Photographed 3 yards away, the fish appear tremendously large. The female is about 70 centimeters (28 inches) long.

Lamprichthys tanganicanus. Photo by Dr. H.R. Axelrod.

water rock labyrinths and caves. We discovered that these fishes, long thought to be nocturnal, are in fact light shy. When near the surface they live in dark recesses; when deep, they wander in the open. In the subdued light of the depths, they occur in large schools.

Cyprinids of the genus *Varicorhinus* are frequently sighted along the surf-washed rocks, as are juvenile *Lates* (Nile perches).

One mormyrid, *Marcusenius discorhynchus*, lives on the rocky slopes far from river estuaries. It is the only mormyrid known from the lake proper. Like all mormyrids, it prefers subdued light or total darkness.

Most of the non-cichlids are much less visible, meaning that they spend most of their life hidden, than are the cichlids. One would thus tend to dismiss them as making up a very small part of the total fish population of the rocky slopes. It is there, however, that they are the most common and, what is also important, are usually the biggest fish in the area. There are rocky slopes where large *Malapterurus* are to be found every other yard, deep in crevices. It is not uncommon to collect ten or twenty very large individuals of *Mastacembelus* with an average weight close to 1 kg in a single one-hour dive. Deeper down schools of *Synodontis* wander on the floor, often 200, 300 or 400 strong. Several thousand *Lamprichthys tanganicanus* are often seen near the rocky shores.

Cichlids: The variety of cichlids is such that we will try to group them according to some of their ecological affinities, without regard to their taxonomic classification.

Feeding and Teeth

1. Grazers—fish equipped with teeth set into a cutting edge or abrasive pads. Examples: *Tropheus, Simochromis, Petrochromis.*
2. Pickers—fish equipped with a set of teeth enabling them to pry food from the rock biocover. Examples: *Eretmodus, Spathodus, Tanganicodus, Lamprologus brichardi,* perhaps *Lamprologus furcifer, L. leleupi, L. schreyeni, L. niger* and the various species of *Julidochromis.*
3. Carnivorous species—with powerful canines. Examples: *Lamprologus compressiceps, L. elongatus, L. lemairei* and *L. savoryi.*
4. Omnivorous cichlids—living off particles in suspension in the water. Examples: *Ophthalmochromis, Cyathopharynx, Limnochromis nigripinnis.*
5. Scale-eaters—with hook-like teeth. Example: *Plecodus straelini.*

Habitat in the Substratum or Off the Slopes

1. Habitat in the substratum—all species of *Julidochromis,* all species of *Tropheus, Eretmodus, Spathodus, Tanganicodus, Petrochromis, Simochromis,* many *Lamprologus* and *Telmatochromis.*
2. Living off the slopes—*Cyphotilapia, Limnotilapia, Limnochromis nigripinnis* and *L. microlepidotus, Ophthalmochromis, Cyathopharynx, Perissodus microlepis, Lamprologus lemairei, L. elongatus, L. compressiceps, L. brichardi* and *L. pleuromaculatus.*

Petrochromis polyodon hovering above a rubble area between larger rocks. Photo by Glen S. Axelrod.

Several *Lobochilotes labiatus*, a mollusc-eating fish of the lake, swimming near the bottom. Photo by Glen S. Axelrod.

Bonds Toward Darkness or Subdued Light

Several fishes show a strong dislike of bright light. *Lamprologus furcifer* is never seen in the open but always against or under big boulders or in caves. *Lamprologus savoryi, L. schreyeni* and *L. niger* are always found in caves or labyrinths.

Bonds Toward Depth

Some species are strictly limited in their vertical distribution, many others are not.

From surface to 3 meters depth: Strictly limited to this habitat with high oxygen level are *Eretmodus, Spathodus* and *Tanganicodus*. Many juveniles of mouthbrooders are also only found in this area: *Tropheus, Simochromis, Petrochromis,* young *Lobochilotes* and *Limnotilapia*. In such cases parents are usually found much deeper.

From surface to 15 meters: Tropheus, Petrochromis and *Simochromis* are very seldom found deeper than 5 or 6 meters. All species of *Lamprologus, Ophthalmochromis, Cyathopharynx* and *Perissodus* occur at this level.

Below 3 meters: Telmatochromis, Lamprologus brichardi, L. savoryi.

Below 6-10 meters: Cyphotilapia, Limnochromis nigripinnis, L. microlepidotus and *Limnotilapia dardennei* adults.

The rock cichlids show various trends toward gregariousness or conversely to individualism. Except for *Lamprologus lemairei, L. elongatus, L. compressiceps* and *Perissodus,* all species living a few meters off the slopes are normally school fish. On the other hand, all fishes living on or in the rocky floor are normally strongly individualistic and do not build communities. Whenever small groups of these fishes are encountered, close observation indicates that they respond to individual stimuli. Very often *Telmatochromis bifrenatus* or *T. vittatus* can be seen a dozen at a time on a small surface. This is simply because the density of these fish is high at this spot. Each is on its own and none will show the typical behavior of school fish. The same is true of *Tropheus* whenever their density is very high. They meet during their wanderings and might travel a few yards together, but they will separate readily and wander off on their own again.

An analysis of the two main littoral cichlid populations—sand and rock—reveals some very striking similarities. Both habitats have fishes living directly on and next to the bottom and, on the other hand, fishes hovering in mid-water off the bottom feeding on particles or prey in suspension (although they use the substratum as their breeding ground). Fishes living in the open, in mid-water, are mostly gregarious or if not are capable of warding off most potential enemies because of their size. Fishes living among the elements of the substrate are, for the most part, highly individualistic. Gregarious fishes, usually wanderers, are mouthbrooders and polygamous as are the fishes which, in their habitat, wander apparently without aim. Sedentary fish, the "settlers," are usually egg-layers on a nest site and monogamous.

The density of fish populations, as should be expected, is directly proportional to the input of edible matter brought into the habitat by local currents and is related to the oxygen level. There is a definite pattern of distribution of species according to depth and related to their oxygen requirements. The richest zone is, by far, from the surface down to about 15 meters.

Many deep-water fishes, including pelagic species, come into shallow water to spawn, and apparently *all* mouthbrooders ascend from their deepest habitats to brood their young according to their specific oxygen needs. Most juveniles grow up along the shallow shoreline, going deeper as they age.

4. Survey of Lake Tanganyika Fishes and Their Endemism

The following list of Tanganyika fishes includes all the species identified as per December, 1975 and has personally been checked by Professor Max Poll.

Several apparently new species or subspecies from the lake are now being investigated by workers in various parts of the world but cannot as yet be included in the present list. Genera and species are listed alphabetically, instead of in the usual phylogenetic order used in systematic classification, for quick reference. Endemic genera and species are marked by an asterisk (*) in front of the name. When the name of the author is between brackets, it means that the species was originally described in a different genus.

FISHES OF LAKE TANGANYIKA

Names preceded by an asterisk are endemics.

No. of Species	Genus	Species	Habitat
Cichlidae			
1	*ASPROTILAPIA	*leptura Boulenger	rock-sand
1	ASTATOREOCHROMIS	straeleni (Poll)	swamps
1	*AULONOCRANUS	*dewindti (Boulenger)	sand
7	*BATHYBATES	*fasciatus Boulenger	pelagic
		*ferox Boulenger	,,
		*graueri Steindachner	,,
		*horni Steindachner	,,
		*leo Poll	,,
		*minor Boulenger	,,
		*vittatus Boulenger	,,
1	*BOULENGERO- CHROMIS	*microlepis (Boulenger)	,,

67

No. of Species	Genus	Species	Habitat
2	*CALLOCHROMIS	*macrops macrops (Boulenger)	sand
		*m. melanostigma (Boulenger)	,,
		*pleurospilus (Boulenger)	,,
1	*CARDIOPHARYNX	*schoutedeni Poll	,,
1	*CHALINOCHROMIS	*brichardi Poll	rock
1	*CUNNINGTONIA	*longiventralis Boulenger	,,
1	*CYATHOPHARYNX	*furcifer (Boulenger)	rock
1	*CYPHOTILAPIA	*frontosa (Boulenger)	,,
1	*ECTODUS	*descampsi Boulenger	sand
1	*ERETMODUS	*cyanostictus Boulenger	rock
1	*GRAMMATOTRIA	*lemairei Boulenger	pelagic
6.	HAPLOCHROMIS	*benthicola Matthes	benthic
		burtoni (Günther)	swamps
		*horei (Günther)	coastal
		*pfefferi (Boulenger)	coastal
		*stappersi Poll	river/swamps
		*vanderhorsti Greenwood	river/swamps
2	*HAPLOTAXODON	*microlepis Boulenger	deep rock
		*tricoti Poll	deep mud
1	*HEMIBATES	*stenosoma (Boulenger)	benthic
5	*JULIDOCHROMIS[1]	*dickfeldi Staeck	rock
		*marlieri Poll	,,
		*ornatus Boulenger	,,
		*regani Poll	,,
		*transcriptus Matthes	,,
35	LAMPROLOGUS[2]	*attenuatus Steindachner	sand
		*brevis Boulenger	sand/shells
		*brichardi Poll	rock
		*callipterus Boulenger	sand
		*christyi Trew. & Poll	rock
		*compressiceps Boulenger	rock
		*cunningtoni Boulenger	ubiquitous

[1]Two other species of *Julidochromis* are being investigated as to their status.

[2]All species of *Lamprologus* in this list are endemic to the lake. Four additional species, all endemic to the Congo basin, have been discovered outside of the lake basin (*L. congolensis*, *L. tumbanus*, *L. mocquardii* and *L. werneri*).

No. of Species	Genus	Species	Habitat
		elongatus Boulenger	ubiquitous
		fasciatus Boulenger	rock/sand
		furcifer Boulenger	rock
		hecqui Boulenger	sand/shells
		kungweensis Poll	sand
		leleupi leleupi Poll	rock
		leleupi melas Matthes	,,
		leloupi Poll	,,
		lemairei Boulenger	ubiquitous
		meeli Poll	rock
		modestus (Boulenger)	ubiquitous
		moorii Boulenger	rock
		multifasciatus Boulenger	rock/shells
		niger Poll	rock
		ocellatus Steindachner	shells
		ornatipinnis Poll	sand
		petricola Poll	rock
		pleuromaculatus Trew. & Poll	sand
		profundicola Poll	rock
		pulcher Poll	rock
		savoryi Poll	,,
		schreyeni Poll	,,
		sexfasciatus Trew. & Poll	,,
		signatus Poll	sand/mud
		stappersi Pellegrin	deep mud
		tetracanthus Boulenger	sand
		toae Poll	rock
		tretocephalus Boulenger	rock
		wauthioni Poll	mud/shells
1	*LEPTOCHROMIS*	*calliurum* (Boulenger)	sand/mud
1	*LESTRADEA*	*perspicax perspicax* Poll	sand
		p. stappersi Poll	,,
9	*LIMNOCHROMIS*[3]	*abeelei* Poll	deep soft bottom

[3]*L. pfefferi* has now been put in the genus *Haplochromis* and *L. otostigma* in a genus of its own, *Triglachromis*. I believe that *L. microlepidotus*, *L. leptosoma* and *L. nigripinnis* should be placed in a genus of their own also.

No. of Species	Genus	Species	Habitat
		*auritus (Boulenger)	,, ,,
		*christyi Trewavas	deep sand/mud
		*dhanisi Poll	,, ,,
		*leptosoma (Boulenger)	,, ,,
		*microlepidotus Poll	rock
		*nigripinnis (Boulenger)	,,
		*permaxillaris David	deep sand/mud
		*staneri Poll	,, ,,
3	*LIMNOTILAPIA	*dardennei (Boulenger)	ubiquitous
		*loocki Poll	rock?
		*trematocephala (Boulenger)	?
1	*LOBOCHILOTES	*labiatus Boulenger	rock
2	*OPHTHALMOCHROMIS	*ventralis ventralis (Boulenger)	,,
		*v. heterodontus Poll & Matthes	,,
		*nasutus Poll & Matt.	,,
1	*OPHTHALMOTILAPIA	*boops (Boulenger)	,,
1	ORTHOCHROMIS	*malagaraziensis (David)	torrents
1	*PERISSODUS	*microlepis Boulenger	rock
5	*PETROCHROMIS	*famula Matt. & Trew.	,,
		*fasciolatus Boulenger	,,
		*orthognathus Matthes	,,
		*polyodon Boulenger	,,
		*trewavasae Poll	,,
4	*PLECODUS	*elaviae Poll	benthic
		*multidentatus Poll	,,
		*paradoxus Boulenger	pelagic
		*straeleni Poll	rock
3	SAROTHERODON	*karomo Poll	estuary
		nilotica (Linné)	swamps
		*tanganicae (Günther)	,, /mud/rock
4	*SIMOCHROMIS[4]	*babaulti Pellegrin	rock
		*curvifrons Poll	,,
		*diagramma Günther	,,
		*marginatus Poll	,,

[4]Two as yet unidentified species of *Simochromis* have been collected by the author.

No. of Species	Genus	Species	Habitat
2	*SPATHODUS	*erythrodon Boulenger	rock
		*marlieri Poll	,,
1	*TANGANICODUS	*irsacae Poll	,,
5	*TELMATOCHROMIS	*bifrenatus Myers	,,
		*burgeoni Poll	,,
		*caninus Poll	,,
		*temporalis Boulenger	,,
		*vittatus Boulenger	,,
1	TILAPIA	rendalli Dumeril	swamps
8	*TREMATOCARA	*caparti Poll	benthic
		*kufferathi Poll	,,
		*macrostoma Poll	,,
		*marginatum Boul.	,,
		*nigrifrons Boulenger	,,
		*stigmaticum Poll	,,
		*unimaculatum Boul.	,,
		*variabile Poll	,,
1	*TRIGLACHROMIS	*otostigma (Regan)	mud
3	*TROPHEUS[5]	*brichardi Nel. & Thys	rock
		*duboisi Marlier	,,
		*moorii Boulenger	,,
1	TYLOCHROMIS[6]	*polylepis (Boulenger)	sand/mud
1	*XENOCHROMIS	*hecqui Boulenger	benthic
10	*XENOTILAPIA	*boulengeri (Poll)	sand
		*caudafasciata Poll	,,
		*longispinnis burtoni Poll	,,
		*l. longispinis Poll	,,
		*melanogenys (Boulenger)	,,
		*nigrolabiata Poll	,,
		*ochrogenys bathyphilus Poll	,,
		*o. ochrogenys (Boulenger)	,,
		*ornatipinnis Boulenger	,,
		*sima Boulenger	,,
		*spilopterus Poll & Stewart	,,
		*tenuidentata Poll	,,

[5]Several local races, subspecies and perhaps species have been discovered lately and are now being investigated.
[6]This genus is also known from the Congo River.

Total of Lake Tanganyika cichlids as per December 31, 1975: 144 (139 species + 5 subspecies) divided among 42 genera of which 35 of them are non-endemic (including 44 endemic species and only 4 species which are not endemic).

The 7 non-endemic genera are: *Astatoreochromis, Haplochromis, Lamprologus, Orthochromis, Sarotherodon, Tilapia* and *Tylochromis.*

NON-CICHLID SPECIES INVENTORY

No. of Species	Genus	Species	Habitat
Lepidosirenidae			
1	PROTOPTERUS	*aethiopicus* Heckel	estuaries
Polypteridae			
2	POLYPTERUS	*endlicheri congicus* Boulenger	,,
		ornatipinnis Boulenger	,,
Clupeidae			
1	*LIMNOTHRISSA	**miodon* (Boulenger)	pelagic
1	*STOLOTHRISSA	**tanganicae* Regan	,,
Mormyridae			
1	MORMYROPS	*deliciosus* (Leach)	swamps/river
1	HIPPOPOTAMYRUS	*discorhynchus* (Peters)	swamps/rock
1	POLLIMYRUS	*nigricans* (Boulenger)	swamps/river
1	GNATHONEMUS	*longibarbis* (Hilgendorf)	,, ,,
1	MARCUSENIUS	*stanleyanus* (Boulenger)	,, ,,
1	MORMYRUS	*longirostris* Peters	,, ,,
Kneriidae			
1	KNERIA	*wittei* Poll	torrents
Characidae			
2	HYDROCYNUS	*vittatus* Castelnau	ubiquitous
		goliath (Boulenger)	,,
3	ALESTES	*imberi* Peters	,,
		macrophthalmus Günther	,,
		rhodopleura Boulenger	,,
1	BRYCONAETHIOPS	*boulengeri* Pellegrin	estuaries
1	MICRALESTES	**stormsi* Boulenger	Lukuga River

No. of Species	Genus	Species	Habitat
Citharinidae			
3	*DISTICHODUS*	*fasciolatus* Boulenger	Lukuga River
		maculatus Boulenger	Malagarazi
		sexfasciatus Boulenger	coastal
1	*CITHARINUS*	*gibbosus* Boulenger	estuaries
Cyprinidae			
18	*BARBUS*	*altianalis* Boulenger	river
		aphantogramma Regan	,,
		caudovittatus Boulenger	,,
		(Typical Congo River species)	
		*euchilus Boulenger	Lufuko River
		eutaenia Boulenger	river
		lineomaculatus Boulenger	,,
		*lufukiensis Boulenger	Lufuko River
		miolepis Boulenger	river
		nicholsi Vinciguerra	Lukuga River
		*oligogrammus David	river
		paludinosus Peters	,,
		pellegrini Poll	,,
		*pojeri Poll	Lukuga outlet
		serrifer Boulenger	river
		*taeniopleura Boulenger	,,
		*tropidolepis Boulenger	,,
		*urostigma Boulenger	,,
		*urundensis Boulenger	,,
5	*VARICORHINUS*	**leleupanus* Matthes	coastal/river
		ruandae Pappenheim	river
		*stappersi Boulenger	coastal/river
		*tanganicae Boulenger	,, ,,
6	*LABEO*[1]	*cylindricus* Peters	sand/coastal
		*dhonti Boulenger	Lukuga outlet
		fuelleborni Hilgend. & Papp.	river
		*kibimbi Poll	,,
		lineatus Boulenger	,,

[1] *L. lineatus* and *L. velifer* are typical Congo River species.

73

No. of Species	Genus	Species	Habitat
		velifer Boulenger	Lukuga outlet
5	BARILIUS	moorii Boulenger	river estuaries
		*neavii Boulenger	coastal
		salmolucius Nich. & Grisc.	river estuary
		*tanganicae Boulenger	coastal
		ubangensis Pellegrin	river estuary
2	ENGRAULICYPRIS	congicus Nich. & Grisc.	Lukuga outlet
		*minutus (Boulenger)	pelagic

Bagridae

No. of Species	Genus	Species	Habitat
1	BAGRUS	docmac (Forskal)	estuary
6	CHRYSICHTHYS	*grandis Boulenger	sand/mud
		*graueri Steindachner	,, ,,
		*brachynema Boulenger	,, ,,
		*platycephalus Worth. & Ricardo	?
		*sianenna Boulenger	sand/mud
		*stappersii Boulenger	,, ,,
1	*LOPHIOBAGRUS	*cyclurus (Worth. & Ricardo)	rock
2	*PHYLLONEMUS	*filinemus (Worth. & Ricardo)	,,
		*typus Boulenger	,,
1	AUCHENOGLANIS	occidentalis (Cuv. & Val.)	ubiquitous
1	LEPTOGLANIS	brevis Boulenger	torrents

Mochokidae

No. of Species	Genus	Species	Habitat
7	SYNODONTIS	*dhonti Boulenger	rock
		*eurystomus Matthes	,,
		*granulosus Boulenger	,,
		*lacustricolus Poll	,,
		*melanostictus Boulenger	river
		*multipunctatus Boulenger	rock
		*petricola Matthes	,,
2	CHILOGLANIS	lukugae Poll	torrents
		pojeri Poll	,,

No. of Species	Genus	Species	Habitat
Amphiliidae			
2	AMPHILIUS	*platychir* (Günther)	torrents
		kivuensis Pellegrin	,,
Clariidae			
1	HETEROBRANCHUS	*longifilis* Cuv. & Val.	sand/mud/rock
1	*DINOTOPTERUS	*cunningtoni* Boulenger	rock
4	CLARIAS	*liocephalus* Boulenger	mud/estuary
		mossambicus Peters	,, ,,
		ornatus Poll	river
		theodorae Weber	mud/coastal
1	*TANGANIKALLABES	*mortiauxi* Poll	rock
Malapteruridae			
1	MALAPTERURUS	*electricus* (Gmelin)	mud/rock
Cyprinodontidae			
1	APLOCHEILICHTHYS	*pumilus* (Boulenger)	swamps
1	*LAMPRICHTHYS	*tanganicanus* (Boulenger)	pelagic
Centropomidae			
3	LATES	*angustifrons* Boulenger	pelagic
		mariae Steindachner	,,
		microlepis Boulenger	,,
2	*LUCIOLATES	*brevior* Boulenger	,,
		stappersi Boulenger	,,
Anabantidae			
1	CTENOPOMA	*muriei* (Boulenger)	swamps
Mastacembelidae			
13	MASTACEMBELUS	*albomaculatus* Poll	rock
		cunningtoni Boulenger	swamps/sand
		ellipsifer Boulenger	rock
		flavidus Matthes	,,
		frenatus Boulenger	,,
		micropectus Matthes	,,
		moorii Boulenger	,,
		ophidium Günther	,,
		plagiostoma Matthes	,,
		platysoma Poll & Matthes	,,

No. of Species	Genus	Species	Habitat
		taeniatus Boulenger	,,
		tanganicae Günther	,,
		zebratus Matthes	,,
Tetraodontidae			
1	TETRAODON	*mbu* Boulenger	estuaries

The non-cichlids in the lake basin are included in 18 families with 43 genera, of which 9 are endemic to the lake. The total number of species is 111, of which 57 are endemic.

ENDEMISM OF THE LAKE SPECIES

If we compare the endemism of cichlids with endemism in other families and try to distribute the species among their different habitats, as far as our present knowledge of the ecology of the fish provides the needed data, we find that the distribution can often be very striking.

Cichlids

The *non-endemic genera* are:

Tylochromis: There is one endemic species in coastal mud bottoms near estuaries.

Sarotherodon: There are two endemic species in the lake, one of which (*S. karamo*) was found in the Malagarazi delta but seems to be more abundant in the upstream swamps; the other (*S. tanganicae*) is found all around the lake, but always coastal. *S. nilotica* lives in swamps and estuaries or their vicinity; it is restricted to the northern part of the lake and is non-endemic.

Tilapia: The only species of *Tilapia* (*T. rendalli*), is not endemic and is restricted to river estuaries.

Haplochromis: The enormous genus *Haplochromis* is represented in Lake Tanganyika by only six species, one of which (*H. burtoni*) is very common in the northern part of the lake basin but is not restricted to the basin. The other five species of *Haplochromis* are endemic to the lake basin, though only three (*H. horei, H. pfefferi* and *H. benthicola*) are really lake species. All the others are coastal and swamp-dwelling species.

Tylochromis lateralis. Photo by G. Marcuse.

Astatoreochromis: There is only one non-endemic species in northern swamps actually in contact with the lake. It is very seldom found in the lake proper, and then only on mud bottoms in front of the swamps. Another species is known from the Lake Victoria and Lake Edward area.

Lamprologus: With 35 of the 40 or so species of the genus recorded only from the lake, the genus *Lamprologus* shows a remarkable endemism.

Orthochromis: One mountain species in the lake basin and another in the lower Congo River rapids make up this genus of torrent-dwelling *Haplochromis* fish.

It is noteworthy that the non-endemic species are restricted to coastal waters, usually on mud flats not very far from estuaries.

Although as yet some data are missing and some species are difficult to assign to one of the three main fish populations mentioned by Prof. Max Poll (littoral, pelagic or benthic), one might say that roughly:

- 30 to 40 species, or about 20% of the total number of species, are open-water fishes and thus are either pelagic or benthic. Among these two genera are notable *Trematocara* (8 species) and *Bathybates* (7 species).

- about 60 species, or about 40% of the total cichlid populations, are bound to rock shores.
- about 30 species, making up about 20% of all of the lake cichlids, are bound to mud or sand floors.

Lamprologus and the related genera *Julidochromis* and *Chalinochromis* represent some 42 species or nearly 30% of the total number of cichlid species. All are egg-layers on substrates. The proportion of mouthbrooders versus egg-layers is thus not overwhelmingly in favor of buccal incubation as it is in most of the Great Rift Valley lakes.

As for endemism, 95% of the species are endemic and the only ones which are not appear to be restricted to shallow or littoral waters still very close to their original river waters. These species have not done well in the lake as a rule.

Non-Cichlids

Of the 43 genera of non-cichlids, nine are endemic to the lake. The 43 genera include 57 endemic and 54 non-endemic species. 50% of the non-cichlids in the lake are thus endemic, but most genera (34) are not. This indicates that some genera, among which are *Lates, Luciolates, Synodontis* and *Mastacembelus*, have adapted very well to the lake conditions while most did not.

Of the nine endemic genera, four (*Limnothrissa, Stolothrissa, Lamprichthys* and *Luciolates*) are pelagic but include a total of only five species. Four genera (*Dinotopterus, Tanganikallabes, Lophiobagrus* and *Phyllonemus*) with only five species consist exclusively of rock-dwelling catfishes. The trend toward rock-dwelling among the lake catfishes is very strong. Most hide in rocky shelters even in the midst of large sand plains. These include species which in rivers are mud-dwellers, such as *Malapterurus*, the various species of *Synodontis, Heterobranchus* and many others.

Many endemic species in the non-cichlid group have succeeded in colonizing most habitats in the lake. Some non-endemic species were as successful, but as a rule the endemic species thrived better and are an important part of the 30 kg of fish per hectare, which recently has been estimated as the average density of fish in the lake (FAO fisheries surveys).

Of the 34 non-endemic genera (some of which have given rise to endemic species) many species, at least about 30, are not in the lake proper but restricted to rivers, mountain torrents and

Lates microlepis. Photo by H.R. Axelrod.

swamps. *Kneria, Amphilius* and *Barbus*, among others, should for this reason be considered as belonging to the lake basin and not to the lake proper.

Some non-endemic genera have, on the other hand, colonized the lake proper and have given rise to entirely endemic species. The most striking examples are, again, *Lates* (3 species), *Synodontis* (7), *Mastacembelus* (13), and *Chrysichthys* (6). Not a single Lake Tanganyika species from these genera has been found outside the lake. They are found in coastal swamps on occasion, but most of the time occur in deeper water far from the shore and often on rock slopes or in the middle of the lake.

The trends among non-cichlids when they colonized the lake were thus very different. They either remained as they were, without any inclination toward speciation, and their spread in the lake was either wide or restricted to habitats they were used to, or they speciated into new forms, including genera, but were not in every case associated with a very broad diversification. Some of the fishes, when they reached the lake waters, did not radiate much "in depth" in a multiple-level cascade of mutations, but showed the same aptitude for diversification as they showed elsewhere (*Synodontis* and *Mastacembelus*).

All in all, the non-cichlids were more successful in their colonization of Lake Tanganyika than they were in any other Rift Lake in Africa, especially when one considers Lake Malawi, the lake closest to Lake Tanganyika as concerns size, depth, ecological and climatic conditions and the ionic properties of the water. With 111 species divided among 43 genera, Lake Tanganyika has more than twice as many non-cichlid species and genera as Lake Malawi. There are eight endemic genera versus only one in Lake Malawi.

This situation is most probably due to several natural factors. Foremost among them is the original stock present in the area supplied for the main part, if not entirely, by the rich Congo basin, and secondly, the possibility of Congo species invading the lake later in its geological history by ascending the Lukuga outlet from the Congo, Lualaba and getting used to progressively higher concentrations of lake water as soon as each mountain torrent confluent with the Lukuga was by-passed during this climb. This is not the case with Lake Malawi and the Shire River which connects the lake to the Zambezi River, because there are impassable waterfalls.

On the other hand, if there are many more species and genera of non-cichlids in Lake Tanganyika which have not descended the

The author photographed during one of his collecting dives in the lake at Bujumbura, Burundi. Photo by Dr. Herbert R. Axelrod.

The surface of the lake as it appeared during a cloudy day. Part of the coastline of Burundi is also seen in the distance. Photo by Dr. Herbert R. Axelrod.

Lukuga outlet toward the Congo River any more than the cichlids did, it is entirely possible that this was due to the high concentrations of minerals to which the lake fish adapted and without which they cannot live any more as well established colonies. It is a well documented fact that it is impossible to keep the lake fish in any water from the innumerable rivers and brooks flowing into the lake. Even if some of the salts they need are present it appears that it is the overall balance of these salts which is all-important for their well-being. The lake water thus acts as a barrier preventing the local species from migrating into the basin rivers or the Congo basin if it does not prevent the gradual migration by the ascension of the Lukuga outlet of some of the Congo populations.

Estuary swamps, slow-moving plain rivers with low pH and oxygen levels, are not good pioneering grounds for the lake fishes. Most of them are used to high pH and oxygen levels. Many fishes from the swamps, on the other hand, only very reluctantly move into pure lake water and then stay confined to the boundaries of river estuaries.

As it is, there is still a poorly investigated "twilight zone" around the estuaries acting as filters where fish are progressively becoming adapted to another type of water and a different ecology.

One might wonder why the lake fishes have not been able to cross the barrier and colonize other basins when they seem to feel at home and breed in hobbyist's tanks. But are they feeling at home? It is much too soon to ascertain whether the stresses they are subjected to (the mineral deficiencies, etc.) will not disturb their genetic equilibrium and lead to the progressive extinction of these transplanted individuals. In nature, these problems are compounded for the migrating populations by the fierce competition from the local species. Intruders thus have a very dim prospect for living, and only the most adaptable survive and eventually become permanently established.

It is along this line of thought that the presence in the lake of river species might perhaps be explained, and it is perhaps not by sheer luck that some of them, like *Mastacembelus* and catfishes of the genera *Synodontis, Heterobranchus, Malapterurus* and *Auchenoglanis*, have colonized the lake in depth. Perhaps they are part of the original or early settlers which got used to the increasing salinity of the water to which latecomers cannot adapt, or they still need time before they can spread everywhere into the lake.

The absence of fossils older than a few thousand years prevents, and most probably will prevent for a long time, a good understanding of the endemism and evolution of the fish populations in the lake.

5. Bridges and Fords

As a professional fish collector in the Congo basin for more than 20 years, the author has had the opportunity of exploring and studying various river systems. The fishes collected have come from virgin forest affluents 1,000 km upstream from Kinshasa as well as from the Stanley Pool marshes, savannah streams, rapids and mangroves at the river mouths.

From all these parts of the Congo River basin about 50% of the fishes collected were identical species which had settled every habitat available. But each area also yielded species specific to that area alone. Fishes from the forest used to cool, soft and very acid waters had been unable to colonize the warmer, more neutral, river stretches in the savannah, nor could the fishes from the rapids populate the low oxygen waters in the swamps.

If the Congo River had been a vehicle for many species which had settled above its whole length, it had also been a barrier for some fishes with special requirements as to the quality of their habitat. So much so, in fact, that most of their fish populations from the affluents from the lower left bank were different from those of the lower right bank across the river. The fishes from the right bank, in the area between Kinshasa and Matadi 300 km down-river, were to some degree related to the Kwilu-Niari River basin, while those from the left bank were not. The small species had been unable to cross the fast-flowing Congo with its many predators and fierce competition.

In another well documented case, in 1962-1963 after especially strong rainy season floods, several species of fishes from cool, acid forest rivers had been washed away to the Stanley Pool and managed to take a slight hold and even started to spawn. Juveniles were collected during two dry seasons afterward. Finally, after a few years, they disappeared entirely from the Stanley Pool. Again, the competition from the local species, often closely related genera, added to the unusual ecological conditions and prevented the intruders from getting more than a precarious hold before they were wiped out.

Ephemeral phenomena such as these are very hard to study singlehandedly, and we thus welcomed the opportunity whenever we chanced to find problems in Lake Tanganyika connected with the notion of the ambivalency of a water system toward the spread of fish populations.

The problem within the lake, of course, was not one based upon different chemical properties of the lake water but on two main facts: first, the gradual drop of oxygen with depth, and second, the bond between the fishes and specific types of rock substrates.

We were very lucky to discover, 8 km south of Bujumbura in the northeastern corner of the lake, an area of rock and sandstone slabs in the middle of huge sand plains. These rocks, on the tip of a slope coming up from 100 meters depth, are totally isolated, both from the shore and the nearest rocky slopes. Between them and the shore lies a one km broad mud flat. The nearest rocky shore is 5 km to the south and consists only of shallow pebble beaches without any big rubble. The first full rocky slope is 15 km away. This area is thus very well isolated and the effects of isolation are here very apparent and noteworthy.

The only rock-dwellers present are a few cichlids, aside from a large population of giant catfishes, among which are many electric catfishes (*Malapterurus electricus*) and very many mastacembelid eels (some reaching 75 cm in length and weighing more than one kilogram). These rock-dwelling cichlids are *Julidochromis marlieri, Telmatochromis temporalis, Telmatochromis caninus, Limnotilapia dardennei* and *Petrochromis polyodon*.

Although these sandstone slabs lie in very shallow water from 1-4 m deep and have been deeply eroded by wave action into crevices and intricate labyrinths, they have not been colonized by the usual shallow-water rock-dwellers of these habitats. In fact, of all the rock-dwelling cichlids present in the lake, only the species mentioned have been able to reach the area. Aside from the cichlids which use a rock floor only for breeding purposes, for example the largest *Lamprologus* (*L. lemairei, L. elongatus, L. tetracanthus,* etc.), these rock-dwellers have found along their migration route either a bridge of properly shaped rocks, a ford, or their bond toward rock is weaker than other rock-dwellers' bonds and thus they can roam farther over open ground.

The results of the lack of competition from the other rock-dwellers have been spectacular, especially in the three species of *Julidochromis* and *Telmatochromis*. One might estimate the pro-

Julidochromis marlieri. Photo by W. Hoppe.

portion of *Julidochromis marlieri* on a more typical rock coast at a few percent of the total cichlid population. In this unusual isolated habitat, however, they probably make up more than 10% of the total cichlid stock. The result of this isolation is such that on a surface area of only a few acres, *Julidochromis marlieri* numbers perhaps 50,000 individuals. In two years time we have collected in excess of 15,000 fishes on these grounds with no apparent drop in the total stock.

It is very interesting to note what happened to the other rock-dwelling cichlids along the way between the rich rocky slopes to the south and the Ruziba shallows to the north. The rocky slopes with their rich variety of habitats—pebbles, rubble, labyrinths, blocks and boulders—and related fish niches give way to gravel and pebble beaches with sparse rubble in shallow water. As soon as the slopes disappear, so do the deep-living rock-dwellers and all those fishes whose niches consist of dark recesses, caves, labyrinths, crevices, etc. Only the surf-dwellers among the pebbles and rubble remain, like *Eretmodus, Spathodus, Simochromis, Lamprologus petricola* and *Haplochromis horei. Tropheus* have become scarce, and *Julidochromis* are infrequent.

As soon as the pebble beaches give way to sand, the above species disappear altogether and are replaced by the sand-dwellers. But *Julidochromis marlieri* must have found in deep water (too deep for the other rock-dwellers) suitable fords and has finally reached the Ruziba shallows, the edge of its range in the northern part of the lake. *Julidochromis marlieri* has been unable to cross the last 8 km to the next rock slabs in the northeastern corner of the lake where *J. regani* has a colony. One might say that this is the boundary of *J. marlieri*, because when *J. regani* and *J. marlieri* are in contact there is interbreeding at the boundary; the offspring are of the *J. regani affinis* Matthes type.

As for the presence on the Ruziba flats of the other rock-dwellers, like *Telmatochromis temporalis, T. caninus, Limnotilapia* and *Petrochromis*, one should note that these cichlids, although closely related to rocky habitats, have a much wider tolerance than the other cichlids toward the quality of their water (they are found on rocks even in the very muddy water which most of the others cannot stand) and to the type of rock they live on. They are thus the most ubiquitous of the rock-dwellers, as their bonds to a specific rock site are very loose.

Julidochromis tolerate muddy water quite well and therefore are able to utilize the recesses which provide them with appropriate shelters and breeding grounds.

The presence of fords acting as stepping stones and bridges between two rocky areas has thus permitted some rock-dwellers to cross open grounds. But apparently these fords were too deep for the upper-layer fishes to cross and of an improper nature for some of the deep-dwelling cichlids.

This is how one might explain the simultaneous absence of *Eretmodus, Spathodus* and *Simochromis* on the one hand, and of fishes like *Telmatochromis vittatus, Lamprologus compressiceps, L. furcifer, L. savoryi* and *L. brichardi*, etc., whose presence in such a type of rock habitat and at such a depth might otherwise be expected.

6. Genetic Dynamism

The cichlids as a group are considered to be among the most versatile and adaptable of all freshwater fishes. In Africa, perhaps even more so than in South America, they are not only represented by a very large number of genera and species but have shown to a remarkable degree a capacity to colonize a wide range of habitats from saturated soda lakes in East Africa to soft, acid rain forest brooks. They spread from the rim of the great Arabian desert in the Jordan valley to South Africa and are known as well from the brackish estuaries of the southern Atlantic Ocean. With similar intensity, other families of African fishes such as the cyprinids (barbs), the Characidae (tetras) and the Clariidae (catfishes) have shown identical adaptability.

But certainly not all the African fish families have shown the same wide diversification in forms. Many seem evolutionarily dormant or nearly extinct with one or only very few species in the family. Cichlids, cyprinids, mormyrids, etc., all seem to be endowed with a powerful genetic dynamism, one might even say instability, giving birth from brook to brook to different species. This remarkable difference in genetic behavior started to attract our attention while we were collecting fishes in the Congo basin; we tried to classify the fish from this basin according to their "radiation potential." They were either:

1. *"Relic"* or *"fossil"* forms, like the famous lungfish (*Protopterus*), the armored *Polypterus*, *Phractolaemus* and the freshwater flying fish (*Pantodon*). There are of course many others, all very ancient and some a hundred million years old.

   All have done well in their habitats, and it is worth noting that they have shared the same type of habitat, swamps, over the years and apparently are not going down the drain of extinction. They are hardy fishes or they wouldn't be here today. Polypteridae, at least, even shows some degree of genetic activity—there are two genera and several species. As a whole though, this group of fishes shows little tendency toward diversification, at least for the time being.

2. *"Static"* or *"dormant"* forms represented by families or genera apparently of more recent origin but which might be considered a dead branch of the genetic tree. In this category we might place the anabantids (labyrinth fishes), notopterids (knife fishes) and certain genera of the cichlids, clarids, mormyrids, etc. These fishes might, by themselves, have a wide distribution without showing any, or only a few, signs of diversification.

3. *"Dynamic"* forms including genera, but not necessarily all genera, of some families (for example the cichlid genera *Tilapia* and *Haplochromis*, the cyprinid genera *Labeo* and *Barbus*, the mormyrid genera *Petrocephalus*, *Marcusenius* and *Gnathonemus*). These fishes diversified into many species when they had the opportunity.

Let us note in passing that mormyrids, like the cyprinodonts, have shown less adaptability to different water conditions and that their proliferation is optimum in soft, warm and acid waters (for mormyrids), or soft, cool and very acid water (for the cyprinodonts). On the other hand, cichlids seem to prefer hard, alkaline waters.

The latest list (June, 1973) of the African fish families compiled by Prof. Poll throws some light on their distribution and genetic dynamism. There are 44 African fish families with a total of 280 genera covering 2,510 species.

Aside from four families of brackish-water fishes and ten ancient families, which together do not add up to more than 60 species, the most important families are:

Cichlidae	675 species
Cyprinidae	561 species
Mormyridae	202 species
Cyprinodontidae	178 species
Mochokidae	155 species (*Synodontis*)
Characidae	122 species (tetras)
Clariidae	102 species (catfishes)
Bagridae	102 species (catfishes)
Citharinidae	82 species

Each of the other families is represented by fewer than 50 species. One might thus say that three groups of fishes (cichlids, barbs and mormyrids) together make up more than 50% of all the African fauna. On the other hand, if we include in this group all the catfishes (families Mochokidae, Clariidae, Bagridae, Amphiliidae, and Schilbeidae) or 446 species, we will reach a total of more than 75% of the African fish fauna for the four main groups. Including brackish-water fishes, of the 44 African families, 23 have no more than five species each, and of these 12 have only one species each. The discrepancy in the genetic dynamism among the 44 families is thus apparent.

The geographic concentrations of catfishes and mormyrids are most important in the western part of Africa, which includes the Senegal, Niger and Congo River basins. In the same area cichlids, in proportion to their main concentration in the eastern half of Africa, are relatively few. Aside from a local concentration of endemic cichlids in Lake Barumbi-Mbo in northern Cameroon, the total cichlid populations between the Senegal River and the Okavambo swamps in South Africa should not exceed about 100 species.

Although the cichlid species of East Africa outnumber their counterparts in West Africa by 5 to 1, they are concentrated mainly in the set of lakes located along the Great African Rift valley. Nowhere else, either in the western or eastern river basins, do they appear to diversify almost at will, as they do in the rift lakes. There, and only there, have cichlids found ideal conditions for speciation.

Petrocephalus bovei. Photo by Gunther Senfft.

Haplochromis cf. *pallidus*, male. Photo by P.V. Loiselle.

But the speciation of cichlid genera is not identical in all lakes. Many lakes, most of them in fact, have only a limited choice of cichlids. Lake Edward, Lake Kivu and Lake Albert have perhaps only about 20 species as an average. Lake Victoria-Nyanza has a cichlid population limited to *Tilapia*, *Haplochromis* and *Haplochromis* derivatives, with the *Haplochromis* making up most of the species in the lake. Lake Malawi has about the same number of species (221), but divided among 26 genera; Lake Tanganyika has only about 140 cichlid species at latest count, but divided among 42 genera. These figures indicate that cichlids have found ideal conditions in these three lakes to put to work their genetic dynamism, sometimes at the expense of other families with which they are too much in competition or perhaps because the lake waters are less favorable to these fishes.

Is this to mean that cichlids in these lakes have shown equally the same radiation potential? Certainly not! To say that cichlids as a whole are highly adaptable is documented beyond doubt. To imply that all cichlids, under any conditions, are endowed with a high speciation potential would be gross oversimplification. In no area, aside from the lakes of the Rift Valley, are there more than a few species of cichlids. Even in the Rift Valley lakes, where they have thrived under ideal conditions, many cichlid genera simply seem evolutionarily dormant and do not show any trend toward diversification. One might wonder why?

Cichlids seem to be of rather recent origin. Few fossils are available to trace them back to their original ancestors. Thus their background is very much an unknown quantity, except for the fact that they have had a marine origin. This might, perhaps, explain their affinity to hard, alkaline waters and why they do not thrive as well in acid, soft waters. In fact, in the whole virgin forest of the central bowl of the Congo basin, in the forest rivers proper and excluding the big rivers, we know of only three cichlids, *Nanochromis dimidiatus*, *Hemichromis bimaculatus* and *H. fasciatus*.

Even if their ancestors are unknown, identifying the genetically active and dormant forms in the cichlids should be rather easy work. Many of them, even though they have a wide geographical distribution (sometimes over most of tropical Africa and most of the important river basins), do not speciate at all. *Hemichromis bimaculatus* and *H. fasciatus*, both probably rather primitive cichlids, seem to suffer from genetic immobility. There are no local races or subspecies. *H. bimaculatus* has only one close relative, *Pelmatochromis thomasi*.

Pelmatochromis thomasi. Photo by R. Zukal.

Leptotilapia tinanti from the Congo River. Photo by P.V. Loiselle.

In the Stanley Pool area of the Congo River and the rapids downstream, the cichlids of the area, for example *Leptotilapia*, *Teleogramma* and *Steatocranus*, seem to be genetically static. In forest areas *Pelvicachromis* (formerly *Pelmatochromis*) has exhibited all over Central Africa a slight measure of speciation. *P. subocellatus*, *P. pulcher*, *P. taeniatus*, etc. are witnesses thereof. But let us realize that they are strictly restricted to the rain forest, do not intrude into the savannah rivers and in fact, over such a huge area, have diversified little. Only *Tilapia* and *Haplochromis* have been capable of considerable speciation when occupying new grounds under different chemical and physical water conditions, different climates and different diets. Both genera have not gone far in colonizing the forest waters. Most cichlids have thus far shown none of the unconditional speciation potential attributed to the family. Many have shown no inclination to settle into ecosystems which are not of their liking and many, even under the best of ecological conditions, simply stay genetically dormant. There are many cichlids in the Rift Valley lakes which don't show the slightest intention of radiating into new forms, at least for the time being, or all genera in these lakes would be represented by several species, which is not the case as we have seen.

On the other hand, *Haplochromis* in Lake Victoria-Nyanza has multiplied and diversified each time it found a new ecological niche in the lake. Each local race, subspecies or species became better equipped to survive than the later intruders. The latter were repelled or forced to extinction.

This process occurring repeatedly, and in various directions according to local conditions, has led to the immense variety of *Haplochromis* species in Lake Victoria, although most probably they have but one common ancestor. In Lake Malawi there are 26 genera of cichlids, most of them tracing back to *Haplochromis*.

There is thus a very big difference between the two lakes, the fish in Lake Victoria having not been in the lake for enough time or not having had the proper speciation conditions to diversify much beyond the species level. The speciation has been "lateral"— one might call it of the "first degree." In Lake Malawi on the contrary, speciation has been at work much longer, or has been accelerated, and the diversification is greater. One might call it a "vertical" or multiple-degree speciation. The differences between the fishes are such that they reach the generic level.

How can we apply this knowledge of variable genetic speciation to the understanding of the Lake Tanganyika fish fauna? Are there also "dormant" and "dynamic" genera? And do they depend totally on isolation?

The overall picture is not clear, but there are some facts tending to show that isolation is not the only force behind the present variety in the lake.

The first problem is that speciation has occurred without isolation or there wouldn't be such a wide variety among the roamers, the perennial wanderers, such as the seven species of *Bathybates*, the sand-dwellers such as the 11 species of *Xenotilapia* and the four scale-eating species of *Plecodus*. On the other hand, *Boulengerochromis*, also a typical roamer, is represented only by a single species.

Genetic dynamism has thus been at work within the pelagic species, but to a varying degree, and in their case isolation was impossible.

Trematocara, with eight species all living in deep or very deep water and perhaps being the most typical Lake Tanganyikan fishes with their sensorial or acoustical drum-like cavities in the head bones, has also shown a remarkable diversification. So have the mastacembelid eels and *Synodontis*.

The rock-dwellers, for which isolation is often difficult to assess as long as their ethology is not totally understood (but nevertheless already well known along broad lines) also show how variable their speciation potential is. If we take for granted that isolation works best and fastest when inbreeding occurs within a small number of fish isolated on new ground away from the main population, individualistic and territorial or sedentary species stand a better chance of diversifying into new local races and then into subspecies, species and finally genera. But we have seen with the migratory pelagic species that this is not always the case. Most of them are gregarious, and crossbreeding between large numbers of individuals within a school, or when different schools mix, is too easy. That there are thus "dormant" and genetically dynamic genera in the lake seems obvious. As for "fossil" forms, the answer is, for the time being, practically impossible to give, at least for the endemic species.

PROBLEMS OF SPECIATION IN THE LAKE

The cichlid populations, when they colonized the lake, did not have an identical response, genetically, to their biotope. If, in Lake Victoria and Lake Malawi, *Haplochromis* had a tremendous genetic explosion, they do not appear to have had the same success in Lake Tanganyika. Only three species have been recorded from the lake proper, *Haplochromis horei*, *H. benthicola* and *H. pfefferi*. A few others, such as *H. burtoni*, are still coastal and bonded to muddy swamps along the shoreline not far from river estuaries. Most of the species are not in the lake proper but in rivers nearby. *Astatoreochromis* lives in estuary swamps and *Orthochromis* belongs to the group of fast-flowing torrent-dwelling *Haplochromis* derivatives. This is not to say that some lake fishes are not related to *Haplochromis* and probably descended from them, for instance, *Telmatochromis* or most mouthbrooders. But the present group of *Haplochromis* species by and large haven't been colonizing the lake lately.

Another genus, on the other hand, has done well. *Lamprologus*, with 35 species at present count, has been genetically the most prolific of all lake genera. Outside of the lake, however, this genus has been found only in the Congo River (represented by a few closely related species). The genus is thus also typical of the Congo River basin, but to decide if they first settled in the lake and then spread into the river basin, or the opposite, is very difficult. Let us say that *Lamprologus* diversified more in the lake than in the river and that they are found on every shore, mud, sand or rock, but with a marked preference for rocky areas.

The sand-dwellers, such as *Callochromis* and *Xenotilapia*, are well diversified and have shown genetic dynamism. Let us remember that they are gregarious wanderers and that isolation is apparently difficult to achieve for such fishes. It is entirely possible of course that variations of the lake level during the past ages has made passages over sand available for these roamers but have now sunk below the present oxygen-bearing layer. This might explain some of the present varieties and why the southern or central parts of the lake harbor races or species which are now different from the northernmost stock.

The same is probably also true for some free-swimming rock-dwellers, such as *Ophthalmochromis* and *Ophthalmotilapia*. Although gregarious and living away from the rocks, but in close relationship with them, they also have diversified differently along the lake shores in the north and south.

As for the sedentary rock-dwellers, there is little doubt that several of them exhibit intense, one might say effervescent, speciation. *Tropheus* for one, according to Dr. Marlier's work, has now reached the status of "symbol of speciation." It might prove of interest to add the latest data available and investigate the case.

As of today, there are four main "types" in the genus *Tropheus:*
1. *Northern type:* comprising the local races described by Marlier from the Zaire coast from Burton Bay to Uvira. These include the following races:
   - all-black from Uvira
   - black and orange stripe from Bemba
   - black and yellow stripe from Mboko
   - black and orange patch from the tip of Ubwari Peninsula
   - black and red patch from Lutunga coast in Burundi
   - another all-black race at Minago on the Burundi coast
2. *Tropheus duboisi:* occurring on the Zaire coast between Uvira and the Burton Bay shore, with one race. Since then two other populations of *T. duboisi* have been found on the eastern coast:
   - a race similar to the one from Zaire, extending south of Nyanza-Lac station in Burundi
   - a broad-banded (yellow and white) race south of the Malagarazi River
3. *Eastern* or Nyanza-Lac (*T. brichardi*) type: extending at least to the Malagarazi delta, with several ill-defined races often banded or striped, even when adult, with an overall yellow-brown color.
4. *Southern* or Zambia type: including at least four dark brown

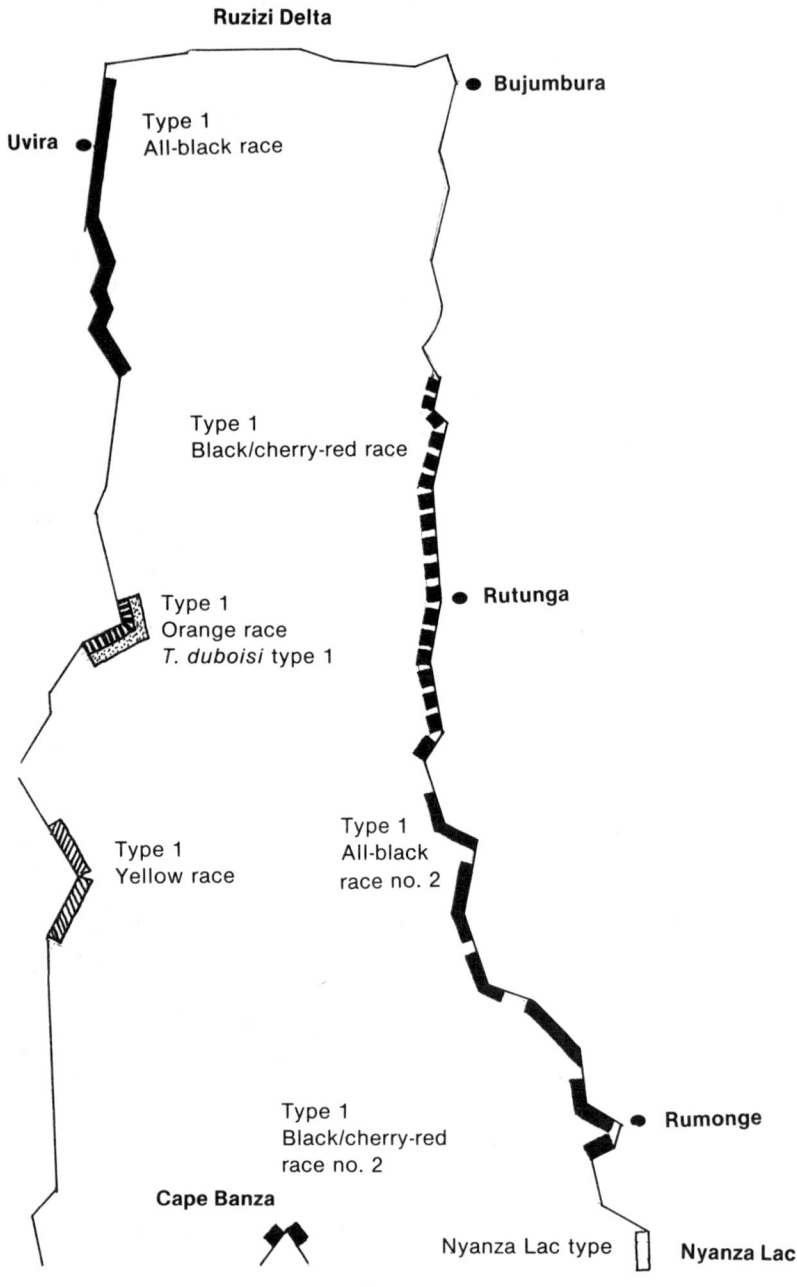

Races of *Tropheus* on the northern shores of Lake Tanganyika.

Tropheus moorii. Photo by E. Roloff.

local races on the true southern or southwestern coasts and two "yellow" races to the southeast.

Detailed study of all these local races and subspecies at all age levels seems in order before we can get a better understanding of the speciation process in *Tropheus*. The problem is not so much adding new local races, and many probably are still missing from the unexplored shores around the lake, but to find the pattern, if there is one, behind the local populations.

T. duboisi, for example, with three local races totally separated from each other by impassable ecological barriers, does not look as much like the local "end" product of *Tropheus* speciation as it once did, but more and more like the result of an already ancient speciation also producing new local races. This will probably be borne out by further studies. It is remarkable that *T. duboisi* from the Zaire coast has the lowest number of anal spines and the narrowest mouth with the smallest number of bicuspid teeth of the races of the *Tropheus* that have been investigated (information provided by Mr. Nelissen, Antwerp University).

Further studies are also in order to determine if races found very far apart, for example the black/red and all-black northern races, are distinct or the same. Should they prove to be identical, although they are separated from each other by impassable biotopes, then one would have to admit that there are patterns in the *Tropheus* speciation. This, under specific circumstances, is still difficult to assess but probably linked to minute local changes in the water composition or perhaps to the availability of different biocovers (which depend on currents). The same races can be created repeatedly in different places along the shores.

Genetic speciation might thus occur along "pre-set" lines, triggered by still undetected ecological conditions. This is not to say that all races of *Tropheus* have been created by pre-set triggers in the biotope.

Let us assume, until all *Tropheus* biotopes have been *systematically* explored (and we have seen that it means the simultaneous study of the biotopes in detail), that the Lake cannot be considered as a whole and always uniformly identical everywhere, but as an endlessly varied biotope. Let us assume also that speciation perhaps isn't always at random, at least as far as *Tropheus* speciation is concerned, and that a few "pre-coded" types might occur along with an odd array of ill-defined races. The problem is to find out how and when speciation works.

Simochromis is another typical rock-dweller with individualistic and territorial habits. Its ecological niche has been repeatedly

Tropheus duboisi. Photo by Dr. H.R. Axelrod.

Julidochromis ornatus. Photo by H. Hansen.

explored underwater and is now well documented. More restricted to shallow water than *Tropheus*, *Simochromis* are found in rubble along the shoreline not much deeper than 3 or 4 meters.

Four species of *Simochromis* have been recorded from the lake, with another as yet unidentified from Nyanza-Lac. No local races have yet been discovered among them. It is premature to decide about the speciation potential of these fishes, but it seems to be less than in *Tropheus*, since explorations covered the same ground where many races of *Tropheus* were discovered. Noteworthy perhaps is their potential for wandering over ground closed to *Tropheus*, which might account for easy crossbreeding.

One of them, *S. diagramma*, reaches the unusual size for *Simochromis* and *Tropheus* alike of about 20 cm (species of *Tropheus* do not exceed 15 cm). It also occurs with *S. babaulti*, the only fish of the two genera found in abundance on rocks in very murky water not far from the river deltas.

Julidochromis, another typical rock-dwelling group of species, apparently swims freely over open grounds, although the habitat is deeper than that of *Tropheus*. They like shade and breed in rocks. The attachment of *Julidochromis* to rock appears to be variable with each species. *J. marlieri* doesn't wander far from rock over sand, but we have seen *J. regani regani* in rubble flee

Julidochromis ornatus in the aquarium will feel at home if a semblance of a rocky habitat is provided. Photo by Jaroslav Elias.

toward sand over long distances (in excess of 20 meters) instead of taking shelter in the rocks as the fish well could. *J. transcriptus* also seems to like deep caves best and is not so much of an open-ground wanderer.

All in all, the species of *Julidochromis* do not appear to be as choosy as *Tropheus* about the purity of their water. They live in rocks near estuaries bathed in very muddy water. This fact, everything taken into consideration, isn't so exceptional. The teeth of *Julidochromis* are not as specialized as the *Tropheus* dentition, and they can prey upon loose material while species of *Tropheus* cannot do so easily. They are thus less restricted to rock covered with a thick layer of biocover than is *Tropheus* (which will not colonize an area where rocks are covered with a muddy slime).

These facts would tend to make the genus *Julidochromis* a poor choice for an example of speciation. Crossbreeding should be easy, as the fish are capable of wandering off their birthplace and are not choosy about the quality of water and food. There is some crossbreeding between different populations of *Julidochromis* apparently occurring at the boundaries of the various species when there are boundaries (*J. transcriptus* may live on the same grounds as *J. marlieri*). There are subspecies of *J. regani*, for example, *J. regani affinis*, near *J. marlieri* grounds which show traces of the latter's vertical bands.

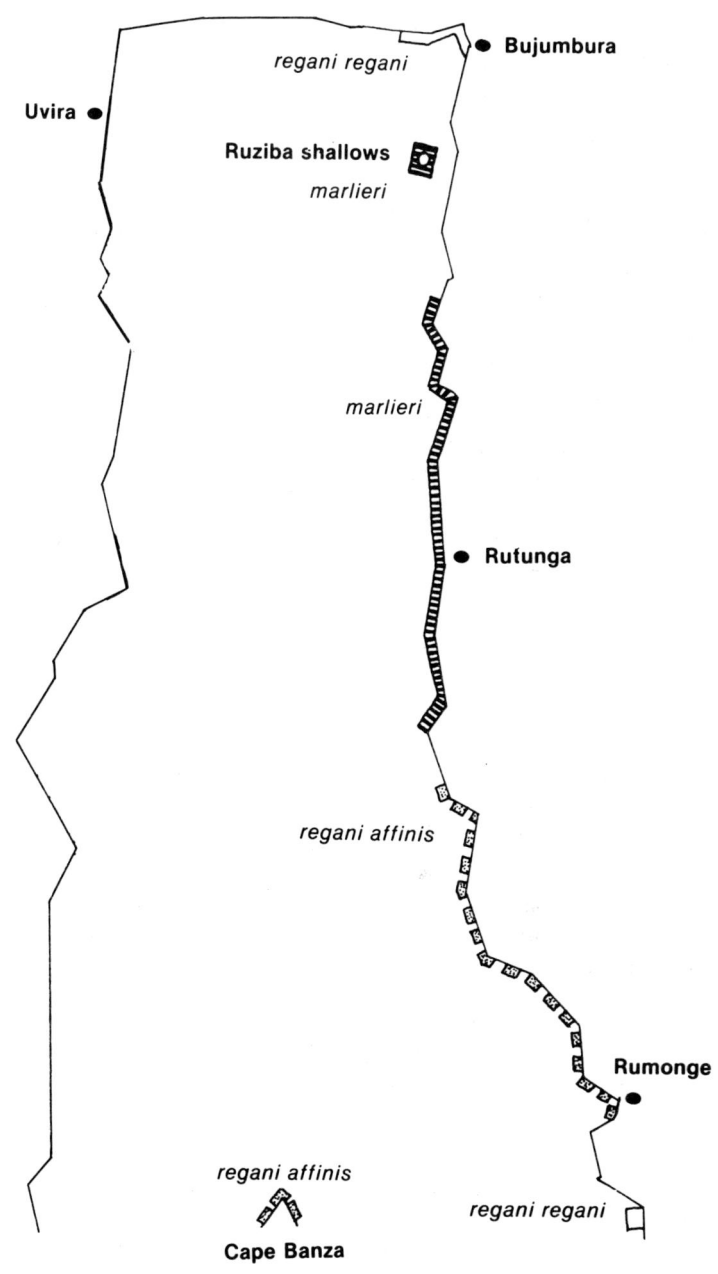

Distribution of *Julidochromis* on the northeastern coast of Lake Tanganyika.

It is not at all impossible that the basic color pattern in *Julidochromis* was composed of horizontal stripes (*J. regani, J. ornatus* and the new species *J. dickfeldi*) without any vertical bands. All the species of *Julidochromis* discovered until now, except for a few "aberrant" individuals of *J. marlieri* found in the northeastern corner of the lake, show these stripes. *J. marlieri, J. transcriptus* and *J. regani affinis* have added the vertical bands. The "aberrant" brown *J. marlieri* has faint bands, and the stripes have become mere lines zigzagging along the body length.

Nowhere are there strong local races, at least in a concentration like the ones observed on narrow coast lines in *Tropheus*. There are three different races of *J. regani regani:*

- *northern* types with brown stripes on a beige body, identified from the Burundi coast and along the area from Nyanza-Lac to Kigoma;
- *southern* type: with black stripes on a light beige body;
- *southern "russet"* type: with reddish-brown stripes on a beige/brown body.

It is remarkable that the northern territory of *J. regani regani* is separated from the next one in Nyanza-Lac by the successive broad habitats of other races or species, first for about 40 km by *J. marlieri* grounds, then by *J. regani affinis* for another 30 km. The latter is found again in Kigoma, 70 km south.

Within their main habitats, the species of *Julidochromis* show little trend toward speciation as there are no local races. Perhaps one might, however, mention a trend toward melanism in a vertical direction. On the same slopes deep-living specimens show more black than white in their pattern. This is constant and a permanent character in the individual, not an only occasionally adaptable mimetism. Populations living in shallow water are constantly lighter in shade. This is especially true with *J. marlieri*. We wouldn't be surprised to discover some day all-black specimens in their deeper habitats, living in the dark recesses of caves and crevices.

The genus *Telmatochromis* is now represented by five species, two of which (*T. bifrenatus* and *T. vittatus*) are so different from the other three that it is rather difficult to understand, except from the systematist's point of view, how they were put together in the same genus. The two "dwarfs" are strictly bound to rather deep (more than 4 meters and at least to 20 meters), very clear (never muddy) water. The other three species are found in shallow, even very murky, water near river deltas. The dwarfs reach a maximum size of 100 mm (very seldom that large in the wild); the others grow well in excess of 100 mm. We collected a 140 mm specimen of *T. temporalis*. The dwarfs are very elongated fish, the others are very stocky.

Dr. Poll stressed the high variability of *T. temporalis* and *T. caninus* and the probability of there being local races, but in these species of *Telmatochromis* it has not been documented since.

The fact that they are omnivorous wanderers, not choosy about their rock habitat, would suggest that crossbreeding must be frequent and local races hard to come by. The large *Telmatochromis* which have often been collected over mud floors (even within the perimeter of large river deltas) are probably the rock-dwelling cichlids with the weakest bond toward rocks, which perhaps, as in some species of *Lamprologus*, are used only for breeding purposes.

On the other hand, the two dwarf *Telmatochromis* species are among the cichlids most attached to a typical rock habitat and are never found anywhere else. Their speciation potential should thus be good, but for the time being none has been detected and local races have not been discovered.

The bond to rock for breeding purposes is a very common one among the rock-dwelling cichlids. It is perhaps the most powerful bond for the gregarious schools (for example *Ophthalmochromis, Cyathopharynx, Ophthalmotilapia*, etc.) living off the slopes in mid-water and feeding on floating particles they could just as well find over sand. It is entirely possible that it keeps species of *Julidochromis* on their habitat, enabling them to have become diversified through isolation into the species and varieties we have recorded.

Why should species of the genus *Julidochromis* be attached by their breeding ethology toward their birthplace? They are the only individualistic fish we know of that probably use the same nesting site (crevices, caves, etc.) during their entire life span. It is for the simple reason that most *Julidochromis* species spawn continuously, in small batches, that the nest is permanently filled with fry at different stages in their development which the parents cannot abandon. The fry, as soon as they grow large enough, wander one by one out of the nest leaving the younger fish behind. *Julidochromis* species, which are not bonded to their habitat by feeding, cleanliness of the water, by oxygen, nor by the absolute need for twilight, are nevertheless incapable of leaving their caves, or at least are very much slowed down, because of the everlasting care of their brood at their nest site. This is one of the reasons behind their isolation.

What can we thus conclude about genetic speciation and isolation in Lake Tanganyika?

1. Many fish have shown little or no trend at all toward speciation. Cichlids, although in what is apparently an optimum biotope, genetically reacted with varying intensity, diversifying at first but afterward appearing "dormant."
2. Some genera (*Tropheus* and *Lamprologus* are the best examples) have shown *"effervescent genetic dynamism."*
3. *Haplochromis* hasn't been as successful in Lake Tanganyika as in the other Rift Valley Lakes.
4. Geographical isolation is not the only trigger behind speciation or there would be little or no speciation in gregarious migratory species.
5. The genetic dynamism of each species is probably the most important single factor behind speciation, perhaps the only one (by genetic instability) among the pelagic and benthic species.
6. Isolation can be achieved by the feeding ethology (*Tropheus*) or nesting ethology (*Julidochromis*).
7. The alternate distribution of some species of the same genus around the lake coasts is, for the time being, very difficult to understand (for example, *Tropheus moorei*, *T. duboisi* and *Julidochromis marlieri*, *J. regani regani*, *J. regani affinis* populations).

7. Reproductive Modes of the Lake Fishes

Until recently, very little was known about the breeding habits and behavior of the Lake Tanganyika fishes. It was only known that many of the cichlids were mouthbrooders. As of today no report on the behavior of the fish in the lake had been made public, although several spawns of cichlids in the aquarium have been related by hobbyists. It is thus interesting and important to know what the breeding behavior of these fishes is and whenever possible to try to find out why they behave as they do.

NON-CICHLIDS

Very few facts are known about the breeding behavior of the non-cichlid fishes of Lake Tanganyika, and there is little hope that information will be forthcoming in the near future. The only systematic studies now under way cover the economically important pelagic fishes such as the plankton-eating clupeids and their predators, *Luciolates*, *Lates* and *Bathybates*.

After several years of systematic survey, one has to admit that the data collected are very few, essentially because the fishes by their very nature are very elusive. They follow migration routes which have only very recently been made apparent, although they are still poorly known, and cover the whole length of the lake. The vertical daily migrations also make observations very difficult. The breeding behavior of the benthic fishes has, until now, not even been subjected to initial study.

As for the non-cichlids living on the lake slopes, not much has been added to what was already known twenty years ago. We are still waiting to see our first spawning (except for *Lamprichthys tanganicanus*, which is now well documented). We haven't seen a single spawning of *Mastacembelus* or any of the catfishes—most probably these fishes spawn at night.

It is apparent, from the fry we have seen, that although the non-cichlids appear to have two peak breeding periods, they spawn, like most littoral fish, through the year. We have a feeling that mating is linked to the climatic seasonal changes of the dry and rainy seasons. At least one of these seasons is more or less in accordance with the annual matings in the Congo basin, which occur at the start of, or just before, the first rains of September-October when the rivers start to fill.

In the Congo basin, this quasi-universal urge to mate seems to be triggered by outside stimuli. During the dry season, as water cools down by more than $4°C$ and at the same time drops several meters, it recedes from the flooded, usually well planted banks and fishes become restricted to the permanent river bed. From day to day the Congo water becomes more foul, laden as it is with silt and organic matter, oxygen levels drop and dangerous parasites like *Ichthyophthirius* or even paratyphoid germs attack the fishes, sometimes reaching epidemic proportions. On the other hand, as the density of fish increases in the remaining river bed the available organic food dwindles with each passing week. At the end of the process in early August, when the waters are at their lowest level, the fishes (except for the predators) are usually emaciated and in poor condition.

The start of the rainy season really flushes the river. As the river level rises, water floods the grassflats and half-dried swamps, making them available as breeding grounds for the fish fauna. All the food accumulated for them on the ground (seeds, fruits, insects, etc.) becomes available. In a few week's time the fishes are conditioned and ready to spawn. The water temperature on these flats has now risen to $27°C$. The second dry season (February-March) is much shorter, less drastic and appears to affect only a few fishes.

On another scale and by different means, but basically the same process, spawning follows the availability of conditioning food in Lake Tanganyika. The drop in water level during the dry season, June to the end of September in the northern section, is only about 50 cm and will be replaced by early December. But the density of suspended matter drops sharply during the dry season months to reach a minimum during August and September. The first big rains at the end of September are followed in short order by a dramatic increase of plankton probably feeding on the minerals and organic matter flushed from mountain slopes by the affluents. Visibility in the lake drops sharply so dense is the plankton bloom.

A few weeks later there are multiple signs of mating activity, the most immediately apparent being probably in the sponges, of which the white patches of young colonies take a grip on every available rock.

The plankton bloom follows the equatorial rainbelt, with its October downpours in the north, to the southern part of the lake which is reached by the rainy season storms during November and early December. There is thus a progressive spread of the plankton bloom from the north to the south of the lake over a 700 km distance. The bloom thus does not occur simultaneously all over the lake surface, and this phenomenon might be one of the reasons behind the pelagic fish migration which have been recently identified across the lake.

CICHLIDS

The underwater exploration of the lake floors reveals the density of the fish populations and fierce competition they have to deal with. Cichlids at best are omnivorous, but more often than not are predatory on fish fry. Protection by the parents of their offspring is therefore a must if the species is to survive. It is really a matter of life or death on these crowded slopes. What are the courses of action and reproduction the cichlids have adopted to insure the survival of the species?

1. *Nest-spawning and breeding:* Most species of *Lamprologus, Julidochromis, Telmatochromis, Boulengerochromis,* etc. are nest-builders. The nests may be constructed in the open (mainly on sand bottoms) when the species is of a fair size (in excess of 150 mm), but more often in sheltered areas when the small size of the fish prevents them from warding predators off the nest site. The sheltered nest is used even when, as an adult, the fish lives in the open.

2. *Buccal incubation:* This type of spawning is used by a very large number of the lake cichlids and in various species tends to show a gradual evolution from nest-breeding to direct incubation without the use of a spawning site. There are thus degrees of buccal incubation.

   - *Monogamous* pairs prepare a nest, usually crater-shaped, on sand bottoms. This is the type used by *Tilapia* and *Haplochromis.*
   - *Polygamous* spawning usually occurs in schooling fishes, either sand- or rock-dwellers. The male builds a nest, usually also crater-shaped or made of small sand cones arranged in a circle. Females enter into the nest one by one, lay their eggs

which are then fertilized by the male and then swim away. The male stays around the nest to attract other females. Species of *Xenotilapia* are typically known for this spawning mode. Spawning is a school affair apparently triggered by group stimuli. All females are fertilized at approximately the same time by the males, and the eggs, incubated in the females' mouths, reach the same development at the same time.

- *Polygamous* spawning occurs *without contact* between the females and the male on the nest site. This very unusual mode is used by *Ophthalmochromis ventralis* and probably by the other species in *Ophthalmochromis, Ophthalmotilapia* and *Cyathopharynx*. The fact that no contact between the partners occurs during the spawning has been observed several times by the author while underwater.
- *Polygamous* spawning also occurs on a makeshift spawning site hastily prepared by the male under some shelter. This is practiced by typical rubble-dwellers like *Simochromis, Spathodus, Eretmodus* and *Tanganicodus*. The pairs are not permanent, spawning occurring when adults happen to meet.

Lamprologus brichardi swimming toward the rocks for cover. Note the collecting net on the right. Photo by Dr. Herbert R. Axelrod.

Lobochilotes labiatus. Photo by Wilhelm Hoppe.

- *Direct buccal incubation* occurs without the use of any spawning site, usually over open ground and most often under the protection of the substratum. The eggs are laid one at a time, picked up by the female at once and eventually fertilized individually when she bumps the side of the male near the sperm duct with her head. This is the mode used by species of *Tropheus* and is probably the most elaborate and the ultimate in evolution of mouthbrooding among egg-laying fishes. Polygamy is the rule, and it is entirely possible that polyandry even occurs occasionally, as spawning occurs at random when individuals meet during their wanderings in and out of the substratum and are of very short duration in the wild.

There is thus a very strong polygamous trend within the lake cichlids. From our data, *all* gregarious cichlids in the lake which we could observe, with the sole exception of *Lamprologus brichardi*, use buccal incubation as their breeding mode. Mouthbrooders *living in schools off the underwater slopes,* in fact in the open either over sand bottoms or rocks, still build nests, sometimes very elaborate, for the spawning site. The only undocumented cases of deep-living mouthbrooders are those of *Cyphotilapia, Lobochilotes, Limnochromis nigripinnis* and *L. microlepidotus.* Some of these gregarious species, essentially sand-dwellers, breed when triggered by group stimuli.

This picture illustrates the presence of fishes near the surface of the water, over the rocks and beneath the rocks in the lake. Photo by Dr. Herbert R. Axelrod.

The rock-dwelling mouthbrooders are usually individualistic and perennial wanderers within the limits of their habitat, territorial only (but not always) when they spawn. In this respect they are in strong contrast with the individualistic, territorial, sedentary species where egg-laying and fry-raising occur on the spawning site. The rule seems to be that when fishes have a territory of their own and are sedentary, they nest; when they are wanderers, they take the eggs along.

Although periodic release of the fry by the female on the substratum has been observed in tank-raised fishes, this behavior, although probable in the wild, has been observed underwater only in two species, *Lobochilotes labiatus* and *Perissodus microlepis*, which release their fry in the open. The other rock-dwellers (*Tropheus* and *Simochromis* are good examples) mentioned as releasing their fry occasionally to feed on the substratum probably release them under the shelter of rubble and pebbles littering the rock slopes.

The following two charts include all species of littoral cichlids which have been discovered on the northeastern coast of the lake. Two pelagic fishes are, however, also included in the list. The first is *Boulengerochromis*, which comes up from the deep waters to nest and breed on sand bottoms. It is a loner, but can easily protect its fry. The second one, *Plecodus paradoxus*, is a very gregarious fish, the schools often numbering several hundreds. It is always on the run and is a scale-eater (it is on the look-out for schools to prey upon), but we never saw the nesting places. The fish are mouth-brooders.

BEHAVIOR OF SAND-DWELLERS

Taxon	Social behavior		Ecology		Sedentarism		Breeding mode	
	Gregarious	Individualistic	Open	Sheltered	Vagrant	Territorial	Buccal incubation	Nesting
Callochromis	★			★		★		★
Xenotilapia	★			★		★		★
Cardiopharynx	★			★		★		★
Aulonocranus	★			★		★		★
Limnotilapia	★			★		★		★
Lamprologus								
„ *attenuatus*		★	★		★			★
„ *pleuromaculatus*	★		★		★			★
„ *tetracanthus*		★	★		★			★
„ *ocellatus*		★			★	★		★
„ *modestus*		★	★		★			★
„ *callipterus*	★		★		★		?	?
Boulengerochromis		★	★		★		★	?
Plecodus paradoxus	★		★		★		★	?

BEHAVIOR OF ROCK-DWELLERS

Taxon	Social behavior		Ecology		Sedentarism		Breeding mode	
	Gregarious	Individualistic	Open	Sheltered	Vagrant	Territorial	Buccal incubation	Nesting
"School fishes"								
Ophthalmochromis	★		★		★		★	
Cyathopharynx	★		★		★		★	
Cyphotilapia	★		★		★		★	
Limnochromis								
„ *nigripinnis*	★		★		★		★	
„ *macrolepidotus*	★		★		★		★	
Lamprologus brichardi	★		★			★		★
"Loners"								
Eretmodus		★		★	★		★	
Spathodus		★		★	★		★	
Tanganicodus		★		★	★		★	
Tropheus		★		★	★		★	
Simochromis		★		★	★		★	

Behavior of Rock-dwellers (continued)

Taxon	Social behavior		Ecology		Sedentarism		Breeding mode	
	Gregarious	Individualistic	Open	Sheltered	Vagrant	Territorial	Buccal incubation	Nesting
Petrochromis	★		★			★	★	
Lobochilotes	★	★			★		★	
Lamprologus								
,, *furcifer*	★			★		★		★
,, *savoryi*	★			★		★		★
,,˙ *shreyeni*	★			★		★		★
,, *leleupi*	★			★		★		★
,, *niger*	★			★		★		★
Julidochromis	★			★		★		★
Chalinochromis	★			★		★		★
Telmatochromis								
,, *vittatus*	★			★		★		★
,, *caninus*	★			★		★		★
,, *temporalis*	★			★		★		★
Perissodus microlepis	★	★			★		★	

Let us explore in detail the breeding habits of these fishes.

Sand-dwellers

The first group of species includes the genera of gregarious cichlids roaming over the vast sand plains. The behavior of *Callochromis*, *Xenotilapia*, *Cardiopharynx*, *Aulonocranus* and *Limnotilapia* is very social, with the typical group stimuli associated with schooling fish such as unidirectional moves and escapes, "explosive" panics, group feeding, etc. The group stimuli during the breeding periods are very well documented for several species of *Xenotilapia*. The whole flock spawns simultaneously on circular nests built by males. The females circling overhead are one by one attracted to the nest, lay their eggs, get them fertilized by the male and resume their position in mid-water. The nests of *X. melanogenys* and *X. ochrogenys* are mixed on the same breeding grounds. The first constructs a flat crater, the second a set of seven or eight sand cones formed into a circle. The two species can be seen spawning at the same time, occasionally on the same grounds, and apparently do not interfere with each other.

In *Xenotilapia* at least, what is remarkable is that not only does a group stimulus for the breeding time exist, but also most probably for the release of the fry. All *Xenotilapia* collected underwater from a single school, and the capture usually numbered in the hundreds, always produced females with fry or eggs in their mouth at the same level of development. Whenever schools of

Note the fry near the head of this benthic mouthbrooder, *Xenotilapia sima*. Photo by P.V. Loiselle.

juveniles were met, all the fish in the school were always very similar in size, indicating that they were of the same age. They were most probably released at the same time by all the females of the school.

This might seem far-fetched, but it is entirely logical. Fry released by individual females would have very little chance to survive in the dangerous open grounds they live on. Moreover, spawned at the same time, living under the same overall conditions as the whole flock and with an identical growth rate, it would be highly improbable that they could have been released by each mother separately.

The spawning process of the other schooling sand-dwellers hasn't been properly investigated until now, but buccal incubation in these fishes has been known for a long time.

A remarkable group is made up of the large *Lamprologus*, for example *L. attenuatus*, *L. pleuromaculatus*, *L. tetracanthus*, *L. elongatus* and *L. lemairei*. The first three are mostly seen over the sand plains and bottoms, and very rarely around rock. They spawn in the sand, digging crater-like nests of very unusual size. They live close to the bottom and are not seen in mid-water, except for *L. pleuromaculatus*.

The last two, *L. elongatus* and *L. lemairei*, are always on or close to rocky bottoms on which they spawn, *L. elongatus* in the open and *L. lemairei* under shelter inside of rock crevices. Both species usually stay in mid-water. The five species are highly individualistic and never seen in groups. Reaching a size of between 20 and 25 cm, these species of *Lamprologus* are armed with powerful canine teeth and are well capable of protecting their fry against most enemies.

It will not be surprising to find males of *Lamprologus* fight in the confines of an aquarium. Photo by Dr. R.J. Goldstein.

We have said that the sand-dwelling species of *Lamprologus* dig large nests. *L. attenuatus* nests reach a diameter of 1½ m, with a depth of more than 50 cm. Those of *L. tetracanthus* are almost as big; spawns may number up to several thousand eggs. Parental protection is practiced; they are very aggressive toward potential intruders. We have not seen any successful attack made on the nests by predators. Usually the parents stand guard separately on opposite stations across the nest. As soon as the fry are free-swimming, the parents assume different stations, one rather close to the fry, the other covering from farther away. In the case of *L. elongatus* one parent stays close to the ground, while the other, several meters away, is in mid-water. All intruders are repelled with incredible savagery by the *L. elongatus* parents, the chase being lightning-fast and covering several meters.

All these species of *Lamprologus* protect their fry over the open grounds for an unusually long time, until they are between 30 and 40 mm long. Most of the fry of the large species of *Lamprologus* stay close to the bottom at first when they are finally abandoned by their parents. *L. elongatus* will, from the very first days of the free-swimming stage, hover well above the protection afforded by the floor and will spend all its life in mid-water.

One might ask what is the wandering potential of these species of *Lamprologus*. We must admit that after four years spent exploring the underwater scenery, we have found no definite answer to this question. Although they might seem to roam at will, either over the vast expanses of sand flats or along the rocky slopes, it is entirely possible that these very individualistic fishes have a territory of their own. Even the sand-dwelling species of *Lamprologus* are very often noted near rocky outcrops or near the rocky slopes. Very few of the sand-dwelling fishes roam the bare sand flats far (or more correctly, independently) from the rocky areas. The only true sand-dwellers are the species of *Callochromis, Cardiopharynx, Limnotilapia, Aulonocranus* and, most of all, *Xenotilapia*. These fishes are essentially roamers.

The same is true of *Boulengerochromis* coming from deep water to spawn in the shallows. This fish lays about 12,000 to 15,000 eggs in the phenomenally large crater it has dug in the sand. Let us note that the crater isn't always dug. When the pair comes to breed on sand patches between rock boulders or slabs in the upper water layer, the protection afforded to the nesting site by the boulder walls seems to be enough for the fish. In that case they will not dig their huge crater but will simply clean the bottom, dig (or not) a shallow depression a few centimeters deep and perhaps 50 cm across and lay their eggs in the middle. They will stand guard at the rim of the walls in mid-water. If the rock walls have openings they will stay close to them. On open ground the fish will stay opposite each other near the bottom, or one will stay in the nest standing close guard, the other fish circling slowly two or three meters from the crater rim. This is a very interesting example of adaptation to local ecology, a full-size nest in open ground being replaced by a shallow depression in sheltered areas. Whenever nature has provided the protection, the parents do not need their nest.

Parental protection of the fry by this giant cichlid stops when the young fish are much smaller (about 2 cm) than the young of the large *Lamprologus* species. One might wonder about this early abandonment, apparently condemning the fry to immediate death. We have seen the extraordinary sight of *Boulengerochromis* fry hovering over a sand plain in the shape of a hemispheric dome more than one meter across and 60-70 cm high. The base of this dome was about 10-20 cm from the floor. The density of the *Boulengerochromis* fry in the hemisphere was such that the dome was totally opaque and seemingly made of solid copper. Far from

Lamprologus lemairei, juvenile, photographed in a tank with the fins extended. This species is known for its voracious appetite, capable of devouring prey approaching its own size. Photo by P.V. Loiselle.

relying on mimicry for protection, the dome was visible several meters away as it moved slowly over the sunlit sand floor. The movement resulted from the forward whirling motion of the fry in the mass. Not a single young *Boulengerochromis* ventured out of the dome! When I thrust an arm into the nearly solid mass of fry, they parted, leaving a neat smooth-walled "tunnel" in the dome. For more than five minutes, literally entranced by this exceptional display, we stood, my daughter Mireille and I, changing the nearly perfect dome into ectoplasmic shapes, with successive thrusts of our hands into the mass. Before leaving the fry on their own, we dipped into the thousands of young fish with a small hand net and caught perhaps two hundred. We kept about a dozen and released the others close to the school, into which they re-integrated at once. Not one of the predators usually attacking young fry molested the young. There is little doubt that for all fish such a shimmering mass is not associated with harmless fry and an easy and tasty snack, but more as a dangerous menace.

Lamprologus modestus belongs, like *L. elongatus* and *L. lemairei*, to the group of ubiquitous species of *Lamprologus* encountered on sand or rock floors. Although exceptional specimens might reach about 18 cm, this fish is usually much smaller. Most probably because they cannot spawn in the open at this size, they try to find something in the sand (it might be an empty mussel shell, a loose pebble or a stone) with which to prop up their tunnel shaft in which they breed. Although they are not infrequent on rocky slopes, we have never seen a *L. modestus* nest in these habitats.

Lamprologus ocellatus is the tiniest and one of the most colorful species of *Lamprologus* on the sand bottoms. We have never seen any specimen more than 5 cm long. The fish hide and breed in empty *Neothauma* shells which do not exceed 4 cm across.

Lamprologus callipterus is the only sand-dwelling species of *Lamprologus* with gregarious habits. Packs of about 20 fish roam close to the bottom and voraciously attack and tear apart any young or sick fish like a pack of wolves. When nothing is in view they dig with their large mouths into the sand, all at the same time, to feed on particles of food, small crustaceans, etc., which they filter from the sand. Ugly, and reaching about 15 cm in size, they are one of the worst predators over open ground and, probably along with *L. lemairei*, among the least enticing cichlids in the lake. Mostly sand-dwellers, they are often found at the rim of the rock slopes, but they seldom venture over bare rock. Breeding was never observed.

Limnotilapia dardennei is a mouthbrooder reaching about 25 cm in length. It is at that size one of the most beautiful fish in the lake, with orange all over the lower part of the body from the mouth on, deep blue sides and multicolored spots in the unpaired fins. Schools of fry and juveniles up to 10 cm in length are found in the shallows. Schools of adults are frequent, but occur much deeper. Individual females mouthbrooding their fry are often seen in more shallow water. Spawning has never been observed by us. The species is of an ecologically uncertain status. They are common over sand plains, but the largest schools were often encountered near rocks. The fish is always on the move and is one of the most ubiquitous fishes in the lake.

If we cover the breeding modes of the sand-dwellers as a whole we might separate them as follows:

1. Buccal incubation is known for all species living in very large schools and roaming over large areas. They feed directly on the bottom. Group stimuli are evident for spawning and perhaps even for the release of the fry. The best example is *Xenotilapia*.
2. Buccal incubation is also known for rather large species, for example *Limnotilapia*, but group spawning has never been observed, and brooding females are often seen alone.

3. Open crater nests are known for fishes, usually loners like *Boulengerochromis* and the big species of *Lamprologus*, capable of protecting their nests. The *Lamprologus* species spawn on their usual grounds, whereas *Boulengerochromis* comes up from deep water to spawn.
4. Sheltered nests are known for the small species of *Lamprologus* that are unable to fight off predators.
5. One species, *L. callipterus*, lives in small packs on the bottom, is a predator and roams. Its spawning and breeding mode has never been checked.

Rock-dwellers

Starting with the gregarious species of rock-dwelling populations we note again, as with the sand-associated species, that all schooling species living in mid-water levels are mouthbrooders.

The spawning of *Cyphotilapia frontosa* and *Limnochromis nigripinnis*, both species living in very deep water, has never been observed in the wild. Both live off the rock slopes or over the sand floors at the foot of the slopes, near the rocks. The first juvenile *Cyphotilapia* are found individually by day at a minimum depth of six meters, with the density and size of the fish increasing with depth. Only once out of more than 200 dives in their habitat have we seen a pair of very large *C. frontosa* at about four meters depth.

Shown are two rock-dwelling fish, *Lamprologus* sp. and *Chalinochromis brichardi* swimming near their hiding place between the rocks. Photo by Dr. Herbert R. Axelrod.

A squirt of fish anesthetic is helpful in capturing them. Photo by Dr. Herbert R. Axelrod.

Both species practice buccal incubation. Spawning should not be simultaneous or triggered by group stimuli, since the spawns collected from a single school belonged to different stages (from eggs to well-developed fry) of development. The release time for *Limnochromis nigripinnis* fry occurs when the fry reach about 1.5 cm in length, for *Cyphotilapia frontosa* when the fry reach a length of approximately 3 cm.

Fry from both species hide under rock shelves and in caves, etc., until they grow up. *L. nigripinnis* and *L. microlepidotus* are especially light-shy, and although juveniles can occasionally be discovered at depths of seven or eight meters they are more common below ten. As they grow up, they will get away from immediate contact with the slope and assume a more distant mid-water position. They are head-standers from an early stage on, although they are usually found upside down on the ceiling in caves.

The other gregarious species of the rock-dwellers are the group composed of *Ophthalmochromis*, *Ophthalmotilapia*, *Cyathopharynx* and *Cunningtonia*. All are "indirect" mouthbrooders. We have seen that this means that they spawn in a nest but practice buccal incubation.

The crater-shaped nest, sometimes a rather makeshift affair, is built by the males on a patch of sand between rock boulders that apparently serve as a protection against eventual predators during the actual spawning. The trouble is that in some well-illustrated cases, such as that of *Ophthalmochromis ventralis ventralis*, no actual spawning takes place in the nest. The females are already carrying eggs in their mouths when in rather quick succession they dive toward the nest, each called by the male, who is already in the nest. The male deposits his sperm in the sand, but evacuates the nest before she comes in to take a mouthful of sperm the fertilization of the eggs. In such a reproductive mode the protection afforded to the nest site by steep rock walls is totally useless.

The example of nest-building by the male *Cyathopharynx furcifer* is even more remarkable. The nest is painstakingly built on top of high boulders, sometimes two or three meters higher than the sand patches nearby. After carefully cleaning the nest site, the male will drop down on the sand, take up a mouthful of sand and bring it to the top of the boulder, where it will be made into a shallow arena 5 cm high and 25-30 cm across.

Why should *Cyathopharynx* go to all this trouble when it could just as well dig such an arena on the sand floor in a matter of minutes? It took us more than a year of observation before we could understand the reason for this supposedly aberrant behavior.

What brought us to some understanding of the matter was the fact that when several boulders were available as nest sites—and there are never two nests on the same boulder—systematically the highest or most visible was always chosen first. The successive "second choice" sites selected by newcomers were the next highest or most visible of the remaining boulders. One might have expected fish to choose the boulder easiest to reach, which means the nearest to the bottom. We decided that fishes are not Einsteins and that the behavior was entirely due to illogical impulses.

It took many more observations before we could understand the "erratic" behavior of *Cyathopharynx* males. As the fish is a mid-water school fish and the males descend to the boulders to start building their nests, the females keep swimming at their own level, circling or staying close to, although higher than, the nest. As such the male with the highest nest will be closer to the female pack and will have the dominant position among the nest-building males, thus having more opportunities to mate than the other males. In shallow shores with sand floors, *C. furcifer* will dig craters.

Let us go back to *Ophthalmochromis ventralis*. We had seen many instances during which a male rising to attract a female toward the crater nest would all of a sudden violently repel the female and select another one. We wondered why the first had been chased away. We thought at first that the "cold shouldered" female wasn't ripe and ready for spawning. Afterwards we discovered that the females following the males to the nest already had eggs in their mouths. There is thus something (which we couldn't quite pin down) in the appearance or behavior of the female with eggs already fertilized that shows the male that she isn't suited for mating. This is why he chases her away so violently.

All in all the mode of reproduction of *Cyathopharynx* and *Ophthalmochromis* gives one the feeling that these fishes were previously nest-breeders at one point in their evolution and that the present nest-building is a kind of carry-over behavior, no longer much needed, since they could use the "direct buccal fertilization mode" of *Tropheus* as well. As it is, the case of *O. ventralis* is, to our knowledge, the first and only recorded example of fertilization of the spawn without the parents ever being in contact with each other.

It has been said that the bright yellow spatulated dots at the tip of the species' long ventral filaments might serve to attract the females toward the sperm duct area, serving the same purpose as the "fake-egg" ocelli on the anal fins of species of *Haplochromis*. We have seen that this is not the case with the *Cyathopharynx-Ophthalmochromis* group of fishes. Let us note that most probably (with the Lake Tanganyika species at least), the presence of anal fin ocelli is not indicative, automatically, of the ocellus-sucking behavior. Several fishes exhibit ocelli, and this mode of egg-fertilization wasn't associated with the species.

Tropheus morphs sometimes have ocelli on the anal fin in *some* male specimens. The ocelli in *Tropheus* species are small, much smaller than the eggs; they are often very faint even in ripe males and of a different color than the egg. Moreover they are situated at the rear of the anal fin, the farthest point from the sperm duct.

Of all the rocky area school fish, *Lamprologus brichardi* is the only one nesting and egg-laying among the rubble—in slits, crevices, caves, etc. It is not a mouthbrooder. Schools of this species, by their unbelievable density, are the most remarkable sight on the Burundi coast where the habitat includes the proper ecological niche. The schools stay on the same grounds month after month. We have collected more than 20,000 *L. brichardi* from an area of 50 X 50 meters and a school of perhaps more than 100,000

The highly successful *Lamprologus brichardi* uses any available niche in rocky area as spawning sites. Occurring in great numbers, they effectively protect the nest from predators. Photo by Dr. Herbert R. Axelrod.

fish. Collecting them in shallow water (between 4 and 6 meters) when the flock extends from 4-40 meters with increasing density hasn't caused any noticeable depletion. Also, because the breeding adults and their fry are sheltered by the rocks, they are protected from our nets.

The breeding pairs descend from the flock hovering permanently 30-100 cm over the substratum and spawn, as we said, in the rocks. It is remarkable that several pairs of adult fish band together and take care of the fry in a kind of community nursery. We have also seen several examples of half-grown fry helping adults in warding off potential intruders.

This is not at all farfetched. This fish, like a few other rock-dwellers in the lake, spawns continuously and takes care of several spawns at various stages of development at the same time. All these fry live with a good relationship to each other.

Tank-raised *L. brichardi* are now common. I would like to say that instances of tank-raised juveniles of the first generation attacking newly hatched fry most probably are caused by the narrow confines of a tank. In the lake, parents chase the first-born out of the breeding site when they might endanger the new spawns. This is also true of *Julidochromis* species.

This photo shows the density of *Lamprologus brichardi* in contrast to other fish species in the rocky parts of the lake. Photo by Dr. Herbert R. Axelrod.

It has not been possible to observe under water whether breeding pairs of *L. brichardi* (nor for that matter many other species) have permanent bonds. Things being as they are with school fishes, we doubt very much that pairs are established for life as they are with many solitary fishes.

The breeding habit of the typical schooling fish, *L. brichardi*, is closely connected to the rock substratum, more so than the other school fishes in this habitat; *L. brichardi* has a very exceptional collective nursery method for rearing its fry. No other fish in Africa, to our knowledge, shares this very unusual breeding mode.

The second group of rock-dwellers is composed of several species, divided among six genera: *Eretmodus, Spathodus, Tanganicodus, Simochromis, Tropheus* and *Petrochromis*. The ecological niche of these species is basically along the piles of pebbles and rubble littering the rocky slopes, the dwarfs (*Eretmodus, Spathodus,* and *Tanganicodus*) dwelling in the upper layers, on the surf-washed shoreline as do the *Simochromis* (although a bit deeper), whereas *Tropheus* and *Petrochromis* live deeper. All are fiercely solitary to the point where it is next to impossible to keep two unpaired *Simochromis, Spathodus marlieri* or *Petrochromis* in the same tank. All these fishes are always on the move, darting in and out of the rock floor. It has been said that tank-kept specimens of *Simochromis* and *Tropheus* are territorial. This can be understood for fish confined in a tank, however large, and where food is added from the outside world by the keepers instead of being searched for and found where it grows in the wild. The behavior of such intelligent fish can be disturbed in captivity and adapted to a new ecology. The fishes are not sedentary in the lake, and their territory is a very temporary one, limited to the mating session.

Tropheus species never assemble in schools, if schooling means a more or less permanent or long-term bond between individuals reacting to group stimuli. There are no group stimuli among the rock-wanderers. They assemble at random as they meet during their wandering and go their own way as soon as they find anything else of interest.

On slopes where they are plentiful, it is not exceptional to see a hundred *Tropheus* at the same time. After a while one understands that they are individuals, each going its own way. One gets the feeling that in the wild spawning is very rapid, preventing perhaps the fertilization of all the eggs released by a female during a single spawn, and that it is entirely possible that one male fertilizes only a very small number of eggs. Some eggs, laid later, are fertilized by another male. The mates are never bonded except for a few fleeting seconds at a time.

Petrochromis is another case. As we remember our dives we don't recall more than three fish together. More often than not we see a single pair hiding under a rock for the spawning session, but usually we see single fish swimming aimlessly in the open.

What remains from these underwater investigations of the rock-wanderers is that they never form pairs. A male might, as is the case with gregarious species, attract a female within the spawning site he has hastily prepared; aside from the breeding time, however, he will resume his wanderings among the rocks.

Spawns of *Tropheus* species are very small, with an average of about 10-12 eggs, often less in wild-caught specimens. The maximum number of developed fry we ever removed from the mouth of a female was 13. We also have data from a German breeder specializing in *Tropheus*. The average spawn for his *T. moorii* was between 8 and 16, with one specimen having an unusual rhythm covering four spawns of 6, 23, 6 and 23, with an average of 14.5 for the four spawns, due perhaps to ovary trouble. These figures come from specimens living far from the predator-infested lake waters, where some eggs are sure to be lost. The maximum spawn

A brooding female *Tropheus moorii* confined in a partioned tank. Photo by Michael Downey.

ever recorded (by Mr. Mueller, Bremen, Germany) was 36—but the eggs were stuck together in the female's mouth and fungused. The Nyanza-lac type *Tropheus* yields from 8-12 eggs per spawn, but this race doesn't reach the size of the regular *Tropheus*. *Tropheus duboisi* produced from 8-19 fry. I was also told about a spawn of 25.

Tropheus eggs are tremendous for the size of this fish, 6 or 7 mm for a maximum adult size of 15 cm. Their spawns, which average between 15 and 20, are thus comparatively small among the lake mouthbrooders.

It has been said that it is impossible to raise fry from eggs removed from the female's mouth. This is not borne out by our own findings. Every daily capture includes brooding *Tropheus* females with either unhatched eggs or fry with the yolk-sac still fully developed. For every stage of development we have been able, without too much trouble, to raise the spawns to adulthood after we had taken them from the female's mouth and placed them into a separate tank. Raised on *Artemia salina* nauplii after they become free swimming, they have, perhaps, even a faster growth rate than the fry in the mother's mouth. Hatching of *Cyphotilapia frontosa* eggs recovered from depths of 25 meters has also been successful.

The release of the fry to the substratum by *Tropheus* and the other species in related genera of rock-grazers has never been observed in the wild. Nor have very young fry, less than about 15 mm, been seen amid the rubble. The first weeks after the release are spent by the fry in deep concealment; the only way they have to survive in a very dangerous world.

Once again the behavior of these fishes, as well as the buccal incubation which is their breeding mode, seems related to the wandering behavior of the species involved.

Buccal incubation is also the breeding mode of two highly solitary fishes which do not spend their lives protected by the rock shelters, as the previous group usually does. They live above the rocky floor, not in it. One of them is *Lobochilotes labiatus*, the second largest cichlid in the lake. Coming from the deeper reaches of the lake, adults seem to move toward the surface to brood. We have never been able to see the spawning of the fish, which perhaps occurs in the deep water, but quite often we have seen brooding females in very shallow water. The fry, numbering several hundreds, are periodically released by the female in sheltered shallows. They feed outside the mother's mouth but return at the first sign of danger. Once we disturbed a very large female looking after her grazing flock. We could see her picking the fry up by the mouthful. She then fled but, as soon as we swam away, dashed back to pick up the stragglers.

A young adult *Lobochilotes labiatus*. The fleshy lips will become progressively thicker as the fish grows older. Photo by Homer Arment.

The second fish to practice periodical release of the fry for outside feeding is *Perissodus microlepis,* a scale-eater. This fish lives in mid-water off the slopes and is always a loner except during the mating season when they form pairs. It is quite unusual to have a monogamous mouthbrooder and a behavior pattern in which the male stays with the female to watch over the brood when it is released in the open for periodical feedings. Another point of interest is that the grazing sites are always situated on top of boulders or large stones well above the rock floor instead of amid the protective low ground. Both parents in nuptial attire, shimmering with metallic blue, protect the 1 cm fry. It is noteworthy that the fry feed on minute organisms grazed from the rock biocover even though the adults are typical scale-eaters, very often seen tearing scales off *Tropheus.*

With these two species we have another variation in the usual mode of buccal incubation. Both practice periodic release of the fry, which has often been reported for riverine species from Africa (for example *Pelvicachromis*), but in one both parents look after the fry, whereas in the other, as is common in the lake, only the female looks after them.

The last, but still very important, group of rock-dwellers includes the egg-layers spawning on traditional cichlid sites, caves, crevices, holes, etc., in the substratum. These fishes guard eggs and fry until the young generation is capable of living by itself, not in schools, but as individuals. The variations of the egg-laying behavior are about as wide as in buccal incubation but limited to four genera, *Lamprologus, Julidochromis, Chalinochromis* and *Telmatochromis.* All of them, taxonomically speaking, are very close.

The most important genus in the lake, *Lamprologus,* is known as a nest-builder. We have seen that the sand-dwelling and ubiquitous species both select either sand or rock as the spawning site. The rock-dwelling *Lamprologus* and the other related genera all breed within the rock shelter, even when they spend their lives hovering or wandering above it.

The nest-builders are perhaps, among the rock-bonded cichlids, those with the best capacity to go deep. It is, in fact, very remarkable that the mouthbrooders (in the lake at least) are either restricted to the top layer or ascend to these layers to brood or deposit their fry, either sporadically or permanently, close to the surface in the most oxygenated water. Even deepwater fishes such as *Cyphotilapia frontosa* are graded down the slopes according to size. When one remembers that the 3-15 meter layer is the one with the fiercest competition, one might wonder why many fishes would choose this zone to leave their fry if it were not for a very pressing reason.

The egg-layers breed deep, and we have found nests of *Julidochromis, Lamprologus brichardi, L. furcifer* and *Chalinochromis* all the way down to 25 meters. We didn't investigate any deeper than this.

It would be very interesting to check if, in Lake Malawi as well, there is a trend in young mouthbrooders to be restricted to the upper water layers and if adult egg-layers have a deeper range both in respect to habitat and breeding sites.

The only egg-layer for which there is an increase in size with depth is *Lamprologus compressiceps*. Although the fish is a roamer, living most of the time above the rock floor, only juveniles or young adults are found in shallow water (of 2-3 meters depth). Adults are seldom seen on these grounds, although they become increasingly common from 5-15 meters. Nests and young of *L. compressiceps*, though, are common at this level, so it is probable that the young fry migrate to the warmer, more oxygenated layers above as they spread from the nest. This is also the only species from the rocks which seems to have definite habits of wandering over a large area and which at the same time is an egg-layer. All other species are strongly territorial and fiercely solitary.

Some species have a very strong bond toward darkness, such as *Lamprologus furcifer, L. schreyeni, L. savoryi* and *L. niger*. As such they spend their lives mostly in caves, slits and crevices or in labyrinths in the rubble. *L. furcifer*, moreover, prefers vertical or overhanging flat walls. This species shares its habitat with *Julidochromis marlieri* on the northeastern coast, and the two often breed on the same site.

Other fishes are indifferent to light, for example *Telmatochromis bifrenatus*, and are seen quite frequently on the bottom, although they breed in slits.

Lamprologus savoryi spawns and breeds among the rubble, out of sight, or in caves and holes. *Chalinochromis brichardi*, a species very close to species of *Julidochromis*, spawns in dark holes like *J. marlieri*. As soon as they reach one centimeter in size, however, the fry are led into the open amid the rubble under careful guard by both parents, which *Julidochromis* does not do. The size of the spawns is, as a rule, much smaller than the several thousand fry produced by the large sand or ubiquitous *Lamprologus* species like *L. attenuatus, L. elongatus, L. lemairei*, etc.

Fishes of several genera found in the lake are recognizable here: *Tropheus*, *Chalinochromis* and *Xenotilapia* in the upper photo; *Tropheus*, *Ophthalmochromis*, *Limnotilapia* and *Petrochromis* in the lower photo. Photos by Glen S. Axelrod.

We have never seen *L. savoryi* with more than a dozen fry, which were in fact quite large (about 3 cm). But whether they were survivors of much larger spawns, or had been originally a very small brood, was impossible to determine. Due to the fact that the fry remain with their parents until they become very large, and also because fry of different ages were always present, we could presume that *L. savoryi* is a continuous breeder like *L. brichardi*. On the other hand, from what we have seen in the lake, *Chalinochromis* and *Julidochromis*, as well as *L. furcifer*, are capable of spawns numbering up to 250 fry. *Julidochromis marlieri* and *J. regani* spawns were checked in our tanks.

Julidochromis transcriptus, J. marlieri, J. regani regani and *J. regani affinis* (we couldn't check on *J. ornatus*) have two modes of spawning. One, like that of most egg-layers, yields a considerable quantity of fry, sometimes as many as 250 for *J. marlieri* and both subspecies of *J. regani*. The second, which was already noted for *L. brichardi* and perhaps *L. savoryi*, is continuous. The female lays eggs every few days, one or two dozen at a time. Both modes are used by *Julidochromis* in the lake as well as in tanks. Although some pairs (and they always pair for life, at least in aquaria) use either the continuous mode or the regular large spawn mode,

In captivity, the creation of a cave-like situation (here, a broken flowerpot) appear satisfactory for the spawning requirement of *Julidochromis ornatus*. Photo by Jaroslav Elias.

Even in the absence of other fishes, the same *Julidochromis* is shown zealously guarding the eggs. Photo by Jaroslav Elias.

others when paired start first with small continuous spawns then progressively space the spawns which then get bigger and bigger. This increase in each spawn does not seem to be restricted to tank-paired specimens, nor is it a general rule. Many young pairs start at once with the periodical, about once in a month, large spawn. Because of this peculiarity in their spawns, it is common to find breeding sites in the lake with a whole set of fry, from freshly hatched 3-mm fry to juveniles ten times as big.

From what we could check in our tanks, the babies are not at all bothered by the previous hatches. The parents seem to know this and don't ward the eldest fry off until they reach over 4 cm in length. *Julidochromis marlieri* and *J. regani* will not venture over open ground until they are well over 5 cm. Up to that time they travel along their native boulder walls, with which they blend very well, out of sight of lurking predators.

Lamprologus furcifer, one of the most fascinating species of rock-dwellers, doesn't seem to have the same peaceful habits as the species of *Julidochromis*. Fry, as soon as they are one centimeter long, start to spread on the "ceiling" of their caves. They blend perfectly with the dark recesses and are very difficult to see because of their dark gray color. Even as tiny fry they are so indi-

Asprotilapia leptura has been found in small numbers on rock shores in the South. Superficially the fish looks very much like *Xenotilapia ochrogenys* but is not as gorgeously colored.

Seen are three fishes swimming very close to the bottom; a *Tropheus*, a *Lamprologus* and an *Asprotilapia* (from left to right). Photo by Glen S. Axelrod.

Astatoreochromis straelini superficially resembles species of *Haplochromis* with which it has been confused before. The species can be positively determined by the number of anal spines and color of the body.

The silvery body of *Aulonocranus dewindti* with iridescent stripes on the dorsal fin and the body blends perfectly with the surf-washed sand floors on which this fish lives.

vidualistic that when they meet they take a threatening stance, their mouths wide open, and are ready to fight. Needless to say, they are very hard to keep together when adults and fight to the death. We have never tried to pair them in tanks, so little is known about the mating process.

We have also observed the wandering habits of *Lamprologus compressiceps*. This species spawns in very narrow slits barely wider than their body. Very young fry, less than 3 cm long, have never been seen in the open.

There is a remarkable change in body color with age. Juveniles, or half-grown adults, are striped and have an overall pale gray-blue color. Fully grown adults are a reddish-brown, perhaps with a very few faint stripes.

The species, with its powerful jaws and canines, should be expected to be a vicious predator. However, we have never seen *Lamprologus compressiceps* in the lake attacking another fish. We have had *L. compressiceps* in our tanks for months and tried to feed them baby guppies and other fry. They never ate one! The problem of their feeding habits is therefore, as far as we know, very much open. We wonder if, like *L. brichardi*, these teeth are not used by *L. compressiceps* to pick invertebrates from the rock biocover.

The attractive dotted body and fin pattern of *Lamprologus compressiceps*, ensure the popularity of this fish among hobbyists. Photo by Wilhelm Hoppe.

Murky conditions in the lake is illustrated in this photograph. One can hardly discern the numerous fishes in the background. Photo by Dr. Herbert R. Axelrod.

Although the rock-dwellers *Telmatochromis temporalis* and *T. caninus* are among the most ubiquitous fishes on their grounds, not a single nest site has been discovered. The smallest individuals collected or seen were already about 2.5-3 cm long. We have observed that these two species are adapted to very murky waters provided the bottom or slopes include some rocky outcrops.

The case of *Telmatochromis bifrenatus* and *T. vittatus* is entirely different. The two species are strictly restricted to their ecological niche, which is essentially composed of large flagstones, slabs, sometimes boulders, but more often than not even sand patches in the midst of rocks. The first and most important requisite is that this habitat be at least three meters deep. They thus share the same layer with *L. brichardi* but do not hover above the ground; they are bottom-dwellers. If they spend their lives in the open they breed in very narrow holes out of reach of any predator except small eels. All species of *Telmatochromis* are certainly sedentary fishes, but *T. bifrenatus* and *T. vittatus* most probably do not wander more than a few meters from their birthplace during their whole life.

Boulengerochromis microlepis, juvenile, 15 centimeters long.

Bathybates ferox is the typical pelagic predator with powerful hinged teeth in several rows rather like a shark's jaw. Some of them grow to about 40 centimeters; all feed on clupeid schools.

This *Callochromis macrops melanostigma* shows the black dots on the body and fins that are characteristic of the subspecies.

An adult *Callochromis macrops melanostigma* in full color. The other subspecies *C. m. macrops* lacks the typical black dots and has never been collected in the northern area of the lake. Photo by Thierry Brichard.

What is remarkable with all the rocky-area egg-laying cichlids is that none of them nest in the open, even when they spend their life above the habitat over open ground. A second point of interest is the very variable number of eggs laid by each species. They can range from several hundred, as in species of *Julidochromis*, to only a very few dozen, as in *Telmatochromis bifrenatus* or *T. vittatus* and *Lamprologus savoryi*. We have identical differences in the mouthbrooders. A third point of interest is the variable cadence adopted by species of *Julidochromis* in their spawns, whether continuous, in which case the females are always ripe, or periodically in one single but huge batch.

As most of the egg-layers, with the probable exception of *L. compressiceps*, are very territorial and sedentary, their spawning behavior seems to be well in line with their ethology. Buccal incubation isn't needed much by such fishes as they breed within their own territory.

Of course this is an oversimplification of the problems involved in the choice between the two breeding modes, but at least there are apparently some keys to this choice, and the keys should be triggered by inner behavioral stimuli.

After all has been said, with our present knowledge of fish reproduction it might be entirely natural that the perennially wandering fish have gone from static nests to carrying their fry along. This is in line with their normal behavior.

Mud-dwellers

We have seen that mud-dwelling fishes in the lake can be divided into two groups. Non-endemic species like *Haplochromis burtoni*, *Astatoreochromis straeleni*, *Sarotherodon melanopleura* or *S. nilotica* live in or close to littoral lagoons and estuarine swamps. These fishes are mouthbrooders as a rule. *Haplochromis horei* and *H. pfefferi* (previously *Limnochromis pfefferi*), found along sand beaches strewn with stones and small boulders, are also mouthbrooders. They are collected in very murky water. We have observed that they are endemic to the lake.

Tilapia tanganicae is present on heterogenous grounds, such as sand with mud patches, in shallow water. In stormy weather thousands of them can be seen at the surface over mud floors gasping for air. They are typical school fish wandering over the floor in search of food. They are also mouthbrooders.

Limnochromis auritus and *Triglochromis otostigma* (previously *Limnochromis otostigma*) are typical mud-dwellers but extend to much deeper water than the non-endemic species or the two species of *Haplochromis* mentioned before. They seem to be egg-layers. Although we collected several thousand of these fishes in four years time, *none* ever had fry or eggs in their mouth. Let us note that until now the only species of *Limnochromis* known to use buccal incubation was *L. nigripinnis*. As this fish already does not fit very well into the taxonomic definition of the genus, it is entirely possible that the different breeding mode is an extra reason to place it in a separate genus.

DECOY EGG OCELLI

Without purporting to decide on the various theories about the use of these ocelli as egg decoys enticing the female to pick up these "eggs" with her mouth, during which time the eggs in her mouth get fertilized by the sperm around the anal fin, I would like to make a few comments on this phenomenon in the lake mouthbrooders.

Several fishes, like *Tropheus* males, have ocelli (sometimes not on the anal fin). These ocelli bear no resemblance at all, by color, shape or size, to the real eggs. The area which the females bump when they get their eggs fertilized is usually on the abdomen of the male, not the fin. In this case one might perhaps say that the ocelli are traces of previous egg decoys but nothing more. The example

In this photograph a pair of spawning *Haplochromis burtoni*, the female seems greatly attracted by the egg spots on the ventral fin of the male. Photo by Ruda Zukal.

Callochromis pleurospilus is a very common fish on sand floors where it lives in small schools.

The color and pattern of all the fins of *Callochromis pleurospilus* are visible in this picture taken by Dr. Herbert R. Axelrod.

A *Cardiopharynx schoutedeni* of undetermined sex (either a female or a young male). Photo by Thierry Brichard.

A female *Cardiopharynx schoutedeni*. This species is more important as a food fish than as an aquarium fish to the native fishermen. Photo by Glen S. Axelrod.

of *Simochromis diagramma* and *S. babaulti*, as documented, shows that if the ocelli (easily visible on these species and close to the real egg in color and shape) are often "picked" upon by egg-brooding females, they are also often overlooked, the female picking sperm on other parts of the anal fin and the abdomen of the male. The example of *Ophthalmochromis ventralis*, which has been illustrated in other parts of this book, shows that the fertilization of the spawn is secured by the female after the male has left the nest, still quite remote from the female. The sperm is transparent and thus cannot be seen by the female, which is probably guided to the spot where the sperm has been deposited by olfactory or gustatory stimuli. The fact is well known that fishes have a strong response to odors. In the case of *Simochromis* the females pick up sperm where it flows, and the anal fin of the male is, of course, in this area. We cannot thus ascertain that the ocelli on the anal fin always serve as egg decoys in the lake mouthbrooders.

DESCRIPTIONS OF THE FISHES OF LAKE TANGANYIKA
Cichlids

The descriptions of the genera and species of cichlids of Lake Tanganyika are given in alphabetical order to make reference to them easier. A resume-type description is given for each genus and the species are illustrated with color photographs whenever possible. Specific details about the ecology and behavior are presented when the information is available.

The genera of Lake Tanganyika cichlids may be identified by the following key updated from Poll, 1957 (*Les Genres Poissons d'eau douce de l'Afrique*).

1. Anal fin with a maximum of 3 spines 2
   Anal fin with 4-10 spines 44
2. Teeth of the outer row more or less tricuspid 3
   Teeth of the outer row not tricuspid, but either bicuspid, conical, or in another shape 10
3. Dorsal fin with XV-XX spines; teeth tricuspid, including, at least partly, the outer row teeth (never conical)......... 4
   Dorsal fin with XII-XV spines; teeth tricuspid or tending to become conical in adult fish or mixed with conical teeth 5
4. 10-16 gill rakers on lower half of first arch; maximum length 120-210 mm .... *PETROCHROMIS*
   18-27 gill rakers on lower half of first arch; maximum length 310-375 mm..................... *SAROTHERODON*
5. 34-43 scales in a longitudinal line 6
   48-64 scales in a longitudinal line; teeth weakly tricuspid tending to become conical, inferior outer teeth pointing forward; maximum size 212 mm ...... *CYATHOPHARYNX*

The forked tail in this *Chalinochromis brichardi* is probably just an abnormality. Photo by Gerard Meola, African Fish Imports.

A spotted form of *Chalinochromis brichardi*. The spots of the juvenile have been retained in the adult pattern. Photo by Gerard Meola, African Fish Imports.

This young *Chalinochromis brichardi* still displays the juvenile body pattern which will disappear when it grows. Very young fry are very similar to young - *Julidochromis*, but the latter keep most of their pattern or have it even more striking with age.

Very closely related to *Julidochromis*, *Chalinochromis brichardi* has been discovered recently on the northern coasts of the lake.

6. Snout slightly protruding; mouth subterminal; teeth tricuspid tending to become conical in adult fish; body depth less than 4 times in standard length 7

    Snout very protruding; mouth inferior; teeth small and tricuspid in 2 narrow bands; body depth 5 in standard length; ventral fins without filaments; maximum length 110 mm .... *ASPROTILAPIA*

7. Teeth anchored, tricuspid or conical, in narrow bands, the inferior outer teeth pointing outward; teeth tending to become conical 8

    Teeth mobile, tricuspid, in more or less broad bands, the inferior outer teeth not pointing outward; teeth tricuspid in adult as well as young fish 9

8. Pharyngeal bone with dental surface heart-shaped, lightly concave, with the anterior blade long and apophysis articulations behind; maximum length 150 mm .... *CARDIOPHARYNX*

    Pharyngeal bone subtriangular, anterior blade rather short and apophysis articulations in line with the rear points of the bone; maximum length 120 mm .... *LESTRADEA*

9. Teeth in many rows, all tricuspid; maximum length 140 mm .... *CUNNINGTONIA*

    Teeth in 3-5 rows, tricuspid except on sides where there is a single row of conical teeth; maximum length 145 mm .... *OPHTHALMOTILAPIA*

10. 27-42 scales in the lateral line 11

    44-96 scales in the lateral line 34

11. Teeth of outer row at least partially bicuspid.............12

    Teeth of outer row not bicuspid 18

12. Mouth terminal, not hooked; jaws more or less equal 13

    Mouth subterminal, snout more or less hooked; lower jaw shorter; premaxillary bones with a set of teeth, bicuspid in front and conical on the sides, followed by a row of small tricuspid teeth; maximum length 195 mm .... *SIMOCHROMIS*

13. Lips normal, dentition variable........................14

    Lips thick, a membranous expansion of the lips turned back on the jaws; 3-5 rows of compressed teeth, outer bicuspid, inner tricuspid in the young fish, all rounded or truncated, without a notch at the tip, in adult fish; maximum length 368 mm .... *LOBOCHILOTES*

14. Frontal area not humped; body pattern without 6 very wide and visible vertical bands..........................15

    Frontal area with a hump, more developed with age; 6 very wide and visible vertical bands present; teeth bicuspid or partially biscuspid and conical, inner teeth identical to the front teeth; maximum size 330 mm.....*CYPHOTILAPIA*

15. Body depth included 2.5-3.75 in length; anal fin with or without ocelli; no very apparent black spot at base of soft dorsal fin; gill rakers few, from 7-14; usually small in size, maximum length 260 mm........................16

    Body depth included 1.75-3.0 times in length; anal fin without ocelli; very visible black spot at base of dorsal fin; 7-9 or 20-27 gill rakers; external teeth bicuspid (sometimes tricuspid in part), inner teeth all tricuspid; maximum size 330-500 mm.........*TILAPIA* and *SAROTHERODON*

16. Caudal fin concave; 10-14 gill rakers on lower limb of first arch; anal fin without ocelli; outer teeth bicuspid or in part conical, inner teeth mostly tricuspid; maximum length 260 mm......................*LIMNOTILAPIA*

    Caudal fin rounded or straight; 6-9 gill rakers (in one case 12-13) on lower limb of first branchial arch; anal fin with or without ocelli; outer teeth bicuspid or conical; not exceeding 185 mm in size..........................17

17. (triplet). Body compressed, depth 2.5-3.25 in length; scales present on cheeks and chest; 3 anal spines (exceptionally 4); anal ocelli in one or two rows; ventral fins with second ray longest; maximum size 190 mm...*HAPLOCHROMIS*

    Anal fin always with 4 spines; anal ocelli always in 3-4 rows; maximum size about 120 mm...*ASTATOREOCHROMIS*

    Body elongate, depth 3.4-3.85 in length; no scales on cheeks or chest; 3 anal spines; ventral fins rounded (second and third rays longest)......................*ORTHOCHROMIS*

18. Less than 20 spines in dorsal fin........................19

    More than 20 spines in dorsal fin......................32

19. Lips normal...20

    Lips thickened, with membranous extensions curling back on jaws; teeth all rounded or subtruncated at the tip, without terminal notch in the adult; outer teeth bicuspid in the young fish; maximum size 370 mm....................
    ....*LOBOCHILOTES* (part)

20. Frontal area not humped............................21

A *Cyathopharynx furcifer* is seen here circling its nest. The fish displays one of the two typical breeding patterns, the "Chaitika" pattern: dark-blue head, blue-white metallic body. The opposite pattern is the "Chipimbi" pattern: blue-white head, deep-blue body. Both differ from that of the northern fish: deep blue and deep green.

Cyathopharynx furcifer, adult. Photo by Glen S. Axelrod.

A closer view of a Chaitika Cape color morph of *Cyathopharynx furcifer*.

The iridescent light blue pattern of this *Cythopharynx furcifer* from the South disappeared as soon as it was collected.

Frontal area increasingly humped with age; outer teeth conical or in part bicuspid, inner teeth conical or in part tricuspid; maximum size 330 mm .... *CYPHOTILAPIA* (part)

21. Frontal, nasal, preorbital, lower jaw and preopercular bones not penetrated by wide ducts with wide openings 22
Frontal, nasal, preorbital, lower jaw and preopercular bones penetrated by wide ducts with wide openings 31

22. Outer soft ray of ventral fins notably longer (about 2 times) than inner ray; teeth variable; no third lateral line 23
Outer soft ray of ventral fins less than twice as long, about equal to or shorter than inner ray; teeth conical, usually pointing forward in outer row of lower jaw; often a third lateral line; maximum size 180 mm....................
.... *XENOTILAPIA* (part)

23. Lower outer teeth not pointing forward, more or less on a horizontal plane 24
Lower outer teeth pointing forward 27

24. Body depth less than 4 times in length, with the exception of three species (which however have more than 19 gill rakers) 25
Body depth 4.5-4.8 in body length; teeth conical and small, larger in outer row; 14-15 gill rakers on lower part of first gill arch; maximum size 150 mm...... *LEPTOCHROMIS*

25. Eye as long as or shorter than snout; less than 35 scales in longitudinal line (except for *Limnochromis microlepidotus* which has 52-57); ventral fin filament without forked spatulate tip 26
Eye large, much longer than snout; 35-37 scales in upper lateral line; ventral fin in male ending in a double spatulate-tipped filament; maximum size 150 mm ....
.... *OPHTHALMOCHROMIS* (part)

26 (triplet). Caudal fin concave or subtruncate; teeth conical in 2-4 rows; lower pharyngeal teeth small, sometimes a bit broader at the rear central part of the bone; maximum size 240 mm .... *LIMNOCHROMIS**
Caudal fin rounded; lower pharyngeal teeth all thin, never broadened; laterally compressed; lowest rays of pectoral fin separate from the fin; no scales on chest; maximum size 100 mm .... *TRIGLACHROMIS*

* *This description applies to all species of* Limnochromis *except* L. microlepidotus.

Caudal fin rounded or subtruncate; teeth in 2-5 rows, the outer with bicuspid teeth, the inner teeth first tricuspid then becoming conical in the adult; lower pharyngeal teeth small except in rear center of the bone where they broaden and are rather molar-shaped; maximum size 190 mm .... *HAPLOCHROMIS* (part)*

27. Teeth separated from each other, in 2-3 rows; inner teeth pointing to rear and of same size as outer teeth 28
Teeth rather close to each other, in 2-5 rows; inner teeth not pointing toward rear and much smaller than outer teeth 29

28. Lower pharyngeal teeth very thin and bunched together in a triangular pattern; maximum size 120 mm .... *LESTRADEA* (part)
Lower pharyngeal teeth very thin and bunched together in a kind of rounded heart-shaped pattern; maximum size 150 mm .... *CARDIOPHARYNX*

29. Lower pharyngeal teeth very broadened, nearly molar-like, in rear middle of bone; 10-12 gill rakers (average 11) on lower limb of first gill arch; body depth less than four times in length; 2 lateral lines; maximum size 160 mm .... *CALLOCHROMIS*
Lower pharyngeal teeth all very thin, even in the rear where at most they are a bit broader 30

30. 12-14 (average 12) gill rakers on lower limb of first gill arch; mouth terminal, jaws subequal; often a spot in middle of dorsal fin; maximum length 100 mm .... *ECTODUS*
17-20 gill rakers on lower limb of first gill arch; mouth subinferior, lower jaw a bit shorter than upper; no black spot on dorsal fin .... *OPHTHALMOCHROMIS* (part)

31. 27-31 scales in a longitudinal line; a single short lateral line (upper); dorsal fin with 8-12 spines; teeth conical and small, forming a band on the jaws; maximum size 45-150 mm .... *TREMATOCARA*
33-36 scales in a longitudinal line; 2 lateral lines; dorsal fin with 11-13 spines; teeth conical and small, those of outer row a bit larger; maximum size 120 mm .... *AULONOCRANUS*

32. Teeth in a single row, with crown not, or only slightly, broadened at tip, rounded, truncated or with a sharp tip 33

* *The above definition applies only to* H. horei.

A pair of *Cyathopharynx furcifer* over a sandy area of the lake. A lone *Cyphotilapia frontosa* is in the foreground. Photo by Dr. Herbert R. Axelrod.

This pair of *Cyathopharynx furcifer* may be in the process of spawning. Photo by Glenn S. Axelrod.

A young adult *Cyphotilapia frontosa* already displaying the hump typical of the species. This specimen is about 20 centimeters long (maximum size is about 35 centimeters). This is one of the most difficult fish to collect because of the great depths at which it lives and the ensuing decompression problems.

An adult *Cyphotilapia frontosa* with a very pronounced frontal hump. Photo by Dr. Herbert R. Axelrod at the Berlin Aquarium.

Teeth in 2-3 rows, spatulate, with a thin stem and a broadened, straight edge; maximum size 75 mm . . . .
. . . . ERETMODUS

33. Anterior teeth relatively short; snout straight, with a terminal mouth, maximum size 90 mm . . . . SPATHODUS

Anterior teeth longer; sloping snout with subinferior mouth; maximum size 65 mm . . . . TANGANICODUS

34. Soft outer ray of ventral fins less than twice as long, as long as or even shorter than inner rays 35

Soft outer ray of ventral fins noticeably longer, about twice as long, than inner rays 36

35. 44-59 scales in a longitudinal line, 6½-8½ above and 12½-14½ below lateral line in a transverse line; 11 or 12 gill rakers on the lower limb of first gill arch; outer teeth of jaw not pointing forward; maximum size 260 mm . . . .
. . . . GRAMMATOTRIA

34-43 scales in a longitudinal line, 3½-5½ above and 8½-10½ below lateral line in a transverse line; 9-18 gill rakers on lower limb of first gill arch; outer jaw teeth usually pointing forward . . . . XENOTILAPIA (part)

36. Teeth in several series, pluricuspid or unicuspid 37

Teeth in one series and of various shapes 41

37. Lower pharyngeal teeth various, but arranged in a triangular pattern; snout equal to or longer than eye; ventral fins usually filamentous, not reaching anal fin 38

Lower pharyngeal teeth thin and bunched together in a nearly circular and concave pattern; snout equal to or shorter than eye, which is large; ventrals with filament in adult fish reaching origin of anal fin; young fish with small tricuspid teeth becoming unicuspid in adult, in 3-5 series, the outer lower teeth pointing outward; maximum size 220 mm . . . . CYATHOPHARYNX (part)

38. Lower pharyngeal teeth all small; body depth 2.7-4.7 times in length; ventral and dorsal shapes rather symmetrical . . . 39

Lower pharyngeal teeth including, in rear of bone, some large, flattened teeth; dorsal profile of body very rounded; ventral profile nearly flat and straight; body depth 2.3-3.0 times (young fish) in body length; teeth small and conical, in 4-5 rows; maximum size 330 mm . . . . TYLOCHROMIS

39. Lower jaw protruding; anal fin with 12-18 soft rays; pharyngeal bone very elongate 40
    Lower jaw not protruding; anal fin with 8-11 soft rays; teeth small, in 3-5 series; outer teeth bicuspid and inner tricuspid in young fish; all teeth conical in adults; maximum size in excess of 650 mm .... *BOULENGEROCHROMIS*
40. Mouth moderately large but slanted upward; teeth conical and small, 90-110 in first row of upper jaw; body depth 2.7-3.3 times in length; 60-72 scales in a longitudinal line; maximum size 280 mm .... *HEMIBATES*
    Mouth large; teeth conical and strong, in 2-4 series, hooked and pointing back, 27-52 in first row of upper jaw; body depth 3.5-5.5 times in length; 60-95 scales in a longitudinal line; maximum size 420 mm .... *BATHYBATES*
41. Teeth of an unusual type, never regularly conical; mouth horizontal or slightly oblique 42
    Teeth small and conical, not or only feebly curved; mouth nearly vertical; lower jaw very protruding; eye very large; maximum size 260 mm .... *HAPLOTAXODON*
42. Teeth flattened and pointing toward back 43
    Teeth unequal in size, with broadened base, transversely compressed toward tip, and with a sharp point on each side of truncated tip; maximum size about 120 mm ....
    .... *PERISSODUS*
43. Teeth small, equal in size, close to each other, compressed, blade-like, front surface slightly concave, the point blunt, and curved toward rear; maximum size 290 mm ....
    .... *XENOCHROMIS*
    Teeth large, unequal in size, separate from each other, compressed, front surface concave, usually with a central groove, blade- or leaf-shaped, and very curved toward back; 18-26 gill rakers on lower limb of first gill arch; maximum size 320 mm .... *PLECODUS*
44. Teeth conical only in outer row 45
    Outer teeth bicuspid in front, conical on sides of jaw; all teeth tricuspid in rear; anal fin with 4-6 spines; maximum size 150 mm .... *TROPHEUS*
45. Teeth all conical but differentiated into canines in front row
    46

At great depth, members of a school of *Cyphotilapia frontosa* swimming away from the rock slopes. The brooding females keep at the same level as the flock; females from other deep-living species often ascend toward shallower waters during the mouth-brooding period.

A pair of *Cyphotilapia frontosa* photographed in their deep-water habitat. Photo by Dr. H.R. Axelrod.

Plecodus straelini fron Sud du Lac mimes not only *Cyphotilapia frontosa* but also *Lamprologus sexfasciatus*.

At 10 meters depth a juvenile *Cyphotilapia frontosa* takes shelter near rock formations. The other fish in the background is *Lamprologus tetracanthus*. This is an example of "mixed habitats" where sand-dwellers and rock-dwellers come in contact.

Teeth in rear rows at least in part tricuspid; front teeth of first row differentiated into canines or not; maximum size 140 mm . . . . *TELMATOCHROMIS*

46. Suborbital ligamentous; more than 21 dorsal fin spines and 6-7 soft rays 47

Suborbital bony; 14-21 dorsal fin spines and 6-12 soft rays; maximum size 310 mm . . . . *LAMPROLOGUS*

47. Genital papillae clearly visible in both sexes; lips thick but not papillose; caudal fin rounded; body pattern permanent from juvenile to adult; maximum size 150 mm . . . . *JULIDOCHROMIS*

No genital papillae visible; lips thick and densely papillose; caudal fin slightly truncate; juvenile body pattern disappearing with age, one black spot remaining at base of dorsal fin; maximum size 150 mm . . . . *CHALINOCHROMIS*

ASPROTILAPIA Boulenger 1901

Boulenger desceibed the only species of this genus, *Asprotilapia leptura*, as follows: "Body elongated, rather feebly compressed, much attenuate in the caudal region; scales ctenoid; two incomplete lateral lines. Teeth small, with very long slender shafts and expanded tricuspid crowns, in two series in both jaws. Mouth inferior, transverse; greater part of maxillary bone concealed under the preorbital. Dorsal with 14 spines, anal with 3. Parietal and occipital crests moderately strong, extending to between the orbits. Vertebrae 35 (16 + 19)"

To which we might add that *A. leptura* has 38 strongly denticulate scales in the lateral line, three series of small scales on the cheek and the caudal fin is forked. There are 36-40 teeth in the upper front row, the snout is very protruding and the mouth is low. The number of gill rakers on the lower half of the first gill arch is 15 or 16.

Habitat: sand and rock
Food habits: not known
Reproduction: mouthbrooder, 20-25 eggs
Maximum size: 110 mm?

No further discussion can be presented due to the lack of knowledge of this fish.

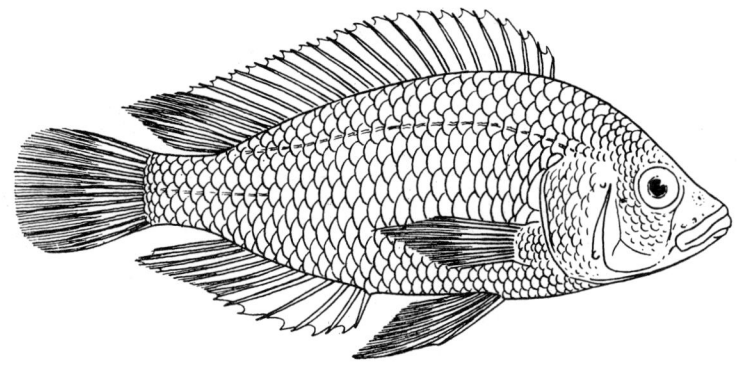

Astatoreochromis alluaudi, from Poll, 1957.

Asprotilapia leptura, from Poll, 1957.

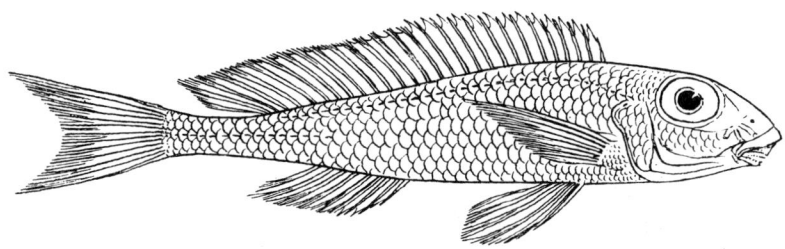

ASTATOREOCHROMIS Pellegrin 1903

The genus *Astatoreochromis* is represented in the Rift lake area by two species, *A. alluaudi*, living to the north of Lake Tanganyika basin around lakes Kivu and Edward, and *A. straeleni*, which has been collected around Lake Tanganyika, but not in the lake itself and only north of the Lukuga outlet.

Astatoreochromis straeleni is a typical swamp-dweller, living in the muddy lagoons and estuaries along with *Haplochromis burtoni*. It is difficult to tell from species of *Haplochromis*, in which genus it had first been placed. The main differences are the number of anal spines, normally 4 instead of the usual 3 for species of *Haplochromis*, and its basic color of a gorgeous yellow-green.

The grounds from which the latest collections have been made indicate that this fish is not as plentiful as *H. burtoni*. Seldom does a full days work yield more than a few dozen fish, and they are usually mixed with hundreds of *H. burtoni*.

Inhabitants of rocky shores in nature, *Eretmodus cyanostictus* will not swim constantly in the aquarium but will stay close to the bottom and merely skip and jump about. Photo courtesy of Wardley Products Company.

An upper surf-washed layer rock-dweller, *Eretmodus cyanostictus*, has been compared to marine gobies because of its behavior among the pebbles in turbulent waters.

Grammatotria lemairei is found on sand floors, sometimes close to rocks. Due to its large size and dull color it is not a very good aquarium fish.

A goby cichlid, *Eretmodus cyanostictus* (striped fish in the center) in its typical habitat. Photo by Glen S. Axelrod.

Breeding *Astatoreochromis straeleni* is by no means any more of a problem than with the other swamp *Haplochromis,* and the fish should by all predictions soon become a favorite among cichlid hobbyists as it keeps its vivid color pattern even when not in nuptial dress.

The fish was originally introduced to the market in very limited quantities a few years back.

AULONOCRANUS Regan 1920

According to Regan, *Aulonocranus* has the frontal, nasal, preorbital, lower limb of preoperculum and lower jaw provided with large channels with wide openings. There are two lateral lines. The teeth are small, conical, the outer row of teeth a little larger. There are less than 20 dorsal fin spines and three anal fin spines. *Aulonocranus* is related to *Trematocara* (which has a single lateral line and the teeth in bands, not rows).

Only one species, endemic to Lake Tanganyika, is presently known.

Body: oblong
Scales: 33-36 in a longitudinal line
Lateral lines: 2, the upper complete
Fins: Dorsal — XI-XIII, 12-14
    Anal — III, 8-10
    Ventrals — with a filament
    Caudal — forked
Teeth: very small and conical, in two rows; 80-90 in outer upper row; outer teeth larger than inner row
Pharyngeal teeth: very small and bluntly conical
Mouth: rather strong
Gill rakers: 17-20 on lower limb of first gill arch
Habitat: shallow water, from the surface to a maximum of 6 meters, mostly over sand or rocky outcrops in sand; a littoral species
Feeding: omnivorous
Reproduction: buccal incubation, eggs 4 mm
Maximum size: 120 mm

Aulonocranus dewindti (Boulenger)

This species, the only one in the genus, is a potentially excellent aquarium fish. It is rather common in coastal waters, where it can be collected with seines. The drawback is, as with many sand-

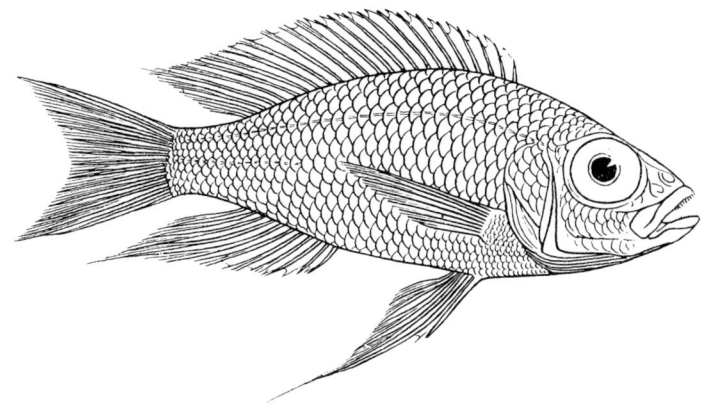

Aulonocranus dewindti, from Poll, 1957.

dwellers, that there are problems in acclimatizing the fish to another type of water.

Seine fishing, when the seines are very long (as they should be on very long beaches), is not very good. This is especially true in Lake Tanganyika, where sand is often very coarse; the fish are rolled in the seines with the sand, become bruised and are difficult to heal afterwards.

Once the acclimatization process is over the fish does not give any more problems. It is not finicky with its food, accepts dried food readily and is a nice addition to a tank.

The eye is especially large for the body size. The color pattern is a light metallic blue with more blue stripes on the head, and the belly and fins are yellow. The anal and ventral fins have filaments.

The fish is always on the move and needs plenty of room. In the lake it is gregarious and lives in schools, although individual specimens have been seen. It is an omnivorous species with an intestine longer than the length of the body.

BATHYBATES Boulenger 1898

The genus *Bathybates* has a long body with ctenoid scales. The teeth are small and irregular, fang-like, in 2-4 rows; the inner teeth are depressible and hinged at the base. The maxillary bone is hidden under the preorbital bone. The dorsal fin has 13-17 spines; the anal fin has 3 spines and 14-18 soft rays. The occipital and parietal crests are strong, not extending forward to beyond the posterior part of the interorbital region. There are 35 or 36 vertebrae.

A *Haplochromis burtoni* in nuptial coloration. Photo by Colour Library International.

Haplochromis burtoni. Photo by Glen S. Axelrod.

Until recently classified among the *Limnochromis*, *Haplochromis pfefferi* is one of the few *Haplochromis* species which has become established in the lake proper. It is found living alone or in pairs along the shores which it seems to prefer. This is a male in full mating color.

A very rare fish, *Haplochromis benthicola* (first discovered in 1962 by Matthes) lives along the rocky slopes. This fish, *Trematocara*, and *Lamprologus niger* all have the same head cavities whose function is still not understood.

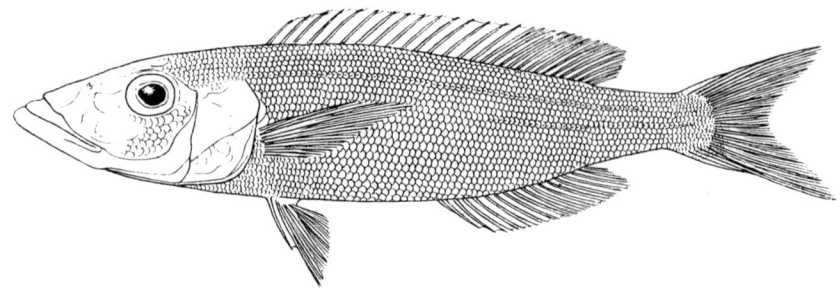

Bathybates leo, from Poll, 1957.

Seven species are known, all endemic to Lake Tanganyika.

Body: elongate, built for speed
Color pattern: marbled, striped or spotted
Scales: 60-95 in a longitudinal line
Lateral lines: 2
Fins: Dorsal — XIII-XVII, 14-18
   Anal — III, 12-18
   Ventrals — short
   Caudal — forked
Teeth: fang-like, inner rows with depressible hinged teeth in 2-5 rows; upper outer row with 27-52 teeth
Pharyngeal teeth: strong, conical, and widely spaced; pharyngeal bone very elongate
Mouth: very large and powerful
Gill rakers: 8-19 on lower limb of first arch
Habitat: pelagic; species of *Bathybates* are among the deepest-living fishes in the lake
Feeding: a typical predator on planktivores such as clupeids
Reproduction: buccal incubation is known for one of the species; eggs were 6.5 mm across, fry 25 mm long
Maximum size: up to 400 mm for one of the species

**Key to the Identification of the Species of *Bathybates*
(after Poll, 1956)**

1. Principal scales for the most part not covered by a layer of small secondary scales 2
   Principal scales for the most part covered by a layer of small secondary scales; eye oval; D. XV-XVI, 15-16; A. III, 14-16;

11-13 gill rakers on lower limb of first gill arch; 77-87 pored scales in lateral line; pattern of male consisting mainly of four longitudinal lateral bands; maximum size 420 mm .... *B. vittatus*

2. Body depth less than 4.6 and head length less than 3.15 in standard length; less than 16 gill rakers; interorbital space 4.7-7.85 in head; caudal peduncle 1.4-2.1 times longer than high 3

    Body depth 4.6-5.5 and length of head 3.15-3.4 in standard length; interorbital space 3.9-4.7 in head; caudal peduncle 2.2-2.5 times longer than high; eye suboval; D. XVI-XIX, 16-18; A. III, 17-19; 16-19 gill rakers; 81-96 scales in a longitudinal line; pattern typical, with transverse bands on sides; maximum size 400 mm .... *B. fasciatus*

3. Dorsal fin without a notch; body depth 3.55-4.75 in body length 4

    Dorsal deeply notched, in two very distinct parts; body depth 3.55-3.85 in body length; interorbital space 4.7-5.0 times in head length; D. XIII-XIV, 15-17; A. III, 17-19; 10-12 gill rakers; 71-86 scales in a longitudinal line; body pattern of four longitudinal lateral stripes; maximum size 210 mm .... *B. minor*

4. 11-15 gill rakers on lower limb of first arch; caudal peduncle less than twice as long as high 5

    8-11 gill rakers on lower limb of first arch; caudal peduncle 2.0-2.1 times longer than high; D. XII-XV, 14-16; A. III, 15-16; 71-87 scales in a longitudinal line; body pattern of short vertical and horizontal stripes and dots; maximum size 270 mm .... *B. horni*

5. Eye oval, 3.3-3.9 in head length; interorbital space 5.9-7.85 in head length 6

    Eye rounded, 3.95-4.8 in head length; interorbital space 5.25-6.0 in head; D. XV-XVI, 15-16; A. III, 16-18; 13-15 gill rakers; 75-88 scales in a longitudinal line; body pattern consisting of vertically elongated spots on anterior part of body and several horizontal stripes posteriorly; maximum size 260 mm .... *B. leo*

6. Body depth 4.0-4.5 in body length; head 2.75-2.95 in body length; D. XIII-XV, 15-17; A. III, 16-19; 12-15 gill rakers; 71-84 scales in a longitudinal line; body pattern consisting of horizontal rows of black dots decreasing in size from back

Haplochromis horei (male above and female below) is a beautiful fish, but unfortunately also predatory and vicious, and will thus not be an ideal community tank fish. Photos by Glen S. Axelrod.

Another *Haplochromis* that has settled in the lake is *H. horei* which lives in the shallows as a predator. Adults in full mating coloration have a deep orange throat, many black stripes on the body, and dots on the cheek and forehead.

Another typical swamp-dweller of the Ruzizi plain; an unidentified *Haplochromis*, very close to *H. burtoni*.

to belly; maximum size 360 mm . . . . *B. ferox*

Body depth 3.55-4.05 in body length; head 2.6-2.7 in body length; D. XIII-XIV, 14-16; A. III, 14-16; 11-13 gill rakers; 60-72 scales in a longitudinal line; body pattern consisting of vertical stripes anteriorly and horizontal stripes posteriorly; two large, conspicuous spots on gill cover; maximum size 250 mm . . . . *B. graueri*

BOULENGEROCHROMIS Pellegrin 1904

The genus *Boulengerochromis* is composed of a single endemic species, *B. microlepis*.

Body: elongate and built for speed, streamlined

Color: three or four spots in a line on the sides; body yellow-green as adult, copper as juveniles

Scales: 74-79 in a longitudinal line

Lateral lines: 2

Fins: Dorsal — XV-XVII, 14-16
    Anal — III, 8-11
    Ventrals — short
    Caudal — large and forked
    Pectorals — large

Teeth: small, in 3-5 rows; outer row bicuspid, the inner tricuspid in young specimens, all becoming conical in adults

Pharyngeal teeth: bicuspid

Mouth: low, horizontal and large

Gill rakers: 13-15 on lower half of first gill arch

Habitat: open water, from the surface to 80 or 90 meters deep; breeding grounds in the shallows, on sand

Feeding: predatory on clupeids

Reproduction: nest-spawner; no buccal incubation; up to 15,000 eggs

Maximum size: in the wild 900 mm or more, maximum recorded weight in excess of 4.5 kilograms

Boulengerochromis microlepis (Boulenger)

Boulengerochromis microlepis is one of the most spectacular and interesting fishes of Lake Tanganyika. But it is certainly not suited for aquarium life as it probably holds the record as the largest cichlid in the world. Specimens of over 800 mm have been reported by anglers.

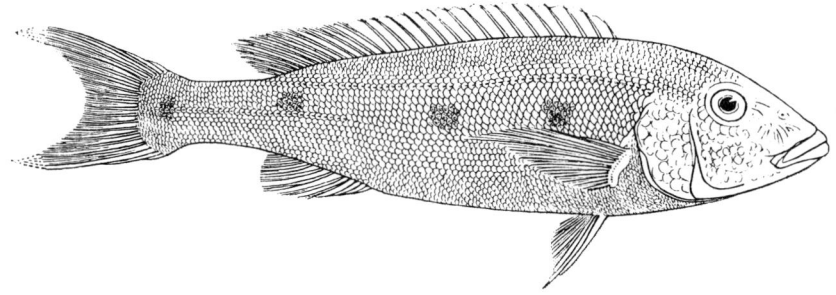

Boulengerochromis microlepis, from Poll, 1957.

Breeding has been reported in detail in another part of this book and in itself would set this species apart from all others.

Research on this species is planned for an excellent reason; the flesh of *Boulengerochromis* is exceptionally good to eat and the over-sized filets are considered a delicacy. As such the fish could have economic value if fry could be transplanted into closed waters suited to their well-being but not their reproduction. It is entirely possible that several endemic fishes from the African Rift lakes, for example this species or *Sarotherodon tanganicae*, could be used in fish farming. They could be allowed to fatten in chemically different types of water and then collected for food. This would prevent the degeneration of premature breeders observed so frequently in fish farms with too well adapted fish species (like most species of *Sarotherodon* and *Tilapia*). This is one of the reasons why *Tilapia* are now considered a bad choice for fish farming in Africa. Of course the fish is predatory, mostly on clupeids, but the size of the species and its value as a first class food warrant the greater research that it has been given as of today. The tremendous quantity of eggs laid by the females, in excess of 10,000 during each spawn, could make a breeding farm on the lake shores a viable enterprise.

CALLOCHROMIS Regan 1920

The genus *Callochromis* contains two species, one of which is broken up into two subspecies. All are endemic to Lake Tanganyika.

Body: deep, compressed, tapering off toward the caudal peduncle; head large

A third member of the dwarf group of *Julidochromis* is the newly described *J. dickfeldi* originating from the southern part of the lake. Photo by Dr. P.A. Lewis.

Julidochromis ornatus is one of the most popular members of the genus among aquarists and is now bred in the United States in great numbers. Photo by Hans J. Richter.

A pair of *Julidochromis dickfeldi* at the Berlin Aquarium display tank. Photo by Dr. Herbert R. Axelrod.

Scales: 32-37 in a longitudinal line
Lateral lines: 2
Fins: Dorsal — XII-XVII, 10-13
   Anal — III, 6-9
   Caudal — forked
Teeth: small, conical, in 3-5 rows, the inner teeth smaller than those in the outer row
Pharyngeal teeth: broadened and molar-shaped
Mouth: very low, horizontal and protrusible
Gill rakers: 10-12 on lower half of the first gill arch
Habitat: directly on sand bottoms in rather shallow water
Feeding: omnivorous, sand-sifters
Reproduction: buccal incubation; up to 50 eggs, each with a diameter of about 2 mm
Maximum size: C. macrops: about 150 mm; *C. pleurospilus:* about 120 mm

Key to the Identification of the Species of Genus *Callochromis*

1. Usually XIV or more spines in the dorsal fin; scales 32-34 in upper lateral line, 16-25 in lower 2
   Usually XII-XIII spines in the dorsal fin (very seldom XIV); scales 22-26 in upper lateral line, 8-10 in lower; body depth 3.33-3.6 times in standard length; pharyngeal bone with anterior blade less than ½ in dental area, teeth of pharyngeal bicuspid .... *C. pleurospilus*
2. Interorbital space 6.2-6.8 in head and 2.0-3.2 in eye diameter; 2 or 3 inners rows of teeth; D. XIV-XVII; male light copper-colored, back dark olive green, black flecks on lateral scales; maximum size about 150 mm ... *C. macrops melanostigma*
   Interorbital space 4.8-6.35 in head and 1.5-2.5 in eye diameter; inner teeth in a single band, not in separate rows; D. XV-XVI (never XIV or XVII); male nearly black all over, with a few silvery flecks on sides; maximum size about 150 mm .... *C. macrops macrops*

The two species of the genus are equally well suited to the aquarium. *Callochromis pleurospilus* is at home in a 20-gallon tank but *C. macrops melanostigma* needs more room as it is a bigger fish. Both species come from sand bottoms and are not seen on rocky slopes as are some other sand dwellers.

Along sandy beaches where there are some sandstone slabs, in

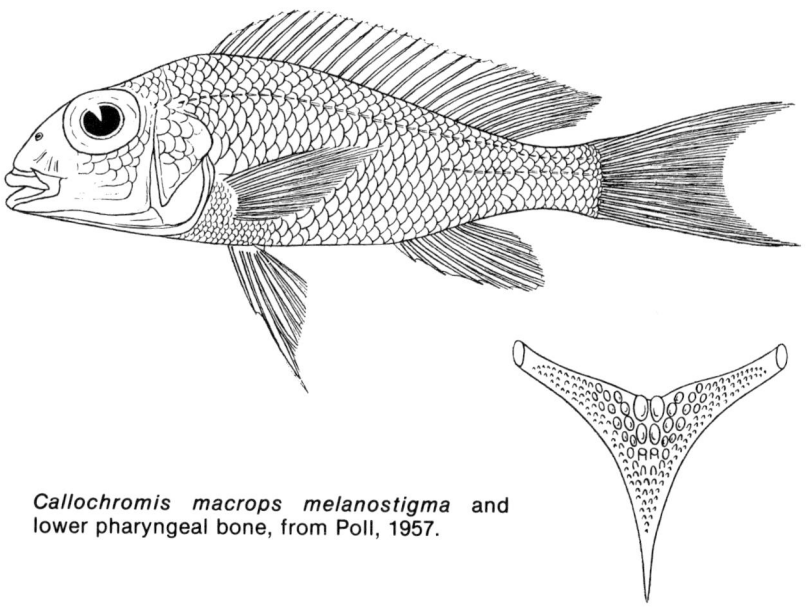

Callochromis macrops melanostigma and lower pharyngeal bone, from Poll, 1957.

the afternoon when the surf is crashing one can see individuals of both species protecting themselves from being smashed against obstacles by sticking close to the walls of narrow recesses. Other sand-dwellers, such as *Aulonocranus* and *Cardiopharynx*, also look for this kind of protection against waves. Otherwise they swim in the open.

The two species of *Callochromis* are bottom-dwellers and are not seen in mid-water. They are not choosy about food and can be kept without any problem and in top condition on dry flakes although, like most cichlids, they relish tubifex worms and other types of live food. Also like most cichlids, they wouldn't hesitate to gobble up any fish small enough to be swallowed. But they are certainly not predatory or vicious, even among themselves.

In the author's opinion *C. pleurospilus* is a very beautiful fish to have in a tank because of its very attractive combination of soft metallic colors on the body. Light green and pink shine on every scale on the sides, the unpaired fins combine opaque white with pink patches and the anal fin is a soft opaque pink visible in young fry when they are 40 mm long. The head is bluish-green with bright blue lips. The throat, chest and belly are pure white. The full colors appear when the fish are about 60 mm long. Seldom does the fish exceed 80 mm, and the bigger specimens are rare.

The body pattern of *Julidochromis ornatus* is quite variable. Note the disrupted yellow band immediately below the fin of this specimen.

A white *Julidochromis transcriptus* in the Berlin Aquarium. Photo by Dr. Herbert R. Axelrod.

A very rare local mutation of Julidochromis marlieri has been found among the regular *marlieri* on the Ruzizi flats in the northernmost part of the lake. Photo by T. Brichard.

The crisscross pattern of vertical and horizontal jet-black stripes on a pale yellow background is typical for *Julidochromis marlieri*, the best known - *Julidochromis* from the lake. Photo by Thierry Brichard.

Spawning has never been observed in the lake but we know the eggs are salmon pink, pear-shaped and about 2-3 mm long.

Acclimatization from the lake water to other water engenders no special problems, although during the first weeks of captivity the colors might not be at their best.

Callochromis macrops melanostigma has a deep golden background spotted with many black spots. The eye, unusually bulging and large, is rimmed with dark red. The unpaired fins are a rich reddish bronze with dark spots. The back is dark olive green. The size, as an average, is between 100 and 120 mm, larger specimens being much rarer. The fry need to be at least 60-70 mm long before they get their adult colors. The eggs are similar to those of *C. pleurospilus*.

CARDIOPHARYNX Poll 1946

The genus *Cardiopharynx* contains only one endemic species, *C. schoutedeni*.

Body: rather elongate and broad; eye very large
Scales: 36-38 in a longitudinal line
Lateral lines: 2, the lower one not complete
Fins: Dorsal — XII-XV, 13-16
   Anal — III, 9-12
   Caudal — well forked
Teeth: tricuspid when young, becoming increasingly conical with age, in 2-3 narrow rows; inner teeth bent backward and of the same size as the front teeth
Pharyngeal teeth: thin and close together, in a heart shaped pattern
Mouth: rather powerful and large; terminal
Gill rakers: 16-19
Feeding: omnivorous
Habitat: 3-15 meters deep over flat sand or mud bottoms; a roamer
Reproduction: buccal incubation, about 60 eggs, each approximately 4 mm in diameter
Maximum size: 150-160 mm

Cardiopharynx schoutedeni Poll

This is a very common fish along sand beaches, sharing the same habitat as *Aulonocranus* but a bit less coastal as it lives in deeper water.

Callopharynx schoutedeni, from Poll, 1957.

It is a very difficult fish to collect properly as it is usually caught by seines several hundred meters long and rolled in the mesh and sand over a long distance before it reaches the beach and can be taken care of. It is one of the food fishes caught by native fishermen because of its abundance.

It could make a suitable aquarium fish even though most of its body is plain silvery and it has only a few outstanding features, such as rows of iridescent scales along the side of the body. The anal and dorsal fins additionally have a large stripe of iridescent metallic hued blue; the ends of both fins turn opaque white. The underpart of the body is pure white, while the chin as well as the caudal peduncle of the male are black. The average size is about 100 mm, although larger fish are not rare.

CHALINOCHROMIS Poll 1974

The genus *Chalinochromis* contains a single species, which is endemic to Lake Tanganyika.

Body: relatively deep, the head and neck profile discontinuous

Scales: 35-36 in a longitudinal line, ctenoid, smaller on the neck and breast, none on cheek

Lateral lines: 2, upper with 12-16 tubed scales

Fins: Dorsal — XXII-XXIII, 6-7
　　Anal — VII, 5
　　Ventrals — rather filamentous
　　Caudal — slightly rounded
　　Pectorals — rounded

Teeth: all teeth conical, four large canines in the upper front row,

A new variety of *Julidochromis,* of the *J. ornatus/transcriptus* group showing a strong trend toward a white color; the fins, except for their edge, have become transparent and the stripes have disappeared leaving only a few black dots. It is probably not a new species but only a freak mutation.

A second variety of *Julidochromis transcriptus*, living in an area 20 kilometers away from the first, has a lighter pattern and at one time was thought to be another species. This specimen, with much white, is typical of the second race.

The northeastern subspecies of *Julidochromis regani, J. regani affinis,* has a body pattern intermediate between *J. marlieri* and the "true" *J. regani*. The color pattern is very strong, especially on the fins.

This very black variety of *Julidochromis transcriptus* has been collected in the same area where the type of the species was first caught. Photo by Thierry Brichard.

2 large canines and 2 small ones on the lower jaw; behind the canines are 4 rows of small conical teeth in both jaws
Pharyngeal teeth: all conical
Mouth: lips remarkably thick and swollen, with thick papillae
Gill rakers: 4 on lower half of first gill arch
Habitat: rocks; not discovered on the western coast of the lake until recently
Feeding: mainly from the rock biocover, omnivorous
Reproduction: nests in rubble; free-swimming fry in the open area guarded by both parents
Maximum size: a bit in excess of 150 mm
Affinities:
 1. With *Julidochromis*, from which it differs by: a) papillose lips; b) absence of a genital papilla; c) changing color pattern between juvenile and adult; d) lack of any body pattern when adult; and e) different breeding ethology
 2. With *Lamprologus*, from which it differs by: a) suborbitals not bony (like *Julidochromis*) and b) more than XXI dorsal spines (also like *Julidochromis*)

Chalinochromis brichardi Poll

This species has been found by the author in the extreme northern part of the species' range in the lake, where it is uncommon if not actually rare. The range seems to extend from 35 km south of Bujumbura, capitol of Burundi, toward Tanzania, where it is more common and is found even in the south of the lake.

At first sight the fish was thought to be a still unknown species because of the quite exceptional pattern of lines on its head and the plain beige body with only a black triangle at the base of the dorsal. The word "*chalinos*" in the scientific name refers to these lines on the head, meaning "bridles" in Greek.

C. brichardi is taxonomically very close to *Julidochromis* and *Lamprologus*, and the spawning behavior is halfway between these two genera. Spawning actions are hidden among the rubble somewhat like those of *Julidochromis*, but unlike species of *Lamprologus* of this size. *Chalinochromis brichardi*, as soon as the fry are one centimeter long, takes them into the open to graze on the rocks. Both of the parents take care of the brood. The fish do not seem to use one of the *Julidochromis* types of spawning (small batches of eggs laid in repeated succession), but have a single spawn composed of several hundred fry. When about 20 mm long

A head-on view of this small school of *Chalinochromis brichardi* shows clearly the extent and arrangement of the "bridles" on the head. Photo by Dr. Herbert R. Axelrod.

or even less, the fry are abandoned and are on their own. Sites of past spawns are identified by a number of fish, up to 30 mm long, spread out in the rubble over a few square meters. Later the fish scatter and are highly solitary and sedentary. The author was able to identify one *Chalinochromis* for about a period of one year on the same boulder.

Very young fry are very strikingly marked. Their body color is a very pale beige with the belly being nearly pure white. The "bridles" are a deep brownish-black. Two dark stripes run along the body toward the tail, and there are five black triangular dots at the base of the dorsal fin. The black stripes on the body progressively break down into spots from the tail toward the front as the fish grows. The dorsal spots disappear one by one, leaving only the last one. When the body stripes disappear altogether, only a small black spot behind the opercle is left. Except for the bridles and the spots near the opercle and on the dorsal, the fish is plain beige with all the tips of the dorsal rays light blue.

Easy to keep in a tank and not vicious toward other fish, *C. brichardi* is an excellent aquarium fish. Pairing them is a problem, however, as fights before pairing are intense when the fish come from pairs broken up during their capture. In one case, after the spawning occurred the male killed the female.

A perfect example of melanistic trends in *Julidochromis* is represented in this *J. regani affinis* as it was called by Dr. Matthes. It is found between Rumonge and Minago on the Burundi coast of the lake. This is not an isolated specimen but a real geographical race, comparable with the much paler eastern and southern races of the same fish.

The "Kigoma" race of *J. regani affinis* has a discolored pattern with a trend toward yellow.

The typical pattern of the unpaired fins is lost in *J. regani affinis* from the South. The fins are now plain.

A magnificent specimen of *Julidochromis regani* of the northern race which is now threatened with extinction by insecticides seeping from cotton fields nearby on its very limited habitat. This race may be a separate species according to investigation now being done. Photo by Thierry Brichard.

CUNNINGTONIA Boulenger 1906

According to Boulenger, *Cunningtonia* has a moderately long body with ctenoid scales. There are two lateral lines, with the upper nearly complete, the lower one not. The jaws have broad bands of minute teeth with curved tricuspid crowns forming a kind of brush pad. The dorsal fin has XIII spines, the anal III. There are 18 + 18 = 36 vertebrae.

The single species, *C. longiventralis*, is endemic to Lake Tanganyika.

Body: moderately long; very large eyes
Scales: 36-41 in a longitudinal line
Lateral lines: 2, the lower one not complete
Fins: Dorsal — XIII, 13-15
 Anal — III, 8-10
 Ventrals — with a long filament
 Caudal — forked
Teeth: mobile, brush-like teeth with curved tricuspid crowns; in many wide bands
Pharyngeal teeth: in a dense, velvet-like pattern
Mouth: wide and terminal
Gill rakers: 15-18

This specimen was photographed and identified by Paul V. Loiselle as *Cunningtonia longiventralis*. The long pelvic fins resemble those of *Ophthalmochromis* and *Cyathopharynx*.

Habitat: from the surface to 15 meters deep over or close to rocks
Feeding: diatoms and microorganisms
Reproduction: buccal incubation of few eggs (3.5 mm in diameter), *Ophthalmochromis* spawning mode
Maximum size: in the wild about 150 mm

CYATHOPHARYNX Regan 1920

The genus *Cyathopharynx* contains a single species, *C. furcifer*, endemic to Lake Tanganyika.

Body: elongated, rather oval, with a very large eye; females have narrow stripes
Scales: 48-64 in a longitudinal line
Lateral lines: 2
Fins: Dorsal — XII or XIV, 13-15
Anal — III, 8-10
Ventrals — with a long filament tipped with a yellow double spatula
Caudal — forked and filamentous
Teeth: small and tricuspid in the young, unicuspid in adults; in 3-5 rows, the outer lower row pointing outward
Pharyngeal teeth: thin and close together in a circular, concave pattern
Mouth: terminal
Gill rakers: 15-18
Habitat: lives in schools in mid-water near rocky slopes, down to about 10 meters
Feeding: omnivorous, but feeds mainly on microorganisms
Reproduction: buccal incubation; the male builds a crater nest on top of big boulders by lifting sand from the nearby bottom (often called the "penthouse nest")
Maximum size: in the wild about 200 mm

Cyathopharynx furcifer (Boulenger)

We have already seen the exceptional behavior of *Cyathopharynx* males when they build their nests under the circling school of females and immature males.

This striking fish, one of the most brilliantly colored aquarium fishes ever, is often the first to be seen when diving on rocky slopes. There are at least four color morphs. In the north the males are an incredible iridescent dark blue, flashing in the sunlit waters, with

Lamprologus callipterus is a typical sand-dweller living in small packs, in essence a scavenger feeding from the sand. It is also on the lookout for sick or dead fish or defense-less fry.

Lamprologus attenuatus can lay as many as 2,000 to 3,000 eggs in crater-like nests dug in sand plains. Photo by Dr. Robert J. Goldstein.

A male *Lamprologus brichardi* with the typical orange dots on the caudal peduncle which the female doesn't show. *L. brichardi* is the most gregarious of all known *Lamprologus*.

A young *Lamprologus brichardi* photographed in a tank by Hans J. Richter.

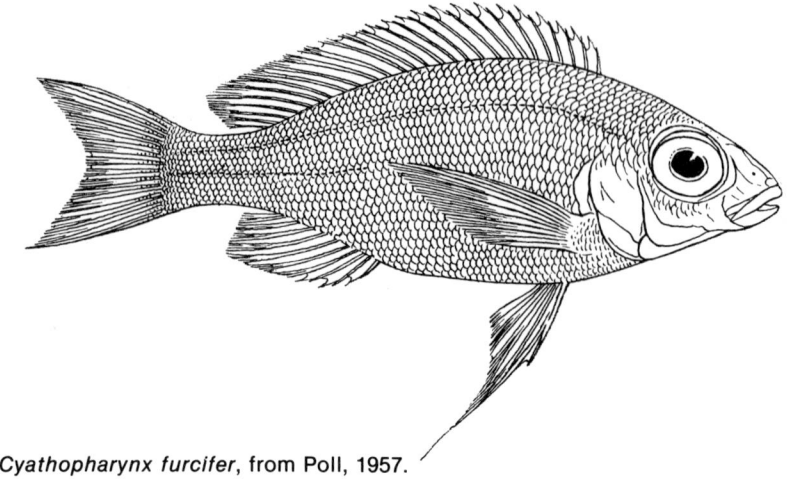

Cyathopharynx furcifer, from Poll, 1957.

the unpaired fins alternating Prussian blue with pure white and orange spots. The ventral filaments, reaching the end of the anal fin, are each tipped with a double yellow-orange spatula. If there is a "fairytale fish," this is it. Close to the border separating Burundi from Tanzania another color morph can occasionally be seen, this one with a chestnut body and orange-vermilion head. In the south there are at least two other color morphs. The first has a pale blue iridescent body with a dark blue head; the second reverses the pattern, with the head light blue and the body much darker. Females of the four color morphs are very similar. They have a silvery, pale green body with several thin dark stripes running down the sides. They lack the brilliant colors of the males and are also much smaller than the 18 cm usually reached by their mates.

Unless given very large quarters, *Cyathopharynx* will not be at ease in a tank; one has to remember that this fish is one of the species hovering slowly in mid-water a bit off the lake slopes and wandering about without being bound to the floor.

This fish will never be common in hobbyists' tanks. It is difficult to acclimatize after capture, from which its soft body usually suffers too much. All thus depends on the careful handling of the fish and constant attention afterward before the fish can be shipped. High air freight rates for such large and delicate specimens add to the total costs, and *Cyathopharynx* for this reason winds up as one of the most expensive fishes to be exported from Lake Tanganyika.

Once it has reached its final destination, the hobbyist's tank, the problems are mostly over. Well fed (the fish is not choosy about food) and with proper quarters (the aquarium should be at least 70-80 cm high), there will be few problems for its well-being.

Cyathopharynx furcifer is a microphage, eating small shrimps and zooplankton floating in the water. As such it will not harm the other fish in a tank, but as it is a cichlid and with an above average size, it should not be trusted with very small fishes.

CYPHOTILAPIA Regan 1920

Cyphotilapia contains one species, *C. frontosa*, which is endemic to Lake Tanganyika.

Body: deep and rather compressed; a hump on the head increasing with age; broad deep blue and white alternating bands

Scales: 32-35 in a longitudinal line

Lateral lines: 2

Fins: Dorsal — XVII to XIX, 8-10
  Anal — III, 7-8
  Ventrals — with long white filament
  Caudal — rounded
  Pectorals — very large

Teeth: external row conical or partly bicuspid, inner row conical or partly tricuspid

Pharyngeal teeth: all very fine, compressed, more or less bicuspid

Mouth: inferior, protrusible and large, not especially powerful

Gill rakers: 10-12

Habitat: coastal, on rocks from 5-50 meters, depth increasing with age

Feeding: omnivorous, eating in part shellfish (snails, mussels) and fish

Reproduction: buccal incubation, about 25 eggs 5 mm in diameter are deposited

Maximum size: in the wild 350 mm

Cyphotilapia frontosa (Boulenger)

This is one of the most magnificent and exciting fish to have reached the aquarium world from Lake Tanganyika.

It is seldom exported, not that it is rare in its native habitat, for thousands of them are caught each day by native fishermen with hook and line. It is in fact a very good fish to eat, and the

The northern race of *Lamprologus compressiceps* is dark brown when adult and the cheeks have a beautiful bronze color.

The eastern race of *Lamprologus compressiceps* shows a beautiful yellow pattern on body and fins.

Lamprologus compressiceps from an unknown locality of the lake. Photo by Glen S. Axelrod.

The southern race pictured here has a very dark pattern, entirely different from the two preceding specimens. Another southern race shows a multitude of striking white dots on body and fins starting from behind the pectoral fins.

native dugouts are often filled to the brim with a half day's catch. The problem is to get them alive, which is very difficult because the fish lives in deep water. The big schools abound in the 30 to 40 meters layer or even deeper. There, in the twilight zone of the lake, the ghostly light blue bands of the fish seem to have a kind of luminescence of their own. The big specimens, often 350 mm long, stand side by side and move around slowly a bit off the greenish-gray slope. To catch the fish at such depths is very difficult. They are quick, and dragging a 36 square meter net between two or three divers in step with the wary fish cannot be done more than three times during a dive. Afterward you have just enough strength left in you to bring the cage with the captured fish a bit higher along the slopes. This must be done slowly as the fish will very quickly show signs of decompression problems.

It is useless also, even if you get the rare opportunity, to catch more than 8-10 fish in the net at a time. They are so powerful that their concerted thrust will lift the net from the ground and they will escape. Not all the fish you thought to be *C. frontosa* will turn out to be them. In the midst of the few fish trapped you will find one or two *Plecodus straeleni* with identical blue and white bands mimicking the 'cyphos' so well that they can mix with the flock unobtrusively and, during a sudden rush, tear a few scales from the *C. frontosa's* sides. It is impossible, without having the *Plecodus* in one's hands, to tell them apart. It is the only such case of mimicry of a species by its predator as yet reported from the lake. We will see, when dealing with *Plecodus*, that there is more to it.

The *Cyphotilapia* thus caught need a long time to be brought to the surface. We have never seen a *Cyphotilapia* brought to the surface alive from depths in excess of 15 meters. If it is not decompressed for several hours and if it is still alive, it will certainly not be in good condition afterward.

To offset this problem we had to develop a new method. We brought a heavy plastic drum down to where we planned to fish, put the captured fish in the drum, filled it with air from our diving bottles, sealed it hermetically and brought it to the surface and our fish compound. The drum had a capacity of about 100 liters (a bit less than 30 gallons), and we could store a maximum of 6-8 middle sized fish in it. The lid had a valve, and every few hours we let some of the air out to decompress the fish. Unfortunately, the system had some drawbacks, the main one being that, after a few uses, the lid could no longer stand the two atmospheres of pressure and leaked.

We then tried metal cylinders. They were strong enough but very heavy. The trouble also was that the inner walls were rough and scraped the fish during the bumpy boat ride back to the fish compound. Another problem was that we couldn't check on the fish; after a while in the confines of these chambers, wounds festered, the water became polluted and fish either died or were in such poor condition that it took a month or more, if we were lucky, to get them into good condition for shipping.

Now we have another less troublesome system. We can get the *C. frontosa* back in a much better condition than before and can check on their health along the way. Even when in the best possible shape they are a bit scratched and the smallest wound is an open door for infection during acclimatization. How do we treat them? With utmost and painstaking care! It is perhaps interesting to tell, for once, a few of the secrets of fish collectors when they are not in the trade exclusively to make money, but also because they like the fish.

Cyphotilapia frontosoa is taken in great numbers by the natives for food, but collecting them alive for the aquarium is a different story. Photo by Gerhard Budich.

Young adult *Lamprologus cunningtonia*. Photo by Dr. Herbert R. Axelrod.

A *Lamprologus niger* about to enter a hole between the rocks. Photo by Glen S. Axelrod.

A *Lamprologus elongatus* hovering over a deep hole. Photo by Glen S. Axelrod.

Lamprologus elongatus belongs to the roaming pike-like group of *Lamprologus*, so powerful that they can raise their fry in the open. This specimen is in full nuptial color.

Each 'cypho,' when out of decompression, is individually checked out of the water. The slightest scratch or bare skin (the tips of the protruding jaws are always a little scraped) is dabbed with iodine. When a fin ray has been broken it is also dabbed, although we know that the place will peel away—but the microbes are killed. The fish are then put into a tank individually. Whether we have 10 or 100 'cyphos,' whatever their size, each is placed in a separate tank. An unusually strong solution of copper sulfate is added to the tank, turning it a light blue. After three or more days, depending on the appearance of the fish in this bath (there is a water change every day), the fish are put into another bath with methylene blue and acriflavine. An antibiotic is put into the water and a sulfa drug added as well. This bath is changed every other day over a two-week period. The fish are fed dried food (in flakes) and tubifex worms (a 200-mm specimen will eat about a bunch of worms the size of a golf ball each day).

When they appear to be healed, which means all wounds cicatrized and covered with skin and all fins smooth and slippery with the mucus replaced on the skin, the fish are considered well enough to be shipped in a few days time. This last quarantine lasts about five days.

At best, a *C. frontosa* in prime condition when caught will thus have to be looked after for about three weeks before being shipped abroad. It will have been handled twice daily during the first two or three days with each wound taken care of, then cured with some costly, or even very costly, drugs. Some of the antibiotics we experimented with cost $2,000 a kilogram (2.2 pounds) wholesale.

When the fish are in poor condition upon arrival they of course need more time, sometimes as long as six weeks, before they are considered in proper condition. We have often had to wait longer than this for ripped fins to grow back. And as usual there are some losses.

Some of the *Cyphotilapia frontosa* taken from the lake are collected by our fishermen. Here, in shallower water where they are less common, they are easier to collect. Our fishermen are not allowed to use SCUBA to fish because of the hazards and latent dangers of this kind of fishing.

Not all the lake fish, fortunately, need such painstaking methods of collecting, though the most valuable fish are all given similar treatment, which explains their price. But it is well worth the effort if excessive losses are to be avoided with species like the

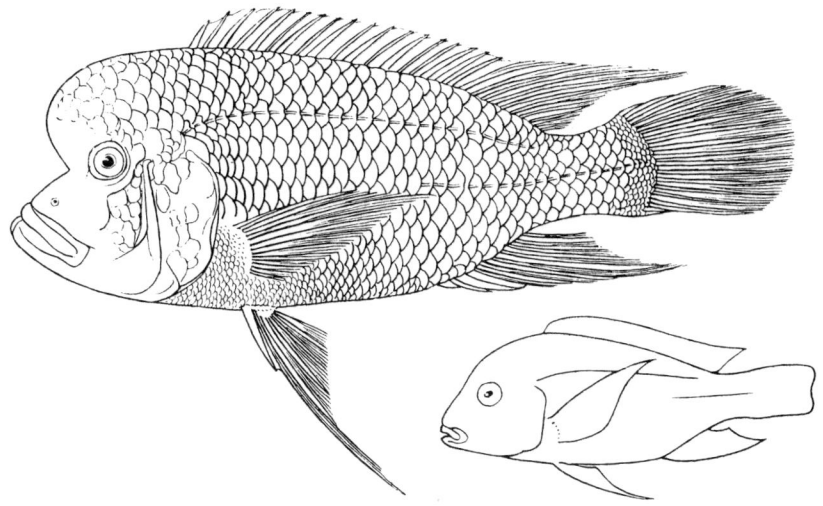

Cyphotilapia frontosa, adult (top) and juvenile, from Poll, 1957.

mouthbrooders from the rocky slopes which cannot multiply in large quantities and cannot thus be collected at random. Losses must be kept low during collecting and acclimatization. When we collected in the Congo basin these losses were less than 3% of the fish collected. We are close to this figure now with our Lake Tanganyika rock-dwellers, and the losses dwindle from month to month.

Let us get back to *Cyphotilapia frontosa*. The schools down deep number between a few hundred to sometimes as many as one thousand individuals, and they include a very large proportion of big adults. The density of the schools and the mean size of individuals dwindle when they are less deep to the point where, at a depth of about 10 meters, there are but a few young fish left, these very seldom venturing into water less than 8 meters deep. Only once during a dive (out of more than 200 dives) did I see a pair at 6 meters depth, and I still don't know what these adults were doing there.

Young fry of less than 50 mm are never seen in the open and seem to spend their lives rather individually, hidden in deep recesses in the same water layer as the big adults. Only a few have as yet been discovered. This is interesting because *C. frontosa*, although a mouthbrooder, seems to stay in deep water to release the fry. Most mouthbrooders go into shallow water either to release the fry or during the incubation time, probably to get

Lamprologus fasciatus is a predator from the South and is never found in the northern part of the lake. It grows larger than 20 centimeters, and shares the habitat of *L. elongatus,* i.e. in mid-water close to the shore.

A young adult *Lamprologus furcifer,* about 9 centimeters long.

Lamprologus lemairei, adult. Compare this specimen with the juvenile on page 103. Photo by Glen S. Axelrod.

Several *Lamprologus* **(possibly** *L. attenuatus* **or** *L. callipterus***) against a wall of big rocks. Photo by Glen S. Axelrod.**

better oxygenation for them.

Most mouthbrooders are near the surface when they incubate the eggs or the fry. Even some deep water fishes, such as *Lobochilotes labiatus*, which lives in the same layer as *C. frontosa*, does this. The fact that *Cyphotilapia frontosa* doesn't might indicate that the oxygen requirements of the fry, and perhaps the adults, are lower than those of most mouthbrooders. There is an advantage to this brooding method: the young fish will live in a layer where many predators don't venture and will thus be capable of surviving the terrific struggle for survival that goes on in the densely populated upper layers. It is very quiet deep down in the lake.

Broods of *C. frontosa* are small for such a huge fish. Seldom have more than 22 to 25 eggs or fry been found in mature females when they are caught, and these figures do not seem to increase much with the size of the fish. The fry are still in their mother's mouth when 25 mm long.

Cyphotilapia frontosa is a ravenous eater with its large mouth capable of engulfing other fishes, but it doesn't appear to be a systematic predator. Fish 40 mm long kept in a tank with a 200 mm long *C. frontosa* were not swallowed whole but were ripped to pieces by the 'cypho,' which we had kept on a diet to see what would happen. Poll mentions that the stomach contents include fish and shellfish.

Most probably *C. frontosa* can be kept with other fishes of similar size without any trouble. It is not a bothersome fish when fed properly and is well worth the trouble.

ECTODUS Boulenger 1898

According to Boulenger, *Ectodus* is characterized as follows. Body moderately long, scales ctenoid; neither of the two lateral lines complete. Teeth conical, in 2-3 rows, those of the outer rows on the lower jaw directed outward and perpendicular to the inner teeth. Maxillary bone entirely hidden under the preorbital bone. A large papillose pad on each side of the pharynx makes a strong protuberance in front of the upper half of the branchial arches. Dorsal fin with XIII or XIV spines, anal with III. Occipital and parietal crests low, extending to between the orbits. Vertebrae 36.

A single species, *E. descampsi*, is endemic to the lake.

Body: elongate, built for speed
Scales: 35-38 in a longitudinal line
Lateral lines: 2, not complete

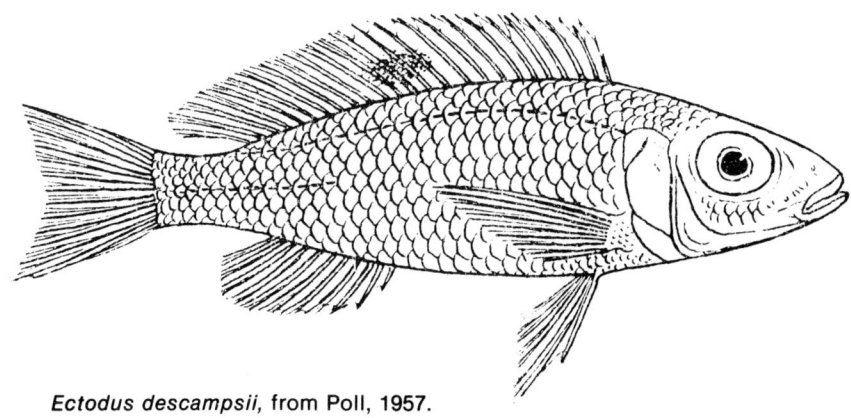

Ectodus descampsii, from Poll, 1957.

Fins: Dorsal — XIII-XIV, 12-15
    Anal — III, 8-10
    Caudal — forked
Teeth: small and conical in 2-3 rows; the outer lower teeth directed outward
Pharyngeal teeth: very thin; there is a crushing cushion on each side of the pharyngeal bone
Mouth: terminal
Gill rakers: 12-14 on the lower half of the first gill arch
Habitat: shallow water over coarse sand bottoms
Feeding: microorganisms, diatoms, algae
Reproduction: buccal incubation; less than 25 eggs (?)
Maximum size: about 100 mm

ERETMODUS Boulenger 1898

A single species, *E. cyanostictus,* is endemic to Lake Tanganyika.

Body: short and stocky, with a blunt, steeply sloping front; several alternating beige-brown bands on the body *extending from the base of the dorsal to the lower part of the body*
Scales: ctenoid, 30-32 in a longitudinal line
Lateral lines: 2, not complete
Fins: short and powerful
    Dorsal — XXII-XXV, 3-5
    Anal — III, 7
    Caudal — rounded

The bright yellow color seen in the wild fish is missing in this much faded specimen of *Lamprologus leleupi.* Photo by Wilhelm Hoppe.

This rather big specimen (15 centimeters long) of *Lamprologus* is probably a new species. A specimen was collected in the northwestern coast three years ago and recently several were collected in the southern part of the lake. Very unusual are: the very long dental and maxillary bones, the short stubby spine at the ventrals, and the very small scales.

The magnificent yellow color of *Lamprologus leleupi* has been captured by the German photographer, Hans J. Richter, in this picture.

Lamprologus leleupi was first introduced to the hobby in small numbers in the late 50's. It is still a very rare fish. Unfortunately, breeding is not easy and as with many Lake Tanganyika cichlids the tank-bred offspring from western breeders do not keep the specimen's bright yellow garb.

Teeth: on a long stem, *each crown typically spatulate with a straight edge* (blade-like) in *separate sets of 2-3 teeth*, those in the front row larger than the inner teeth. A typical grazer dentition.

Pharyngeal teeth: uniform in size; subconical

Mouth: very low, broad and straight

Gill rakers: 10-12

Habitat: very shallow, amid rubble and pebbles in the surf-washed shoreline; not below 3 meters depth

Feeding: from the rock biocover

Reproduction: buccal incubation of about 25 ovoid, pink, 2 mm diameter eggs, incubated until fry are about 8-10 mm long

Maximum size: 70-80 mm exceptionally

Eretmodus cyanostictus Boulenger

Along with *Spathodus erythrodon* and to a lesser degree *Tanganicodus irsacae*, this species is one of the most common, if not the most common, fishes on the surf-washed pebble shorelines in Lake Tanganyika.

It is also one of those cute little cichlids that one falls in love with at first sight. Perhaps it does not correspond to what one usually thinks of as a cichlid; the colors are not especially bright and the shape is rather plump and stocky. Therefore it is no winner in a beauty contest, but it does have a lot going for it as an aquarium fish. It is not big, usually not more than 60 mm and with a maximum size of 80 mm. It has brown stripes on a lighter brown background and a few blue dots on the head, mainly on the cheeks. And what a snout! There is a long, wide, sloping front, so wide we called it the 'tapir fish' at once, while some call it 'schnozolla.'

Eretmodus stays on the bottom of the tank in the open, jumping from place to place with a jerk as if incapable of prolonged swimming. In fact, it is unable to swim properly in mid-water. It is too heavy and the swim-bladder doesn't seem to give it enough buoyancy, with good reason. Since *Eretmodus* lives in the surf near the shoreline, a lightweight body would be the last thing it needs; the fish would be smashed against the rocks. With its stocky, heavy body it is happy to jump from stone to stone. As the waves break around it, it seeks shelter among the rubble. Many people compare *Eretmodus* with marine gobies, and perhaps they are right.

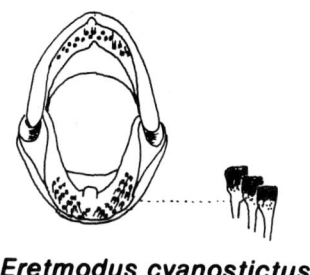
Eretmodus cyanostictus

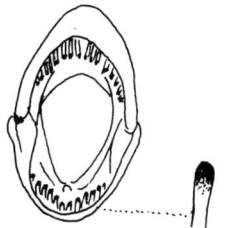
Spathodus erythrodon

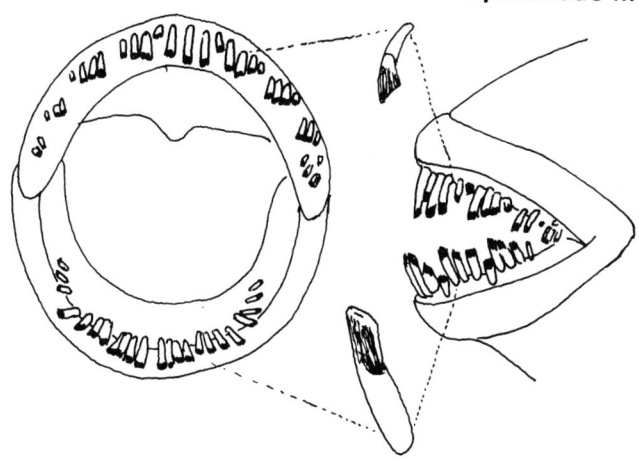
Spathodus marlieri

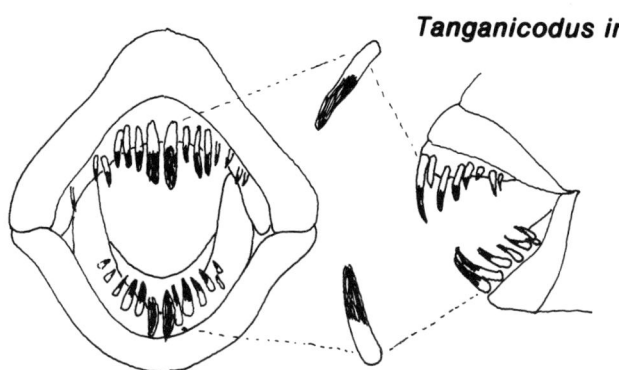
Tanganicodus irsacae

Teeth of four species in the genera: *Eretmodus*, *Spathodus* and *Tanganicodus*, from "Exploration Hydrobiologique duLac Tanganyka Poissons Cichlidae" by M. Poll.

The southern race of *Lamprologus modestus* has yellow pectoral fins as seen in this fish. The northern type has pale blue translucent pectorals.

Lamprologus moorii is another species known only from the South. It is very beautiful with velvet-black body and fins and the tail edged in light blue. It is a rock-dweller.

This *Lamprologus* is still unidentified and most probably it is a new species. A few specimens of this striking species with a pure white chin, beige yellow body and bright orange yellow fins have been found by the author along southern rocky coasts.

A new species of *Lamprologus*. It is a very gregarious species like *L. brichardi* and *L. pulcher*.

For my part I would put *E. cyanostictus* along with *Steatocranus*, the "buffalo-head" from the Congo basin, because of the overall similarity between the two body shapes (except for the *Steatocranus* hump), the heaviness of the body and the habitat. *Steatocranus* also lives in very turbulent waters in the powerful Congo rapids, also jumps from place to place, and is also incapable of reaching mid-water without jerky, spasmodic swimming.

The habitat of *Eretmodus* doesn't extend below 3 meters of depth under the best of conditions, and only the largest adults live that deep. The fish are always on the move from rock to rock and it is next to impossible to determine whether they have a territory or like *Tropheus*, they wander about within the narrow limits of their habitat. They are found exclusively around pebbles and rubble and never on boulders. When the habitat is suited to their needs the density of these fish is remarkable, several of them per square meter.

They are mouthbrooders, the eggs numbering about 25. The fry are still in their mother's mouth when a good centimeter long.

In the tank *Eretmodus cyanostictus* is the perfect community tank fish, not bothersome to other fishes and even liking the company of the mid-water species. Feeding is easy, and the fish can be kept happy even on dry food alone. It is not a plant-eater as are so many cichlids from some of the Rift Valley lakes.

GRAMMATOTRIA Boulenger 1899

Grammatotria contains a single species, *G. lemairei*, which is endemic to Lake Tanganyika.

Body: elongated, built for speed
Scales: ctenoid, 44-59 in a longitudinal line
Lateral lines: 3, none complete
Fins: Dorsal — XV-XVI, 13-16
　　Anal — III-IV, 9-12
　　Ventrals — short
　　Pectorals — long
　　Caudal — well forked
Teeth: conical, in 4-6 rows, the outer large, the inner very small, each row a narrow band
Pharyngeal teeth: very large and molar-like, with 2 very large oval molars at the back of the bone; conical teeth on the rear corners of the bone
Mouth: terminal and with powerful jaws

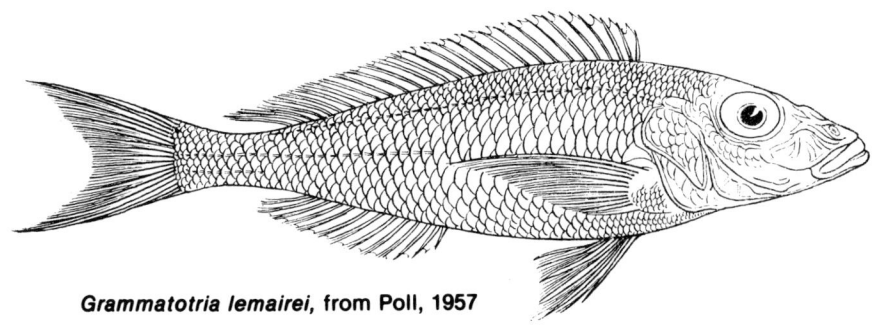

Grammatotria lemairei, from Poll, 1957

Gill rakers: 11-12
Habitat: medium depths from 5-20 or 30 meters, apparently gregarious, over sand; semi-pelagic
Feeding: diatoms, insects, shellfish, etc.
Reproduction: buccal incubation; 60-90 eggs, 4.5 mm in diameter
Maximum size: 260 mm

Grammatotria lemairei Boulenger

This fish has occasionally been seen by the author in seine hauls by native fishermen, but was never discovered underwater. It is apparently not a littoral species but probably is a bottom-feeder since its diet includes diatoms and molluscs.

This powerful and swift species, reaching well over 250 mm in length, with poor colors and strong jaws, is certainly not a good aquarium fish.

HAPLOCHROMIS Hilgendorf 1888

There are five species of *Haplochromis* endemic to the lake basin, of which three are in the lake proper; one non-endemic species (*H. burtoni*) inhabits coastal delta swamps.

Body: moderately long, dorsal and ventral profile convex
Scales: all ctenoid
Lateral lines: 2, not complete
Fins: Dorsal — always with less than XX spines
    Anal — with III or IV spines
    Ventrals — with first ray longer than the others
    Caudal — rounded
Teeth: in one or two rows, usually bicuspid
Pharyngeal teeth: molar-shaped in central part of the bone, conical on the sides

At present *Lamprologus niger* has not yet been found on the northeastern coast of the lake but only on the northwestern coast. The fish belongs to the *L. leleupi* group which is associated with a substratum of caves and labyrinths. It has never been seen yet in the open, but was caught quite by accident. It is not exceedingly rare. The checkerboard pattern on the fins along with the deep orange vermillion body color is quite beautiful. A brown variety of *L. niger* is shown below.

Lamprologus ornatipinnis is a very rare fish (less than six have been taken in 5 years of collecting) because of its peculiar habitat. This dwarf species (not exceeding 6 centimeters) belongs to the shell-dwelling group of *Lamprologus* living in the sand plains of the lake.

Lamprologus ocellatus is a good-looking fish but unfortunately also difficult to collect. They live in empty snail shells and they get crushed between the shells gathered in the net during collection. Photo by Thierry Brichard.

Mouth: end of maxillary bone exposed when mouth is closed
Habitat: in Africa, multiple adaptations; in the lake, except for
  H. benthicola, always in shallow water and coastal; in the case
  of *H. horei* specimens have been collected in river estuaries,
  showing a trend toward colonization of rivers; all, except for
  the two species found in the lake proper, are river-dwelling
  fishes
Feeding: Haplochromis benthicola: not ascertained
  H. horei: predatory
Breeding: Haplochromis benthicola: not known
  All others exhibit buccal incubation

Key to the Identification of the Species of *Haplochromis*

I. Species inhabiting the lake proper (including hard bottoms)

1. Cheek scaleless; snout long, 2.15 to 2.45 times in head; interorbital space 5.0 to 6.3 times in head; D. XIV-XVII; 10-13 gill rakers; pharyngeal teeth thin, broader in the rear; head spotted with very distinct black spots .... *H. horei*
   Cheek scaled (3 to 6 rows) 2

2. Four to six rows of scales on cheek; lower jaw 2.65-2.9 times in head; 14 to 16 scales in lower lateral line; 13 to 14 gill rakers; eye small, 5.0-5.75 times in head, 1.95-2.25 times in snout; 3-5 rows of teeth on upper jaw; pharyngeal bone shaft short, with conical teeth sparse posteriorly; XVII dorsal fin spines; color plain brown; size to 160 mm; habitat deep and rocky........................ *H. benthicola*
   Three rows of scales on cheek; lower jaw 2.0-2.5 times in head; 10-12 scales on lower lateral line; 10-13 gill rakers; head very narrow, 2.4-2.6 times in length; mouth very narrow; pharyngeal bone with all teeth conical and slender; XV-XVI dorsal fin spines; color dark olive on back and sides with dark vertical stripes; size to 120 mm; habitat mainly rocky, but also found on mud .... *H. pfefferi*

II. Species inhabiting rivers, estuaries and swamps

1. Caudal peduncle 1.2-1.4 times longer than high; 30-48 teeth on outer row of upper jaw; 0-2 ocelli (seldom more) on anal fin; maximum size 130 mm .... *H. stappersi*
   Caudal peduncle about as high as long.................... 2

2. Dorsal with XIII spines; head and snout as broad as long;

pharyngeal bone shaft ⅔ as long as bone surface; pharyngeal teeth thin; 28-30 scales in upper lateral line; 4-5 rows of scales on cheek; 7-10 gill rakers; color various, blue or green with strong horizontal darker stripe; size 120 mm; inhabits swamps and possibly estuaries . . . . *H. burtoni*

Dorsal with XVI-XVII spines; snout very short, 3.3-4.0 times in head; head 2.7-3.2 times in standard length; pharyngeal bone shaft short, ⅓ to ¼ bone surface; pharyngeal teeth broad and molar-like in the center and rear; colored much like *Astatoreochromis straeleni* including the 5-6 rows of red scales behind the pectoral base, but without the blue cheeks and lips; maximum size 130 mm . . . . *H. vanderhorsti*

Haplochromis benthicola Matthes

The last *Haplochromis* to have been discovered in the lake, *H. benthicola*, is a very seldom seen species, less than 20 specimens of which have been collected since its discovery in the early 60's. More than any other Tanganyikan species of *Haplochromis*, it is a typical deep-living rock-dweller. The shape and behavior of the species is atypical for a species of *Haplochromis* from Lake Tanganyika, as the fish is often in hiding in the rubble instead of, as with *H. horei* or *H. pfefferi*, in the open along the shoreline.

The few specimens collected by the author were rather large, about 160 mm long, and of a deep brown color without any striking marks on the body.

This species is rather peculiar for a *Haplochromis* because it is equipped with several skin-covered cavities (enlargement of the mucous canals) in the head very similar to those which have been discovered in species of *Trematocara*, which also live in deep or very deep water in the lake; such cavities are also one of the features of *Lamprologus niger*. The fact that *H. benthicola* is so different from *Trematocara* but is endowed with these drum-shaped cavities might tend to indicate that fishes living in deep water, without much light to identify their neighbors, might have developed an additional warning system amplifying either pressures or noises so that they would be aware of what happens around them.

The rarity of *H. benthicola*, the problems involved in its occasional capture because of decompression and the drabness of its body pattern, as well as its carnivorous diet, will never make it anything other than one of the lake oddities.

Lamprologus species (male above, female below). This still unidentified species is found in the southern part of the lake in small schools close to the rocks.

Lamprologus pleuromaculatus, with alternate yellow and blue stripes on the body and fins, is one of the most colorful species of *Lamprologus* along with *L. tetracanthus*. Unfortunately, although not bothersome with large fish, it will prey upon fishes one-third its size.

Lamprologus pleuromaculatus with unusual coloration.

Haplochromis horei (Gunther)

One of the three endemic species of *Haplochromis* from the lake proper (the other two being *H. benthicola* and *H. pfefferi*), *H. horei* is a coastal species living very close to the shoreline. It does not venture deeper, perhaps, than one meter, for it has as yet never been seen in deep water in its habitat.

The species is predatory on other fishes and can swallow a good sized fish with its huge mouth.

The adults are very beautiful, with the lower part of the body a deep orange-red and the belly a strong yellow. The species is easy to identify because of the many black spots on the head, mainly on the cheeks and the front. It is not a good aquarium fish because of its large size and vicious temper.

The species uses buccal incubation as its breeding mode, the eggs and fry being small and numbering well over a hundred.

Haplochromis pfefferi (Boulenger)

This fish until very recently was classified in the genus *Limnochromis*. It is better adapted to the lake than *H. horei*, is found over rocky slopes far from river estuaries and has been seen at depths of 10 meters. It is a ubiquitous fish, having been collected close to sand beaches as well. Never abundant, it is nevertheless common everywhere and lives a solitary type life until pairing for mating purposes. Afterwards each adult resumes its solitary wanderings. The fish doesn't seem to be territorial, unless its territory is very large. It doesn't live in the substratum, but on top of it, close by.

The unusually small mouth and the very narrow body makes it an unusual cichlid. Seen from a few meters away it might be mistaken for *Lamprologus compressiceps*, whose habitat it often shares.

The fry are very black and look a little like *Lates niloticus* fry. The unpaired fins also are very dark. This color pattern changes as the fish grows into a thinly striped olive-green body and a darker hued green-blue head. The colors of sexually ripe fish become much more attractive, although the fish are never dull.

Buccal incubation has been observed in this species. The fry, when they are released by the parents for good, stay together for a while in a close bunch which might number between 40 and 50.

Although not a nuisance to other fishes in a tank, the species is reported by Prof. M. Poll as being carnivorous, with a diet of clupeids and shrimps. Stomach content examination revealed some pieces of fish.

HAPLOTAXODON Boulenger 1906

According to Boulenger the body is elongate, strongly compressed and covered with small ctenoid scales. There are two lateral lines, the upper complete. The mouth is nearly vertical, sloping upward, with a single series of small, conical equal teeth; maxillary is exposed at the end. Dorsal fin with XVII or XVIII spines, anal with III. Occipital and parietal crests strong, extending to between the orbits. Vertebrae 38.

There are two species, *H. microlepis* and *H. tricoti*, in this genus, both endemic to Lake Tanganyika.

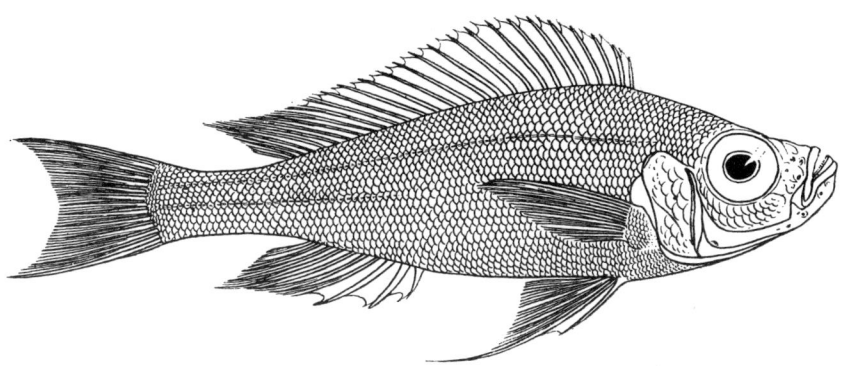

Haplotaxodon microlepis, from Poll, 1957.

Body: elongate, deep, laterally compressed; eye very large
Scales: ctenoid, small, 64-79 in a longitudinal line
Lateral lines: 2, only the upper complete
Fins: Dorsal — XVII-XIX, 11-13
    Anal — III, 8-10
    Ventrals — with short filament
    Caudal — forked
Teeth: a single row of small conical, sometimes curved, teeth
Pharyngeal teeth: conical and very sharp
Mouth: lower jaw protruding, both jaws nearly vertical, pointing upward
Gill rakers: 20-29 on lower limb of first gill arch

Lamprologus savoryi is not a rare fish in the lake but it is a very secretive species and not very many are caught. Photo by Dr. Herbert R. Axelrod.

An unidentified *Lamprologus* from the South which bears some resemblance to *L. savoryi* but is different, probably a new species.

Lamprologus sexfasciatus closely resembles *L. tretocephalus* but has four vertical bars under the dorsal fin instead of three which is characteristic for *tretocephalus*. It grows to approximately 18 centimeters on its native rock slopes in the South, but has never been found in the North as yet.

Lamprologus tretocephalus is one of the most valuable cichlids from the lake, although breeding in captivity appears to be exceedingly difficult. It is easily distinguished from *L. sexfasciatus* by the three (not four) vertical bars under the dorsal fin.

Habitat: average depth perhaps 10-20 meters; along rocky coasts, probably gregarious
Feeding: carnivorous, usually preying on clupeids and copepods
Reproduction: not known
Maximum size: about 250 mm

Key to the Identification of the Species of *Haplotaxodon*

Head length more than 3.0 in standard length; eye less than 3.0 in head; interorbital space more than 1.4 in eye length; 3 rows of scales on cheek; more than 60 scales in lateral line . . . .
. . . . *H. microlepis*

Head less than 3.1 in standard length; eye more than 3.0 in head; interorbital space less than 1.4 in eye length; 2 rows of scales on cheek; less than 60 scales in lateral line . . . . *H. tricoti*

HEMIBATES Regan 1920

There are two species of *Hemibates*; one is *H. stenosoma*, endemic to Lake Tanganyika and a second one now being identified by Dr. M. Poll.

Body: stocky and rather short
Scales: 60-72 in a longitudinal line
Lateral lines: 2, the upper complete
Fins: Dorsal — XV or XVI, 13-14
   Anal — III, 12-13
   Caudal — forked

Hemibates stenosoma, from Poll, 1957.

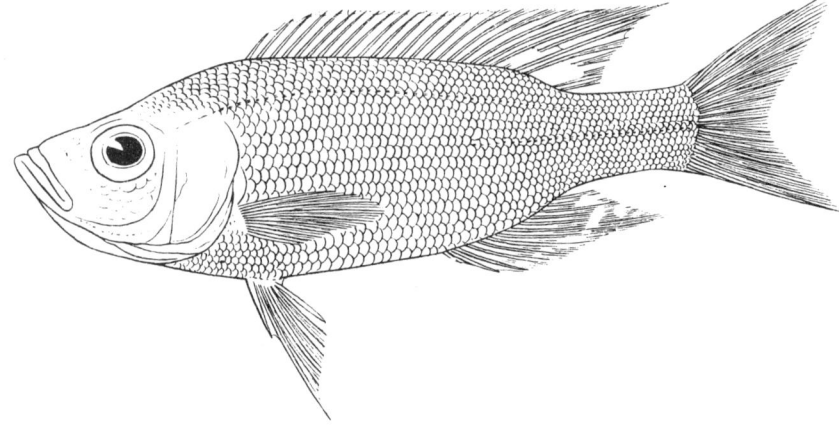

Teeth: small and conical, in 2-3 rows; 90-110 teeth in upper front row

Pharyngeal teeth: subconical and rather weak

Mouth: rather large, lower jaw protruding and turned upward

Gill rakers: 27-31 on lower limb of first gill arch

Habitat: pelagic, often in front of river estuaries and over mud bottoms

Feeding: predatory on other fishes

Reproduction: not known, but the size of the eggs (7 mm) along with the roaming pelagic habitat tend to indicate buccal incubation as probable

Maximum size: 280 mm

JULIDOCHROMIS Boulenger 1898

In the genus *Julidochromis* there are five species, all endemic to Lake Tanganyika, plus several subspecies and local races.

Body: elongate and cylindrical; color pattern always including horizontal stripes from the head to the caudal peduncle; sometimes vertical banding also present

Scales: very denticulated; very small on the nape; 31-36 in a longitudinal line for *J. marlieri, J. regani* and *J. transcriptus,* and 45-50 for *J. ornatus* (not known for *J. dickfeldi*)

Lateral lines: 2, not complete

Fins: Dorsal — XXI-XXIV, 6-7
Anal — VII-IX, 4-6
Ventrals — outer rays rather long but not filamentous
Caudal — rounded
Pectorals — usually yellow or orange

Teeth: conical, in narrow bands with strong, curved canines; hind teeth more or less tricuspid

Pharyngeal teeth: all small and conical

Gill rakers: 2-5 according to the species

Habitat: always among rocks; common in rubble, caves or labyrinths from about one meter to at least 35 meters deep; very seldom horizontal when in the substratum, most of the time a headstander or upside down; horizontal in the open or swimming at a 45° angle when threatened; the amount of venturing over open ground is variable with each species

Feeding: omnivorous in the wild, feeding mostly on microorga-

Lamprologus staecki is a new *Lamprologus* from the southern coasts that is very close in shape to *L. modestus*. The slate gray body and yellow pectorals are typical.

Lamprologus toae, a dark phase or variety. Photo by Glen S. Axelrod.

Lamprologus toae (black fish) in a shallow channel between two boulders. Photo by Glen S. Axelrod.

Lamprologus toae has never been seen on the northeastern coast, but it is not rare on the northwestern coast. The fish is peaceful and a good community tank dweller.

nisms picked from the rock biocover.

Reproduction: egg-layer in caves, slits or crevices; two modes, continuous spawns of a few eggs every few days or large spawns about once a month

Maximum size (in the wild): a) *J. marlieri, J. regani regani, J. regani affinis:* about 150 mm; b) *J. ornatus, J. transcriptus* and *J. dickfeldi:* apparently not more than 60 or 70 mm

Affinities: With *Lamprologus,* from which it differs by having (a) suborbital ligamentous (bony in *Lamprologus*), (b) dorsal fin with XXI or more spines, XXI being rare (*Lamprologus* usually have less than XX, only one species reaching XXI). With *Chalinochromis,* which has (a) body color pattern absent in adults, (b) a different breeding ethology

The genus *Julidochromis* would be one of the most difficult to separate into the various species already named were it not for the typical (diagnostic) color pattern of each species. All of them share very similar taxonomic features, with most of them overlapping. There are, however, two main evolutionary stems in the genus. The first includes three species which do not grow larger than 70, perhaps 80, mm. This group includes *J. ornatus, J. transcriptus* and *J. dickfeldi* (found in the southern part of the lake). The second group includes species which grow in excess of 100 mm and might reach 150 mm. This group includes *J. marlieri, J. regani* and what is called *J. regani affinis.* There are several local varieties in each group.

We have seen that the range of some species in both groups is very hard to determine, more so because of the several local races. They do not occupy successive habitats; on the contrary, the species seem to alternate around the lake shores. One might wonder also why there are "dwarf" julies and "giant" julies and what the basic pattern of the body colors really is.

As far as these patterns are concerned, all *Julidochromis* species have the horizontal stripes in common, sometimes two on each side with a third on the dorsal (*J. ornatus* and *J. transcriptus*), sometimes only two on the sides and none on the dorsal (*J. dickfeldi*), and sometimes three, more or less complete (*J. marlieri, J. regani regani* and *J. r. affinis*). In both groups some species have added vertical bars (*J. transcriptus, J. marlieri*) to the basic pattern. Of course it is impossible to say if these vertical bands were there first and then disappeared afterward, or the reverse. One subspecies, *J. regani affinis,* which probably should be put aside as a distinct species, in all its populations around the lake shows a trend (or is it traces?) to vertical bars and is thus halfway between the two patterns. One species, *J. transcriptus*, has two local races, one close to the grounds of *J. ornatus* and having widely spaced black vertical bars and a pure white chin, chest and belly; and the second, way down the coast and far from *J. ornatus* territory, is nearly all black, the vertical black bars having taken over most of the white patches (which have become mere "slits"). The chest and belly of this race are totally black. All other features of the species are common to the two races.

One would say that in the lake there is no relationship between *J. marlieri*, *J. regani regani*, and *J. regani affinis* when one puts together the most differentiated races of the three fishes. But it is a fact that where pure black and white *J. regani affinis* from the grounds where they breed true are in contact with *J. marlieri* populations, they crossbreed with *J. marlieri* at the border between the two flocks. This is apparent from the color patterns of some (but not many) of the *J. marlieri* in this place.

On the other hand, when one sees specimens from the Tanzanian border, instead of the black and white color pattern of *J. regani affinis* in the north, they have the overall brown-beige color and body shape of *J. regani regani*. In the north and west *J. regani affinis* is a plump fish, like *J. marlieri*, but in the southeast it is a bit more elongate, like *J. regani regani*.

Crossbreeding in tanks between *J. regani regani* and *J. regani affinis* is no harder than between each subspecific race. It would be interesting to study the result of crossbreeding between the various pure, well established species. This would perhaps throw some light on the speciation which occurred in the lake and which is perhaps still underway.

Julidochromis marlieri Poll

Julidochromis marlieri is one of the most beautiful fishes to have come from Lake Tanganyika in recent years. Since its first exportation in 1971, it has reached worldwide popularity among aquarists. The fish are hardy, peaceful toward other species (in fact in the lake they are microfeeders and not carnivorous at all) and highly intelligent. It is unbelievable to see how quickly they get used to surface-feeding on dry flakes when one knows they often live in deep water and never come to the surface for feeding in the wild. They never swim in mid-water but are typical rock-dwellers. They do venture into the open, but never far from the rock cover.

These photos show *Lamprologus tretocephalus* guarding young in the natural habitat. The fry are hiding along the lower edge of a large boulder. Photos by Glen S. Axelrod.

An unidentified *Lamprologus* species in the Berlin Aquarium. Photo by Dr. Herbert R. Axelrod.

Lamprologus tetracanthus guarding its brood in the aquarium. Photo by Glen S. Axelrod.

They breed in crevices and caves, as has already been mentioned. The behavior of the fry is not standardized. Sometimes they spread outside of the cave as soon as they are 15 mm long, and one might discover them 30 or 40 strong in broad daylight on vertical cliffs. When threatened, they do not hide in the nearby breeding cave but flee along the boulder wall. At other times the fry remain inside of the cave and apparently do not venture out until they are much larger.

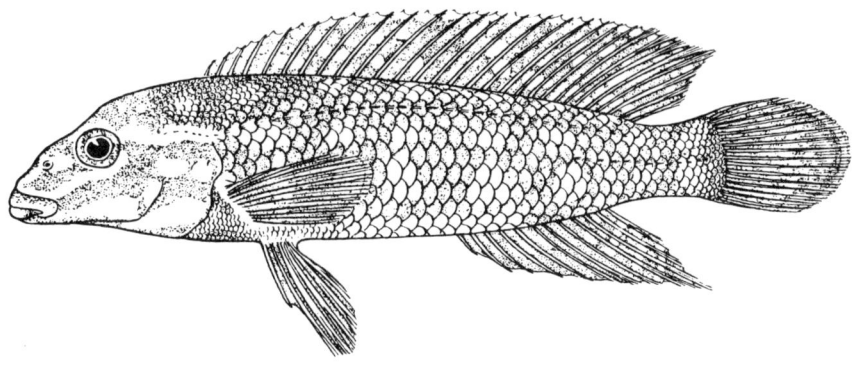

Julidochromis marlieri, from Poll, 1957.

We have seen that there are two methods of spawning: the large batch once a month or so and spawning in quickly repeated bursts of a few eggs at a time. We have never seen young adults have an initial big batch. Usually they start with several small ones a few days apart, then afterward might turn to large widely spaced spawns. Some adults never seem to have the large periodic broods and keep laying a few eggs every few days without ever stopping.

Pairing adults in aquaria is tricky, especially if the fish are in narrow confines and there is only one of each sex. Pairs in the wild appear to be formed for life. Females are often larger than their consort, but it is, by far, not the rule in the lake. Very large pairs of *J. marlieri, J. regani regani* and *J. regani affinis* have both partners of the same size.

Julidochromis regani Poll

The habitat of this species and its behavior seem to be a bit different from those of *J. marlieri*. *Julidochromis regani* likes to live in the open and ventures quite a lot over sand in the shallows. This is also the case with *J. marlieri*, but with a difference. Whenever *J. marlieri* is chased, it will swim away, sometimes over very long distances (in excess of 20 meters), but always over rock. If surprised over sand, it will seek refuge among the nearest rocks. The behavior of *J. regani* is quite different. It will most of the time swim toward the sand patches, even when it was surprised over rubble. This is not to say that *J. regani* is a sand-dweller, far from it; the fish has a close relationship with rocks, but this difference in behavior was worth mentioning.

Another difference is the habitat, which is much shallower, unless I am mistaken, than the one in which the biggest populations of *J. marlieri* are found. The author has never seen *J. regani* deeper than 5 meters, although it is entirely possible that there are some fish deeper. The pattern of the fish, light beige with deep brown stripes, blends very well with the bright coastal sand floors near the tan rocks, and the fish are very hard to see whenever small particles drift in the water.

Julidochromis regani, the type with narrow brown stripes on a light beige background, has up to now been found only in two

Species of *Julidochromis* adapt to tank conditions very easily and the author considers them as one of the many "intelligent" fishes of the lake.

This *Lamprologus tetracanthus* variety, with black-tipped dorsal fin, is a regular sight over sand floors where it roams and nests individually. A good aquarium fish under some conditions, it should not however be trusted with small fishes.

Lamprologus tetracanthus with red-tipped dorsal fins can be found in the same areas as the black-tipped variety.

A school of juvenile *Limnotilapia dardennei* swims over a sandstone slab isolated in a sand plain. In the foreground a *Telmatochromis temporalis* flees toward the entrance of a cave.

Limnotilapia dardennei. Photo by Dr. Herbert R. Axelrod.

small areas of Lake Tanganyika. It is possible, however, that another local race has been found in the far south with an identical pattern.

It is remarkable how the fish blends with the sandstone slabs, the only type of rock on which it has been found as yet. These slabs (which are in very shallow water) are a pale pinkish beige when bathed in bright sunlight on their lightly colored biocover. The stripes on the body of *J. regani* are an excellent camouflage for the fish, even in recesses, since they break up the body shape. *J. regani* is less visible in its habitat than *J. marlieri* because the whitish spots of *J. marlieri* literally "shine" in the dark.

Julidochromis regani is perhaps also less of an upside down type of *Julidochromis* than is *J. marlieri*. It is most commonly seen in the regular fish position, even in recesses, which *J. marlieri* very seldom assumes unless wandering in the open. Both fish however, when hunted from above, will flee slightly turned on one side so that they can have full vision of their enemy while they look for shelter.

This and other behavior are what make the species of *Julidochromis* such interesting pets. One cannot help but like them. Although they like dark recesses in the lake, they are not shy and learn very quickly. When a fish has been chased around several times over a few weeks, it will become more and more difficult to catch. And, as with *Tropheus* species, the memory of the hunt will stay engraved in their brains for several weeks, and they will adapt their behavior so that they might be capable of warding off further attempts at capture.

Every hobbyist knows that fish have different ranges of intelligence. Some are dumb and never learn anything. They act according to the imprinted behavioral codes which they received from their forebearers. Other fishes show remarkable adaptability to a wide range of conditions. None show more intelligence than some of the cichlids of Lake Tanganyika. Among them, the species of *Julidochromis*, as well as *Tropheus*, are outstanding and well worth more detailed research.

Julidochromis ornatus Boulenger

Julidochromis ornatus is one of the mysteries of speciation around the lake. It is present in the extreme northwest and deep south of the lake and no other grounds around the lake. It is very hard to understand how two populations, without any apparent specific or subspecific differences, can be separated by perhaps 1,500 miles of linear coastline when one knows of their attachment to rocky areas and the shallow life-supporting layer in the lake.

J. ornatus is one of the dwarf species of *Julidochromis*, and the one with the basic horizontally striped pattern with no vertical

Julidochromis ornatus with the basic horizontal stripe pattern. Photo by Hilmar Hansen.

bars. It is also the only species of *Julidochromis* with a deep yellow background, which none of the other species in the genus have.

Some reports mention that fish bred in captivity from tank raised parents sometimes practice polygamy, with a male breeding alternately with two females and the three fish living peacefully together. This spawning behavior has never been noted for any species of *Julidochromis* in the wild. It is of course not at all impossible that this might happen in wild fish as well as other species of the genus. It is also possible that this apparently aberrant behavior is the result of genetic disturbances in individuals with a long ancestral background of captivity.

No *J. ornatus* have been exported from the lake shores in at least five years and all the fish now in aquaria result from very few specimens sent to breeders years back. These fish often show visible traces of a degenerative process under way, such as paler colors and broken stripes.

Breeding fish from wild-caught specimens is an important part of the hobby, and by selection it often results in magnificent varieties. But it is perhaps worth mentioning that past breedings of some Tanganyika cichlids in the late 50's, like *Lamprologus leleupi*, started from a very small number of breeders and resulted very quickly in the production of drab, worthless offspring. The causes of this failure were twofold: (1) too few breeders with too much interbreeding resulting in degeneration; and (2) poor water quality with many trace elements or essential minerals missing.

A half-grown *Limnochromis nigripinnis*.

Leptochromis calliurum, the only *Leptochromis* recorded from the lake, lives in deep water on sand floors and is not often caught because of the problems involved in deep fishing. This is unfortunate as the fish is beautiful with striped unpaired fins and alternating brown and mother of pearl stripes on the body. It has never been bred in captivity, although under the proper conditions it should not be too difficult.

Limnochromis microlepidotus is one of two species of the genus which I believe is not properly classified. They are typical mouthbrooders and schooling fish. The fish ascend from deeper to shallower waters to brood and release the fry.

Limnochromis nigripinnis has the same habitat and exhibits the same behavior as *L. microlepidotus*.

With recent exports from the lake area it is probable that this situation will improve and the quality of the tank-raised fishes will become very similar to the quality of wild fish. But it is not at all sure that this will be true with all species.

Julidochromis transcriptus Matthes

Julidochromis transcriptus is the second of the dwarf species of *Julidochromis* discovered in Lake Tanganyika. From the hobbyist's point of view, and mine, it is probably the best looking (along with the "pure" *J. regani*). The fish has everything going for it: a jet black background as well as the unpaired fins; a pure white belly in one race (called *J.* "kissi" in the aquarium trade), jet black in the second variety. The chin is pure white, and the unpaired fins are edged with a nearly fluorescent light blue. The spots on the sides, often mere slits, are white and in the "black" race turn a smoky black. Most probably careful breeding with selected specimens could result in a jet black fish with blue edges to the fins, a white chin and without any other white on the body.

The trend toward melanism is sometimes apparent in *J. marlieri* when they live in very deep water in some very small areas of the rocky slopes. We have seen once, at 30 meters depth, an individual *J. marlieri* with half the body jet black. There are always specimens in this layer with a different type of white spotting. The regular type of white spotting in *J. marlieri* is not, in fact, white, but is a grayish yellow. Some specimens, on the same grounds as *Lamprologus leleupi*, orange *Tropheus* and *L. niger*, have the

Julidochromis transcriptus, probably the variety known as "kissi" in the aquarium trade. Photo by Hilmar Hansen.

lighter parts of the body more yellow than in other areas of the lake. But the deep-living *J. marlieri* have the light spots rimmed with a very thin pure white line which gives these spots a "frosted" look. In reverse, *J. marlieri* living in the sunlit shadows have paler black stripes and bars, and the pale spots are larger. The intensity of the colors in these specimens doesn't change much in tanks, and these variations are permanently inbred in the fish.

Julidochromis dickfeldi Staeck

The latest species of *Julidochromis* from the south, although belonging to the dwarf *Julidochromis* group, is apparently a species standing well apart from all the others in the genus. One feature strikes the collector at once: the dorsal fin is much higher than in all other species of *Julidochromis* and does not have the same shape.

All in all the whole group of *Julidochromis* species is one of the most exceptional additions to the aquarium world, providing the hobbyist with several enticing, very good looking fish with the little something that sets them apart from all the other African and South American cichlids. And, for a change, not one of them is a mouthbrooder.

LAMPROLOGUS Schilthuis 1891

Lamprologus is the most important cichlid genus of Lake Tanganyika for the number of species (35) constitutes almost 25% of the number of cichlid species in the lake. It also places together, under apparently narrow morphological definitions, what is in fact a very heterogeneous and artificial group of species.

The main characteristics of this genus are:
- denticulate scales (ctenoid)
- bony suborbital
- cheek devoid of scales most of the time
- teeth conical and in several bands; the front teeth of the first row on each jaw enlarged into powerful canines
- pharyngeal teeth all conical, some of them a bit broader in the rear; a few species with two large molars in the center of the bone
- IV-XII anal fin spines; XIV-XXI dorsal fin spines

Some of these generic features are very broad indeed, such as the variability of the dorsal and anal fin spines, not only between the species but also within a given species.

The presence of the large canines backed up posteriorly by

When young, *Limnochromis nigripinnis* has bright yellow fins. Photo by Dr. Warren E. Burgess.

A small sample of *Limnochromis leptosoma*. Photo by Glen S. Axelrod.

This photograph shows very clearly the rows of scales (like mother-of-pearl) along the sides of *Limnochromis auritus*. Photo by Dr. Robert J. Goldstein.

Limnochromis auritus can be easily maintained in the aquarium but requires plenty of room. Photo by Dr. Herbert R. Axelrod at the Berlin Aquarium.

conical teeth, might have been one important feature if the teeth were used by all *Lamprologus* in a way associated with these teeth, which is to seize and hold prey. The ethology of many *Lamprologus* species cannot be linked to predatory carnivorous feeding habits, however.

The *Lamprologus* are divided among three, perhaps four, biotopes: (1) open water (carnivorous, even voracious, species); (2) sand bottom (sand sifters and voracious species together); (3) mud bottom (shell-dwellers); and (4) rock bottom (small invertebrate pickers on the rock biocover). Their teeth thus should reflect various ways of seizing food according to the type of food and where it is to be found. Their various feeding patterns are apparent in underwater observations. For this reason the study of the pharyngeal bones and their teeth is all important. There are probably three different types of pharyngeal bones in the known species of *Lamprologus*, one with all conical teeth, one with molar-like teeth associated with conical teeth and one, in *L. profundicola*, with a very unusually shaped bone very similar to that of *Bathybates*.

It is thus very difficult at the present time to give a definitive key to the identification of the species of *Lamprologus* as they do not fit into clear-cut standards. This is borne out by the list below, which is restricted to only a few morphological features (after Poll 1956).

ANAL FIN: The number of spines varies from IV to XII. Nine species have a variability of three anal spines, three other species have a variability of four spines. The number of spines is thus very variable within the same species, not to speak of the genus. The entire genus *Haplochromis* (a grouping of several hundred species) has a variability of only two, usually having three spines and seldom four.

Of the 33 species of *Lamprologus* in Poll's list, it might be interesting to note the most frequent number of spines found in each species: one species has only 4 spines; 10 species most frequently have 5 spines; 10 species most frequently have 6 spines; 4 species most frequently have 7 spines; 6 species most frequently have 8 spines; no species has 9 spines; one species always has 10 spines and one species has from 10-12 spines (10 being most frequent).

There are thus 30 species with an average number of spines between 5 and 8. The two species with 10 or more anal spines are *L. fasciatus* and *L. compressiceps*; these, also because of other features, should probably be put in a genus of their own.

DORSAL FIN: The number of dorsal fin spines varies from XIV-XXI. The variability covers a spread of three spines in 10 species and four spines in two species. As for the most frequent number of spines in each species we might say that: one species has as few as 14 spines (maximum 15); one species always has 15; 24 species have the most frequent number of spines between 17 and 19 (although some species included in this group might have up to 21 spines) and six species have predominantly 20 spines (although some of them might have a count as low as 19).

When the total number of rays (soft and spiny) are considered, one discovers that four species have less than 25. All other species of *Lamprologus* have an average above 25 rays.

SCALES: The number of scales in a longitudinal line, in the 33 species considered, varies all the way from 25 to more than 70. By itself, this variability should indicate a wide range of ecological and behavioral conditions. A very high number of scales, at least in African fishes, might be associated with speed, not only in open-water roamers but also in predators lying in wait for prey to pass by.

As it is, the 33 species of *Lamprologus* listed by Poll are as follows: one species (*L. ocellatus*) has between 25 and 30 scales; 23 species have 30-40 scales; one species has 40-45 scales; 4 species have 45-60 scales; and 4 species have more than 60 scales.

The following species are open-water predators (with high scale counts): *L. elongatus* (65-75 scales); *L. attenuatus* (65-75 scales); *L. cunningtoni* (60-70 scales); and *L. profundicola* (60-65 scales). It is possible that *L. christyi* and *L. pleuromaculatus*, by their biotope and ethology, are also part of this group, although they have only 50 to 60 scales in a longitudinal line.

Species of *Lamprologus* with a small number of scales would thus contain species directly in contact with the substratum. This appears probable from our underwater observations.

Absence of scales on the body: Many species of *Lamprologus* do not have scales on the lower part of their body. Although additional studies are in order, it can already be deduced from Dr. Poll's descriptions that: 13 species do not have scales on the body between the ventral and pectoral fins; 10 species have at least part of the thorax scaleless and five species are devoid of scales on the nape, although the other species of *Lamprologus* have nape scales (however, always small).

Most species have scaleless cheeks; five have a few small scales

The southern race of *Lobochilotes labiatus* has less vertical bars and more horizontal yellow stripes.

The northern race of *Lobochilotes labiatus* with distinct vertical bands.

An adult *Lobochilotes*, probably a female in the early stages of buccal incubation, wanders into the upper water layer, amidst the rubble. The foreground boulder has an exceptionally thick biocover.

This *Lobochilotes labiatus* is unmistakably of the northern race. All the vertical bars in the body pattern are visible. Photo by Gerhard Marcuse.

on the cheek and two species have several rows of scales (*L. leloupi* has 4-5 rows, *L. profundicola* has from 18-20).

Scales on dorsal and anal fins: The presence of scales on the dorsal and anal fins of several species of *Lamprologus* has already been noted by Prof. Poll, but this significant feature has not as yet been systematically explored. These scales extend up on both sides of the fin's base, creating a kind of sheath into which the fins can fold. They also occur along the fin spines and often on the membrane linking the rays. In several species they might even grow on the soft posterior part of the fin.

Most *Lamprologus* species, however, do not have such scales on their unpaired fins and, along with other significant features such as presence or absence of scales on the nape, thorax or cheeks, this feature might help establish a new subdivision of this over-extended genus.

The study of *Lamprologus* is, in the author's opinion, one of the most urgent and important taxonomic tasks to be undertaken. This genus, along with *Telmatochromis, Julidochromis* and *Chalinochromis*, includes nearly 40% of all the Tanganyika cichlids, all of them nesters, not mouthbrooders. Recent discoveries, as yet not added to the present classification, will increase the number of species in each of the four genera by more than half a dozen species. Very probably more are in store with the gradual extension of the intensive exploration of the shoreline. The four genera include many rock-dwelling species, and it is in this habitat that most discoveries are going to be made, especially among the fishes which spend most of their lives well hidden in the substrate.

The second habitat which might yield new species of *Lamprologus* is the deeper reaches of the life-bearing layer where six species have already been previously found, most of them living in empty shells. This habitat is very difficult to explore with SCUBA gear or the traditional trawl nets. As the nest-brooders appear to depend less than mouthbrooders on high oxygen levels, it is not at all impossible that the proportion of new species to be discovered in this habitat might tip in favor of *Lamprologus*-related species.

The present classification is by all means not definitive. It has been made with an eye toward the need for further updating. It has been impossible with the present state of the genus to avoid entirely internal identification features such as the pharyngeal bones and teeth and to rely solely on outer morphological features such as scales, dorsal and anal spines, etc. The field worker will thus have to refer to the full description when in doubt.

Key to the Species of the Genus *Lamprologus*

1. Ten or more spines in the anal fin 2
   Less than ten spines in the anal fin 3
2. Body short; depth 2.45-2.9 in standard length; 31-34 scales in a longitudinal line; 22-27 scales in upper lateral line and only 5-9 in lower lateral line; D. XX-XXI spines; A. X-XII spines; maxillary pedicel long; mouth oblique; size about 130 mm .... *L. compressiceps*
   Body elongate; depth 3.7-3.9 in standard length; 35 scales in a longitudinal line; 27-29 scales in upper lateral line and 20 in lower lateral line; D. XVIII-XIX spines; A. X spines; body yellow with several broad black patches, sometimes "y"-shaped, on upper part; size about 130 mm .... *L. fasciatus*
3. At least 42 scales in a longitudinal line 4
   Not more than 40 scales in a longitudinal line 12
4. More than 35 scales in upper lateral line and more than 15 in lower lateral line 5
   23-42 in upper lateral line, but less than 15 in lower lateral line 11
5. 18-20 rows of scales on cheek; 63-65 scales in a longitudinal line; 39-55 scales in upper lateral line, 20-25 in lower; eye very small; body depth 3.4-3.7 in standard length; pharyngeal bone usually "y"-shaped; dorsal fin with XVIII spines, anal fin with V; 9 gill rakers; size 300 mm .... *L. profundicola*
   Cheek naked or with only a few scales 6
6. 61-73 scales in a longitudinal line; 46-60 scales in the upper lateral line, 21-31 in the lower 7
   46-60 scales in a longitudinal line; 36-47 scales in the upper lateral line; 15-27 in the lower 9
7. 8-10 canines in upper jaw, 6-9 in lower; 66-73 scales in a longitudinal line; 49-55 scales in upper lateral line, 21-31 in lower; D. XVII-XVIII spines; A. always V spines; body depth 3.5-4.5 in standard length; 11-14 gill rakers; mottled with rows of tiny pure white stripes; size about 200 mm .... *L. elongatus*
   4-6 canines in each jaw 8
8. 6-8 gill rakers; 61-71 scales in a longitudinal line; 48-54 scales in upper lateral line, 21-25 in lower; D. XX-XXI spines,

Ophthalmochromis ventralis, southern race.

An *Opthalmochromis ventralis* in the display tank of the Berlin Aquarium. Photo by Dr. Herbert R. Axelrod.

A totally barren rock area in Nyanza-Lac, Burundi. Devoid of any noteworthy biocover it is also depleted of significant fish life. The only fish present here, *Ophthalmochromis ventralis ventralis,* do not live on the biocover.

The yellow tips of the ventral fins of *Ophthalmochromis ventralis* help greatly in identifying this fish under water. Photos by Glen S. Axelrod.

A. IV-V spines; cheeks naked; body depth 4.15-4.3 in standard length; size 290 mm .... *L. cunningtoni*

13-17 gill rakers; 66-73 scales in a longitudinal line; 46-60 scales in upper lateral line, 22-29 in lower; D. XVII-XIX spines, A. IV-VII spines; cheeks naked; body depth 4.5-5.5 in standard length; color plain gray; size 150 mm .... *L. attenuatus*

9. 5-6 gill rakers; 50-60 scales in a longitudinal line; 37-41 scales in upper lateral line, 19-20 in lower; D. XIX-XX scales, A. IV-V scales; cheeks with a few scales; 6 canine teeth in each jaw; pharyngeal teeth tending to be molar-shaped; tail with very long lobes; size about 140 mm ....*L. christyi*
   9-14 gill rakers....................................... 10

10. 46-54 scales in a longitudinal line; 39-47 scales in upper lateral line, 15-27 in lower; D. XX spines, A. IV-VI spines; 6 upper canines and 4 lower; caudal lobes long and broad, dorsal and anal fins with long, broad ends; pharyngeal teeth conical; 11-14 gill rakers; body deep purple, all fins very dark or even orange; eye very yellow and globular; size 150 mm .... *L. furcifer*
    47-60 scales in a longitudinal line; 36-45 in upper lateral line, 17-26 in lower; D. XVII-XIX spines, A. V-VII spines; 6-8 canines in upper jaw, 4-8 in lower; pharyngeal teeth all very thin and sharp; 9-12 gill rakers; scales on cheek; all unpaired fins striped with yellow, body with alternating horizontal yellow and light blue stripes; black spot in middle of body; size 120 mm .... *L. pleuromaculatus*

11. 45-55 scales in a longitudinal line; 23-42 scales in upper lateral line, only 6-12 in lower; D. XVIII-XIX spines, A. VI-VIII spines; cheek naked; 4-8 canines on each jaw; 8-13 gill rakers; caudal fin rounded; size 80 mm ....*L. hecqui*
    42-46 scales in a longitudinal line; 28-34 in upper lateral line, 5-12 in lower; D. XVIII spines, A. VII; cheek bare; upper jaw with 6-8 canines, lower 6; 11-12 gill rakers; one or two rows of black spots on body; size 70 mm ....*L. meeli*

12. 18-21 gill rakers; 30-40 scales in a longitudinal line; 17-20 scales in upper lateral line, lower lateral line absent or with up to 5 scales; D. XVIII-XX spines, A. VII-IX; cheek naked; 4-6 canines on each jaw; pharyngeal teeth thin and very dense; body depth 2.9-3.25 in standard length; size 50 mm .... *L. brevis*

Less than 18 gill rakers 13
13. Several rows of scales on cheek 14
    Cheeks naked or scales very sparse 15
14. 31 scales in a longitudinal line; 23 scales in upper lateral line, 8 in lower; 4-5 rows of scales on cheek; D. XVII spines, A. VI spines; 6 canines on each jaw; 6 gill rakers; body depth 3.25 in standard length; caudal fin (typical): four successive stripes, two black then a white one edged in black; size 60 mm .... *L. leloupi*
    31 scales in longitudinal line; 19 scales in upper lateral line, 6 in lower; 6 rows of scales on cheek; D. XVII spines, A. IX spines; 6 canines on each jaw; 6 gill rakers; body depth 3.5 in standard length; head 2.9 in standard length; size 150 mm .... *L. stappersi*
15. Pharyngeal teeth not molar-shaped 16
    Pharyngeal teeth molar-shaped 29
16. Caudal in form of deep crescent; filamentous tips to all unpaired fins 17
    Caudal fin straight, rounded or truncate 18
17 (triplet). 33-35 scales in a longitudinal line; 26 scales in upper lateral line, 11 in lower; cheek naked; D. XVIII-XIX spines, A. VI-VII spines; 6 canines on upper jaw, 4-6 in lower; 8-10 gill rakers; body depth 2.7-3.0 in standard length; pharyngeal teeth conical, larger to the rear; deep purple body with several darker bands; size about 90 mm .... *L. savoryi*
    32-36 scales in longitudinal line; 20 scales in upper lateral line, 5-8 in lower; cheeks naked; D. XIX-XX spines, A. V-VII spines; 6 canines in upper jaw, 4-6 in lower; 7-14 gill rakers; body depth 3.2-3.7 in standard length; pharyngeal teeth conical and thin; body pale beige, eventually with orange spots at the rear; all unpaired fins with long white filaments; black stripe from eye to opercular bone; size 90 mm (usually much less)................. *L. brichardi*
    Identical to *brichardi* but with body beige, each scale with orange spot; black opercular stripe replaced by two separate vertical stripes, one on preopercle, other on opercle; size 80 mm .... *L. pulcher*
18. 11-15 gill rakers; 35-37 scales in a longitudinal line; 25-27 scales in upper lateral line, 9-15 in lower; D. XVIII-XX spines, A. VI-IX spines; 6-10 canines in each jaw; cheeks

251

Perissodus microlepis, one of the scale-eaters in the lake, uses buccal incubation. Both parents look after the fry during periodic releases of the young to graze on the biocover.

Instead of hiding the fry amongst the rubble, *Perissodus* releases them on top of a prominent boulder, well in the open. This is most unusual for mouthbrooders in the lake.

naked; pharyngeal teeth all sharp and thin; body depth 3.35-4.15 in standard length; body yellowish with dark gray mottled patches; scales are exceptionally rough and raised; size 160 mm .... *L. callipterus*
Less than 11 gill rakers 19
19. Never more than IV anal fin spines; 36-40 scales in a longitudinal line; 27-32 scales in upper lateral line, 11-22 in lower; D. XVIII-XX spines; 6-8 canines on upper jaw; 4-6 on lower; cheek naked; 6-9 gill rakers; pharyngeal teeth conical; body depth 3.35-3.95 in standard length; body beige-brown with several horizontal rows of pearly scales on sides; dorsal and anal fins edged with white and with ray tips black or red; caudal with pale spots; size 190 mm .... *L. tetracanthus*
V-IX anal fin spines................................ 20
20. Lower lateral line missing or with less than 15 scales....... 21
Lower lateral line with 15-20 scales, upper with 25-31; 33-37 scales in a longitudinal line; D. XVIII-XIX spines, A. VII-IX; 4-6 canines in each jaw; cheek naked; 6-11 gill rakers; pharyngeal teeth conical and sparse; body depth 3-3.45 in standard length; head 2.5-2.65 in standard length; interorbital space narrow, 6.2-7.8 in head length; color gray with 3 or 4 wide irregular bands on body; scales very rough and raised, like *L. callipterus*; size 230 mm .... *L. lemairei*
21. Only 2 canines on each jaw; 29-31 scales in a longitudinal line; 10-22 scales in upper lateral line, 0-3 in lower; D. XVII spines, A. VI-VII spines; cheek naked; 6-10 gill rakers; pharyngeal teeth all very thin; body depth 3.2-3.4 in standard length; head 2.65-3.1 in standard length; eye 3.0-3.3 in head; interorbital space 4.25-5.25 in head; 10-12 vertical stripes on body; caudal rounded; size 35 mm .... *L. multifasciatus*
4 or more canines in each jaw 22
22. Interorbital width 4.0-4.7 in head; D. XIX-XX; 7-10 gill rakers 23
Interorbital width 6.2-10.0; D. XIV-XIX; 4-9 gill rakers ... 24
23. 33-34 scales in a longitudinal line; 22-25 scales in upper lateral line, 4-10 in lower; D. XIX-XX spines; A. always VI spines; 6 canine teeth in upper jaw, 4 in lower; cheek naked; 8-10 gill rakers; pharyngeal teeth broader to the rear, but

conical; body depth 3.3-3.6 in standard length; head 2.75-2.85 in standard length; interorbital space 4.0-4.7 in head; body, including all fins, deep orange, eye light blue; caudal fin rounded; size 90 mm .... *L. leleupi leleupi*

31-34 scales in a longitudinal line; 22-26 scales in upper lateral line, 4-8 in lower; D. XIX-XX spines, A. V-VI; 7-9 gill rakers; other features as in *L. l. leleupi*; body entirely black, sometimes with a few faint stripes; fins all black except pectorals which are bright orange; soft portions of unpaired fins often orange; eye blue with upper and lower rim orange; sometimes lower part of body deep orange; size 90 mm .... *L. leleupi melas*

24. 8-20 scales in upper lateral line; lower lateral line absent or with only 1-2 scales................................25

17-26 scales in upper lateral line; lower lateral line present, with 1-12 (usually more than 3) scales 27

25. 30-34 scales in a longitudinal line; A. V-VI spines 26

25-30 scales in a longitudinal line; A. VII-IX spines; 10-20 scales in upper lateral line, lower one missing or with a maximum of 2 scales; D. XVI-XVIII spines; 6 canines in each jaw; cheek naked; 5-8 gill rakers; pharyngeal teeth all very thin; body depth 3.15-3.5 in standard length; head 2.45-2.85 in standard length; eye 2.8-2.9 and interorbital space 8.5-9.6 in head length; strongly upturned, oblique mouth; a large spot in middle of the dorsal; caudal fin rounded; size 58 mm .... *L. ocellatus*

26. 30-33 scales in a longitudinal line; 11-19 in upper lateral line, lower lateral line absent; D. XIV-XV spines, A. VI spines; canines very long and thin, in shape of fangs, 7-8 in upper jaw, 10-12 in lower, all of about same size; 4-5 gill rakers; pharyngeal teeth all very thin and sharp; cheek naked; body depth 3.7-3.9 in standard length; head 2.85-3.05 in standard length; eye 2.6-3.0 and interorbital space 8.0-9.5 in head length; caudal rounded; a single large black spot in the middle of the dorsal; size 34 mm ....*L. kungweensis*

32-34 scales in a longitudinal line; 8-16 in upper lateral line, which might be broken; lower lateral line absent, seldom with a maximum of 2 scales; D. XVII-XIX spines, A. V spines; cheek naked; 5-6 canines in upper jaw, 4-6 in lower; 9 gill rakers; pharyngeal teeth conical, stronger in rear and in center; body depth 4.0-4.4 in standard length;

Perissodus microlepis is one of the scale eaters in the lake, but also a very beautiful and elegant fish.

Petrochromis fasciolatus collected from Sud Lac.

An unidentified *Petrochromis* from the southern shores.

Petrochromis fasciolatus is one of the most common and largest rock-scrapers in the lake.

head 2.6-2.9 in standard length; eye 3.65-4.3 and interorbital space 6.2-7.1 in head; caudal rounded; body brown, unpaired fins darker and mottled; size 43 mm ....*L. schreyeni*

27. 32-36 scales in longitudinal line; 4-6 gill rakers; head 3.0-3.65 in standard length................................28

    30-31 scales in longitudinal line; 20-26 scales in upper lateral line, 7-12 in lower; D. XVII-XVIII spines, A. VI spines; 6-8 canines in each jaw; 6-7 gill rakers; cheek naked; pharyngeal teeth conical; body depth 3.4-3.5 in standard length; head 2.6-2.8 in standard length; eye 2.5-3.0 and interorbital space 6.0-7.0 in head length; all unpaired fins with ocelli; caudal rounded; size 53 mm ....*L. wauthioni*

28. 32-36 scales in a longitudinal line; 20-26 scales in upper lateral line, 3-10 in lower; D. XV-XVIII spines, A. V-VIII spines; 5-6 canines in upper jaw, 8-10 in lower; 4-6 gill rakers; cheeks naked; pharyngeal teeth conical, broader at the rear, with two nearly molar-shaped teeth in center of the bone; body depth 3.5-4.2 in standard length; head 3.0-3.65 in standard length; eye 2.3-2.7 and interorbital space 6.5-7.5 in head; all unpaired fins strikingly striped with black lines; caudal rounded; size 75 mm ....*L. ornatipinnis*

    35 scales in longitudinal line; 17-24 scales in upper lateral line, 1-7 in lower (which is broken); D. XV spines, A. V spines; 4-6 canines in each jaw; cheek naked; 4-5 gill rakers; pharyngeal teeth conical, larger in the rear; body depth 3.9-4.4 in standard length; head 3.0-3.25 in standard length; eye 2.3-2.9 and interorbital space 7.25-10.0 in head; body with a few indistinct stripes; caudal straight with rounded upper and lower tips; size 53 mm ....*L. signatus*

29. 10-14 gill rakers....................................30

    4-9 gill rakers.......................................32

30. 6-8 canines in upper jaw, 4-8 in lower; D. XVII-XIX spines; A. V-VII spines 31

    10-12 canines in upper jaw, 7-10 in lower; D. XIX-XXI spines, A. VII-IX spines; 33-35 scales in a longitudinal line; 24-26 scales in upper lateral line, 7-9 in lower; cheeks naked; pharyngeal teeth conical, becoming molar-shaped in the rear; 10-14 gill rakers; body depth 2.25-2.4 in standard length; head 2.75-3.0 in standard length; eye 3.2-4.0 and interorbital 3.2-3.9 in head; body and fins entirely velvety black; unpaired fins edged with striking bright blue; caudal rounded; size 100 mm .... *L. moorei*

31. 34-37 scales in longitudinal line; 22-28 scales in upper lateral line and 8-12 in lower; D. XVII-XIX spines, A. V-VII spines; cheek naked; 6 canines in upper jaw, 4 in lower; 11-13 gill rakers; pharyngeal teeth conical, molar-shaped in rear center (including two big flat molars in center); body depth 2.6-3.1 in standard length; head 2.5-2.8 in standard length; eye 3.0-4.0 and interorbital 4.7-5.7 in head; six dark blue bands on light blue background, four of which are on dorsal fin length; caudal rounded; size 110 mm .... *L. sexfasciatus*

    29-33 scales in longitudinal line; 24-25 scales in upper lateral line, 12-14 in lower; D. XVII spines, A. V-VI spines; cheeks naked; 6-8 canines in each jaw; 13-14 gill rakers; pharyngeal teeth conical, tending to become molariform in the rear, with two strong molars in center of the bone; body depth 2.8-3.0 in standard length; head 2.6-2.8 in standard length; eye large, 2.75-3.0 and interorbital space 4.4-5.5 in head; several faint and irregular bands on olive green body; mouth unusually straight for *Lamprologus;* canines not visible when mouth is closed; caudal straight; size 10 mm .... *L. toae*

32. IV-VI anal fin spines 33

    VIII-IX anal fin spines; 36-38 scales in a longitudinal line; 25-30 scales in upper lateral line, 9-10 in lower; D. XX spines; 6 canines in upper jaw, 4 in lower; many minute scales on rear of cheeks; 7-9 gill rakers; pharyngeal teeth thin but tending to become molariform in rear and center; several cavities in head bones (as in *Trematocara* and *Haplochromis benthicola*); body depth 3.3-3.4 in standard length; head 2.6-2.7 in standard length; eye 4.25-4.6 and interorbital space 5.0-5.1 in head; juveniles deep orange to reddish (including fins); adults black with red pectorals, eventually all fins red; caudal rounded; size 90 mm .... *L. niger*

33. 23-29 scales in upper lateral line, 7-14 in lower; interorbital space 3.0-4.5 in head length 34

    29-31 scales in upper lateral line, 9-14 in lower; interorbital

Petrochromis polyodon from the northern rocky shores.

Another specimen of *Petrochromis polyodon,* possibly a female. Photo by Dr. Herbert R. Axelrod.

Another unidentified species of *Petrochromis* from the North.

A still unidentified species of *Petrochromis* from the South.

space 4.8-6.1 in head length; 33-35 scales in a longitudinal line; D. XVII-XIX spines, A. V-VI spines; cheeks naked; 6-8 canines in each jaw; 6-8 gill rakers; pharyngeal teeth conical, molar-shaped in rear and center, especially two very broad, flat ones in center; body depth 2.85-3.15 in standard length; head 2.6-2.9 in standard length; eye 2.9-3.85 in head; six dark blue bands on light blue background (like *L. sexfasciatus*) but only 3 on dorsal fin length; metallic green hue on opercle; caudal fin rounded; size 140 mm . . . . *L. tretocephalus*

34. 34-37 scales in longitudinal line; 23-29 scales in upper lateral line, 7-12 in lower; D. XVIII-XXI spines, A. IV-VI spines; cheeks naked; 5-6 canines in each jaw; 4-7 gill rakers; pharyngeal teeth conical but molariform in center and rear of bone; body depth 3.0-3.8 in standard length; head 2.8-3.4 in standard length; eye 3.5-4.7 and interorbital 3.25-4.5 in head; body beige with several indistinct broad bands; caudal rounded (juveniles with a truncate caudal exist but might belong to another species, *L. mondabu*, placed by Poll in the synonymy of *L. modestus*); size about 120 mm . . . . *L. modestus*

33-36 scales in longitudinal line; 26-28 scales in upper lateral line, 11-14 in lower; D. XIX-XX spines, A. V spines; cheek naked; 6 canines on each jaw; 5-6 gill rakers; pharyngeal teeth conical, becoming molars in center and rear; body depth 2.8-3.35 in standard length; head 3.15-3.6 in standard length; eye 2.65-4.25 and interorbital space 3.0-3.8 in head length; faint vertical bands on a dark brown body; caudal rounded; size 130 mm . . . . *L. petricola*

Lamprologus attenuatus Steindachner

Lamprologus attenuatus is a poor aquarium fish with predatory habits, large size and a drab color pattern. It belongs to the group of *Lamprologus* species that roam over sand plains down to at least 20 meters.

Its nest is dug in the sand, in the open, with the fish being quite capable of fending off predators. The mating behavior has not been observed in the field, but spawns totalling 2,000-3,000 eggs are known to be deposited in crater nests in the open. The fish are solitary.

The intestine is only ⅓ of the standard length, indicating a

Lamprologus attenuatus. Photo by Paul V. Loiselle.

carnivorous diet, as do the large canines and the conical pharyngeal teeth which are usually large at the front of the bone.

Lamprologus brevis Boulenger

One of the smallest fish in Lake Tanganyika, *L. brevis* would be a good aquarium fish if it could be made available. Unfortunately, it is seldom collected since it lives over sand and mud bottoms too deep for traditional collecting methods. *Lamprologus brevis* stands apart from the other species of *Lamprologus* because of its unusually high number of gill rakers (18-21). The coiled intestine attains 80% of the standard length.

Lamprologus brichardi Poll

Lamprologus brichardi is an excellent aquarium fish, one of the best from the lake. This is not so much because of the color, which is a plain, although deep, beige, but because of the elegant shape of the body and the very long and graceful filaments on the unpaired fins. *Lamprologus brichardi*, very peaceful among themselves and toward other fish, is the most gregarious of all species of *Lamprologus*. They are microfeeders, picking small crustaceans and other invertebrates from the rock biocover. They reach a maximum size of 90 mm. Mating occurs among the rock rubble, and the fry are often kept under guard by several adults in a kind of communal nursery.

An oral view of the head of *Petrochromis polyodon* showing the arrangement of the teeth. Photo by Glen S. Axelrod.

As mentioned elsewhere, *Petrochromis* are solitary fishes and are not to be seen in schooling formation. Photo by Glen S. Axelrod.

An unidentified *Petrochromis* species lingering alone in a favorite spot among the rocks. Photo by Glen S. Axelrod.

A male *Petrochromis polyodon* in full breeding color (brown head, olive green body) is looking around, over the large rocks, for mature females.

The intricate pattern on the unpaired fins of this *Lamprologus brichardi* is nicely silhouetted in this picture. Photo by Wilhelm Hoppe.

This *Lamprologus callipterus*, which is a bottom digger in the lake, looks unhappy in a bare holding tank. Photo by Paul V. Loiselle.

Lamprologus callipterus Boulenger

This is a poor aquarium fish with a voracious appetite and carnivorous, predatory habits. Although their main diet seems to be crustaceans hidden in the sand, which they dig up by taking mouthfuls of sand, they might be called scavengers of the sand plains. They live in small herds (about 20 strong) near the sand floor and tear apart all the sick or dying fish they chance to fall upon. Breeding has never been observed underwater. They are one of sand floor associated species of *Lamprologus* seldom wandering over rocks. The coiled intestine attains ½ of the standard length. The maximum size is 150 mm.

Lamprologus christyi Trewavas and Poll

Lamprologus christyi is also a poor aquarium fish because of its predatory habits, large size (140 mm) and roaming ways. It stands out from the main group of species of *Lamprologus* by several unusual features: several scales on the cheek, a rather powerful set of pharyngeal teeth, including two big molars, and the coiled intestine reaching ⅔ of the standard length. The stomach contents of wild specimens include insect larvae, crustaceans and mollusc shells. The molar-shaped teeth on the pharyngeal bones seem to be used as shell crushers.

Lamprologus compressiceps Boulenger

This is one of the best aquarium fishes from the lake and one of the most famous. Some local races have multiple rows of pearly dots on the body and fins. Although the powerful jaws would tend to indicate predatory behavior, never during more than 200 underwater observations of this fish have we seen it attack another fish. Guppies put in tanks where several *L. compressiceps* were kept were unharmed after several weeks. The pharyngeal teeth are conical and larger toward the rear of the bone. The coiled intestine is rather long, about 80% of the standard length. The stomach contents of wild fish include shrimps and crabs. The fish thus seems to be peaceful toward other fishes.

Lamprologus compressiceps has a very high number of spines in the anal fin (10-12), which sets it apart from the other species of *Lamprologus* (except *L. fasciatus*).

Lamprologus cunningtoni Boulenger

Totally unsuited for aquarium life, this species reaches about

This *Plecodus straelini* with an unusual color pattern was seen in the wild as it is pictured here. The fish was collected in Bulu Point, South of Kigoma and photographed by Glen S. Axelrod.

Plecodus straelini is the only species of *Plecodus* that lives on rocky slopes and not in open water. It is a scale eater and is capable of mimicking its victim's body color pattern.

A southern variety of *Plecodus straelini* mimics not only *Cyphotilapia* but also *Lamprologus sexfasciatus*.

The vertical bars on this *Plecodus straelini* are well marked. Photo by Dr. Wolfgang Staeck.

300 mm in length and is a roamer. The pharyngeal teeth tend to be molar-shaped. It is a carnivorous fish, which is borne out by the inventory of the stomach contents. *L. cunningtoni* is one of the few cichlids in the lake to eat crabs.

The number of scales in a longitudinal line (67-71) indicates it is a roamer.

Lamprologus elongatus Boulenger

Lamprologus elongatus is totally unsuited for aquarium life, although not bad looking with its rows of pearly scales on a slate gray background, because of its large size and predatory diet. This individualistic species hovers one or two meters from the substratum, never far from rock. It breeds in the open on sand patches between or near the rocks. Because of their large size, the parents succeed in protecting their fry very effectively until they are quite large. Stomach contents consist of shrimp and fish; the coiled intestine reaches 50% of the standard length.

Lamprologus fasciatus Boulenger

Only three specimens of this species were collected during the 1946-1947 exploration, and none since. There is thus very little to say about this fish but for the fact that it is the second known species of *Lamprologus* (along with *L. compressiceps*) with ten spines in the anal fin.

The diet seems to be algae and shrimp. It has been seen only in the south of the lake.

Lamprologus furcifer Boulenger

Lamprologus furcifer is a species with one of the strictest bonds toward a given type of habitat in the lake. It is never found anywhere other than against big rock slabs, most of the time under them in dark niches and crevices but often also on the well-lit sides.

It is the typical upside-down cichlid in the lake and is very seldom seen in a normal position. The fish would be hard to find in the dark caves were it not for its large yellow bulging eyes and the vicious-looking white canine teeth.

This fish never wanders from its habitat in close contact with rocks. For this reason they are hard to detect and harder to collect. They do not tolerate each other, and young fry 40 mm long already engage in fights when they meet in a tank. They are not hard to feed in captivity, even on dry food, and usually don't

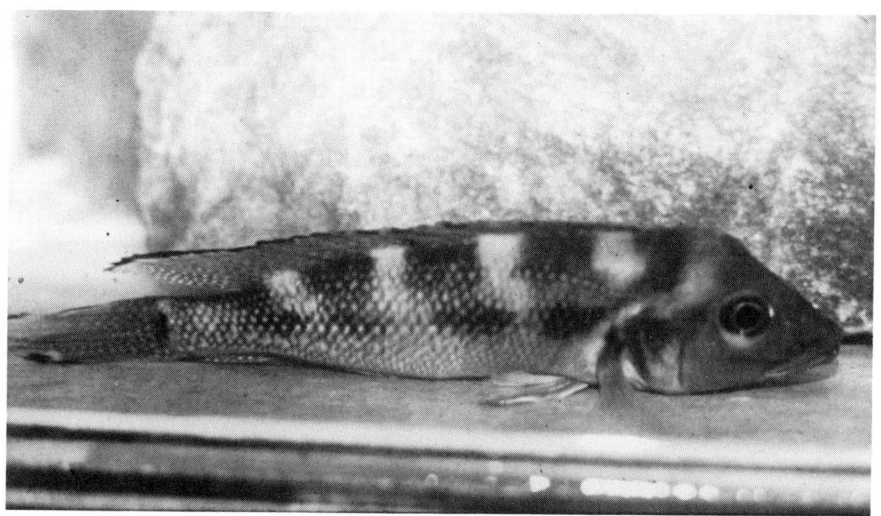

A species like *Lamprologus furcifer* normally found inhabiting cave-like situations, should be provided with a similar type situation in the aquarium. This specimen seems desperate for a hiding place. Paul V. Loiselle.

bother the other fish. Because of the large sail-like unpaired fins and their deep purple color, they are one of the most sought-after species from Lake Tanganyika and are a valuable addition to the aquarium for the advanced hobbyist. Breeding in captivity has not been reported.

Lamprologus hecqui Boulenger

This species is another of the dwarf species of *Lamprologus*, reaching a maximum size of less than 80 mm. The fish has never been collected in the northern part of the lake nor observed underwater. Many data are thus missing on the behavior of the species. It is reported by Poll that this species eats fishes and crustaceans in spite of its small size. The coiled intestine reaches ½ the standard length.

Lamprologus kungweensis Poll

One of the species which does not fit into the normal generic pattern is *L. kungweensis*. Its unusual specific characters are as follows: no scales on the thorax, behind the pectorals or on the nape; interorbital space exceedingly narrow; canine teeth shaped like snake fangs, very thin, very long and curved, numbering 7 to 8 in the upper jaw and 10 to 12 in the lower (no other species of *Lamprologus* has as many in the lower jaw). The pharyngeal teeth, far from being molar-shaped as in the shell-eating species,

This fish, *Plecodus paradoxus,* is equipped with a special type of dentition for removing the scales of its prey. Photo by Dr. Herbert R. Axelrod.

Sarotherodon tanganicae, unlike other species of the genus, can be found in areas of the coast not associated with a mud bottom. Photo by Glen S. Axelrod.

Simochromis babaulti, a rock-scraper, is rather common on shallow pebble and rubble shores; a nice-looking but a bad-tempered fish. Males of the southern race have rows of red dots on the sides which those of the northern race lack.

An unidentified species of *Simochromis* from the southern coast. The red dots on the sides are typical. It is one of the smallest species of the genus, seldom exceeding 6 centimeters, and lives in the same habitat as the well known *S. babaulti.*

are very thin and sharp. The diet should thus be something special, and Poll notes that stomach contents include copepods and water mites. We could thus have here a very specialized species as far as feeding is concerned.

Nothing else is known about this dwarf species of *Lamprologus* which does not exceed 38 mm.

Lamprologus leleupi Poll

This is one of the most famous Lake Tanganyika fishes with yellow-orange body and fins as if it had been dipped into a pail of paint. Only the eye is light blue. A second subspecies, *L. leleupi melas*, with a very deep brown color and blue eyes, has been reported from the north-west coast but has not been collected* recently. *L. leleupi*, if not exceedingly rare near the surface, is at least not very common. Its normal habitat is deep, and it is only around 40 meters depth that the species becomes abundant. Unfortunately the fish is very elusive and hard to collect, moreso than any other fish of the genus, and much time is lost chasing it around. A second problem when fishing deep is decompression. All cichlids are very sensitive to sudden extreme changes of pressure, especially when you catch them, because the nervous exhaustion or a kind of shock prevents them from adjusting their air bladder to the lesser pressure. The swim bladder then expands, stops blood from circulating through the hind part of the body, pushes the bowels through the gullet and, in very bad cases, eventually explodes. All cichlids are to be handled very cautiously when caught in deep water. Those which get into a kind of nervous shock, like *L. compressiceps* and *Cyphotilapia frontosa*, are next to impossible to bring up alive unless put into cumbersome decompression chambers at the depth they were caught and then decompressed very gradually. The process might take 24 hours or longer for very deep-caught fish, with inherent infection problems.

Lamprologus leleupi, although not suffering from shock when collected, cannot be brought up during the same dive (40 meters is much too deep) and thus are collected in small numbers when they are found nearer the surface.

Cichlids from the lake are more or less prone to this shock phenomenon, which is identifiable whenever a fish literally "curls" its body into an arch. When put back into the water the fish stays in this posture, motionless for several seconds, before straightening up and being able to swim normally.

Breeding *L. leleupi* was successfully achieved in the late 1950's when the first commercial collecting started in Lake Tan-
* *New localities have been found lately.*

Lamprologus leleupi. Photo by Wilhelm Hoppe.

ganyika, but it was soon discovered that the fry, away from their native waters, lost most of their brilliant yellow color from one generation to the next and became very drab. Spawns in captivity have again been reported recently, and perhaps with better knowledge it will be possible to breed the fish with their original magnificent dress.

L. leleupi seems to belong to a group of several species of *Lamprologus* that are very close according to their habitat preference and behavior. Among these we might include, from underwater observations, *L. niger* and *L. schreyeni* as well as an as yet unidentified species of *Lamprologus* with a deep brown coloration. The four fish have a typical crescent-shaped yellow stripe under the eye.

The diet of *L. leleupi* is essentially composed of small shrimp picked loose from the rocks and probably also small snails, according to the molar teeth they have on the pharyngeal bones (as reported in *L. niger*). Their coiled intestine is about 60% of the standard length.

Lamprologus leloupi Poll

Only one specimen of this fish was collected during the 1946-1947 exploration, and very little is known about this species. The

With the fins extended, the fin markings on this *Simochromis babaulti* are displayed. Photo by Dr. Herbert R. Axelrod.

Simochromis babaulti with a pale body background and distrupted body bars.

Depending upon tank conditions, the wild coloration of most fishes like this *Simochromis curvifrons* does not show up. Photo by Glen S. Axelrod.

Simochromis curvifrons is a very funny-looking fish with a very high head, very low and small mouth, and very compressed body. It is never very common.

fish has never been seen underwater. It stands apart from the other species of *Lamprologus* by having 4 or 5 rows of scales on the cheek.

Lamprologus lemairei Boulenger

Again, one of the most voracious and predatory species of the genus and not suited for the aquarium. It has a very big head with an enormous mouth allowing it to swallow fish nearly its own size. They are not roamers and are ill-equipped for speed with their short and stocky body. They are very often seen near rocks, sometimes lying on the floor in the open, motionless. They are highly solitary, and pairs are seldom seen. The female lays eggs in rock recesses, and the fry are taken care of by the female only.

We have never seen a pair guarding the spawn. The diet is, of course, carnivorous and composed exclusively of fish. The coiled intestine attains 50% of the standard length.

Lamprologus meeli Poll

This fish has never been collected nor seen underwater in the northern part of the lake. It is one of the few species of *Lamprologus* with more than 40 scales in a longitudinal line and is also one of the dwarfs—the maximum size being 67 mm. The diet is microcarnivorous (insect larvae and copepods), which is reflected by the length of the intestines (60% of the standard length).

Nothing is known about the behavior.

Lamprologus modestus Boulenger

Lamprologus modestus is one of the most common and ubiquitous fish in the lake. Seen over sand as well as on rock, but usually near the surface and near the shore. The normal color is pale beige, with the edges of the unpaired fins a pale blue. The southern race has unusual opaque yellow pectorals which the northern race lacks.

Their nests have never been discovered among rocks, although they are easily identified when the fish live in sand plains. They dig a deep tunnel propped against a big shell or a stone in the open even when nearby rock outcrops could help them in the building of their shaft. Both parents watch over the fry. The central pharyngeal teeth are molar-shaped, which agrees with stomach content inventories that include snail shells. The intestines reach 70% of the standard length.

Lamprologus moorii Boulenger

Lamprologus moorei has not been discovered in the northern part of the lake, and seems restricted to southern shores. This species has several unusual features for *Lamprologus*, including the very high number of canines in both jaws (the upper in excess of 10) and a very long intestine (200% of the standard length). This should indicate a very different diet from the one normal to all *Lamprologus*, i.e. flesh in every form. This feature seems borne out by the stomach contents of *L. moorii*, which consists of algae and ostracods. This fish is one of the best looking fish in the wild, with flowing fins, jet-black body and a sky-blue edge at the tail.

Lamprologus multifasciatus Boulenger

This is the smallest species of *Lamprologus* found in the lake, with a maximum recorded size of 35 mm. It has several interesting features. Only two canines are present on each jaw, there is only one lateral line, the other being quite short and there are always XVII spines in the dorsal fin. Most species of *Lamprologus*, as we have seen, have a very variable number of spines in the dorsal and anal fins.

Nothing is known of the ecology or behavior, the species never having been observed underwater.

Lamprologus niger Poll

We have seen that this species is a close cousin of *L. leleupi* and inhabits the same rocky slopes on the northwestern coast of the lake. It should be a very good aquarium fish because of its colors, from orange-brown to deep brown with the dorsal and anal fins lined with light blue, and small size (not more than 90 mm). The big difference between the two species, when the specimens tend to have the same body color, is that the fins of *L. niger* are checkered with black and the eye is red. Large specimens often have the pectorals deep brown or even red.

Like *L. leleupi*, *L. niger* has no scales on the thorax or the belly. Like *L. leleupi*, *L. brichardi*, *L. savoryi* and a few others, this species has scales on the dorsal and anal fins. There are some small scales on the back of the cheek, which the others have bare.

The diet, reflected by the enlarged pharyngeal teeth, includes molluscs and insect larvae.

Unfortunately for the aquarium world, this beautiful little fish is rare and hard to collect.

Simochromis diagramma is easily identified by the series of oblique bars on the body. Photo by Dr. Herbert R. Axelrod.

Note the characteristic continuous dark band on the dorsal fin that is typical of *Simochromis marginatus*. Photo by Glen S. Axelrod.

An unidentified *Simochromis* from the southern shores that is found with *S. babaulti*.

Another unidentified *Simochromis* from Nyanza Lac with a totally different body pattern than other *Simochromis*. It will probably be considered a new species.

Lamprologus ocellatus (Steindachner)

This is one of the most unusual of the lake *Lamprologus* because of several uncommon features: the very narrow interorbital space (the narrowest by far in the genus), the mouth turned upward at a very steep angle (the steepest among the *Lamprologus*), the unusually large eyes and the long filaments on the ventral fins. The habitat is empty shells. The size is small, less than 60 mm, and the color is a beautiful light beige with a blue edge to the dorsal and anal fins, a large black spot on the opercle, a bright mauve stripe under the eye and the filaments of the ventrals pure white.

It could become one of the favorites from the lake if only it weren't so hard to collect. In four years of collecting, only a few specimens have been brought back alive. They usually die when they are rolled between snail shells in the net, whenever they are caught.

Lamprologus ornatipinnis Poll

This dwarf species of *Lamprologus* would also be an exceptionally good aquarium fish if only it could be collected in large numbers. Only four or five specimens have been taken during our more than four years of collecting. The body color is a rather drab gray, but the fins are strikingly striped with black and white in a quite unusual pattern. The small size of the species, with a maximum of 74 mm recorded, prevents it from being dangerous to other fishes. The diet, as indicated by the short intestine (40% of the standard length), consists of copepods, so the species is considered microcarnivorous.

As a matter of fact, all species of *Lamprologus*, whether macrocarnivorous with a diet consisting of other fish, snails, shellfish or even crabs, or microcarnivorous, with a diet consisting of the smallest crustaceans or insect larvae, adapt very readily to dry food in captivity. The only occasional exception is *L. compressiceps*, which might refuse to eat anything in captivity.

Lamprologus petricola Poll

This very beautiful species of *Lamprologus*, with a maximum size of 130 mm and a very beautiful yellow body, could also be one of the species best suited for the aquarium. The fish has never been collected by the author in the northern part of the lake nor seen during my dives. The habitat thus seems to be restricted to the southern basin. The features of the species are as follows: 6 canines in each jaw and pharyngeal teeth tending to be molar-shaped in the rear center of the bone, possibly indicating a diet composed, at least in part, of molluscs. In fact, examination of the stomach contents revealed the presence of insect larvae. The coiled intestine attains a length of about 70% of the standard length.

L. petricola belongs to the group of *Lamprologus* species with scaleless belly and thorax.

Lamprologus pleuromaculatus Trewavas and Poll

This is perhaps one of the best middle-sized species of *Lamprologus* for the aquarium, provided it is not kept with fishes it could swallow. *L. pleuromaculatus* reaches only about 110 mm in length but has a powerful set of canines and is predatory on small fishes. The colors are bright alternating stripes of blue and light yellow. The fish is easily fed on dry food, and there is no problem in keeping it in top condition. The species has an unusual feature for the group; several scales are present on the cheek, but the nape, chest and belly are scaleless. The coiled intestine reaches 75% of the standard length.

This species prowls over bare ground in the huge sand plains of the lake, but just as often near rocky slopes or outcrops. Breeding has not been reported for captive fish nor observed underwater, though it is known that the pair dig crater-nests.

Lamprologus pleuromaculatus. Photo by Paul V. Loiselle.

Spathodus erythrodon, one of the smallest typical rock-dwellers, lives close to the surface in rubble and pebbles. This variety was found in the south end of the lake.

Spathodus erythrodon is colorful and in addition a peaceful fish in the tank. It accepts the usual aquarium fish food. Photo by Dr. Herbert R. Axelrod.

Tanganicodus irsacae, like *Spathodus* and *Eretmodus*, is also a rock-dweller in shallow water and is one of the very best aquarium fish from Lake Tanganyika.

Spathodus marlieri found around Nyanza Lac grows to about 8 centimeters and differs very much in ethology from *S. erythrodon*, swimming in pairs or alone over the rocky floor and not hidden between the rocks. With a very bad temper and drab dark color it makes a poor aquarium fish. The shape of the snout is unusual.

Lamprologus profundicola Poll

This species is another of the *Lamprologus* species which doesn't fit very well with Schilthuis' 1891 definition of the genus. The unusual specific features include: 18-20 rows of scales on the cheek (bare on most species of *Lamprologus*); a very unusually shaped pharyngeal bone (a deep "V" instead of the usual rounded triangle) with conical teeth longer in front instead of in the rear and even on the front extension toward the tip of the bone. In shape the pharyngeal bone looks like the pharyngeal bone of *Bathybates*.

The species also had, from the five specimens which were studied by Poll, a very definite number of spines in the dorsal and anal fins, with no variation from fish to fish.

The eye also is unusually small for a *Lamprologus*. The coiled intestine is 55% of the standard length, and stomach contents indicate that the fish is predatory.

Lamprologus pulcher Poll

This species was at first considered a subspecies of *L. savoryi* but was set apart as a distinct species by Poll (1974). Aside from the preserved specimens, little was known about the ecology of the fish, and no specimens had been observed, much less caught, underwater, until I discovered it in the south.

The fish is known to be a rock-dweller and is probably microphagous like *L. brichardi*, to which it seems to be closely related.

Lamprologus savoryi Poll

Not at all a bad looking fish, *L. savoryi* has a very nasty temper that makes it a poor aquarium fish unless kept with larger fish. This is not too difficult because the maximum size of *L. savoryi* doesn't exceed 80 mm by much. The color is dark blue with very dark blue bands. The fins are elongated into filaments, not as long, however, as those of *L. brichardi*.

The fry and the adults hide in the rock rubble and are never seen in the open. The fish spawn in deep, dark recesses, a few fry being hatched in each spawn. We never saw more than a dozen fry, which is extremely low for egg-layers and for a species of *Lamprologus*. The fry are watched over by the parents until they are quite large, at least 30 mm long. At that size the young *L. savoryi* can easily be mistaken for young *Cyphotilapia*, with the lighter bands, the head and the lips being a pale blue, contrasting with the deep blue bands.

Unlike *Lamprologus brichardi, L. savoryi* is not too common in the aquarium trade. Photo by Paul V. Loiselle.

It is one of the most secretive fish in the lake because of its hiding places and is seldom captured although not at all uncommon in its habitat. The diet, according to examination of the stomach contents, included Diptera, copepods and vegetable matter (quite unusual for the genus). The coiled intestine reaches 70% of the standard length, which would indicate a rather omnivorous diet. The southern race instead of being bluish-pink is smoke-colored and shows no bands in the wild.

Lamprologus schreyeni Poll

Lamprologus schreyeni is one of the dwarf rock-dwelling species of *Lamprologus* living deep inside rock crevices. It is never seen in the open where its very small size would make it an immediate victim of the predators of the "outside" world.

The species belongs to a group of small rock-dwellers, like *L. niger*, which are never very common in their habitat and spend all of their time in hiding, being discovered only by chance. Their capture can only be made during underwater SCUBA explorations made at leisure.

If new species of *Lamprologus* are discovered in Lake Tanganyika they would most probably be among these tiny, shy rock-dwellers.

Telmatochromis vittatus, from the southern part of the lake, has only one stripe under the eye, a conspicuous dot at the base of the tail, the fins a bit shorter than those of *T. bifrenatus*, and the oblique body stripes less visible. Its maximum size is about 9 centimeters.

An adult *Telmatochromis bifrenatus*. Note the conspicuous oblique stripes on the body. Photo by Dr. Herbert R. Axelrod.

One of the two dwarf species in the genus, *Telmatochromis bifrenatus* is an excellent aquarium fish. It reaches a length of 7 centimeters and inhabits deep rocky slopes.

Telmatochromis bifrenatus with the secondary stripe between the lateral stripe and the dorsal fin. Photo by Glen S. Axelrod.

The species, although quite small, has a high number of dorsal fin spines (XVII-XIX) and a low number of anal spines (V). The pharyngeal teeth include two enlarged molar-shaped teeth in the center rear which would tend to indicate a diet including, perhaps, small snails or clams. This is not at all out of line with their habitat—among rocks with a rich biocover.

Breeding has never been researched. The number of fry seems to be about 20, perhaps more; they are watched over by both parents. The nests appear to be very narrow slits in the rocks, out of reach of any other fish except young mastacembelid eels or *Telmatochromis bifrenatus*.

Lamprologus sexfasciatus Trewavas and Poll

This species is without doubt one of the most spectacular fishes in Lake Tanganyika, with its rich deep blue bands alternating with pale blue, the iridescent green and electric blue spot on the opercle and the striking pale blue edges to the unpaired fins. The species is very close to *L. tretocephalus*, but it is very easy to tell them apart.

Both species are found on the same type of substratum (rocks), but they are never found together. None have been discovered in the northeastern coast of the lake, although they are rather abundant on the eastern coast from the Tanzanian-Burundi border toward the south. On the northwestern coast they are common but not abundant. This is one of the striking examples of the variety of coastal fish populations around the lake.

L. sexfasciatus is distinguished from its close relatives by the fact that it has 6 dark bands (of which 4 start along the dorsal length), whereas *L. tretocephalus* only has five (of which three start along the dorsal length). The two species have peculiar flat molar teeth on the center and rear of the pharyngeal bone, which has a different shape in *L. tretocephalus*—and an unusual one at that.

Both species live over the rubble, not in it. The size of *L. sexfasciatus*, according to specimens in collections, is said not to exceed 90 mm, but I caught some which were 12 cm long.

The diet is said to include snails, among them *Neothauma*. The shell of this snail is very hard and it is thus in line with this diet that the pharyngeal bone and teeth are so strong. The coiled intestine reaches nearly 90% of the standard length, which is quite long.

Lamprologus signatus Poll

A very low number of gill rakers (4-5), of dorsal (XV) and anal (V) spines and a naked chest, belly and nape are the features of this dwarf *Lamprologus*. On each jaw there are two outsized fang-shaped canines. The eye is very big and the interorbital space very narrow (7.25-10 times in head length). The habitat is reported to be deep water on soft, muddy bottoms. The fish feed on small shrimp. The maximum size of collected specimens was 53 mm, at which size the fish were mature. Nothing else is known of this species.

Lamprologus stappersi Pellegrin

This species, never collected or seen underwater by the author, doesn't seem to exist in the northern part of the lake. Taxonomic features include six rows of scales on the cheek, which is not in line with Schilthuis' definition of genus *Lamprologus* (1891). The species also lacks scales on the belly and has a high number of anal spines (IX). Nothing is known about the ecology or ethology of the species.

Lamprologus tetracanthus Boulenger

Lamprologus tetracanthus is one of the best looking sand-dwelling species of *Lamprologus*, with its alternating rows of pearly and beige scales, four or five vertical bands and long ventral and anal fins, the latter spotted. The caudal and dorsal fins are also spotted and have a white or yellow band at the edge. Each ray of the dorsal fin is tipped either with bright red or black. Unfortunately, *L. tetracanthus* grows to a maximum size of nearly 200 mm and of course is not to be kept with other fish of a size it might swallow. Two molars at the back of the pharyngeal bone, stomach content inventories including mainly snails and fish, and the coiled intestine reaching 90% of the standard length would lead us to believe that the species is not one of the typical predators of the lake.

Breeding has been observed in the open on sand flats in a crater-nest dug from the floor. The fry number several hundred and are closely watched by the parents. We don't remember having seen the fish over rock.

Lamprologus toae Poll

The author and his team didn't see a single *L. toae* on the

Telmatochromis caninus is one of the most common fish in the lake. It is associated with rocks but at ease in murky water (which most rock-dwellers are not).

Close-up view of the head of *Telmatochromis caninus*. Photo by Dr. Herbert R. Axelrod.

Positive identification of *Telmatochromis caninus* and *T. temporalis* usually requires the examination of the teeth for these species greatly resemble each other externally. Photo by Dr. Robert J. Goldstein.

Telmatochromis temporalis in captivity. It has lost some of the color usually seen in the wild. Photo by Aaron Norman.

northeastern coast of the lake in four years and more than 500 individual dives. But the fish is rather common along the northwestern coast just across the lake on identical habitats. This again shows the variability of fish populations from coast to coast. The species is a rock-dweller, living in the open. It is rather small (maximum size 100 mm). The fish doesn't look like a typical *Lamprologus* at first. It is difficult to say, but there is something different in the appearance of the fish which is not all unattractive, with its very big eye, the fins well erect, and the scales in a horizontally contrasting pattern. Only a few specimens have been collected, and nothing is known about their breeding behavior.

The canines are not very sturdy, nor are they very much differentiated from the other teeth or from each other. The mouth is also straight in front instead of oval as in most species of *Lamprologus*.

The coiled intestine reaches 60% of the standard length, and the diet is reported to be mainly aquatic insect larvae. It is certainly not a predatory species.

Lamprologus tretocephalus Boulenger

Much has been said already about this species in the discussion of *L. sexfasciatus*. The fish is said to reach about 140 mm and has a diet consisting of shells and aquatic insect larvae. The coiled intestine is only 30% of the standard length in contrast to *L. sexfasciatus* where it reaches 90%. The species are certainly differentiated by their basic diet, although *L. tretocephalus* is also reported to eat some clams; in the lake most molluscs of this type usually have thin and brittle shells. This is perhaps as good a reason as any to explain the huge difference in intestine length.

L. tretocephalus is of course one of the best Lake Tanganyika additions to the aquarium fish inventory. It is peaceful toward other fish, although fights might occur between them when too crowded in small tanks.

Lamprologus wauthioni Poll

Again, this species is one of those elusive species which have never been observed in the northern part of the lake, although rather frequently collected by Poll in the central part. The species, as reported by him, lives in snail shells (*Neothauma*) on mud floors in rather deep water.

The species has a constant number of anal fin spines (VI), few gill rakers (6 or 7) and 2 large, stubby canines on each jaw. The color pattern includes several spots on the sides forming, more or less, two rows. Ocelli are present at the end of the dorsal and anal fins and, what is unusual, on the tail near the caudal peduncle.

The diet consists of shrimp, as in the case of so many dwarf and middle-sized species of *Lamprologus*, and the coiled intestine reaches about 50 % of the standard length. *L. wauthioni* seems to belong to the same group as *L. ocellatus*.

LEPTOCHROMIS Regan 1920*

One endemic species in Lake Tanganyika.

Body: very elongate and rather cylindrical, with horizontal rows of very brilliant scales

Scales: 37 to 39 in a longitudinal line

Lateral lines: 2, not complete, the lower short

Fins: All unpaired fins are striped, the dorsal and anal fins with oblique stripes
Dorsal — XVI to XVIII spines and 10-12 rays
Anal — III spines, 7-9 rays
Ventrals — outer rays longer than inner rays
Caudal — forked

Teeth: small, conical, in 3 to 4 rows in a single band, the teeth in the outer row larger (sand-sifter?)

Pharyngeal teeth: subconical and very fine

Mouth: rather large and terminal; upper jaw slightly protruding; protractile mouth

Gill rakers: 13 to 15

Habitat: rather deep, down to at least 20 meters, although coastal, over mud and sand floors

Feeding: omnivorous, but not predatory

Reproduction: no buccal incubation discovered; ripe females had 200 eggs of 2 mm diameter

Maximum size: about 150 mm

Leptochromis calliurum (Boulenger)

This is rather seldom collected because of the depth at which it seems to live. It is normally found over deep mud floors and has been collected only exceptionally in shallow water. It is probably not rare in its habitat, but it is difficult to collect with any kind of efficiency in deep water because one can spend perhaps only half

*Reganochromis

Triglachromis otostigma. Photo by Homer Arment.

Triglachromis otostigma is a typical mud-dweller, never seen close to rocks. Nothing is known about its breeding habits and the fish has never been bred in captivity. It is assumed to be an egg-layer and not a mouth-brooder as not a single specimen was collected with eggs or fry in its mouth. It is an excellent aquarium fish.

The original *Tropheus duboisi*. This adult has lost the thin stripe usually found in *T. duboisi*.

Another local race of *Tropheus duboisi* of the Nyanza-Lac type, collected in Tanzania around Kigoma.

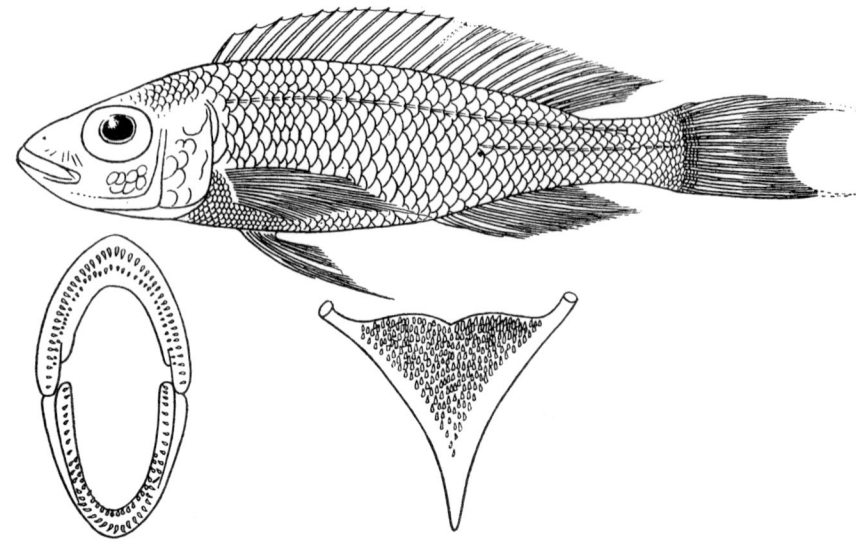

Lestradea perspicax perspicax, buccal dentition (left) and lower pharyngeal bone (right), from Poll, 1957.

an hour at these depths. One cannot move large nets without getting too exhausted for safety, and one has to find the fish before the real collecting can start. Fishes from the depths are thus neglected by collectors.

The diet of the fish, as reported by Poll, consists of the largest shrimps available in the lake (about 2.5 cm long) and fry of the Nile perch (*Lates*). In a tank the fish doesn't bother other fish and is peaceful. The mouth, about 7 mm across when wide open, is not big enough for swallowing large fishes. I must say that I have never seen a fish in Africa that wouldn't gobble fry whenever given a chance, including even the mormyrids (which nobody would dare call predators), much less cichlids, which are omnivorous at best.

Leptochromis would be a good aquarium species if it could be bred. The shape is very elegant, there are three rows of shiny mother-of-pearl scales on the body and the unpaired fins are decorated with strongly contrasting black stripes. Better yet, the fish is hardy and not too choosy about food. The diet, as with most of the lake cichlids, can be based entirely on flake food. Like most lake cichlids, the fish doesn't eat plants.

LESTRADEA Poll 1943

One endemic species (*L. perspicax*) including two subspecies.

Body: elongated; very large eye
Scales: 37 to 40 in a longitudinal line
Lateral lines: 2, the upper complete
Fins: Dorsal — XIII to XVI spines and 13 to 16 rays
Anal — III spines and from 9 to 11 rays
Caudal — forked
Teeth: 2 or 3 rows of conical teeth, the inner bent backward, all of the same size
Pharyngeal teeth: thin, close together in a triangular pattern
Mouth: terminal
Gill rakers: from 15 to 19
Habitat: shallow, over sand floors
Feeding: microorganisms
Reproduction: buccal incubation of more than 20 eggs of 2 mm in diameter
Size: about 140 mm

Lestradea perspicax stappersii, lower pharyngeal bone (left) and buccal dentition (right), from Poll, 1957.

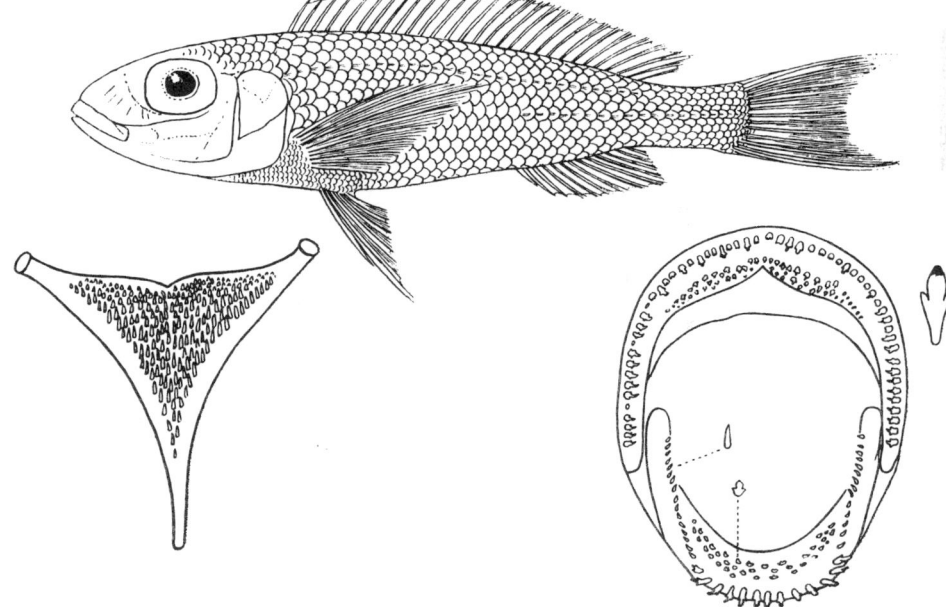

The white-dotted pattern is the characteristic juvenile pattern of *Tropheus duboisi*. Photo by Peter Chlupaty.

Juvenile dotted pattern of the original race of *Tropheus duboisi* found on the northwestern coast of the lake.

The white vertical bar in adult *Tropheus duboisi* is variable as seen in the fish on the left with an incomplete bar. Photo by Glen S. Axelrod.

The striking white dots on the head of *Tropheus duboisi* betrays the identity of this fish even when photographed at a good distance under water. Photo by Glen S. Axelrod.

LIMNOCHROMIS Regan 1920

Nine endemic species.

Body: elongated to very elongated, cylindrical or compressed

Scales: usually 30 to 42 in a longitudinal line (one species with from 63 to 71)

Lateral lines: 2, the upper complete

Fins: Dorsal — XIV to XVII spines and 8-10 rays
   Anal — III spines and 7-9 rays
   Ventrals — often with a filament
   Caudal — forked or rounded

Teeth: conical, set in from 2 to 4 rows; no canines

Pharyngeal teeth: small

Mouth: terminal or low

Gill rakers: 10-18 (21 to 24 in *L. nigripinnis*, *L. leptosoma* and *L. microlepidotus*)

Habitat: mud for all species except *L. nigripinnis*, *L. leptosoma* and *L. microlepidotus*, which live off of rocky slopes

Feeding: omnivorous; some species have specialized feeding (copepods)

Reproduction: apparently egg-layers, except for *L. nigripinnis*, *L. leptosoma* and *L. microlepidotus*, which use buccal incubation

Maximum size: variable depending on the species

Affinities: Limnochromis nigripinnis, L. leptosoma and *L. microlepidotus* should be put together in another genus.

Limnochromis permaxillaris, from Poll, 1957.

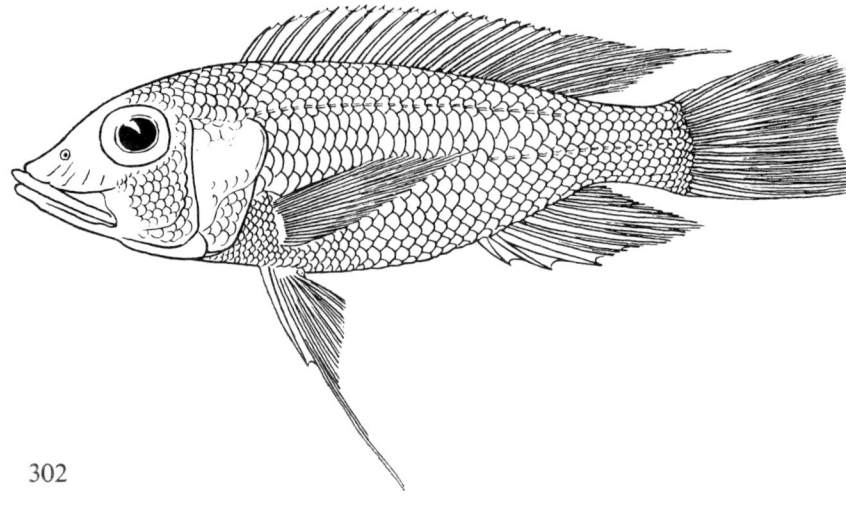

Key to the Identification of the Species of *Limnochromis*

1. Body very elongate, height at least 4 times in standard length; a single row of teeth; 28 or more elements in dorsal fin, of which at least 13 are soft rays; 20 or more gill rakers; no opercular spot; pharyngeal bone long and thin, with fine conical teeth at posterior edge only 2

   Body rather stocky, height less than 4 times in standard length; several rows of teeth; 25-27 elements in dorsal fin, of which at most 11 are soft; less than 20 gill rakers; opercular spot present; pharyngeal bone with conical teeth on dental area
   3

2. (triplet). More than 60 scales in longitudinal line; more than 50 scales in upper lateral line and 15-23 in lower lateral line; 2 rows of scales on cheek; 15 to 16 rays in anal fin ....
   .... *L. microlepidotus*

   39-40 scales in longitudinal line; 29 or 30 scales in upper lateral line and 11-14 in lower lateral line; 2-4 rows of scales on cheek; 11 to 12 rays in anal fin .... *L. nigripinnis*

   39-42 scales in longitudinal line; 27-33 scales in upper lateral line, 11-15 in lower lateral line; 2 rows of scales on cheek; 13 to 15 rays in anal fin .... *L. leptosoma*

3. Snout very short, 3.75-3.9 times in head length; eye very large, 2.5-2.75 times in head length; 1 or 2 rows of scales on cheek; mouth very oblique; DXIV-XV, 9-10; 13-15 gill rakers; 32-34 scales in longitudinal line; 23-34 scales in upper lateral line, 9 to 14 in lower lateral line; pelvic fins with filaments; tail rounded .... *L. dhanisi*

   Snout 2.25-3.5 times in head length; eye 2.5-4.3 times in head length; 3-5 rows of scales on cheek; mouth terminal or slightly oblique; DXV-XVIII; 34-42 scales in longitudinal line; pelvic fins without filaments; caudal fin straight or concave 4

4. Pharyngeal bones with central teeth molar-shaped 5
   Pharyngeal bones with central teeth conical 6

5. 11-13 gill rakers; dorsal spines XVI-XVII; caudal fin well notched, with angular lobes; body depth 3.0-3.4 times in standard length; 6.5/9.5-10.5 scales in transverse line; pharyngeal bone triangular; size 140 mm .... *L. auritus*

   13-15 gill rakers; dorsal spines XV; caudal fin concave with rounded lobes; body depth 2.8-3.0 times in standard length; 3/11 scales in transverse line; pharyngeal bone elongate;

The newly discovered form of *Tropheus duboisi* with the broad yellow-white band across the body. This local race was discovered in Tanzania south of the Malagarazi delta and is thus very well isolated from other *T. duboisi* found on the northern shores.

An adult *Tropheus duboisi* eyeing intently a boulder with biocover. Photo by Glen S. Axelrod.

An unusual *Tropheus moorii* with a distinctly blunt snout and bright yellow paired fins. Photo by Glen S. Axelrod.

Tropheus polli is a new species recently described by Glen S. Axelrod and thus it is not included in the author's list. Photo by Glen S. Axelrod.

size 200 mm.............................*L. staneri*
6 (triplet). Snout long, only 2.25-2.7 in head length; maxillary pedicle reaching interorbital space; mouth large and very protractile; lower jaw 2.0-2.3 in head length; teeth in 2 or 3 rows in front, only one row on side of the jaws; caudal peduncle 1.2-1.35 times as long as high; pharyngeal teeth few and thin; 33-37 scales in longitudinal line; maximum size 150 mm ....*L. permaxillaris*
Snout rather short, 2.7-3.5 in head length; maxillary pedicle reaching only to nostrils; mouth not very protractile; lower jaw 2.3-2.5 in head; teeth in 3-4 rows, even on the sides of the upper jaw, and bent backward; caudal peduncle slender, 1.3-2.0 times as long as high; body height 3.3-3.5 in standard length; head 2.6 to 2.9 in standard length; eye 3.1-3.7 in head; gill rakers 14-15; scales in longitudinal line 36-39; caudal fin concave; size 110 mm .....*L. abeelei*
Snout rather short, 3.3 in head length; maxillary pedicle and mouth like *L. abeelei*; teeth in 2 or 3 rows on upper jaw, 2 only on the lower, a single row on sides; caudal peduncle short, 1.2-1.4 times as long as high; body depth 2.6-2.8 in standard length; head 2.5-2.7 in standard length; eye smaller, 3.9-4.3 in head; gill rakers 16 or 17; scales in longitudinal line 44 to 49; caudal fin truncate; size 130 mm.......
....*L. christyi*

Limnochromis auritus (Boulenger)

Limnochromis auritus is a common species in the deeper waters of around 40 to 60 meters. This fish fortunately also reaches higher levels in the mud and sand slopes on which it lives and can thus be collected.

The overall color is a pinkish mauve with lighter bands of a pale yellow. As in many Lake Tanganyika cichlids, the sides are brightened by two or three rows of contrasting mother-of-pearl scales. The tips of the dorsal, anal and caudal fins are black.

It is a good aquarium fish, not nasty and easy to feed. With a maximum size of 140 mm, this husky fish will need room. Breeding of the species in captivity has not been reported. It is rather delicate to ship and the freight is costly, which explains why they are neither cheap nor common in tanks.

This is one of the problems with the Lake Tanganyika cichlids, and perhaps the *most* important problem with them. They come from an isothermic lake where they spend all their lives in a

Limnochromis auritus. Photo by Homer Arment.

constant temperature of 25-27° C. Because of this feature they cannot stand a sudden drop, even of a few degrees, without danger to their well-being. The temperature during their trip to foreign importers cannot drop lower than 18°C (65°F) without causing heavy losses. Under 20°C (68°F), the fish when unpacked will be subject to a kind of thermal shock and will have to be brought back to standard tropical temperatures during a painstaking process of mixing their packing water with tank water very gradually.

This is one of the problems which the author had to face during the initial exporting of fishes from Lake Tanganyika after reports of unexplainable losses during unpacking started to come in. Hundreds of bags of fishes were packed as if they were going to be shipped abroad. The fish were kept in the plastic bags for up to 60 hours, during which time they were overheated, chilled, anesthetized, etc. Afterwards they were put back into their tanks to determine what could be wrong with the packing methods, during the trips or when the fish were unpacked and stored in the importer's tanks.

These experiments were conducted very thoroughly, with every bag being checked every few hours, day and night, during the entire experiments. A record was kept on each individual bag of fishes. It took two years until a set of rules covering every eventuality could be given to the importers, and it took an unaccounted quantity of specialized manpower, a five-figure amount of dollars,

A *Tropheus moorii* fry with the yolk sac still not completely absorbed. Photo by Glen S. Axelrod.

Tropheus brichardi is one of three endemic *Tropheus* species in the lake. Photo by Dr. Herbert R. Axelrod.

Juvenile color pattern of the all-black northern race of *Tropheus moorii*. The fish is still grayish-yellow.

One of the varieties of *Tropheus moorii* from the eastern coast of the lake.

and a transit station in Europe started at a cost of $10,000 to overcome the shipping problems of the normally "too hard to ship" Lake Tanganyika cichlids. But now the Lake Tanganyika fishes reach their destination in perfect condition and their health cannot be better. These are probably, because of their special temperature needs, the hardest fish in the world, marine or fresh water, to ship—and they are certainly not for novice collectors.

Limnochromis microlepidotus Poll

Limnochromis microlepidotus is one of the most outstanding fishes to come from the lake, perhaps among the 10 best species, and a very peculiar one. It is the only cichlid as yet discovered that lives off the floor along rock slopes but comes from very deep water to breed in shallower coastal water. Its regular habitat is far in excess of 40 meters, and the schools which are seen in shallow water are probably only a fraction of the main schools in deep water. This is perhaps one of the reasons why they are so difficult to decompress when they are collected below 10 meters, which appears to be their upper range for breeding.

Young fish, with their bright yellow and always erect unpaired fins, can be discovered on the ceilings of grottos and small caves, which shows that they are released there by the mouthbrooding mothers. At this time they are very tiny but already very beautiful, the slate gray body being in violent contrast to their bright fins. When adult, which means at about 80 mm long, their very narrow and slender body is a darker gray, rather drab, and the dorsal, anal and caudal fins are gray-blue and yellow.

What happens to this fish when in breeding color is unbelievable. The body of the male becomes the base on which large patches of blue-black, electric blue and yellow spread and change places in a matter of hours. It is hard to understand how such changes can be triggered, as none of the breeding colors stay at the same place on the body of any specimen. The dorsal fin follows the same trends: one hour the huge blue-black patch is in front, the next the patch is on the back of the long dorsal. The other unpaired fins are also deep blue and bright yellow. The head and front of the body are a shimmering iridescent light blue. No photograph has yet depicted the fish in its full brilliancy.

The other very unusual feature of *L. microlepidotus*, also uncommon in open-water cichlids, is that it is a head-stander, like a South American *Leporinus*. Never do you meet the fish on an even keel. In open water all the fish in a school are at approximately a 45° angle. When in caves they assume every conceivable position, head down or up, body on the side or upside down.

In a tank all specimens, from very young fry to the largest adults, will adopt any position: along the leaves of *Vallisneria*, head down or up, or even floating belly up at the surface of the water.

The problem when these odd fishes are collected is the decompression process, which might take days. It is very difficult for them to cross the last few meters below the surface of the lake. Even in tanks, after a few days *L. microlepidotus* which had been in perfect condition and properly decompressed might all of a sudden have problems with their bladder again and die. It is of course quite a problem, and one which has not found a proper solution, unless one were to build a huge decompression chamber with heavy plate glass and have at hand other rather expensive equipment.

In a hobbyist's tanks this species should not be kept alone. There ought to be several, at least 5 or 6, *L. microlepidotus* together, as the fish will otherwise feel lost and ill at ease. It is one of the most gregarious cichlids in Lake Tanganyika and needs company.

The diet consists mainly of copepods, and the fish is reported by M. Poll to be a zooplankton eater. We have had some problems feeding them on dried flakes, but once adapted to this food the fish is not a problem.

Limnochromis nigripinnis (Boulenger)

A close cousin of *L. microlepidotus*, from which it can be distinguished by the smaller number of scales in a longitudinal line, this species shares the same habitat and the same problems of decompression when brought to the surface. The youngsters are endowed with magnificent yellow unpaired fins, but the fish changes to a drab blue-gray body and dark unpaired fins with age, hence its scientific name.

LIMNOTILAPIA Regan 1920

Three endemic species.

Body: moderately elongated and deep
Scales: 32 to 37 in a longitudinal line
Lateral lines: 2
Fins: Dorsal — XVIII to XX spines and 9 to 11 rays

The so-called "blue-eyed" *Tropheus* found around Kigoma with a strong yellow-green dorsal patch is another race of the Nyanza-Lac or eastern type of *Tropheus moorii*.

A juvenile *Tropheus moorii* of the Nyanza-Lac type with the typical bands of the juvenile. Some specimens will keep the bands until the adult stage. Banded and unbanded individuals are often seen in the same areas.

Tropheus moorii, green variety with yellow stripes.

The eastern or Nyanza-Lac type of *Tropheus moorii* with characteristic stripes on an adult fish. This type from Nyanza-Lac doesn't grow more than 9 or 10 centimeters.

Anal — III spines and 7 to 9 soft rays
Caudal — straight or slightly forked
Teeth: in one or several rows, the front row composed of a sharp edge of bicuspid teeth, becoming more or less conical toward the sides of the jaws
Pharyngeal teeth: small, thin and bicuspid
Mouth: terminal and rather large
Gill rakers: 10 to 14
Habitat: coastal, over sand and rock; shallow for juveniles, deeper —down to 20-25 meters—for adults
Feeding: omnivorous
Reproduction: buccal incubation
Maximum size: about 260 mm

Key to the Identification of the Species of *LIMNOTILAPIA*

(From Dr. M. Poll, "Poissons Cichlidae," Mission Hydrobiologique au lac Tanganyka 1946-1947)

1. D. XVIII-XX; cephalic sensorial orifices of the lateral line not enlarged..2

   D. XVI; cephalic sensorial orifices of the lateral line enlarged
   ....*L. trematocephala*

2. Body depth 2.8 to 3.25 times in length; 35 to 37 scales in a longitudinal line; a double row of black spots on the back; maximum size 260 mm....................*L. dardennei*

   Body depth 2.33-2.5 times in length; 30 to 32 scales in a longitudinal line; traces of vertical stripes on sides of body, maximum size 100 mm ....*L. loocki*

Limnotilapia dardennei (Boulenger)

The only species of *Limnotilapia* found as yet in the northern reaches of the lake, *L. dardennei* as a young fish lacks the bright color pattern usually associated with the Rift Lake cichlids. Until at least 18 cm long, it is a silvery fish with vertical stripes stopping midway down on the sides and of a drab olive green on the back. It is only later, when the fish goes to live in deeper water than the shoals it spent its early years on, that it will all of a sudden start to get a totally different color pattern that makes it one of the most beautiful sights in the lake. By then *L. dardennei* will have a deep blue body with yellow on the belly and bright orange-red on the throat. The pelvic fins will be a deep blue and the anal and tip of the dorsal a rich Prussian blue with yellow-orange stripes or dots.

Limnotilapia dardennei. Photo by Dr. Herbert R. Axelrod.

The fish will occasionally be seen higher up along the rock slopes, but these will always be females incubating fry in their mouth, and very seldom a male. The habitat of the adult fish is thus around the 20-25 meter layer, or deeper, and these depths are prohibitive for regular fishing. This is why *L. dardennei*, after the first exports, saw its popularity dwindle when people, seeing the drab looking youngsters, didn't realize they had a very special fish if only they could be a bit patient.

LOBOCHILOTES Boulenger 1915

One endemic species.

Body: narrow, elongated, body tapering off toward the tail; powerful head; vertical stripes very apparent

Scales: 33-35 rather large ctenoid scales in a longitudinal line

Lateral lines: 2, neither complete

Fins: Dorsal — XVII to XIX spines and 10-11 rays
  Anal — III spines and 7 or 8 rays
  Caudal — straight
  Pectorals — powerful

Teeth: all rounded or truncated, outer teeth bicuspid in the young

Pharyngeal teeth: conical, rounded or molar-like at the back of the bone

Tropheus moorii, bronze variety.

Tropheus moorii, mottled copper-black variety.

Regular orange variety of *Tropheus moorii*.

Adult *Tropheus moorii* of the orange variety.

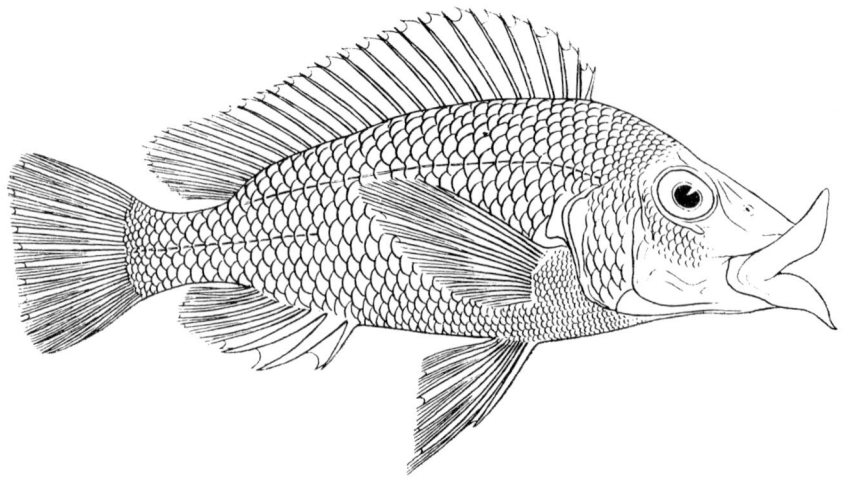

Lobochilotes labiatus, from Poll, 1957.

Mouth: terminal; lips fleshy when young, becoming very thick and folding back on maxillary, perhaps prehensile, with age
Gill rakers: 18-22
Habitat: always close to rock; adults in rather deep water
Feeding: omnivorous on invertebrates, shellfish and crabs
Reproduction: buccal incubation with several hundred eggs
Maximum size in the wild: about 400 mm, the second largest cichlid in Lake Tanganyika

Lobochilotes labiatus Boulenger

This large fish, one of the largest cichlids in the lake (or anywhere), has very peculiar lips. Very fleshy when the fish are young, they start to thicken more when the fish grows older, becoming more and more like a kind of rubbery tubing all around the jaws. When adult, the fish has a set of very thick lips curling back on the outside of the mouth. These lips are in no way immobile, and the fish can control them to some extent. Seeing the fish eat in the lake, one gains the impression that the lips might be prehensile and thus very useful in helping the fish dig the shells from the sand floors in which they are embedded, and perhaps even more to seize the crabs which are a regular part of the fish's diet. The pharyngeal teeth of the species are very thick and flattened and used as crushers where the shells are broken down into pieces, the body being swallowed and the shell fragments spit out.

There are places in the lake on rock slopes where the floor is littered with a vast quantity of freshly broken bivalves. It is highly probable that *Lobochilotes*, the only mollusc-eating fish of such size in the lake living on these same grounds, is responsible for these big meals. What is noteworthy is the fact that these broken shells are always concentrated on huge flat boulders, protruding like a table from the nearby sand slopes. They appear thus to have been brought there deliberately.

Lobochilotes when young is a striking fish in any tank because of a number of deep green vertical stripes on the body as well as a mottled array of dots and small stripes of deep green and orange brown. For this reason the fish has gained a lasting popularity among hobbyists. Feeding has presented few problems, nor does breeding present problems provided one is ready to accommodate the fish in large quarters.

This fish again illustrates the trend of buccal incubators to come up with their fry from the deep layers to the upper, well oxygenated, layer. It is then that the diver can see the big adults looking over their hundreds of youngsters in very shallow water. The juvenile fish will spend their first year in this habitat, individually and not in a school like those of *L. dardennei*. Later on they will move down the slopes, to 40 meters and more, apparently to wander in the semidarkness.

The curled thick lips of this *Lobochilotes labiatus* are typical for an adult fish. Photo by Dr. Herbert R. Axelrod.

Tropheus moorii of the red type from the southern part of the lake. Photo by Glen S. Axelrod.

A very large specimen (14.5 centimeters) of *Tropheus moorii* of the northern type red-black race. The red stripes on the ventrals are unusual because they extend to the base of the fins.

Juvenile *Tropheus moori* are often striped, although the pattern disappears in most local varieties of the northern type when the fish become adult. Adults of the Nyanza-Lac type often remain banded and the same areas have banded or plain specimens. This is a juvenile of the red-black northern type.

Pure red-black northern type of *Tropheus moorii*.

OPHTHALMOCHROMIS Poll 1956

Two endemic species with two subspecies.

Body: oblong, rather elongated, rather broad
Scales: 36 to 40 in a longitudinal line
Lateral lines: 2, the upper complete
Fins: Dorsal — XII-XIV, 13-16
   Anal — II or III, 9-11
   Ventrals — outer ray with a very long filament extending to the caudal fin, sometimes tipped with a forked spatula (in the male)
   Caudal — very forked, each lobe ending with a filament
Teeth: conical, in 2 or 3 rows; outer teeth larger, in a continuous edge
Pharyngeal teeth: in a dense velvet-like cushion
Mouth: lower jaw shorter than the upper, which in *O. nasutus* ends in a narrow proboscis about 5 mm long, increasingly apparent in the male with age
Gill rakers: 17-20 on the lower half of the first arch
Habitat: from 2 to at least 10 meters depth, in mid-water, always over hard floors
Feeding: various microfoods
Reproduction: buccal incubation of a few 4 mm eggs
Maximum size: O. nasutus about 180 mm, *O. ventralis* about 120 mm

Ophthalmochromis nasutus Poll & Matthes

The species belonging to this genus are known to have developed into several geographical forms, and the present fish was finally recognized by Poll and Matthes as a distinct species. This is apparent to the casual diver as soon as he has been able to see *O. nasutus* and *O. ventralis* in their respective habitats.

O. nasutus lives on the northernmost rocky shores along the Burundi coast and can be separated from *O. ventralis* by its larger size (about 180 mm), the drab gray body color in both male and female (the male darker) and the proboscis extending from the upper jaw and protruding slightly in front of the mouth. The male has two very long pelvic filaments extending well beyond the base of the anal fin, both filaments being forked at the tip and widened into yellow spatulae. We have seen in the chapter devoted to the breeding behavior of lake fishes that these yellow spatulae don't

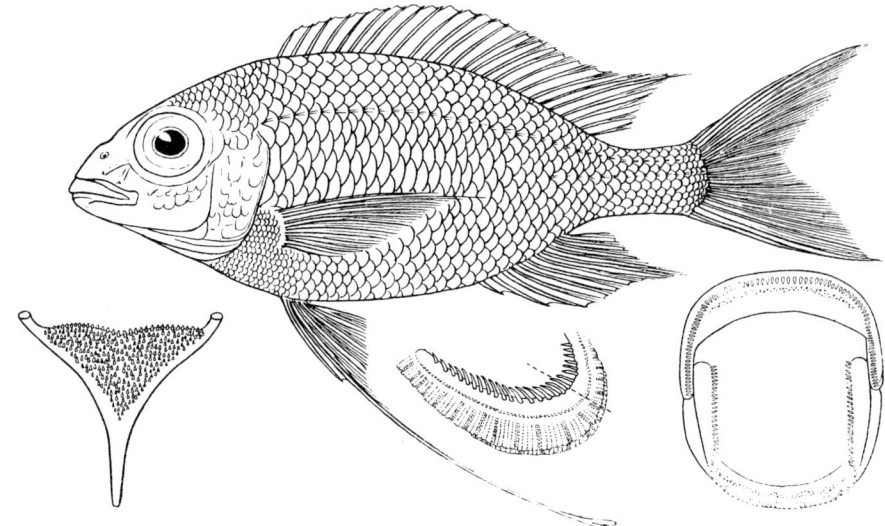

Ophthalmochromis ventralis, lower pharyngeal bone (left), first gill arch (middle), and buccal dentition (right), from Poll, 1957.

serve as dummy eggs, as males and females are never in contact with each other during spawning.

The depth range of *O. nasutus* is approximately between 2 and 15 meters. The species is very common along the rocky slopes. It is difficult to keep alive during acclimatization if they have been bumped around in the slightest way during transport over rough water or bad dirt roads.

Buccal incubation and polygamy are the modes of reproduction.

As an aquarium fish *O. nasutus* will always be rare due to its size and freight costs, unless devoted aquarists succeed in spawning the fish.

Ophthalmochromis ventralis (Boulenger)

The second species of *Ophthalmochromis* has been divided into two geographical subspecies by Dr. M. Poll, of which only *O. ventralis ventralis* has been found on the Burundi coast and southward toward Kigoma in Tanzania. The other subspecies, *O. ventralis heterodontus*, appears to live farther south.

O. ventralis ventralis is a very beautiful mid-sized species of *Ophthalmochromis*, the biggest specimens not exceeding 120 mm at most. The males, like all the species in the genus, have very long

A *Tropheus moorii* about to enter a hole among the rocks. Photo by Glen S. Axelrod.

Another geographical race with the same over-all body pattern as the "Chaitika" is the "Kabeyeye" variety of *Tropheus* with yellow dorsal and anal fins instead of the red and blue fins.

The so-called "rainbow" *Tropheus* recently discovered in the southern part of the lake.

The "Chaitika Cape" variety, also called the "rainbow" *Tropheus*, has an unusually bright body color pattern. The head is raspberry-red with many tiny white or light green dots while the body is bright pale yellow-green with greenish-white stripes.

pelvic filaments, also forked like *O. nasutus,* but the tips are without spatulae (although they are a pale yellow like those of *O. nasutus*). Males in full nuptial gown are a sight to behold: they are steel blue all over the body, including the unpaired fins, and have the most peculiar painting of the top of the head ever seen in any African cichlid. The space between and behind the eyes, the neck and the forehead are covered with an opaque pure white coat which seems to have been painted on the fish. This patch, in strong contrast with the overall deep blue color of the body, makes the fish visible yards away. Swimming in the open as they do, there is little doubt that this unusual color pattern helps attract females to the ripe males. The males not ready for spawning which swim in the midst of the female swarm don't have the white patches on the head.

To get the breeding colors of the male in a color picture has proved impossible with captive fish, unfortunately, as it has with *O. nasutus* and *Cyathopharynx furcifer.*

The problems of acclimatization of *O. ventralis* are as difficult as with *O. nasutus* and compounded by the distance the fish have to travel before they can reach their final destination. They will thus never be a common sight in the Western World unless bred by devoted hobbyists.

Once acclimatized, the fish stand a good chance of surviving for a long time, as they adapt readily to dried flake food. In the lake they live on the floating particles drifting in mid-water, and thus have a better balanced diet than many specialized feeders from the lake.

OPHTHALMOTILAPIA Pellegrin 1904

A single endemic species, *O. boops*

Body: oblong, rather broad
Scales: 62 to 74 in a longitudinal line
Lateral lines: 2
Fins: Dorsal — XII or XIII spines and 14 to 16 rays
　　Anal — III spines and 8-10 rays
　　Ventrals — outer rays with a very long filament reaching to the caudal fin base, forked into a spatula at the tip
　　Caudal — forked and filamentous
Teeth: all tricuspid, in from 3 to 5 rows, except on the side of the jaws where there is only one row of conical teeth
Pharyngeal teeth: very thin, close together in a felt-like cushion
Mouth: terminal

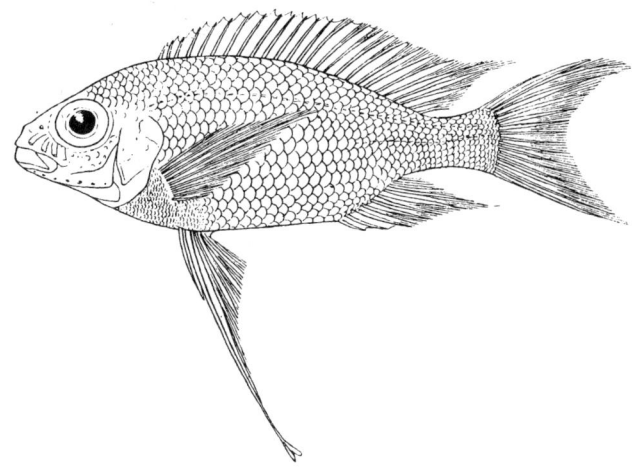

Ophthalmotilapia boops, from Poll, 1957.

Gill rakers: 16 or 17 on lower half of first arch
Habitat: in mid-water over rock floors
Feeding: microorganisms
Reproduction: buccal incubation
Maximum size: about 150 mm
Affinities: with *Ophthalmochromis*, from which it differs by the far larger number of scales and the tricuspid instead of conical teeth in from 3 to 5 rows instead of 2 or 3

ORTHOCHROMIS Greenwood 1954

One endemic species from mountain torrents (*O. malagaraziensis*) and another from the Congo River Basin (*O. polycanthus*).

Body: elongate, progressively tapering toward the tail; *cheeks, chest and sides of chest without any scales*
Scales: ctenoid on the body, small *cycloid scales on the ventral surface* deeply embedded in the skin
Eyes: supralateral, giving a goby-like appearance
Lateral lines: 2, not complete
Fins: Dorsal — XVI-XX spines and 9-12 rays
   Anal — III spines and 8-10 rays
   Ventrals — the fins are rounded with the second and third rays longest
   Caudal — rounded

The juvenile form of the "Chipimbi Cape" *Tropheus* looks very much like the young Kamba Bay *Tropheus*, but the red stripe in the caudal peduncle is already visible.

The fourth variety of *Tropheus* collected by the author in the southern part of the lake is the "Chipimbi Cape" variety, so-called after the cape on the western coast where it was discovered. The color pattern is entirely different from any other *Tropheus* so far found in the lake. It has a bright red stripe on the caudal peduncle.

Among the several new *Tropheus* varieties collected by the author in the southern part of the lake, this one, called the "Kamba Bay" race from the shore where it was found, is especially beautiful with strongly contrasting white or green stripes, orange fins and deep yellow belly.

A fish belonging to the same *Tropheus* variety but with the juvenile and dotted V-V pattern.

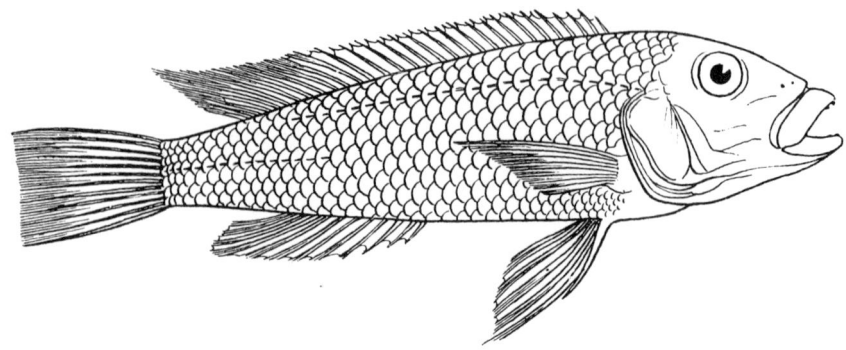

Orthochromis malagaraziensis, from Poll, 1957.

Teeth: outer row primarily bicuspid anteriorly, unicuspid at the side and the back of the jaw
Pharyngeal teeth: small and cuspidate
Mouth: horizontal, with thickened lips
Habitat: mountain torrents flowing into the Malagarazi or Congo River rapids (*O. polyacanthus*)
Feeding: probably omnivorous
Reproduction: not known for *O. malagaraziensis*; *O. polyacanthus* from Kinshasa Regina Falls is a mouthbröoder
Maximum size: about 120 mm for *O. malagaraziensis*; *O. polyacanthus* reaches 150 mm
Affinities:
- with *Haplochromis* from which the genus differs by:
    1) the scaleless cheek and chest, the embedded cycloid ventral scales,
    2) the rounded pelvic fins;
- with *Telmatochromis* from which it differs by having:
    1) undifferentiated outer teeth,
    2) only 3 spines on the anal fin

PERISSODUS Boulenger 1898

One endemic species.

Body: elongated and built for speed
Scales: 65 to 70 very small scales in a longitudinal line

Lateral lines: 2, not complete
Fins: Dorsal — XVIII spines and 11-13 rays
    Anal — III spines and 9-10 rays
    Caudal — forked
Teeth: A single row of a few large teeth that are broad, the crown low and concave, with a small but sharp point on each side; the broad edge of the tooth faces forward; the teeth, as in all scale-eaters of the lake, are buried in the gums at rest
Pharyngeal teeth: scarce, small and pointed
Mouth: strong and powerful
Gill rakers: 18-21 on the lower half of the first arch
Habitat: over rock, usually in mid-water
Feeding: juveniles are omnivorous, grazing on the rock biocover; adults rip scales from other fish, often *Tropheus*; in captivity the fish can get used to dried food
Reproduction: buccal incubation; up to 300 young, one of the biggest broods registered in the lake, even more remarkable taking into account the small size of the fish
Maximum size: approximately 120 mm

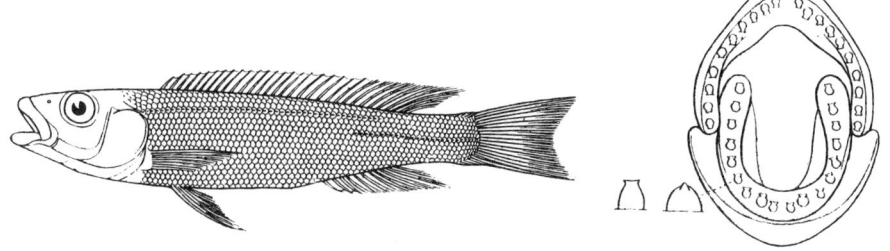

Perissodus microlepis and buccal dentition, from Poll, 1957.

Perissodus microlepis Boulenger

One of the more interesting species in Lake Tanganyika because of its peculiarly predatory diet, *P. microlepis* is a scale-eater and thus not suited for aquarium life.

Torpedo-shaped, not unlike several *Lamprologus*, this species of *Perissodus* lives near the rocky slopes, poised in mid water, waiting to strike at an unwary victim. The author was lucky to observe such swift attacks (which started from four to five yards away) on

This *Xenotilapia* was identified by the author as *X. boulengeri*. The specimen was collected and photographed by Dr. Herbert R. Axelrod during an earlier trip to Lake Tanganyika.

Xenotilapia spilopterus is the latest species of the genus to have been described from the lake. It appears to be restricted to the southern part of the lake.

This *Xenotilapia*, as yet unidentified, seems to be restricted to the northern part of the lake. With a size not exceeding 8 to 9 centimeters and a pale mauve body with bright yellow dorsal fin, it should become a popular aquarium fish.

A closer view of the same fish shown above.

Tropheus moorii. The victim apparently didn't mind much, although scales were ripped off the strong plating of the fish, and with a fast shrug went on whatever chore it was attending to when attacked by *Perissodus*.

This predator can be seen down to at least 15 meters, always solitary, always in mid-water and not near the rock shore. As already mentioned, both parents look after the fry, which is unusual with mouthbrooders from the lake, and like to release their offspring periodically on top of a high stone among the rubble. When this happens their behavior is similar to the typical substratum breeders, but the periods when the fry are free-swimming are probably much shorter than the time spent in their parent's mouth. It has not been possible by observation to note if both parents take the fry in their mouth or only the mother.

PETROCHROMIS Boulenger 1898

Five endemic species.

Body: stocky, rather broad; head large, blunt
Scales: 32 to 36 in a longitudinal line
Lateral lines: 2, the upper complete
Fins: Dorsal — XVII-XX spines and 8-11 rays
     Anal — III spines and 7-8 rays
     Caudal — rounded

Perissodus microlepis. Photo by Paul V. Loiselle.

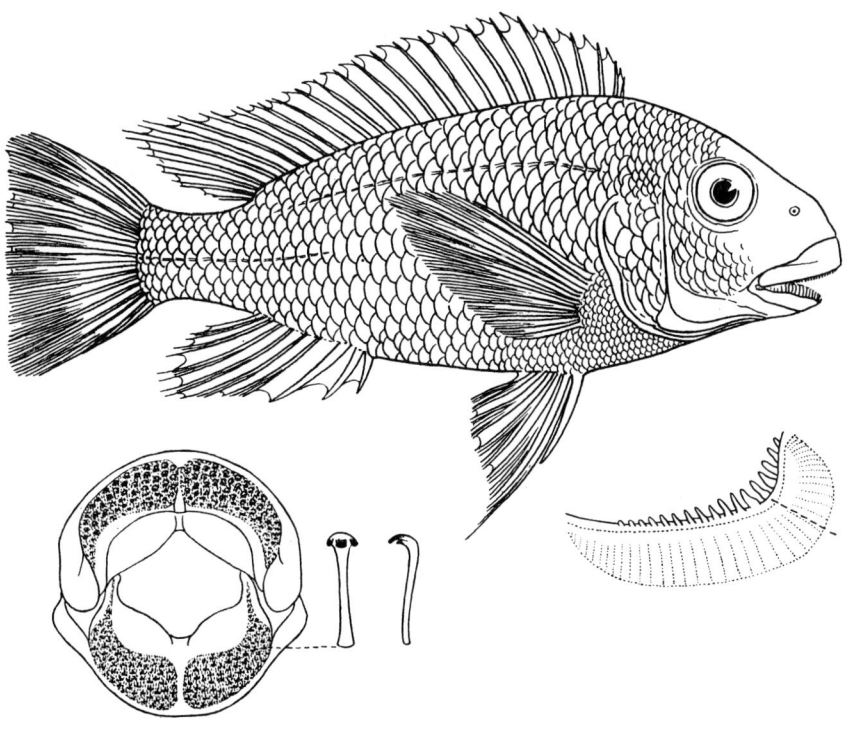

Petrochromis polyodon, buccal dentition (left) and first gill arch (right), from Poll, 1957.

Teeth: tricuspid, on a very long stem and hinged at the base, the crown curved backward; very close together in a wide, brush-like pad

Mouth: very broad and very low, with very thick lips; the lower jaw shorter. The fish curls the lips back when feeding, applies the tooth pads against the rocks and scrapes the rock clean of the overgrowth when it vigorously closes its jaws

Gill rakers: 10 to 16 on the lower half of the first gill arch

Habitat: always over rock

Feeding: rock biocover

Reproduction: buccal incubation; approximately 50 eggs, 5 mm in diameter, per spawn

Maximum size: about 200 mm

The species of *Petrochromis* are difficult to tell apart by their counts and proportions. These numbers and averages of all the

Like many sand-dwelling cichlids in the lake *Xenotilapia ochrogenys ochrogenys* is one of the most strikingly colored, but a very delicate fish to handle when collected.

Close-up of the head region of *Xenotilapia ochrogenys ochrogenys*.

Sand-dwelling *Xenotilapia* such as these *X. ochrogenys* blend so well with the sand bottom that they seem not to be there. Photo by Glen S. Axelrod.

Xenotilapia sima is one of the largest and least colorful species of the genus. Noteworthy is the large size of the yellow-rimmed eye which is often the first part of the fish to be seen when it is swimming over the sand.

species are very close and sometimes even overlap. This might be due on one hand to the relatively small quantity of specimens which have been used for the identification of each species and on the other hand to the evolution of the *Petrochromis* species which might not have reached its final stages.

This eventual evolution toward better differentiated species is, in our opinion, apparent:

- in the shape of the mouth, with the lower or the upper jaw protruding;
- in the shape of the pharyngeal bone and its tooth-bearing surface, either triangular or more or less heart-shaped;
- in the trend toward scaleless cheeks
- in the very specific body color patterns of four of the five known species.

Teeth and dental pads, number of gill rakers, number of rays in the dorsal and anal fins, shape of the fins and number of scales in a longitudinal line vary from species to species in narrow limits and tend to overlap.

Key to the Identification of *Petrochromis*

1. Jaws equal, or the upper jaw protruding 2
   Lower jaw protruding; color pattern of several broad bands, alternating light blue and orange-brown, and a large number of orange-brown spots on body and fins ... *P. fasciolatus*
2. 8 or 9 vertical rows of 6 or 7 white dots; dots also on unpaired fins .... *P. trewavasae*
   Without rows of white dots 3
3. Pharyngeal bone more or less triangular in shape, with concave sides; 3 to 5 rows of small scales on cheek; 33 to 35 scales in a longitudinal line; body and fins of a plain deep chocolate color.. *P. polyodon*
   Pharyngeal bone more or less heart-shaped, with lightly convex or rounded sides; 2 to 4 rows of small scales on cheek 4
4. 31 to 33 scales in a longitudinal line; body plain deep chocolate brown; caudal fin lightly checkered .... *P. famula*
   28-31 scales in a longitudinal line; rear corners of pharyngeal bone not protruding from rear side plane; color pattern very striking—head and body to pectoral fins deep chocolate brown, rest of body pale olive green; three white or pearl gray stripes across head, first on nose ...... *P. orthognathus*

Petrochromis fasciolatus. Photo by Wilhelm Hoppe.

Petrochromis is very close to *Tilapia*, from which it differs by the mouth, which has broad bands of teeth on the jaws which are visible when the mouth is closed. All the teeth are very slender with tricuspid crowns. The stems are bent backward, hinged at the base and very irregularly implanted.

This genus has about the same distribution as *Tropheus*, both vertically in respect to its oxygen requirements and with regard to the type of rock substratum the fish live on. However, *Petrochromis* are also found around rubble in muddy water not far from river estuaries, areas from which *Tropheus* is absent.

All species of *Petrochromis* are highly solitary and are never found in schools or even the ephemeral groupings of *Tropheus*. The most one can discover together wandering among the rubble are two or three males chasing a ripe female, and more often than not this ends in a short but furious fight. Pairs are often discovered among the rubble; as females often wander about with their fry in their mouth, it might be assumed that these pairs are hiding during the actual mating.

Petrochromis are typical grazers on the rock biocover, on which they apply their extendable thick lips and maxillary tooth pads before vigorously closing the mouth. A few bites like this and

A pair of *Xenotilapia longispinnis* either spawning or showing aggression towards each other. Photo by Glen S. Axelrod.

Another view of the same fishes above a flat-topped boulder. Photo by Glen S. Axelrod.

Xenotilapia melanogenys is one of the those species which is not exported due to losses during acclimatization. Photo by Aaron Norman.

Xenotilapia longispinis longispinis can reach a maximum size of about 16 centimeters. Photo by Glen S. Axelrod.

the rock is scraped clean. As a result *Petrochromis* are among the few lake cichlids considered as plant eaters and thus not very well suited to the regular community tank with its heavy plant growth.

Although not bothersome to other species, even of the same genus, the species fight to the death among themselves. If they cannot be provided with abundant algal growth on the tank sides, and they eat ravenously, they will soon start to graze on the other fishes' sides with devastating results or they will progressively starve to death. As such, *Petrochromis* with their unusual body patterns, but for *P. trewavasae* with its striking chocolate brown body, dotted with a large number of pearly white dots and fins with long flowing filaments, make poor aquarium dwellers and will never become very popular. *P. trewavasae* is an outstanding fish, but needs lots of algae to be kept in good health.

Local races and geographically restricted species are the rule, with the fish in this genus apparently in active evolution; from the southern shores there are at least three species yet to be described.

PLECODUS Boulenger 1898

Four species endemic to the lake.

Body: usually elongate and built for speed, except for *P. straeleni* which is stocky, with a high body and very different behavior and ecology

Scales: 58-78 small cycloid scales in a longitudinal line

Lateral lines: 2, the upper nearly complete

Fins: Dorsal — XVIII-XX spines and 12 to 15 rays
  Anal — III spines and 11 to 13 rays
  Caudal — moderately forked

Teeth: a single row of few large, sometimes uneven teeth shaped like a curved, narrow leaf with a central groove and pointing backward; as with *Perissodus* the teeth are embedded in the gums at rest

Pharyngeal teeth: few and conical, sometimes bicuspid; in several species the teeth are also embedded in a wrinkled skin

Mouth: large and powerful, lips thick

Gill rakers: 18 to 26 on the lower half of the first gill arch

Habitat: P. paradoxus—from shallow to very deep water (220 meters); *P. straeleni*—over rock, off the slopes or floors, very often in association with *Cyphotilapia frontosa*, which it mimics with the same color pattern. All other species of *Plecodus* have been collected over sand floors and probably

share the habitat of *P. paradoxus*
Feeding: scale-eaters preying on other fish
Reproduction: buccal incubation
Maximum size in the wild: in excess of 200 mm except for *P. straeleni*, which probably does not reach more than 160 mm in length, and *P. multidentatus*, which reaches 114 mm

Key to the Identification of the Species of *Plecodus*
(From Dr. M. Poll "Poissons Cichlidae"
Mission Hydrobiographique au Lac Tanganyka. 1946-1947)

1. Body depth included more than 3 times in length; more than 61 scales in a longitudinal line; less than 10-12/22-24 scales in a transverse line; more than 44-46/24-32 scales in the lateral lines 2

   Body depth included 2.5-2.95 times in length; 58 to 61 scales in a longitudinal line; 10-11/22-23 scales in a transverse line; 44-46+2/2+24-32 scales in the lateral lines; dental formula 17-21/15-16; maximum size 160 mm . . . . . *P. straeleni*

2. Less than 33-40/30-35 teeth on the two jaws; more than XVI-XVII spines and 11 or 12 rays in the dorsal fin 3

   33-40/30-35 teeth on the two jaws; D. XVI or XVII, 11-12; A.iii, 10; 69 to 73 scales in a longitudinal line; 7-8/20-22 scales in a transverse line; 56-63/34-46 scales in the lateral lines; maximum size 114 mm . . . . *P. multidentatus*

3. 18-20/12-15 teeth on the two jaws; D. XVIII-XX, 13-15; A. III, 12-13; 68 to 78 scales in a longitudinal line; 7.5-8.5/18.5-20.5 scales in a transverse line; 57-69/39-46 scales in the lateral lines; maximum size, 290 mm . . . . . *P. paradoxus*

   22-37/18-23 teeth on the two jaws; D. XVII-XIX, 11-13; A. III, 10-11; 64 to 67 scales in a longitudinal line; 5-6/16-17 scales in a transverse line; 54-58/36-38 scales in the lateral lines; maximum size 320 mm . . . . *P. elaviae*

This genus shares with *Perissodus* the dubious feature of being composed entirely of scale-eaters. Most species of *Plecodus* are pelagic and thus very hard to observe under water, the schools of these fish moving at will in the vast expanses of the lake often at considerable depths. *Plecodus paradoxus* has been caught down to 250 meters!

Fortunately this species also roams over shallow sand flats or near the rocky shores where it is possible to observe the schools

Polypterus endlicheri with a close-up of the head in the lower photo. Photo by Glen S. Axelrod.

Micralestes stormsi is the smallest of the characins in the lake, living not far from the shores.

Citharinus gibbosus, battered and with a considerable loss of scales, is seen here in the typical position when feeding in the mud.

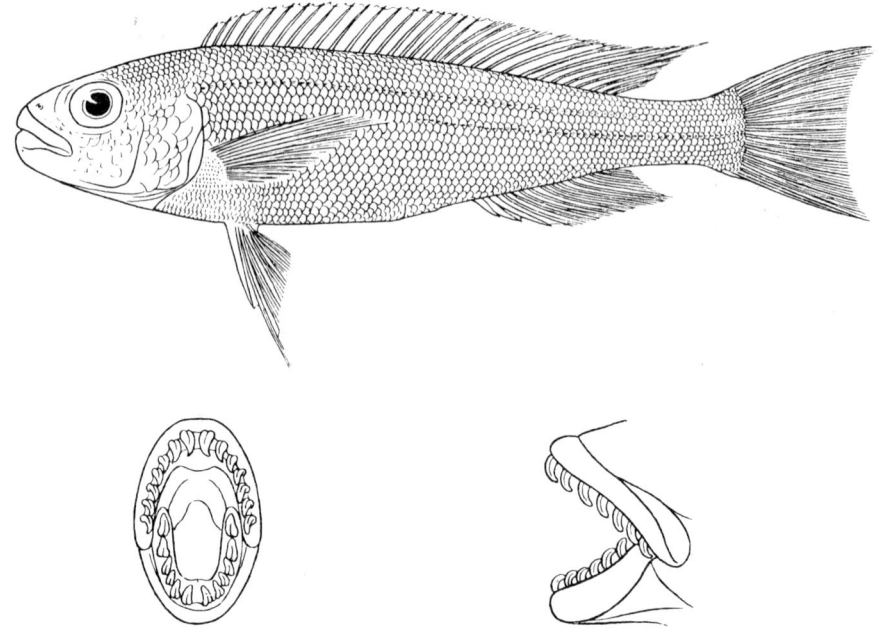

Plecodus paradoxus, frontal view of buccal dentition (left) and lateral view of buccal dentition (right), from Poll, 1957.

passing by. It is seldom that these torpedo-shaped fish stand still. In the poor visibility of shallow sand flats one can see their hazy shapes pass swiftly by, made apparent only by a longitudinal thin black stripe and the black spot on the caudal peduncle. Schools of these fish have been counted whenever possible and often number close to 500 or more individuals.

P. paradoxus was "paradoxical" because of the peculiar shape of its teeth, formed as leaf-shaped blades (with a groove in the middle) lying transversely on a long stem. These teeth, when the mouth is closed, are embedded in very thick gums and protrude from the jaw only when the fish opens its mouth and retracts the gums. By then these formidable hooks are ready to slide between the victim's scales and skin to take the scales off. The scales will be digested, leaving only the cartilaginous tissues, and are stacked like dishes until fully digested.

When brooding, the individual females come close to shore. It is not at all impossible, although it has never been ascertained, that they might release the fry periodically (as does *Perissodus*) under the guard of both parents. *Plecodus paradoxus* fry have been found near the shore in shallow water. As soon as they are released they mix their schools with schools of mid-water species of similar size.

Plecodus straeleni is the second species of *Plecodus* to be found on rocky shores but, contrary to *P. paradoxus*, it is always solitary. Apparently a mouthbrooding female has never been seen by the author's team in five years of diving. The fish most probably lives alone, at least in respect to its own species, because *P. straeleni* as a scale-eater lives near its future victims and as such has shown the only case of mimicry as yet recorded from African fresh waters.

P. straeleni has a color pattern consisting of several broad vertical bands on a lighter background. There are two basic colors which apparently the fish can change at will, the first occurring when the fish is in shallow water over rubble-strewn slopes in broad sunlight among commonly beige or russet fishes (like *Lamprologus brichardi, L. compressiceps, L. modestus, Telmatochromis*, etc.). In that case *P. straeleni* has beige bands on a dirty white background. This camouflage blends very well with the landscape and the fish, mainly *L. brichardi*, near which it is most often found.

When they are found deeper, which is common, it is always near, or even in the middle of, schools of *Cyphotilapia frontosa*. In this case *P. straeleni* bears dark blue vertical bands, of exactly the color of the *C. frontosa* bands, on a pale blue background, again similar to the luminescent body of *C. frontosa*.

As *P. straeleni* has a shape very close to that of young *Cyphotilapia frontosa*, (i.e. a deep body), the victims don't seem to be capable of identifying the intruder and most probably don't even understand why one of them tears their scales off from time to time.

The *P. straeleni* way of swimming, in slow motion or standing still as most *Cyphotilapia* do when undisturbed, makes it most difficult for even a careful diver to identify the fish, and it is only when one has seized *P. straeleni* in his hands that it is possible to tell the predator from its victim. It is an extraordinary case of a predator capable of mimicking not only one but several of its victims. This is not a case where the dim light of the deeper layers might have fooled a diver, as many *P. straeleni* have been brought to the surface along with *Cyphotilapia frontosa*. These still displayed for a day or so afterward a part of the color pattern they had when they were caught.

Distichodus fasciolatus. Photo by Dr. Herbert R. Axelrod.

Distichodus sexfasciatus. Photo by Gerard Meola, African Fish Imports.

Labeo lineatus. Photo by Dr. Herbert R. Axelrod.

One of the most common coastal labeos in the lake, *Labeo cylindricus* is seen occasionally on, and more often in, crevices between sandstone slabs near river estuaries.

SAROTHERODON Ruppell 1854/TILAPIA Smith 1840.

Key to the Identification of the Species of Sarotherodon/Tilapia

The recent subdivision of *Tilapia* into *Sarotherodon* and *Tilapia* according to the presence or absence of buccal incubation has not been taken into account for taxonomic identification.

1. Gill rakers 18 to 27 on lower part of first gill arch; outer teeth bicuspid or tricuspid.................................2

   Gill rakers 7 to 9 on lower part of first gill arch; outer teeth bicuspid and larger than the inner teeth; maximum size 330 mm; non-endemic...................*Tilapia rendalli*

2. Teeth in wide strips tricuspid only (even in front row), or with a few bicuspid teeth 3

   Teeth bicuspid in the front row, tricuspid in the rear, in narrow strips; gill rakers 21 to 27 on lower part of first gill arch; pharyngeal teeth in a felt-like pad, with a sharp angle in front; maximum size 500 mm; non-endemic ....
   ....*Sarotherodon nilotica* var. *eduardiana*

3. Very broad felt-like dental pad; pharyngeal teeth surface also like felt but not pointed in front; gill rakers 18-20 on lower part of first gill arch; snout 2.0-2.8 times longer than eye; maximum size 320 mm; endemic to the Malagarazi River, not in the lake proper beyond the river delta ....
   ....*Sarotherodon karomo*

   Felt-like dental pad not as broad; felt-like surface of pharyngeal teeth heart-shaped and with a point in front; gill rakers 23-27; snout only 1.1. to 2.4 times longer than eye; maximum size 440 mm; endemic to the lake proper ....
   ....*Sarotherodon tanganicae*

S. tanganicae is the only species of *Sarotherodon/Tilapia* found on coastal floors far from river estuaries. It is also the only *Sarotherodon/Tilapia* commonly found over sand and rock and not associated systematically with mud floors in the lake. *S. karomo* is found in the Malagarazi River delta, but is more abundant upstream. *T. rendalli* has a range in the south of the lake basin but has been transplanted for fish-farming purposes into the Ruzizi River valley. This fact explains its presence along the northern

Tilapia rendalli. Photo by Gerhard Marcuse.

Sarotherodon nilotica. Photo by Klaus Paysan.

Barilius ubangensis. Photo by Dr. Jacques Gery.

Phyllonemus typus seen here with its typical black feather-like barbels extended is one of the very few bagrids suited for aquarium life.

Lophiobagrus cyclurus is one of the dwarf bagrids living in rocky shelters and never out in the open. The body exudes a poisonous slime when the fish is threatened. This poison repels fishes and kills them in confined situations (like a pail). The quantity exuded by such a small fish is quite exceptional.

Lophiobagrus cyclurus. Photo by Dr. Herbert R. Axelrod.

shores of Lake Tanganyika but not in the lake proper. It has not been found, as yet, on the western or eastern shores.

S. nilotica is represented along the northern shores by the Lake Edward and Lake Kivu subspecies, *S. nilotica eduardiana*, but has not been discovered in the southern part of the lake.

Another species of *Sarotherodon*, first believed to be *S. nilotica*, was identified from a single specimen in the Malagarazi River delta on the central eastern coast. Other specimens of the species were discovered around the mouth of the Lukuga River outlet where it arrived from the Congo River from the Upemba depression in Zaire. This species is called *S. upembae* Thys van den Audenaerde, 1964, and is not actually a part of the lake fauna.

Of the *Sarotherodon* and *Tilapia* species identified in Lake Tanganyika and its basin, only *S. tanganicae* has been able to colonize the whole length of the lake and can be considered as a true lacustrine species. Many adult schools have been discovered in the south along rocky shores and were seen grazing on the rocks in typical *Tropheus* or *Petrochromis* style.

SIMOCHROMIS Boulenger 1898

Four endemic species.

Body: stocky and broad, with a blunt head
Scales: 30 to 35 in a longitudinal line
Lateral lines: 2, none complete
Fins: Dorsal—XVII to XIX spines and 8 to 11 rays
   Anal — III spines and 6 to 9 rays
   Caudal — two slight lobes
Teeth: one row of bicuspid teeth in front, conical teeth on the side of the jaw, with up to 6 rows of tiny tricuspid teeth behind
Pharyngeal teeth: tiny, more or less bicuspid
Mouth: very inferior, lower jaw shorter, broad
Gill rakers: 5 to 13 on the lower half of the first gill arch
Habitat: rubble in shallows along the shoreline; probably not occurring deeper than 5 meters
Feeding: grazing on rock biocover
Reproduction: buccal incubation, about 40 eggs of 6 mm diameter
Maximum size: *S. diagramma:* about 200 mm; *S. babaulti*, about 110 mm; *S. curvifrons:* about 140 mm
Affinities: with *Tropheus*, from which it differs by: 1) having no

more than III spines in the anal fin, 2) having less than XX spines in the dorsal fin, 3) the number of bicuspid anterior teeth (excluding the conical teeth on the sides of the jaw) averaging always less than 40, except for the largest *S. diagramma* in which the total is more than 40, and 4) the mouth which is rounded or oval and not straight as in *Tropheus*. With *Petrochromis*, from which it differs by: 1) having bicuspid teeth in a row and conical teeth laterally (*Petrochromis* has slender tricuspid teeth on a stem, in pads), 2) by the mouth which is thin and does not have thick lips, and 3) the shape of the head, which is narrow and not broad.

Key to the Identification of the Species of *Simochromis*

1. Gill rakers 10-13 on lower limb of first gill arch 2
   Gill rakers 5-8 on lower limb of first gill arch 3
2. Head with slope slightly convex; 40 (juvenile) to 61 teeth in outer row of upper jaw; total number of rays (spiny and soft) in dorsal fin 27-30 and in anal fin 10-12; 9 to 12 transverse (oblique) stripes on body; maximum size about 200 mm . . . . *S. diagramma*
   Head with a nearly vertical slope; 36 to 41 teeth in outer row of upper jaw; total number of rays (spiny and soft) in dorsal fin 25-28 and in anal fin either 11 or 12; body with vertical stripes; maximum size about 140 mm . . . . *S. curvifrons*
3. Depth 2.55 to 2.95 times in body length; eye 1.35 to 1.7 times in snout length; usually 8 anal rays; a black band reaching to 7th or 8th spine of dorsal fin in the male; maximum size 105 mm . . . . *S. babaulti*
   Depth 2.4 to 2.6 times in body length; eye 1.0-1.3 in snout length; usually 7 anal rays; a continuous black band extending the whole length of dorsal fin; maximum size 90 mm . . .
   . . . . *S. marginatus*

*N.B. Another species discovered on the northeast coast has not been described as yet.

The genus *Simochromis* includes a group of fishes closely related to *Tropheus* in morphology, behavior and habitat. There are, however, some differences. *Simochromis* has only three anal spines, whereas *Tropheus* always has four or more. The number of teeth on the jaws is much smaller in *Simochromis* than in *Tropheus*

Two unidentified *Chrysichthys* species collected and photographed by Dr. Herbert R. Axelrod.

The male and female *Synodontis eurystomus* display the same type of vermiculated pattern on a brown background, but the male's pattern (lower photo) is well-outlined, the body a bit more slender and the white edge of the black fins stronger.

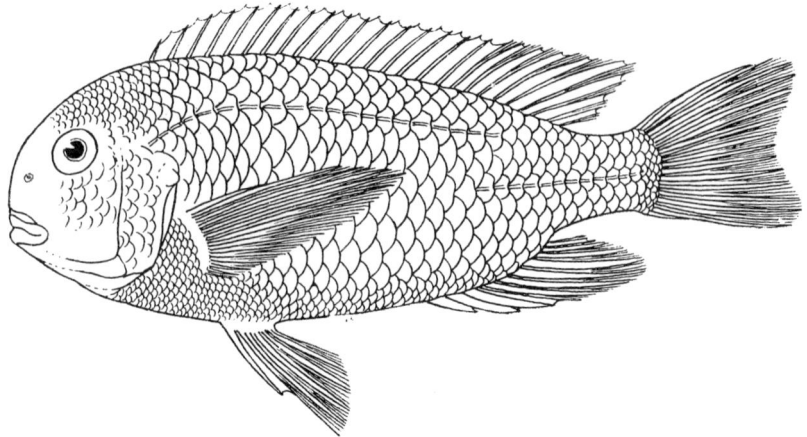

Simochromis curvifrons, from Poll, 1957.

in specimens of the same size. The habitat of *Simochromis* is very shallow water probably not in excess of 5 meters for the deepest living species; *Tropheus* go down to about 15 meters. *Simochromis,* although preferring clear water, are also found on rock rubble in murky water, and the horizontal range of the genus is thus broader than that of *Tropheus.* This might explain why few if any geographical races or varieties of *Simochromis* have been discovered around the lake. Both fishes graze on rock and appear to be unable to live on sand bottoms.

Simochromis diagramma is the largest species of *Simochromis,* reaching over 200 mm in total length. It is also the species of the genus most adaptable to murky water and is thus found everywhere, provided there is rock rubble or boulders. They can be seen darting in and out of the crevices on the shoreline in the surf in groups of three and four, males chasing females. The youngsters avoid the crashing surf and stay a bit deeper in quieter waters.

Simochromis babaulti is probably the shallowest-living *Simochromis,* often being found among rubble and pebbles when the water is quiet in 20 or 30 cm, but a bit deeper where the waves crash. The alternating slate-grey and bright yellow bands of the male and somewhat paler colors of the female, as well as their size—which seldom exceeds 100 mm, would make them attractive aquarium fish if their temper was a bit better. Solitary fish in the wild, they don't accept other fish of their kind and not many other cichlids either!

Breeding the species in captivity is easy, but reports from scientific institutions indicate they tend to show a rapid degeneration after a few generations. As with some of the most typical Lake Tanganyika endemic cichlids, this might be due to a lack of vital minerals or lack of the type of food they find in lake waters which was not duplicated when the fish were raised in captivity.

Simochromis curvifrons as yet has seldom been found in the northernmost part of the lake. I was believed recently, by some research people, that this fish might be a *Tropheus*, but the most recent data available tend to suggest that *S. curvifrons* should be placed in a separate genus.

Simochromis marginatus has not been found on the northern shore.

SPATHODUS Boulenger, 1900

Two endemic species.

Body: stocky and short; no vertical bands; two or three rows of blue dots on the body (*S. erythrodon*) or none at all (*S. marlieri*); head of *S. marlieri* with a hump extending to between the eyes

Scales: 30 or 31 in a longitudinal line

Lateral lines: 2, not complete

Fins: Dorsal — XXI to XXV spines and 4-8 rays
Anal — III spines and 6 or 7 soft rays
Caudal — rounded

Teeth: a single row of unevenly sized large and long teeth, with a rounded brown crown; typical set of teeth for a "picker" from the rocks

Pharyngeal teeth: small, thin, subconical and uniform in size

Mouth: contrary to *Eretmodus*, the head is not blunt but is rather pointed, and the mouth is narrow and terminal rather than low

Gill rakers: 12 or 13 on the lower half of the first gill arch

Habitat: *S. erythrodon* is found at the very edge of the pebble or rubble shoreline; *S. marlieri* lives deeper, to about 2 meters

Feeding: picking microorganisms from the rock biocover

Reproduction: buccal incubation

Maximum size in the wild: *S. erythrodon*: not more than 70 mm;

Positive identifications of some synodontids can only be established by examination of teeth and proportional measurements. Shown are two views of *Synodontis petricola*. Photos by Dr. Herbert R. Axelrod.

As *Synodontis multipunctatus* grows larger, it also becomes darker. This specimen is about 18 centimeters long.

Young *Synodontis multipunctatus* are lighter in color than the adults. The few irregular spots in this specimen (3 centimeters long) will increase in number and the very pale yellow colored body will become copper colored with age.

S. marlieri: about 100 mm

Affinities: with *Eretmodus* and *Tanganicodus*, from which it differs by: 1) the body lacking stripes, and 2) the teeth, which are very long, in a single row and with a blunt tip.

Spathodus erythrodon Boulenger

This genus, composed of two species, is very close to *Eretmodus* and *Tanganicodus* and shares the same type of habitat, the shoreline strewn with pebbles and small rubble, where it darts from rock to rock between crashing waves. Even more than the two other genera, *Spathodus erythrodon* lives in very shallow water. We have never discovered any specimen deeper than one meter. Most are seen in less than a foot of water. *S. erythrodon* in the lake is a little jewel; the body is a rosy pink with mauve, blue or green dots on the head and body depending on the light. It is unfortunate that the fish loses some, but not much, of its basic rosy body color in a tank to become a beige-brown. Although known to reach the same maximum size as *Eretmodus*, most *Spathodus erythrodon* are much smaller, seldom exceeding 50 mm in total length.

They are peaceful companions in a tank and are not afraid to wander about in the open, as they are used to living in open sunlight in the wild. They are not choosy about their diet and will thrive on dried flakes although, as rock pickers, brine shrimp, frozen or alive, would be a welcome addition for their well being.

Spathodus marlieri Poll

This fish has been discovered and exported lately from the southernmost part of the Burundi coast in the northern part of the

Spathodus erythrodon and buccal dentition, from Poll, 1957.

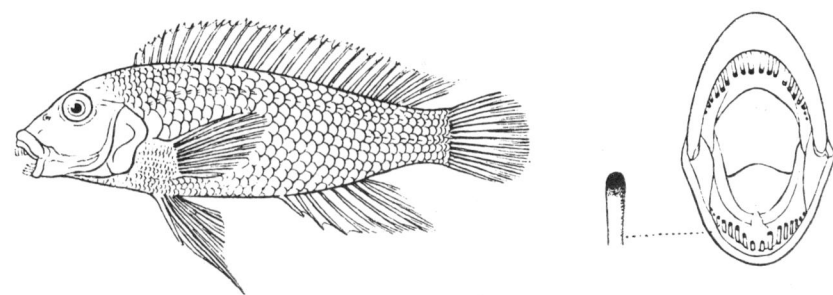

lake near the Tanzanian border.

The behavior of this species is quite different from that of *S. erythrodon*. *S. marlieri* can be seen swimming over the rock bottom for long distances, alone or in pairs, instead of jumping from place to place between the pebbles as *S. erythrodon* does. *S. marlieri* is larger and averages between 60 and 80 mm in length. In the lake the basic color is nearly black with a few green spots on the head and none at all on the body. The temper of the fish is awful toward its own kind and not very good toward other fishes. As such it will never become one of the aquarium favorites.

Although geographical races have not as yet been discovered among the *Spathodus*, it is remarkable how, on the northeastern coast, their populations are restricted to a few bays instead of being spread out along the pebble coastline (as in *Eretmodus*). Along the first 40 km from north to south on the east coast only one bay shelters *Spathodus erythrodon*, and not a single specimen has been found in the other bays and coves, although *Eretmodus* has been discovered in large numbers along the entire coastline. The fact that not a single *S. marlieri* has ever been found along the same stretch might be explained by the long sand beaches separating the southernmost rocky coast of Burundi, where it lives, from the northern habitat.

TANGANICODUS Poll 1950

One endemic species.

Body: stocky and short, with vertical stripes only on the lower half of the body, a black dot at midlength along the base of the dorsal, blue stripes and spots on the head and blue spots in two rows on the upper half of the body and dorsal fin; head rather pointed, but a bit less than in *Spathodus*.

Scales: 30 to 32 in a longitudinal line

Lateral lines: 2, the upper complete

Fins: Dorsal — XXIII or XXIV spines and 4 or 5 rays
Anal — III spines and 7 rays
Caudal — rounded

Teeth: very long and tusk-like with pointed tips; irregular in size, the largest in front, in a single row

Pharyngeal teeth: subconical or bicuspid, the largest at the back of the bone

Mouth: rather narrow, but less so than in *Spathodus*

Synodontis species. Photo by Dr. Herbert R. Axelrod.

In the wild *Chiloglanis* is an efficient and powerful algae scraper. It could starve in captivity because a strong algal cover is missing in a tank. Photo by Aaron Norman.

This picture of an *Amphilius platychir* on its back shows the shape and size of the pectoral and pelvic fins; the first ray is thick and rubbery so that the fish can hold tightly to the rocks in fast-flowing torrents.

Heterobranchus longifilis, a catfish that grows to gigantic size in the lake. Photo by Dr. Eugene Balon.

Gill rakers: 11 or 12 on the lower half of the first gill arch
Habitat: very close to the shoreline in shallow water, over rocks in the rubble
Feeding: on rock biocover
Reproduction: buccal incubation
Maximum size: about 70 mm
Affinities: with *Eretmodus*, from which it differs by the following: 1) tusk-like teeth in a single row, 2) body striped only on the lower half, with 2 rows of blue dots on the upper half and a black spot on the dorsal, 3) mouth narrow and not broadened terminally, and 4) head without the long snout so typical of *Eretmodus*. With *Spathodus*, from which it differs by the following: 1) teeth not arranged in sets and not blunt, and (2) color pattern having half stripes on the body and the black spot which *Spathodus* lacks.

Tanganicodus irsacae Poll

Tanganicodus irsacae is, along with *Eretmodus cyanostictus* and *Spathodus erythrodon*, one of these queer surf-dwellers, spending their lives among the pebbles on the very shoreline. The three genera have been separated because of the very peculiar nature and setting of their teeth, which are constructed to pick edible matter, mainly tiny crustaceans that are attached to the rocks. They are thus not grazers as their teeth are used mainly as tweezers. In appearance *Tanganicodus* shares the stocky and

Tanganicodus irsacae and buccal dentition, from Poll, 1957.

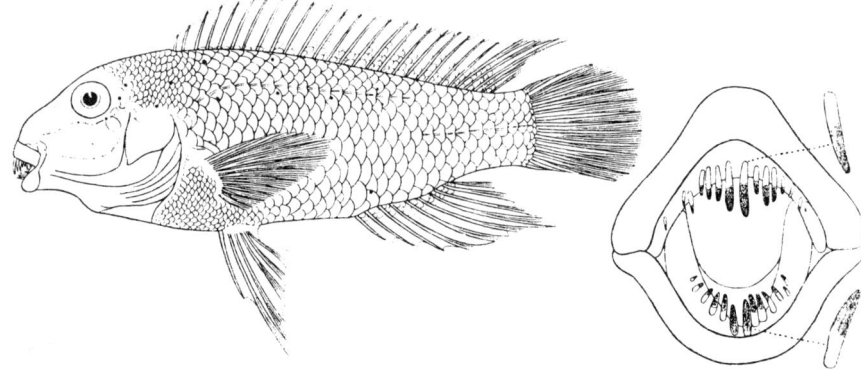

heavy body of its cousins, which need all their muscles to resist the tear and push of the breakers. These fish live in the oxygen saturated surf, and it is probably because of this that they are unable to descend into calmer layers, where they would suffocate.

As for the color pattern, *Tanganicodus* is halfway between *Eretmodus* and *Spathodus*. Only the lower half of the body has the vertical stripes of *Eretmodus*, upper half being a plain beige but with the upper rows of blue-green dots of *Spathodus*. A conspicuous black spot at the middle of the dorsal fin base as well as the yellow and pink crisscrossing pattern on the unpaired fins make identification of the species easy.

Much rarer than *Eretmodus* or *Spathodus erythrodon*, *Tanganicodus* has never reached the hobby's tanks in large numbers. The behavior of the fish, its size, which is seldom over 6 cm, the ease with which it adapts to prepared foods, its peaceful disposition and, needless to say, its colorful garb should help make *Tanganicodus* one of the most popular African dwarf cichlids in the aquarium world.

Breeding is by buccal incubation as with the other species of surf-dwellers.

TELMATOCHROMIS Boulenger 1898

Five endemic species.

Body: elongate to very elongate, with the occipital crest becoming a slight hump; diagonal stripes on the body; two species, *T. bifrenatus* and *T. vittatus*, are very slender fish

Scales: 31 to 37 in a longitudinal line, very denticulate

Lateral lines: 2, not complete

Fins: Dorsal — XVIII to XXII spines and 6 to 10 rays
Anal — V to VIII spines and 5 to 8 rays
Ventral — long
Caudal — rounded
All unpaired fins are usually tipped by a filament

Teeth: outer teeth always conical, often including from 6 to 8 canines; inner rows made up of small tricuspid teeth

Pharyngeal teeth: conical or subconical

Gill rakers: 3 to 9 (*T. vittatus* and *T. bifrenatus* have 3-4)

Habitat: always rock; although *T. vittatus* and *T. bifrenatus* are always in very clear water, the other three might be found on rocks in muddy water

Feeding: microorganisms, omnivorous

Malapterurus electricus, the electric catfish. Photo by Dr. Herbert R. Axelrod.

Front view of *Malapterurus electricus*. Photo by Gerhard Marcuse.

Perhaps the most beautiful fish in the lake and the whole of Africa, *Lamprichthys tanganicanus* is also one of the most delicate to handle, which explains why it is seldom seen in a tank. New acclimatization methods make it likely that they will soon be available in larger numbers.

This picture clearly shows the beautiful pattern of *Lamprichthys tanganicanus*. Photo by Dr. Herbert R. Axelrod.

Reproduction: no buccal incubation

Maximum size in the wild: *T. vittatus* and *T. bifrenatus* reach 60 mm; the other species of *Telmatochromis* are about 120 mm

Key to the Identification of the Species of *Telmatochromis*

1. Body depth included less than 4 times in standard length; head included less than 3.35 times in body length 2

   Body depth included more than 4 times in standard length; head length included more than 3.35 times in body length 4

2. Teeth of inner rows all tricuspid 3

   Teeth of inner rows increasingly conical with their distances from outer edge of jaw; 5-10/4-10 canine teeth; oblique stripes on sides, more visible on hind part of body; maximum size 120 mm .... *T. caninus*

3. 7-20/7-21 canines in front of jaws; without oblique stripes; maximum size 100 mm .... *T. temporalis*

   6/6 canines in front of jaw; 2 long horizontal stripes; maximum size 51 mm .... *T. burgeoni*

4. Body depth included 4.3 to 4.4 times in standard length; head included 3.7 to 4.0 times in body length; eye included 4.55 to 4.65 times in head length; 12-15/12-13 canines in front of jaw; 2 black horizontal stripes along sides of body, upper at base of dorsal fin; maximum size 86 mm .... *T. vittatus*

   Body depth included 5.3 to 5.7 times in standard length; head included 3.35 to 3.65 in body length; eye 3.9 to 4.0 times in head length; 8-10/6-8 canines in front of jaw; body with 2 horizontal stripes; maximum size 53 mm(?) ... *T. bifrenatus*

The genus *Telmatochromis* is very close to *Lamprologus* and *Julidochromis*, two other egg-laying groups of cichlids from the lake, and like them have several powerful canines on each jaw and a relatively high number of anal spines. Two of the five species appear to have developed a strict bond toward a certain type of rocky habitat in very pure lake water, whereas the other species, *T. caninus*, *T. temporalis* and *T. burgeoni*, have been discovered over many types of rock substrates even in very muddy water and are, in fact, among the most common and ubiquitous fishes of the lake.

Telmatochromis temporalis and *Telmatochromis caninus*

Telmatochromis caninus. Photo by Dr. Herbert R. Axelrod.

were among the first fish to be exported from the lake a few years back and both are now established as regular aquarium cichlids. Both species have been bred without much problem. As in their native habitat, the fishes are not light shy and swim in the open. Because of their behavior in the lake, where they might prey upon small fishes, they should not be trusted with much smaller fishes in the aquarium.

Telmatochromis bifrenatus and *T. vittatus* are so different from these other two species that it is with reluctance that one accepts their grouping under the same generic name. Both fish live in rather deep water for such small species, specimens having been found as deep as 20 meters, although they seem to prefer a range between 5 and 10 m. Although most of the time specimens are discovered wandering in the open close to the rocks or over coarse sand between rock patches, they never assemble in schools, even small ones. The fish, although often very close to neighbors, lead solitary lives. When in danger they will seek shelter between the piled-up rubble or in the tiniest hole wide enough for them to enter.

The metallic sheen on the body of *Aplocheilichthys pumilum* is retained by the fish even while in captivity. Photo by Dr. Herbert R. Axelrod.

Aplocheilichthys pumilum is a typical swamp fish of eastern Central Africa, never found in the lake proper.

Lates mariae, juvenile. Photo by Dr. Herbert R. Axelrod.

Lates angustifrons: note the rounded tail. Photo by Dr. Herbert R. Axelrod.

Telmatochromis bifrenatus. Photo by Paul V. Loiselle.

It is also in these miniature caves that they will mate and rear their young. In the danger-strewn world they live in, amidst countless enemies, the fry don't wander into the open until they are capable of fast escape. Not before they are at least 15 mm long can one discover them along with mature fish.

As dwarf aquarium fish, it is difficult to imagine a better pair than *T. bifrenatus* and *T. vittatus.* With a maximum size of about 60 mm, their elegant and slender shapes not unlike that of *Julidochromis* and the ease with which they adapt to aquarium life, not hiding but swimming in the open and readily accepting most types of commercial food, one might say that they have everything going for them. It is unfortunate that after a few spawnings the original striking color pattern, with its two longitudinal black stripes on a very pale beige background, tends to become dull and much less appealing.

TREMATOCARA Boulenger 1899

Eight endemic species.

Body: moderately elongate
Scales: 27 to 31 cycloid scales in a longitudinal line
Lateral line: only one, the upper, which is reduced to a few tubes
Fins: Dorsal — VII-XII spines and 10 to 13 rays

Anal — III spines and 8 to 11 rays (rays longer than spines)
Ventral — long
Caudal — forked
Pectoral — large

Teeth: very minute; conical, in a single narrow band

Pharyngeal teeth: subconical, conical, bicuspid; in some species the central posterior teeth are rather molar-like

Mouth: terminal; *the bones of the head* (nasal, frontal, pre- and suborbitals, preopercle and mandible) *with rows of excavations*, separated by narrow bridges, *and covered by a thin skin*

Gill rakers: 9-25 on the lower half of the first gill arch

Habitat: deep, along the coast line, sometimes to 200 meters. All the species seem to tend toward a nyctemeral vertical migration, ascending at night into shallower waters

Feeding: microorganisms

Trematocara unimaculatum and head (upper left), heads of *T. nigrifrons* (lower left), *T. marginatum* (upper right) and *T. stigmatum* (lower right), from Poll, 1957.

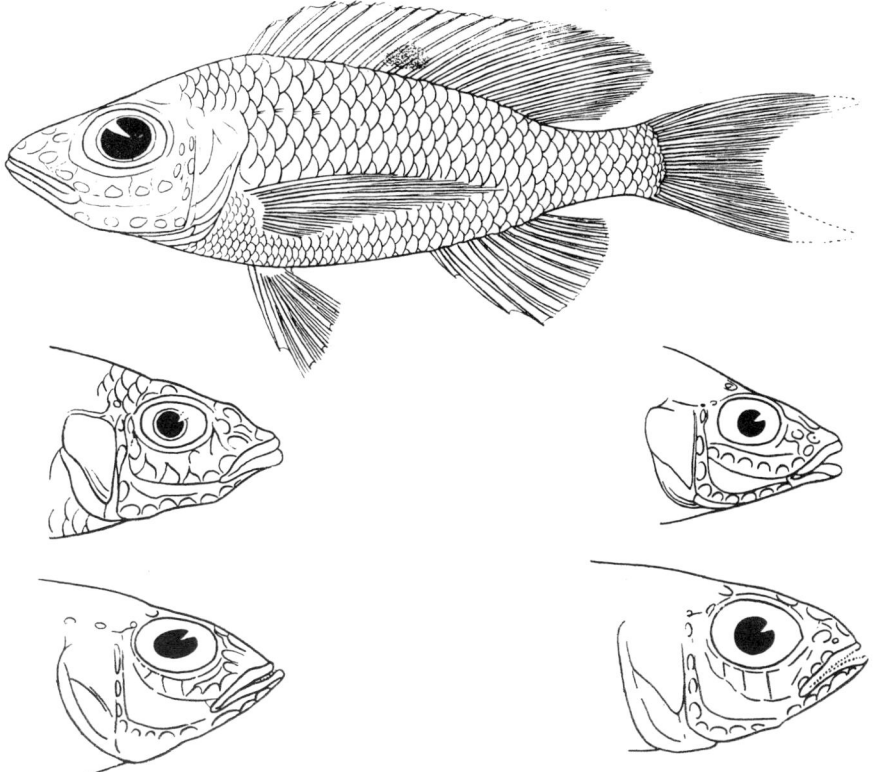

Lates microlepis (juvenile): note the truncated or straight tail. A close-up of the head is shown below. Photos by Glen S. Axelrod.

The easternmost *Ctenopoma* of Central Africa is *C. muriei* which is not a lake-dweller but lives in swamps nearby. The shape is very similar to that of *C. davidae*, but the black dots on the brown body are typical of the species.

One of the most common and largest of the spiny eels in the lake, *Mastacembelus flavidus*, lives among the rubble and rock crevices.

Reproduction: nothing is known of their behavior except for the fact that captures commonly involve many specimens

Maximum size in the wild: depending on species, from 50 mm to 150 mm

Key to the Identification of the Species of *Trematocara*

1. 15 to 25 gill rakers on lower part of first gill arch; 3 to 9 sensory organs on pre- and suborbital bones; caudal peduncle 1.35-2 times longer than high 2
   9 to 12 gill rakers on lower part of first gill arch; 8 (seldom 9) sensory organs on pre- and suborbital bones; jaws equal and lips rather thick; dorsal fin edged with black stripe along its entire length; maximum size 100 mm ...... *T. marginatum*
2. Body depth included 3.0-4.2 times in body length; head length included 2.5 to 3.0 times in standard length; 3 to 9 sensory organs on pre- and suborbital bones (except in *T. variabile*, which has only 5 sensory organs but on the other hand has 15-17 gill rakers) 3
   Body depth included 3.7-4.1 times in standard length; head length included 2.75-3.0 times in standard length; 5 hypertrophied sensory organs; lower jaw protruding; a typical black spot on chin, more visible in female; 17 to 21 gill rakers on lower part of first gill arch; maximum size 115 mm .... *T. nigrifrons*
3. Minimum of 4 sensory organs on pre- and suborbital bone 4
   Only 3 sensory organs; caudal peduncle very narrow, twice as long as high; body depth included 3.8 to 4.2 times in standard length; an elongate black spot at front of spiny dorsal; maximum size 68 mm .... *T. kufferathi*
4. A full row of 8 or 9 hypertrophied sensory organs 5
   An incomplete row of 4 to 7 hypertrophied sensory organs 6
5. Body depth included 3.0 to 3.25 times in body length; eye included 2.5-3.0 times in head length; maxillary not reaching to middle of eye; teeth not set on external part of lips; dorsal fin with median spot; maximum size 150 mm ....
   .... *T. unimaculatum*
   Body depth included 4.1 to 4.2 times in body length; eye included 3.5 times in head length; maxillary reaching middle of eye; teeth set in part on external part of lips; dorsal fin without anterior black spot; maximum size 45 mm ....
   .... *T. macrostoma*

6. Only 4 hypertrophied sensory organs on pre- and suborbital bones 7

   5 to 7 hypertrophied sensory organs on the pre- and suborbital bones; body depth included 3.4 to 4.1 times in body length; 15 to 17 gill rakers on lower part of first gill arch; black spot on anterior part of dorsal fin; maximum size 87 mm .... *T. variabile*

7. Eye oval, included 2.65 to 2.95 times in head length; 15 to 20 gill rakers; dorsal edged with black band in anterior part of fin; maximum size 75 mm .... *T. stigmaticum*

   Eye round and very large, included 2.3 to 2.65 times in head length; 21 to 25 gill rakers; dorsal with broad black band at mid-height; maximum size 67 mm .... *T. caparti*

TRIGLACHROMIS Poll & Thys van den Audenaerde 1974

A single species.

Body: elongate

Scales: absent from in front of the ventral fins, as well as around the base of the pectorals; 35 to 37 on a longitudinal line; oblique, alternate rows of pearly scales on the body

Lateral lines: 2, the upper complete

Fins: Dorsal — XV or XVI spines, each tipped with a soft filament, and 8 to 10 rays

Anal — III spines and 7 or 8 rays

Ventrals — first rays with a filament

Pectorals — *lower rays free from the fin;* the next rays partially welded into the fin

Caudal — rounded, not forked as in *Limnochromis*

Teeth: conical, in 2 or 3 rows, the outer row well apart from the next row and with much larger and rather horizontal teeth

Pharyngeal bone: very small rather bicuspid teeth

Mouth: low, horizontal and broad

Gill rakers: 12 to 14

Habitat: typical mud-dweller, coastal, from shallow to rather deep water

Feeding in the wild: diatoms and microorganisms, but also omnivorous

Reproduction: the breeding mode is unknown; buccal incubation has not been reported

Maximum size in the wild: not in excess of 100 mm

A *Mastacembelus plagiostomus* slides into the open in quest of food. More often they poke their head from a crevice, like a moray eel does, to snap at fish passing by. Photo by Thierry Brichard.

Crescent-shaped stripes are characteristic of *Mastacembelus ellipsifer*. Photo by Thierry Brichard.

A young *Mastacembelus moorii* displays a vermiculated pattern, a deep brown network on a beige background. The body is muscular when compared to that of *M. tanganicae* and *M. ophidium*. It is the largest of all African eels.

The ferocious-looking head of *Mastacembelus ophidium*, like a viper's head, makes the fish recognizable.

In contrast with many other eels from the lake, the head of *Mastacembelus ophidium* is broader than the slender body.

Triglachromis otostigma. Photo by Dr. Herbert R. Axelrod.

Triglachromis otostigma (Regan)

It is quite by accident that in 1972 the author, while experimenting with new packing tranquilizers for this fish, discovered the very unusual feature which led Pr. Thys van den Audenaerde to separate *T. otostigma* from *Limnochromis*.

T. otostimga has the lowest rays of the pectoral fin separate from the other rays of the fin and not bound together by a membrane. These independent rays can be bent down by the fish, and it is possible, although it hasn't been proved, that they might act as feelers when the fish, in its very muddy habitat, has very poor visibility. Unless I am mistaken, it is the only case of separate pectoral rays reported from African freshwater fishes.

One of the staple fish to come from Lake Tanganyika to the aquarium world, *T. otostigma* has never been a problem as far as acclimatization is concerned. It is more surprising that, at least to the author's knowledge, there have been no reports of breeding the fish in captivity.

T. otostigma is again one of those unusual Lake Tanganyika cichlids with much less color than many of the better known varieties of Lake Malawi, but with body color patterns not often found anywhere else. The appeal of the fish depends on its metallic copper background with contrasting oblique golden stripes; this pattern is strongly enhanced by the white paired fins and the black edge on the tail.

Much smaller than most Rift Valley cichlids, *Triglachromis otostigma* is a good community tank fish provided, as with all cichlids, that its companions are of comparable size.

TROPHEUS Boulenger 1898

Three endemic species and several local races.

Body: deep in front, tapering off toward the tail; head blunt and broad; body stocky and broad

Scales: denticulate, 31 to 32 in a longitudinal line

Lateral lines: 2, neither complete

Fins: Dorsal — XX or XXI spines, 5 or 6 rays
  Anal — IV to VI spines, 5 to 7 rays
  Ventrals — with short filament
  Caudal — truncated, slightly forked
  Pectorals — long

Teeth: an outer row of bicuspid teeth with a continuous cutting edge; the sides of the premaxillary bone with strong, curved conical teeth

Pharyngeal teeth: more or less bicuspid, thin and compressed

Mouth: very low, very straight and transverse

Gill rakers: 11 or 12 on the lower half of the first gill arch

Habitat: restricted to rocky slopes with a heavy biocover; to 15 m deep

Feeding: typical rock-grazer

Reproduction: buccal incubation; about a dozen eggs (maximum number of eggs in a wild caught specimen 14), 7 mm in diameter

Maximum size in the wild: T. moorii : 145 mm; *T. duboisi:* about 100 mm. *T. brichardi:* unknown

Affinities: with *Simochromis,* from which it differs by having: 1) more than 3 anal spines; 2) never less than 20 spines in the dorsal fin; and 3) a deeper habitat, never in muddy water

As of this writing, three different species of *Tropheus,* each with several local varieties (some of them probably deserving subspecific status), have been discovered over a distance of about one-fourth of the total lake shoreline. It thus appears that the most famous genus of Tanganyika cichlids has not yet wound up surpris-

One of the best spiny eels for the aquarium from the lake is *Mastacembelus tanganicae*, seen here against a background of some plants.

A *Mastacembelus* slithering close to the walls of a rock in the lake. Photo by Glen S. Axelrod.

ing us with a seemingly inexhaustible supply of unusual color morphs. Perhaps, after the full inventory has been completed, in the years to come the genus itself will have to be split.

Aside from *T. duboisi*, of which two new local races have been discovered on the eastern coast, the northern type, *T. moorii* has been known since Pr. Marlier's work to have at least 4 geographical races. One of them, the orange, is the only *Tropheus* as yet to present multiple variations, including marbled specimens, in body pattern of the same population.

The eastern *Tropheus*, whose type was first discovered in Nyanza Lac, Burundi, and now has been described as *T. brichardi*, is represented by at least two other geographical races. Some southeastern populations might belong to this group also. The southern type includes at least one deep brown "type" with a red stripe on the caudal peduncle, which includes 6 races, and one rainbow "type" on both sides of the Lufubu River confluent with the lake toward Mpulunou, with 3 races.

All species of *Tropheus* share common traits such as strong individualism and a restricted habitat, both in vertical range and type of substrate (which has to be heavily covered with the indispensable biocover). This means that the rocks have to be stable and therefore cannot be small pebbles or small enough to go rolling over the slopes. There must be hiding places among the rubble between which the fish can wander. *Tropheus* species do not live in caves, but in the open close to the floor. Because of the available food, populations of *Tropheus* might be dense, giving an impression of schooling, but in fact these groups are ephemeral, disbanding progressively, without any bond between the members of the group other than the chasing of a female.

Kept in tanks, *Tropheus* very strongly resent the presence of their own kind and, unless their quarters are very roomy, will fight until only one is left. One can artificially overcome this individualism by putting together two dozen or more *Tropheus* in a very small aquarium. The crowd will inhibit their combative mood. The eastern type is far more intolerant of its own kind than the northern type and thus even more solitary.

It has been said from tank observations that *Tropheus* is somewhat territorial. This is not born out by multiple underwater observations in the lake. A *Tropheus* tank should be a very large tank with few individuals and many hiding places in it, and it still is a poor duplicate of the rocky lake habitats. Therefore one cannot talk with authority about territorial behavior of the genus from observations in captivity.

It has been said that *Tropheus moorii* doesn't penetrate as deep as *T. duboisi*. It is true, as with most mouthbrooders, especially the rock-grazers, that the habitat of both species of *Tropheus* doesn't exceed 15 meters. Pr. Marlier stated than on the northwestern coast *T. moorii* didn't go deeper than 10 meters. By checking with a depthmeter we found them, although in much reduced numbers and only very large specimens, still swimming complacently at 15 meters.

It is probable that their vertical range is not limited by oxygen levels, which at such a depth on current washed shores are still high, but probably because of the scarcity of the type of diet they prefer, which may not be found in the deeper layers.

As several local populations have been found quite far apart, with signs of a long separate evolution, it might indicate that *T. duboisi* is the offspring of an already remote common ancestor shared with *T. moorii* instead of being the result of a relatively recent mutation. This species has proven, contrary to *T. moorii*, to be rather delicate and hard to acclimatize in tanks. Needless to say,

A trio of young *Tropheus duboisi.* Note the developing body stripe on the uppermost fish. Photo by Wilhelm Hoppe.

Fighting *Tropheus moorii*. Photo by Wilhelm Hoppe.

T. duboisi is probably the most striking *aquarium* fish to have come from the lake in recent years, but only as a juvenile. When it reaches adulthood the fish unfortunately looses its striking white dots and often even the white vertical stripe in the middle of the body. Only the new broad banded variety coming from south of the Malagarazi keeps a very striking attire as an adult, with its half yellow, half pure white band on the dark blue body.

The Nyanza Lac type *Tropheus* is probably the *Tropheus* with the most pronounced differences with *Simochromis*. It has the highest number of anal spines, the broadest head and the largest number of teeth. This type is equally interesting because it shows a trend, as yet undetected in the other species of *Tropheus* except when very young, to be banded. The Nyanza Lac type shows a remarkable variety of color morphs on the grounds where it was first collected, and it is not rare to see three or four morphs at the same time. The most typical has an oval olive-green, grass-green or lemon-yellow spot on the back toward the end of the dorsal on a chocolate brown background. The eye is of the same color as the oval spot. Other forms are banded, alternating grass-green and chocolate or bright yellow with orange-brown bands. Some specimens are all chocolate.

A few hundred meters away, further down the coast, the color pattern might again be different, such as broad deep brown bands alternating with emerald green stripes that are broader on the back.

These color morphs are seen only during underwater observations and never come back when the fish are kept in tanks. This is why, with such a shy fish, no satisfactory picture of these color morphs was taken successfully in the aquarium.

TYLOCHROMIS Regan 1920

One endemic species in the lake (*T. polylepis*), five others in the Congo Basin.

Body: deep and narrow, laterally compressed, the head large and deep, the body tapering off strongly toward the caudal peduncle

Scales: 32-60 in a longitudinal line

Lateral lines: 2, both complete

Fins: Dorsal — XIV-XVI spines and 13-15 rays
   Anal — III spines and 7-9 rays

Tylochromis polylepis and lower pharyngeal bone, from Poll, 1957.

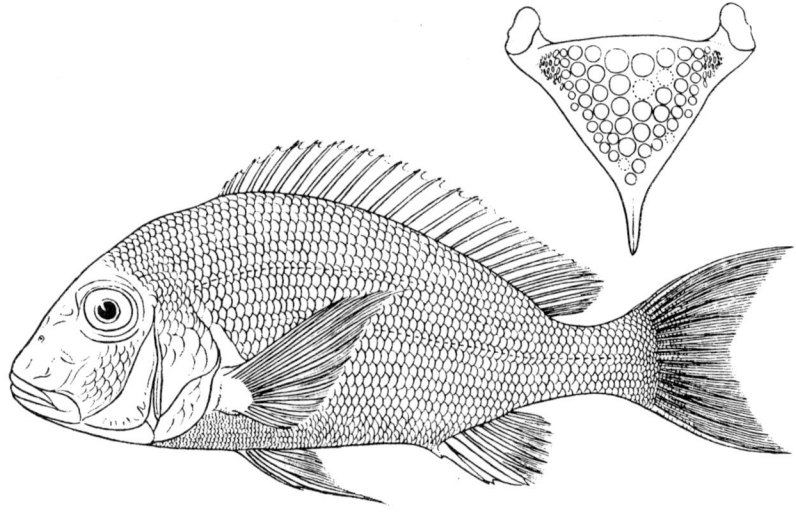

Ventrals — with a small filament on the first rays
Caudal — slightly forked
Teeth: small, conical, in 4 or 5 rows
Pharyngeal teeth: molar-shaped, larger on the central and rear areas of the bone
Mouth: inferior
Gill rakers: 14 or 15 on the lower half of the first gill arch
Habitat: strictly coastal, most often found in front of or close to river estuaries, into which the fish also penetrate; always over sand or mud bottoms
Feeding: omnivorous but with a preference for plants
Reproduction: buccal incubation
Maximum size: in excess of 300 mm

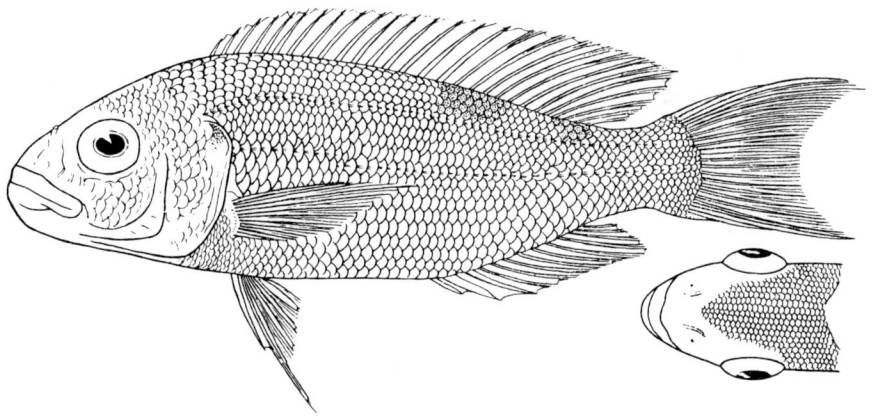

Xenochromis hecqui and top view of the head, from Poll, 1957.

XENOCHROMIS Boulenger 1899

One endemic species (*X. hecqui*).
Body: elongate; two black ocelli at the base of the dorsal
Scales: small and cycloid, 57-65 in a longitudinal line
Lateral lines: 2, the upper nearly complete
Fins: Dorsal — XVI-XVII spines and 11 or 12 rays
   Anal — III spines and 9 to 11 rays
   Caudal — slightly forked

Teeth: small, compressed and blade-shaped, a bit concave in front and very curved in the rear, close together, rather blunt, in a single row close to the jaw edge

Mouth: terminal, powerful

Gill rakers: 47-57 on the lower half of the first gill arch

Habitat: deep to very deep water over mud floors and perhaps sand—a benthic species

Feeding: all specimens collected were feeding on copepods

Reproduction: nothing definite except for the fact that immature females had a minimum of 600 eggs, 2.5 mm in diameter, in their ovaries

Maximum size: probably close to or in excess of 300 mm

XENOTILAPIA Boulenger 1899

Thirteen endemic species and subspecies.

Body: elongate, with a large and deep head, body tapering off from the nape to the caudal peduncle, which is narrow

Scales: 34 to 43 in a longitudinal line

Lateral lines: 3, the upper complete, the other two not

Fins: Dorsal — XIII-XV spines and 11 to 19 rays
Anal — III spines and 7 to 18 rays
Ventrals — *the outer rays always shorter than the inner rays*
Caudal — forked

Teeth: very small, conical teeth in 2 or 3 rows; outer teeth of the lower jaw pointing forward (typical of sand-sifters)

Pharyngeal teeth: in two papillose cushions located on the sides of the bone

Mouth: low, straight and small, but protractile

Xenotilapia sima, from Poll, 1957.

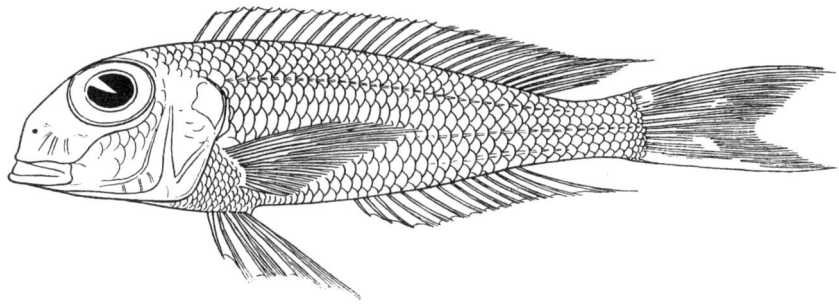

Gill rakers: 9-18 on the lower half of the first gill arch
Habitat: not deep, *always over sand,* even on sand patches between rubble on rock slopes
Feeding: copepods, small shrimps
Reproduction: buccal incubation involving up to about 50 eggs, size 3 mm
Maximum size: about 150 mm, but many species much less

Key to the Identification of Species of *Xenotilapia*
(From Dr. M. Poll)

1. Teeth set in a minimum of 2 rows, the teeth from lower front row pointing more or less in horizontal plane; pharyngeal teeth rather molar-shaped, at least in central part of bone; interorbital space 4.8-8.25 in head length 2
   Teeth very thin and miniscule, in one row at edge of each jaw, the row on lower jaw not pointing in a well defined direction; pharyngeal teeth all thin; interorbital space included 3.8 to 4.6 times in head length; maximum size 80 mm .... *X. tenuidentata*
2. Body depth included less than 5 times in standard length; slope of head always rather convex; anal fin with fewer than 15 soft rays 3
   Body depth included 5.0 to 5.9 times in standard length; slope of head straight or barely convex; 13 to 18 gill rakers on lower part of first gill arch; D. XIII-XV, 16-19; A. III, 15-18; maximum size 150 mm .... *X. melanogenys*
3. Body depth included 4.25 to 4.85 times in standard length; ventral fins with inner ray longer than outer ray; maximum size about 110 mm 4
   Body depth included 3.3 to 4.1 times in standard length; ventral fins with inner ray equal to or longer than outer ray; maximum size in excess of 125 mm 5
4. Gill rakers 9-12 on lower part of first gill arch; caudal peduncle 1.65 to 2.0 times longer than high; eye 2.5-3.75 times in head length; maximum size 110 mm .... *X. ochrogenys ochrogenys*
   Gill rakers 11-14 on lower part of first gill arch; caudal peduncle 1.9 to 2.5 times longer than high; eye 2.3 to 3.1 times in head length; maximum size 103 mm .... *X. ochrogenys bathyphilus*

5. Gill rakers 13-18 (seldom 13) 6
   Gill rakers 9-14 (seldom 14) 9
6. Dorsal fin with spines longer in middle (in the male) 7
   Dorsal fin with spines increasing in length from first to last .. 8
7. Longest dorsal spine shorter than half head length; inner ray of ventral longer than outer ray; no spots on anterior part of dorsal fin; maximum size 163 mm .... *X. longispinis longispinis*
   Longest dorsal spine equal to or longer than half head length; inner ray of ventral fin about equal to outer ray; dorsal fin with several small black spots in front; maximum size 173 mm .... *X. longispinis burtoni*
8. Gill rakers 13-15 on lower part of first gill arch; A. III, 8-10 (usually 9); caudal peduncle 1.9-2.1 times longer than high; ventral fin with inner ray longer than outer ray; maximum size 130 mm .... *X. nigrolabiata*
   Gill rakers 15-17 on lower part of first gill arch; A. III, 7 to 9 (usually 8); caudal peduncle 1.65-1.9 times longer than high; ventral fin with inner ray equal to or barely longer than outer ray; maximum size 125 mm .... *X. ornatipinnis*
9. Lower jaw not protruding 10
   Lower jaw very protruding; 11-14 gill rakers on lower part of first gill arch; D. XIV-XV, 11 to 14; A. III, 10-12; ventral fin with inner ray longer than outer ray; maximum size 164 mm .... *X. sima*
10. Dorsal fin with more than 12 soft rays 11
    Dorsal fin with XIV or XV spines and 10 to 12 rays; A. III, 7-9; 9 to 11 gill rakers; ventral fin with equal rays; male with striped caudal fin; maximum size 156 mm .... *X. caudafasciata*
11 (triplet). 11 to 14 (usually 12) gill rakers; D. XIII to XV, 13-15; A. III, 10-11; ventral fin with inner ray longer than outer ray; maximum size 153 mm .... *X. boulengeri*
    13 gill rakers; D. XIV, 14; A. III, 10; ventral fins with inner and outer rays equal; maximum size 104 mm .. *X. lestradei*
    12-13 gill rakers; D. XII-XIII, 13-14; A. III, 8 or 9; ventral fins with inner ray shorter than outer ray; body depth 3.3 to 3.6 in S.L.; large black spot in middle of dorsal; dorsal fin with spines number 8 to 11 longer than other spines .... *X. spilopterus*

Body elongate with ctenoid scales; 3 lateral lines, only the upper complete. Mouth small, low, horizontal and very protractile. Teeth very small and conical, in 2 or 3 rows, the outer row on the lower jaw directed forward and perpendicular to the inner rows. Maxillary folding under the preorbital. Large papillose pad in front of the upper half of the branchial arches. Dorsal fin with 13 to 15 spines; anal with 3. Inner ventral rays largest. Occipital and parietal crests strong and extending between the orbits. Vertebrae 34 or 35.

Of all the species of fish Lake Tanganyika shelters, none are more elusive for a frustrated fish collector than the 13 species of *Xenotilapia*. This is not because the fish are rare. Many species along the northern shores are caught with seines by professional fishermen in very large quantities, one might say by the tens of thousands each day.

The problem with this kind of seine fishing is that the fish never survive the catch because the seines are of a peculiar type. They are very high and are laid very far from shore in water ten or even fifteen meters deep, where they sink and are then hauled back to shore with ropes hundreds of meters long by a score of fishermen. Rolled between the mesh, bruised or crushed by pieces of wood and pebbles and finally dragged into shallow water over coarse sand, the fish are damaged beyond rescue. Worse still, at the depth at which they were captured by the net it is impossible for them to reach the shallow water near the beach without a strong case of the "bends" (decompression sickness), with an inflated bladder and the intestine protruding from the mouth or the anal orifice.

For years we have bought the best looking fish by the hundreds from the fishermen, but to no avail; losses were too high. When we were very lucky we saved one percent of the fish thus collected.

We tried to see what could be done. But over these vast expanses of sand floors with a light slope, the turbidity of the water was such that no one could see more than a few feet. The colors of *Xenotilapia* blend wonderfully well with their biotope. Of this we felt sure after a while, because the only way to see any was to put the eyes at sand level and try to see the shape of the fish against the lighter background of the water. Even so, the problem was to find a sizable school, to get the other divers that were looking around on their own back to the school, to stretch the net into the proper direction and then try to chase the fish into the net.

Xenotilapia sima is rather unattractive and not in demand as an aquarium fish. Photo by Dr. Herbert R. Axelrod.

We were lucky when out of four dives with the full diving team we could collect one or two hundred *Xenotilapia*. The acclimatization process then began and, as with most sand-dwellers, we had more trouble and losses of course with them than with the much hardier rock cichlids. When everything was over and the fish were ready to be shipped abroad, they just didn't show off in the importers' tanks as they did in ours.

It is a fact that most sand-dwelling cichlids from Lake Tanganyika, although they are sometimes the most beautiful fishes in the lake, suffer from minute changes in the mineral contents of the water they have been put in and lose most of their appeal. This is certainly the case with *Xenotilapia ochrogenys*, one of the most gorgeous cichlids in the world, but next to impossible to bring back alive until someone finds a way. It is very difficult to ship and has a high mortality rate during the acclimatization process and travel.

Xenotilapia species are also apparently localized on the lake sand floors. Many species probably have as yet not been found in the northernmost part of the lake north of the Ubwari Peninsula. Of the four species so far identified, one appears to be new (to be described by Pr. Poll) because of its beautiful deep yellow dorsal fin. Oddly the best picture I succeeded in taking of any *Xenotilapia* is of this one. This fish was the only one of its genus we had less trouble in getting for a while, for we succeeded in stumbling upon a habitat where they assembled in shallow waters and were able to round them up regularly.

Xenotilapia melanogenys at breeding time is also incredibly beautiful, and it is difficult to have a better looking fish at mating time. The male's head and chest is a combination of Prussian blue patches with metallic blue and emerald green areas; the cheek is deep orange, the throat jet black, the lips pure white or light blue; the whole body an iridescent blue and pink, and the fins are gorgeously striped with deep orange and white. *X. melanogenys* unfortunately is a bit too big and delicate to be shipped economically and, as losses during acclimatization are high, we have abandoned collecting the fish altogether.

We have only once succeeded in discovering a huge school of the fish mixed with another of *X. ochrogenys* in shallow water over favorable grounds for catching them, but as the fish were busy nesting and spawning on this site, we preferred to enjoy the sight. Once again with these deep-living fish, often deeper than 60 meters, it is apparent that they come up the slopes to mate in shallow water and it is there that the schools stay after mating has taken place. The females can then incubate the eggs and fry in their mouths in the upper, oxygen-rich, layer. Once the fry have grown and have been released, these buccal incubators will migrate back to the deep layers where they spend their lives.

Xenotilapia sima is the least appealing species of the genus, with an outsized head, big bulging eyes, colorless body and faint yellow fins. Its size, well in excess of 150 mm, makes it a poor aquarium dweller.

All *Xenotilapia*, once used to tank life, will thrive on common types of food and will present no problem to the average hobbyist. They need some space since they are roamers, but they will not bother any fish unless it is really a very small one. Breeding them in captivity has as yet not been reported.

In the wild it appears that all females in the same school are ripe at the same time and mate, incubate and probably release their fry on the same spot at the same time. The fry are thus formed into a communal school of assorted sizes as are the adult schools. Needless to say, *Xenotilapia* are very gregarious and respond to all the group stimuli of very gregarious fishes. In a very recent observation of a spawning school, we followed one female who repeatedly went down in several male's nests—spawned—got their eggs fertilized and swam away. The eggs of one female were thus fertilized by different males.

Non-Cichlids

The 110 non-cichlid fishes of Lake Tanganyika are divided among 18 families and 43 genera if one takes into account the species living in the lake affluents or the Lukuga River outlet toward the Congo river and the torrential affluents of this river. Most certainly this list is not complete, and more species of non-cichlids will be discovered in the rivers as well as in the lake proper.

The keys for the identification of the genera and species, whenever possible, have been written to help identify the fish by their external taxonomic features, and as little as possible by features which can be ascertained only by dissecting the fish. When in doubt, it is necessary to go back to the full taxonomic description of the fish as it stands today.

In this regard this book is thus only a field guide.

Family LEPIDOSIRENIDAE

The lungfish *Protopterus aethiopicus* has never been collected by us. It is not seen in the lake proper, but always in river estuaries and swamps. Like all other *Protopterus*, the paired fins developed into flexible spikes with a membrane on the rear side of the fin. The pectorals and ventrals are well separated from each other. *P. aethiopicus* is separated from the other African lungfishes by the fact that its dorsal fin starts midway between the occipital crest of the head and the anus. The four geographical races the author has seen (as far as the color pattern is concerned) are as follows:

1. *Congo River:* marbled or reticulated with blue-grey on a whitish background
2. *Congo River albino* (*Kinshasa*): red eyes, light pink body, eventually with dark grey spots on the tail and hind part of the body
3. *Lake Edward:* gray or yellow-gray, sometimes with orange-vermilion tail; tiny black stripes on body. Maximum size in Lake Edward about 2 meters
4. *Lake Tanganyika:* drab gray with faint reticulations

It has not been possible to ascertain if *P. aethiopicus* makes cocoons in the lake area whenever the swamps it lives in dry out.

This fish, because of its size and nasty habits, is definitely not an aquarium fish. Large specimens should be handled with utmost care and, if possible, not by hand. The powerful teeth and strong canines can cause painful wounds. Specimens in excess of 1 meter have been known to cut off all the fingers of a hand in one lightning fast stroke. This is also the only African fish the author knows of which, when escaping a hold by a rearward motion of the body, will rush forward to bite. The apparent sluggishness of the fish is very misleading.

In captivity the lungfish will eat all kinds of worms, including garden worms, chopped meat and even tadpoles.

Family POLYPTERIDAE

Polypterus are identified by their paired fins mounted on a peduncle with the rays radiating into a fan. The scales are rhomboidal and thick. The dorsal fin is divided into separate strong spines, each with a membrane behind.

Key to the Identification of Polypterids of the Lake Tanganyika Basin

Snout much longer than lower jaw; eye included 8.5 times in head; X or XI dorsal spines, first spine well behind pectoral fin; 62 or 63 scales in a longitudinal line, 24 to 25 between occiput and first dorsal spine; Malagarazi River . . . .*P. ornatipinnis*

Snout much shorter than lower jaw; eye included 8 to 14 times in head; XII-XV (more often XIII or XIV) dorsal spines, first very close to pectoral fin; 55 to 59 scales in a longitudinal line, 11 to 15 between occiput and first dorsal spine; river estuaries . . . . . .
. . . .*P. endlicheri congicus*

The presence of *P. ornatipinnis* in the Malagarazi delta was one of the major discoveries of the 1946-47 Hydrobiological Mission to the lake. This species is typically from the Congo River basin (it is very abundant in the Stanley Pool rapids in Kinshasa), and its presence on the eastern coast in the Malagarazi was quite a surprise. As the species has been collected nowhere else around the lake and is of course one of the most ancient fish living in Africa, it looks like it had been a dweller in this river for quite a long time before the lake started to fill in. If this line of thought is correct, it would corroborate the theory that the Malagarazi is an affluent

Polypterus ornatipinnis. Photo by Helmut Pinter.

from the Congo River, from which it was cut off when the lake floor started to sink across the river bed.

Reaching an impressive size, none of the *Polypterus* would be much of an aquarium fish, but when caught young their very unusual shape and the romantic appeal of having a "prehistoric" specimen in one's tank have always made them favorites among hobbyists. It is a hardy fish, as one would expect from it's being a swamp-dweller, but is best kept with fishes it cannot swallow. Little is known about the spawning habits of the Protopteridae and their ethology. The author has seen *Polypterus endlicheri* twice on rocky coasts far from rivers, in the south of the lake.

Family CLUPEIDAE

The clupeids are recognized by their serrated belly made up of keeled and angular scales, the lack of an adipose fin and the lack of mouth barbels. The two genera of the lake are distinguished as follows:

- *Limnothrissa* — teeth present on the palatine bones and on the tongue; maxillary bone as broad in front as in the rear (*L. miodon*);
- *Stolothrissa* — no teeth on the palate or on the tongue; maxillary bone narrower in front than in the rear (*S. tanganicae*).

The clupeids are the most important food fishes in the whole lake area. Thanks to the plankton, these small fishes are so abundant that they account for most of the animal protein available to millions of Africans in Zaire, Burundi, Tanzania and Zambia. Some of their many schools have been estimated at a weight of 50 tons, and when the "Ndakala" or "Ndagaa" or "Kapenta" (as they are called) are available, every flat, sandy patch on the lake shore is covered with the drying fish. The Africans dry them in the sun so that this delicacy might reach the most remote village markets without spoiling.

After years of research, nothing is known about the breeding habits of these economically important fish, which is still one of the main mysteries of the lake. As nobody knows how, when and why they spawn, the danger of overfishing is ever present.

Because of these clupeids, a whole host of species have multiplied in the lake, all of them preying on the luckless schools. Among these predators may be included seven species of *Bathybates*, two *Haplotaxodon*, one *Hemibates*, one *Boulengerochromis*, three *Lates* and two *Luciolates*. Altogether sixteen species in the lake prey on clupeids as their main diet, not counting of course the other occasional predators. All of them—except *Boulengerochromis*, for which no data are available—are also school fishes and make up the other portion of all fishes caught by man in the lake.

Although they are very important as food fishes, the two clupeids never reach the aquarium hobbyist. The fish are not

Stolothrissa tanganicae, palate (left) and head (right), from Poll, 1957.

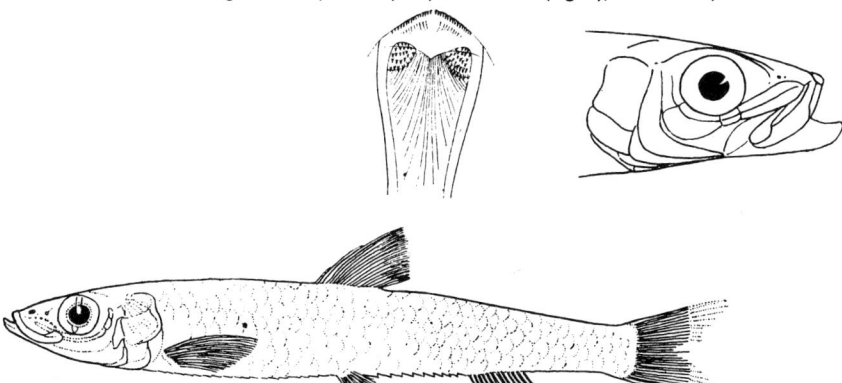

beautiful, just being silvery, and are incredibly difficult to handle. As soon as the fish is taken out of the water, it dies. When clupeids are netted one has to put a pail in the net, chase the fish into the pail underwater, and then lift the pail to have a chance to see the fish survive for a few minutes.

Being fast roamers, they need a very high level of oxygen and room to spare. No one other than specialized government agencies has tried to keep the fry alive for eventual seeding of other lakes—and even the agencies have not met with much success as yet.

Family MORMYRIDAE
Key to the Identification of the Genera of Mormyrids in the Lake Tanganyika Basin (from Taverne)

1. Very long dorsal fin................................*Mormyrus*
   Short dorsal fin 2
2. Mouth in a tube-like extension..........................3
   Mouth not at tip of a tube-like extension 4
3. With chin barbel at end of tube ....*Campylomormyrus*
   Without chin barbel at tip of tube...........................
   ....*Mormyrops (Oxymormyrus)*
4. Chin bulge fleshy and globulous ....*Marcusenius*
   No fleshy chin bulge 5
5. Caudal fin with very short lobes; body very elongate; 10-36/10-36 bicuspid teeth on each jaw; teeth of palate and tongue reduced ....*Mormyrops*
   Caudal fin with elongated lobes; body rather short; never more than 10 teeth on lower jaw; well developed palate and tongue teeth....................................6
6. Large *bony* chin, made up of recurved lower jaw bones; upper jaw protruding over lower jaw ....*Hippopotamyrus*
   No bony chin................................*Pollimyrus*

The Lake Tanganyika mormyrids do not, with the exception of *Hippopotamyrus discorhynchus*, live in the lake proper but in the affluent river swamps and estuaries. It was a very big surprise to discover *Hippopotamyrus* far from these usual mormyrid habitats, hidden in the dark recesses of rocky slopes more than 40 km from the nearest river mouth. Most mormyrids appear to have come up from the Congo River Basin through the Lukuga outlet but have not as yet been very successful as settlers in the lake. The example of *Hippopotamyrus* shows at least that this settlement is not impossible for other species as well.

As aquarium fishes, the lake mormyrids cannot compete with the colorful elephant-nose mormyrids from the Congo River.

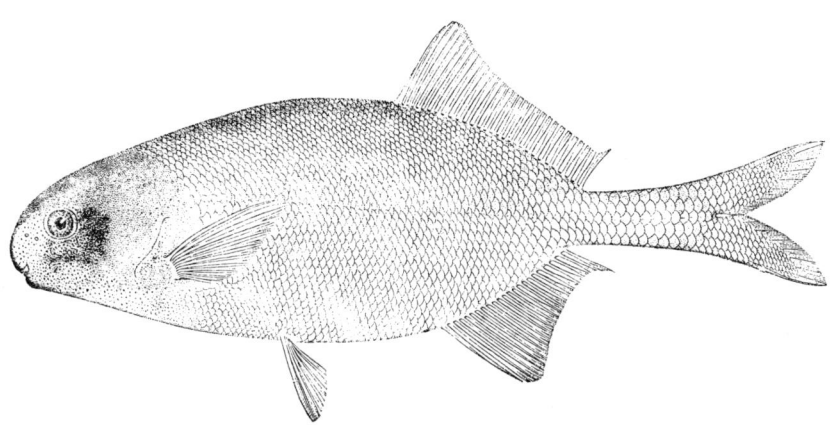

Marcusenius discorhynchus.

Family KNERIIDAE

The main feature of these very special torrent-living tiny fish is the male's suction disk on the sides of the head. Sometimes quite colorful, *Kneria* are found only in the mountain rivers of East Africa. The Kneriidae could become excellent aquarium fishes if they were not so difficult to collect. Only one species, *K. wittei*, has been discovered in the lake basin. There could be more.

Characteristics of *Kneria wittei:* body depth: 4.6 times in body length; head length: 5 times in standard length; snout: 3.25 times in head length; eye: 3.75 times in head length; interorbital space: 2.6 times in eye length; dorsal fin $3+7+1$, originating in the second half of the S.L. of the body; anal fin: $3+7+0$; ventral fins: $1+7$; pectoral fins: $1+15$; scales: 76 in a longitudinal line (very small); caudal fin: lobed.

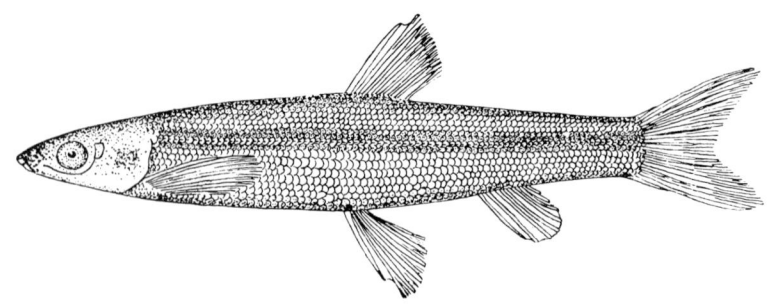

Kneria wittei, holotype, 50 mm long, from Poll, 1946.

Family CHARACIDAE

Key to the Identification of the Genera of Characidae from the Lake Tanganyika Basin (from M. Poll)

1. Pluricuspid teeth in 2 or 3 rows on each jaw.................2
   Unicuspid teeth, sharp and very large, in a single row on each jaw.......................................*Hydrocynus*
2. Teeth in 2 rows on upper jaw; first dorsal ray above or behind ventral fins 3
   Teeth in 3 rows on upper jaw; first dorsal ray in front of ventral fins................................*Bryconaethiops*
3. Upper jaw teeth of inner row conical; lower jaw with only 2 inner teeth; lateral line complete ....*Micralestes*
   Upper jaw teeth of inner row obliquely truncated or molar shaped; only two inner teeth on lower jaw; lateral line complete, large size as adult....................*Alestes*

Key to the Species of the Genus *Hydrocynus*

Body longitudinally striped with several rows of black-spotted scales; A. III, 10-13; 8 to 10 gill rakers; size to 800 mm ....
....*H. vittatus*
Body without horizontal rows of black-spotted scales; dorsal as well as the lower caudal lobe yellow or red; A. III, 13 to 16; 10 to 12 gill rakers; size about 150 mm...............*H. goliath*

The famous African tiger fishes live in the lake proper, but only near river estuaries. None have been caught, according to available records, in the northern part of the lake (*H. vittatus* has been seen), although they are abundant to the south. They are considered good game fish because of the tremendous fight they display when hooked and because of their formidable size (the author has seen in Kinshasa a *H. goliath* measuring 1.5 m and weighing 35 kg—and much bigger ones have been recorded).

The species of *Hydrocynus* are pelagic roamers with a fantastic appetite. The adult fish appear to live in pairs, and it is not uncommon when hooking a tiger fish to see its mate rush to the splashing victim and swallow half of it in a single bite. In one such instance the remaining half weighed close to 10 kg and was about 70 cm long. The typical tiger fish bite, crescent-shaped and clean, showed that the hind part of the fish had been swallowed tail first before the attacker closed its jaws. The teeth, up to 30 mm long, pointed like a needle and with sharp edges, interlock with those of the opposite jaw, resulting in a clean cut without the need for tearing.

Fortunately *Hydrocynus* does not attack man, except by mistake in murky waters. Years ago the author in the Stanley Pool, part of the Congo River, barely escaped an attack by a tiger fish. While waterskiing I suddenly felt pressure waves against my chest and a moment later a tiger fish, which had turned off at the last second, jumped out of the water and disappeared. There has been at least one record of an attack on an angler standing wasit-deep in shallow water. The calf of his leg was entirely cut off.

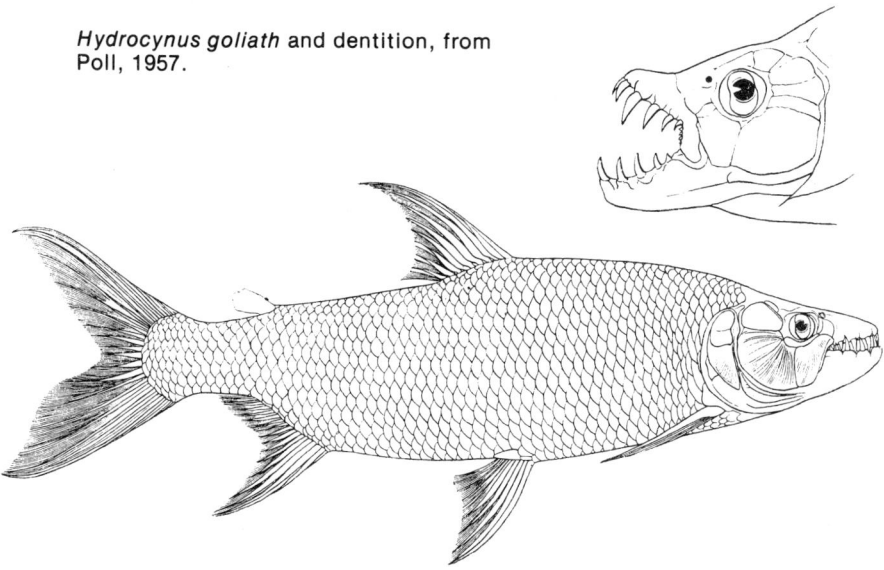

Hydrocynus goliath and dentition, from Poll, 1957.

Tiger fish thus are not for the aquarium and as they are characins and show a remarkable degree of adaptation to many different types of water (they are distributed all over Tropical Africa) they should never be allowed to be imported into countries like the United States where local conditions might suit their basic needs. Only responsible public aquariums should be allowed to handle them.

Key to the Species of the Genus *Alestes*

1. Dorsal fin II, 8; anal fin III, 12-16; scales in a longitudinal line 23-29 2
   Dorsal fin II, 8; anal fin II, 16-20; scales in a longitudinal line 39-45; no peduncle spot .... *A. macrophthalmus*
2. First rays of dorsal fin above ventrals; scales 23-29; peduncle spot present; body deep .... *A. imberi*
   First ray of dorsal fin well behind base of ventrals; 28-29 scales; peduncle spot present; snout to dorsal fin profile straight .... *A. rhodopleura*

None of the rather large species of *Alestes* from the lake are good aquarium fishes because they lack the brilliant colors of their dwarf cousins, the *Micralestes,* and smaller characins so common in tropical Western Africa. The other characids from the lake,

Bryconaethiops boulengeri, from Poll, 1957.

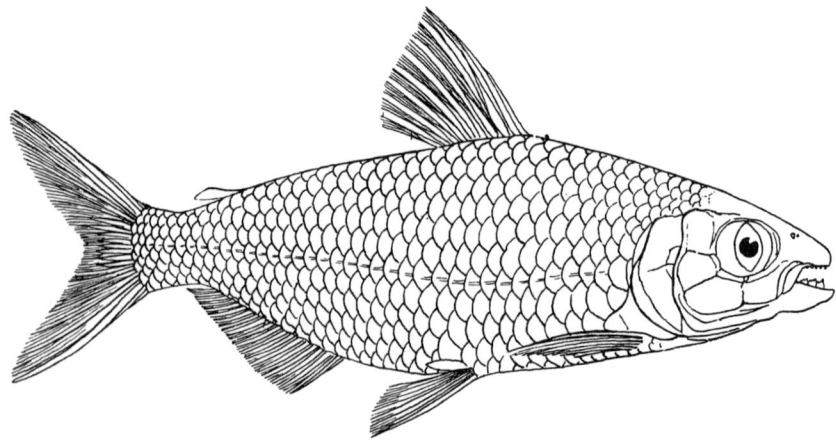

with the exception of *Bryconaethiops boulengeri,* also lack the qualities to make them good aquarium fishes.

It does not appear that the characins have been successful in the lake, and one might say that the family as a whole is more at ease and shows the greater speciation in soft, acid forest brooks and rivers than it does in hard, alkaline waters. It is in the virgin forests of Africa that the dwarf characins feel most at home. In the lake the characins have settled in wide open waters as well as along the shore line, but they don't form a significant part of the lake fish population.

Family CITHARINIDAE
Key to the Identification of the Genera of Citharinidae of the Lake Tanganyika Basin

Scales cycloid; body very deep and laterally compressed, maximum twice as long as high.................................*Citharinus*
Scales ctenoid; body more than twice as long as high, moderately compressed ....*Distichodus*

Key to the Identification of the species of *Distichodus*

1. Eye small, 5.7 times in head length........................2
Eye large, 3.2 times in head length; body long, 2.7 to 3.0 times longer than high; snout short, included three times in head length; teeth in two rows on each jaw, 28 in outer row of upper jaw, 24 in outer row of lower jaw; 11 anal rays, 18 dorsal rays; 70 scales in a longitudinal line; origin of dorsal fin in front of ventral fins; large spots all over the sides; size about 350 mm ....*D. maculatus*
2. Body very deep only 1.7 to 2.2 times in standard length; head large, 4.0 to 4.3 times in S.L.; 16 to 18 teeth in outer row of upper jaw; 60 to 68 scales in a longitudinal line; about 6 vertical black bands on yellow-orange body; all fins red (juvenile); the pale background darkens with age as do the fins; maximum size in excess of 1000 mm....*D. sexfasciatus*
Body elongate, depth 2.5 times in S.L.; head small, 4.8 times in body length; 2 rows of teeth; upper jaw with 29 teeth, lower with 25; 68 to 78 scales in a longitudinal line; 18 to 20 thin vertical bands on a dark green body; maximum size about 350 mm...............................*D. fasciolatus*

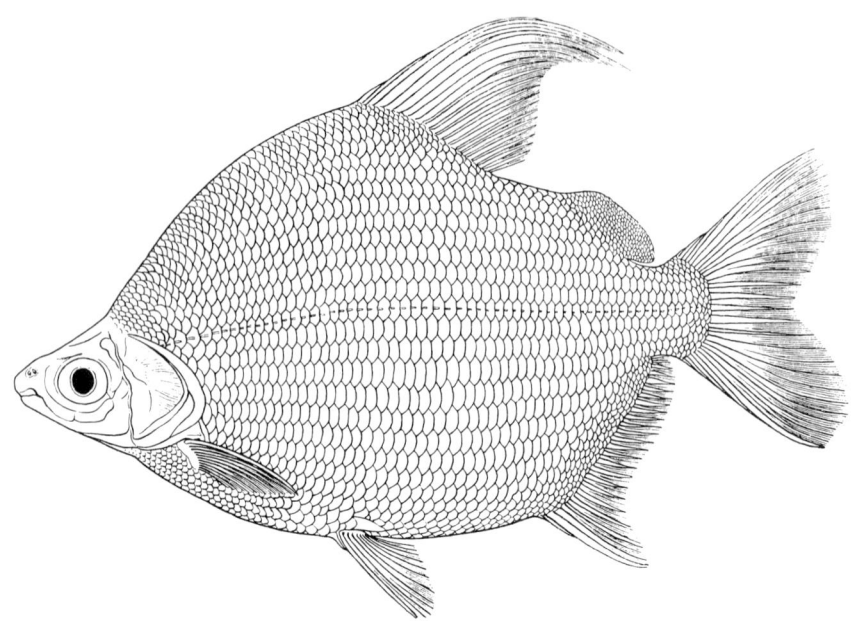

Citharinus gibbosus, from Poll, 1957.

The Citharinidae are poorly represented in the lake, and none of them wander into the lake proper. They stay near the river estuaries or in them or, as with *D. sexfasciatus* (the *Distichodus* from the Congo river basin), in the mouth of the Lukuga. *Distichodus* are typical vegetarians, which is a well known fact to the native fishermen in the Congo River. They are probably the only fish in Africa to be caught on hooks baited with banana slices or manioc meal. It is not rare, however, to catch one on a worm-baited hook, which would indicate that they are not so strictly plant-eaters as is commonly thought.

The species of *Distichodus* as a whole have not been very successful in colonizing the lake and are still restricted to habitats much like their original birthplace—mud swamps with a low pH and alkalinity. They don't appear to like the lake water with its high pH and salt content and rather poor plant growth.

In the genus *Citharinus, C. gibbosus,* very common in the Congo River mud bottoms, is a typical mud-eater, which means that it is a diatom and microfeeder. The fish has a silvery, nearly circular body and is very difficult to keep for a long time in a tank. Without its specialized food, it slowly starves to death. During the dry season, in drying swamps on Congo River sandbars, it is one of the last fishes to die from lack of oxygen, along with *Protopterus* and the electric catfish. They are rather common in the lake, especially in the southern part, and are caught deep down on mud floors.

Family CYPRINIDAE

Although the lake basin has 35 cyprinids, few of them have colonized the entire lake, the exceptions being the coastal *Varicorhinus*, *Labeo* and *Barilius* species. When they are found, even along rocky shores in the wave-battered boulder area, they are not numerous. The habitat of the cyprinids in this area is more the swamps of the river estuaries and the mountain torrents. It is in these habitats that some of them are known to live, with a few of the largest species coming up from the lake to spawn. This feature shows that many of them are still strongly bound to the type of habitat they previously lived in, and that their acclimatization in the lake is not, as yet, quite complete.

All in all, few of these fishes are potential aquarium fishes, either because they grow to a tremendous size or because they lack the fancy color patterns of their Asian counterparts.

Key to the Genera of Cyprinidae of the Lake Tanganyika Basin

1. Dorsal fin entirely in front of anal fin; anal fin with maximum of 7 branched rays 2
   Dorsal fin at least partly extending beyond origin of anal fin, which has a minimum of 10 branched rays 4
2. Mouth terminal or inferior, with more or less developed lips 3
   Mouth inferior, without lips; lower jaw with a cutting edge in a horny sheath .... *Varicorhinus*
3. Mouth inferior, with very well developed sucking lips and with an inner cutting edge covered in a horny sheath; first rays of dorsal fin always well in front of first rays of ventral fins .... *Labeo*
   Mouth terminal or inferior; lips relatively large, not shaped as a sucking organ, with or without a cutting edge; first rays of dorsal fin somewhat in front or somewhat behind the first ventral rays .... *Barbus*
4. First ray of dorsal fin in front of first ray of anal fin .... *Barilius*
   Dorsal fin entirely above anal fin .... *Engraulicypris*

Key to the Identification of the Species of *Barbus* From the Lake Tanganyika Basin

1. Scales longitudinally striated 2
   Scales radially striated 7
2. Number of scales in lower lateral line not more than 40 3
   Number of scales in lower lateral line between 44 and 47; 5 or 6 scales between lateral line and base of ventral fins; 16 scales around caudal peduncle; single barbel on side of mouth; maximum size 100 mm .... *B. tropidolepis*
3. Not more than 3 scales between lateral line and base of ventrals 4
   3½ to 4 scales between lateral line and base of ventrals; 34 to 39 scales on lateral line; dorsal well forward; 2 long barbels on each side of mouth; maximum size 360 mm .... *B. urudensis*
4. Maximum of 32 scales in lateral line; less than 3 scales between lateral line and base of ventral fins; anal fin doesn't reach tail; first dorsal ray soft and thin; 2 barbels 5
   34 to 35 scales in lateral line; 3 scales between lateral line and base of ventrals; anal fin reaching tail; first dorsal ray thick and bony; 2 long barbels at least equal to eye, which is very small (5.0 to 5.5 times in head length); maximum size 500 mm; affluents .... *B. altianalis*
5. Eye included 4.0 to 4.25 times in head length 6
   Eye very small, 5.7 times in head length and 2.16 in snout length; lips thick, with median lobe; 2 barbels on each side; first dorsal ray soft and smooth, shorter than head length; 26 to 32 scales in a longitudinal line; a dark stripe on upper and lower edges of tail; maximum size 27 mm; Congo affluents, lake and Lukuga River .... *B. caudovittatus*
6. Body depth 4.0 in standard length; head length 3.5-4.0 in standard length; interorbital space 3.0-3.3 in head length; eye 4.0 in head length; 2 short barbels on each side; D. IV, 10; last single dorsal ray thin, soft and smooth; maximum size 85 mm; Lukuga River and its affluents .... *B. euchilus*
   Body depth 3.5 in standard length; head length 4.0-4.5 in standard length; interorbital space 2.6 in head length; eye 4.0-4.25 in head length; 2 short barbels on each side; D. III, 10; last single ray of dorsal bony at its base, segmented at its tip, soft and smooth; maximum size 180 mm;

Lukuga River and its affluents .... *B. pojeri*
7. Lateral line complete 9
   Lateral line not complete, reduced to at most its anterior half
   8
8. Maximum of 3 scales in lateral line (which might be totally missing); last single dorsal ray short, strong, bony and serrated, a bit more than half head length; 21 to 23 scales in a longitudinal line; 10 scales around caudal peduncle; one barbel; maximum size 48 mm; affluents of Malagarazi River .... *B. aphantogramma*
   4-13 scales in lateral line; 12 scales around caudal peduncle; 2 barbels on each side; maximum size 57 mm; high affluents of the Malagarazi River; other features very similar to *B. aphantogramma* .... *B. oligogrammus*
9. Not more than 32 scales in lateral line 10
   34-39 scales in lateral line; 6½-7½/5½-6½ scales in transverse line; 16 to 18 scales around caudal peduncle; last single dorsal ray bony, serrated, as long as head; 2 barbels on each side, second as long as eye. Maximum size 120 mm; Lukuga, East and South Africa ...... *B. paludinosus*
10. 22 or 23 scales in lateral line; base of ventrals entirely under dorsal fin; maximum size 140 mm; Central Africa, Lukuga River .... *B. nicholsi*
    24 to 32 scales in lateral line; base of ventral fins, at least in part, in front of first dorsal rays 11
11. At least 4½/3½ scales in a transverse line; 2 scales between lateral line and base of ventral fin; 10 scales around caudal peduncle 12
    3½/2½ scales in transverse line, 1½ between lateral line and base of ventral fins; 8 scales around caudal peduncle; 24 very narrow and very high scales in the lateral line; dorsal III, 7-8; last single ray bony, thin, smooth and equal to head length; 2 short barbels; black spot behind opercle; scales edged in black; maximum size 110 mm; western affluents of the lake .... *B. lufukiensis*
12. Last single ray of dorsal strong, bony and serrated 13
    Last single ray of dorsal thin, soft, segmented and smooth .. 16
13. At least 24 scales in lateral line and 4½/4½ in transverse line
    14
    23 scales in lateral line, 4½/3½ in transverse line; eye, snout and interorbital space approximately 3 times in head

409

length; dorsal III, 8; base of ventral fins under first dorsal rays; caudal peduncle 1.5 times longer than high; 12 scales around caudal peduncle; only 2 scales between lateral line and base of ventrals; maximum size 70 mm; Congo River Basin and affluents of the lake ....*B. miolepis*

14. Base of ventral fins partly in front of dorsal 15

    Base of ventrals well in front of dorsal fin; caudal peduncle 1.5 times as long as high, surrounded by 11 to 14 scales; 2 barbels about size of eye; dorsal III, 7, placed midway between eye and tail; 24-28 scales in lateral line, 4½/4½ in transverse line; 2 or 2½ scales between lateral line and base of ventrals; black stripe from eye to tail; East and South Africa and lake affluents; size 90 mm ...*B. eutaenia*

15. Caudal peduncle 1.5 to 2.0 times longer than high; 28 to 30 scales in lateral line; 4½/4½-5½ scales in transverse line; 2 or 2½ scales between lateral line and base of ventrals; 12 scales around caudal peduncle; 2 barbels, second very long; 3 black spots on body, second spot sometimes double, the three spots sometimes connected by black line; Lakes Edward and Kivu, and Upper Malagarazi; maximum size 115 mm ....*B. pellegrini*

    Caudal peduncle 1.5 to 1.6 times longer than high; 26 to 30 scales in lateral line; 4½-5½/4½-5½ scales in transverse line; 2½ to 3 scales between lateral line and base of ventrals; 12 scales around caudal peduncle; 2 barbels, second very long; a thin black stripe along body ending in a small black spot on caudal peduncle; Lakes Edward and Kivu, and various affluents of the lake; maximum size 120 mm
    ....*B. serrifer*

16. Dorsal III, 8 branched rays 17

    Dorsal III, 7 branched rays; caudal peduncle 1.5-2.0 times longer than high; 25 to 30 scales in lateral line; 4½/4½ in transverse line; 2½ or 3 scales between lateral line and base of ventrals; 12 scales around caudal peduncle; rounded black spot at base of caudal fin .....*B. urostigma*

17. Dorsal well in first half of body length; caudal peduncle twice as long as high, with 12 scales around peduncle; 27 to 32 scales in lateral line; 4½-5½/4½ scales in transverse line; 2½ to 3 scales between lateral line and base of ventrals; 2 barbels, second long; 4 to 7 black spots in a line above lateral line; sometimes a black stripe on dorsal ridge in front of dorsal fin; maximum size 66 mm; East Africa and

lake affluents...................B. *lineomaculatus*
Dorsal halfway between eye and tail; caudal peduncle 1.6 to 2.0 times longer than high, with 12 scales around peduncle; 27 to 29 scales in lateral line; 4½/4½ in transverse line; 2½ scales between lateral line and base of ventrals; black stripe meeting lateral line on caudal peduncle; maximum size 90 mm; various lake affluents
.................................B. *taeniopleura*

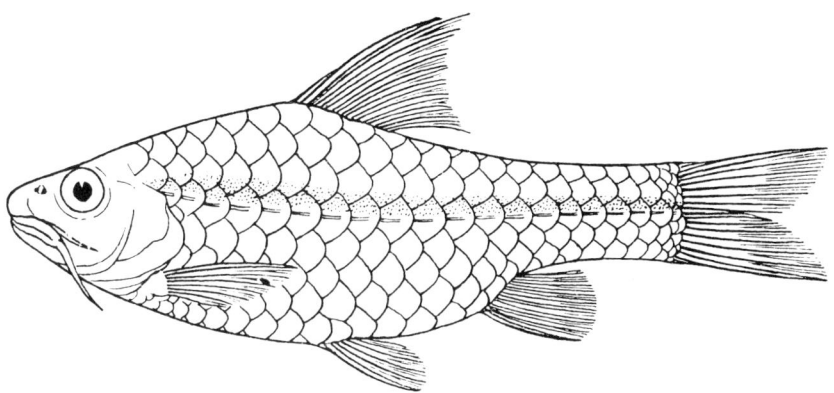

Barbus nicholsi from Poll, 1957.

The taxonomic differences between the species of *Barbus* of the Lake Tanganyika basin are mainly between species with longitudinally striated scales and those which have radially striated scales. In both groups, but especially in the species which have radially striated scales, the differences are often minute and the measurements overlap. The color patterns are often unreliable as a means of identification for they might vary from place to place and might even be completely absent.

Key to the Identification of the Species of *Varicorhinus* of the Lake Basin

The identification of the various species in this genus is based essentially on the number of scales and dorsal and anal rays.

1. Number of scales in lateral line fewer than 40 2
   Number of scales in lateral line more than 40..............3
2. Dorsal fin IV, 10; anal fin III, 5; 34 to 36 scales in lateral line; 5½/5½ scales in transverse line; 3 scales between lateral

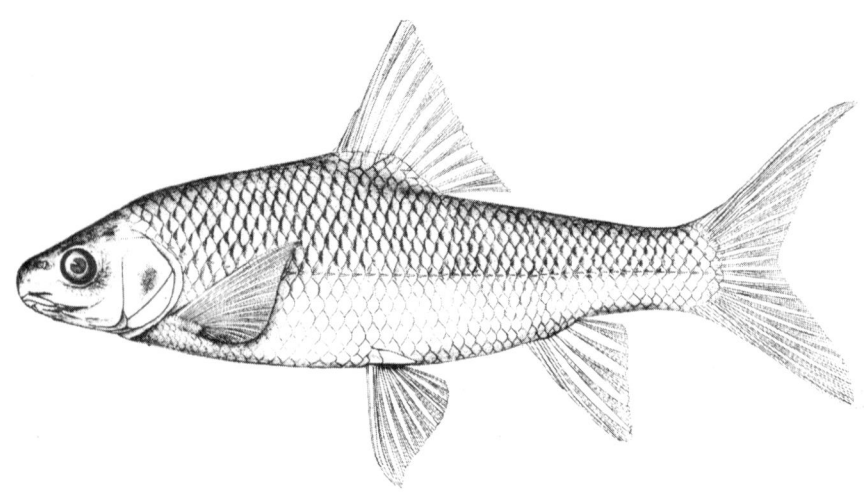

Varicorhinus leleupanus, from Poll and Matthes, 1962.

line and base of ventrals; maximum size 210 mm ....
.... *V. ruandae*
Dorsal III, 10; anal II, 5; 30 or 31 scales in lateral line; 4½/5½ scales in transverse line; 2½ scales between lateral line and base of ventrals; maximum size 310 mm .... *V. stappersi*
3. Dorsal III, 10; anal III, 5; lateral line with 46 scales; 8½/8½ scales in transverse line; 5½ between lateral line and base of ventrals; maximum size 270 mm .... *V. leleupanus*
Dorsal IV, 8-10; anal III, 5, 64 to 70 scales in lateral line; 13½-14½/14½-15½ scales in transverse line; 9 or 10 between lateral line and base of ventrals; maximum size 550 mm .... *V. tanganicae*

Key to the Identification of the Species of *Labeo* From Lake Tanganyika

The number of scales of the Tanganyika basin labeos and their dorsal and anal finnage are very similar. Noteworthy are the shape of the caudal peduncle and, for some species, the shape of the body, the inner surface of the lips, the placement of the eye in the head and even the shape of the dorsal.

1. Transverse folds on inner side of lips 2
    No transverse folds on inner side of lips; caudal peduncle twice

as high as long; dorsal fin halfway between snout and tail; D. III, 11, with a convex shape; anal fin reaching the caudal fin; fin red, red dots on each lateral scale; maximum size 780 mm; Congo basin, Lukuga outlet ...... *L. lineatus*

2. 16-18 scales around the caudal peduncle 3
   12-14 scales around the caudal peduncle; D. III, 10-11 with upper edge concave; maximum size 400 mm ..... *L. dhonti*
3. D. III or IV, 8-10; anal fin III, 5 4
   D. III, 12-13; anal fin II, 5; dorsal fin with upper edge very convex; anal fin very long; caudal fin well notched; 37 scales in lateral line; 5½/6½ in transverse line; 4 scales between lateral line and base of ventrals; 16 scales around caudal peduncle; maximum size 700 mm; Congo and Lukuga Rivers .... *L. velifer*
4. Caudal peduncle as high as long 5
   Caudal peduncle 1.3 to 1.5 times longer than high; body depth 4.0 to 4.6 in standard length; head 4.7 times in standard length; eye median; 38-39 scales in lateral line; 5½-6½/6½-7½ scales in transverse line; 3 or 4 scales between lateral line and base of ventrals; 16 to 18 scales around caudal peduncle; maximum size 400 mm; overall color olive green; East Africa lake affluents and in the lake proper
   .... *L. cylindricus*

Labeo velifer and mouth, from Poll, 1957.

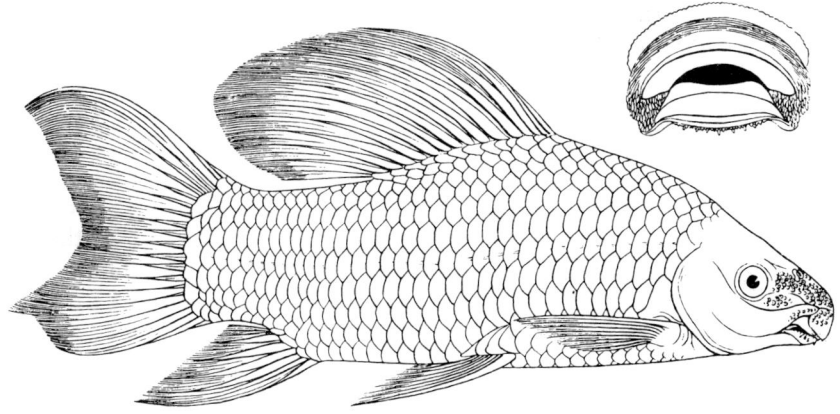

5. Eye small, entirely lateral and toward rear of head, included at least 7 times in head length; caudal peduncle 1.5 times higher than long; snout long and very protruding, 1.5 times in head length; D. III, 11, with upper edge convex; 3 scales between lateral line and base of ventrals; color green with red dots, fins red; maximum size 680 mm; Lukuga River only .... *L. kibimbi*

Eye superolateral, less than 7 times in head length; caudal peduncle as high as long; D. III-IV, 9-10, with upper edge straight or a bit concave; 4 scales between lateral line and base of ventrals; maximum size 235 mm; Lake Rukwa and upper Malagarazi affluents .... *L. fuelleborni*

Key to the Species of *Barilius* from the Lake Tanganyika Basin

1. More than 50 scales in lateral line 2
   Less than 50 scales in lateral line 3
2. 82 scales in lateral line; $13\frac{1}{2}/7\frac{1}{2}$ in transverse line; 4 scales between lateral line and base of ventrals, 26 around caudal peduncle; snout very pointed, 1.5 times in head length; mouth reaching rear of eye; 16 to 17 vertical bands on body; anal fin III, 17; maximum size 260 mm ...... *B. tanganicae*
   54 to 61 scales in lateral line; $9\frac{1}{2}$-$11\frac{1}{2}/6\frac{1}{2}$-$7\frac{1}{2}$ scales in transverse line; $2\frac{1}{2}$-$3\frac{1}{2}$ scales between lateral line and base of ventrals; 18 to 20 scales around caudal peduncle; 6 to 14 vertical bands on body; anal fin III-IV, 12-15; maximum size 210 mm .... *B. moorii*
3. Maximum of 45 scales in lateral line 4
   46 to 48 scales in lateral line; $8\frac{1}{2}/4\frac{1}{2}$ in transverse line; 2 or $2\frac{1}{2}$ scales between lateral line and base of ventrals; 16 to 18 around caudal peduncle; dorsal III, 9; anal III, 13 to 15; mouth reaching posterior $\frac{2}{3}$ of eye; dorsal fin clear, red edge to tail; maximum size 175 mm .... *B. salmolucius*
4. Caudal peduncle with 14 scales; 3 scales between lateral line and base of ventrals; 42 to 45 in lateral line; $7\frac{1}{2}/4\frac{1}{2}$ scales in transverse line; dorsal fin II, 9-10; anal III-IV, 11-16; eye 4.0 to 5.75 times in head length; 8 or 9 bands on body; dorsal blackish; maximum size 190 mm; affluents of Upper Malagarazi .... *B. neavii*
   Caudal peduncle with 15 or 16 scales; $1\frac{1}{2}$ to 2 scales between lateral line and base of ventrals; $8\frac{1}{2}/4\frac{1}{2}$-$5\frac{1}{2}$ scales in transverse line; 41 to 44 scales in lateral line; dorsal III, 9; anal

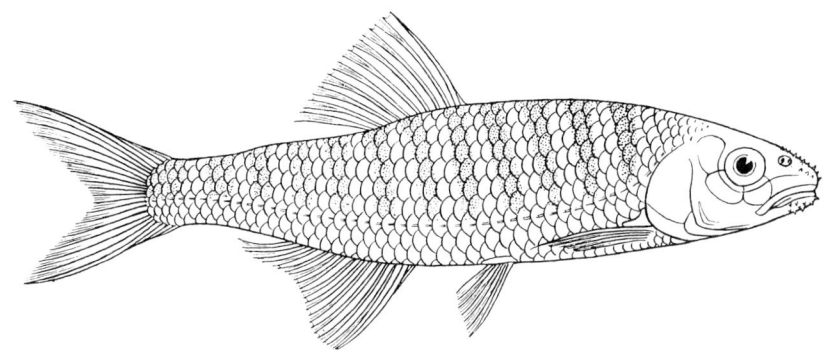

Barilius ubangensis, from Poll, 1957.

III, 13; eye 3.5 to 4.5 times in head; 8 to 13 bands on body; rear edge of dorsal black; origin Congo River, only found in Lukuga outlet; maximum size 130 mm ...... B. *ubangensis*

Key to the Species of *Engraulicypris* from the Lake Tanganyika Basin

Body depth 4.5 to 5.5 times in standard length; anal fin III, 16 to 18; transverse scales 6½/2½; first rays of anal fin just in front of first rays of dorsal fin; origin Congo River, affluents of the Lukuga outlet; maximum size 70 mm .... E. *congicus*
Body depth included 5.5 to 6.5 times in standard length; anal fin III, 18 to 20; transverse line with 7½/1½ scales; origin of anal well in front of first dorsal rays; maximum size 75 mm .... E. *minutus*

Engraulicypris minutus, from Poll, 1953.

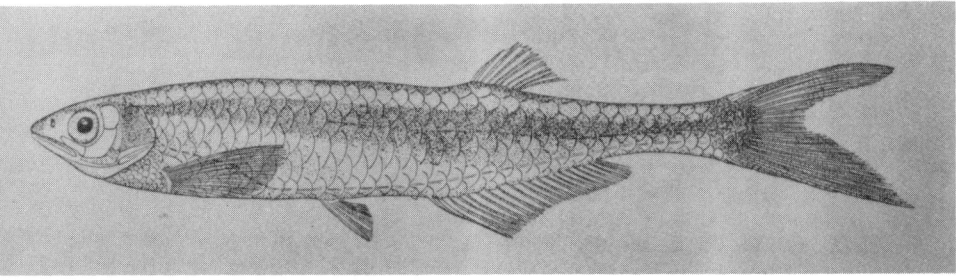

Family BAGRIDAE

One of the most interesting families in the lake and its affluents, the Bagridae includes some of the giants of the African fish world (*Bagrus*, *Chrysichthys* and *Auchenoglanis*) as well as some of the smallest (*Lophiobagrus* and *Phyllonemus*).

The giants as well as the dwarfs live in the lake proper, sometimes quite deep, as their requirements concerning the oxygen levels are low. Although these fishes have been traditionally associated with mud in Africa, the author was quite surprised to find these giants hidden in the deep recesses of rock labyrinths, in holes or crevices, and never on the open floors. This doesn't mean that the fish don't perhaps wander over open ground by night, but the stomach contents of specimens which were collected showed that the diet very often consisted of crabs and rock fishes.

Once again the discovery of the lacustrine bagrid habitat throws some light on the habitats of their river cousins. Very often in the Congo River at the Kinshasa rapids the author discovered large specimens of members of this family in the middle of rock caves or between huge overhanging boulders. Very big specimens are rare in the lake. In Kinshasa, for example, the author was once fortunate enough to see a 190 kg, more than 2 meters long, *Chrysichthys grandis*. Such a tremendous animal has never been recorded from Lake Tanganyika.

Lophiobagrus cyclurus is an endemic bagrid from the lake, seldom more than 100 mm long, but with a very unusual character. Whenever such a fish is upset, as when it is caught and taken in the hands, its body exudes a very sticky, easily flowing transparent mucus. This slime mixes with the water and, if the specimen is put into a pail along with other fish, it will poison the latter in a matter of minutes. It is as yet the only example of such a skin-exuded poison in Lake Tanganyika.

Phyllonemus are also a bit unusual, having a flattened and narrow body, long square-cut head and very long whiskers. *P. typus* has the tip of its very long barbels widened into a black feather-like membrane. The fish holds this barbel with the tip facing forward—which is also unusual. Because of its small size this rather rare fish, which has a nice metallic copper body, white belly and graceful shape, is one of the rare bagrids suited for aquarium life. But both species of *Phyllonemus* are seldom seen.

Leptoglanis belongs to a highly adapted group of torrent-living catfishes. As such, the lake basin species is not found in the lake proper, but in the high affluents cascading down the

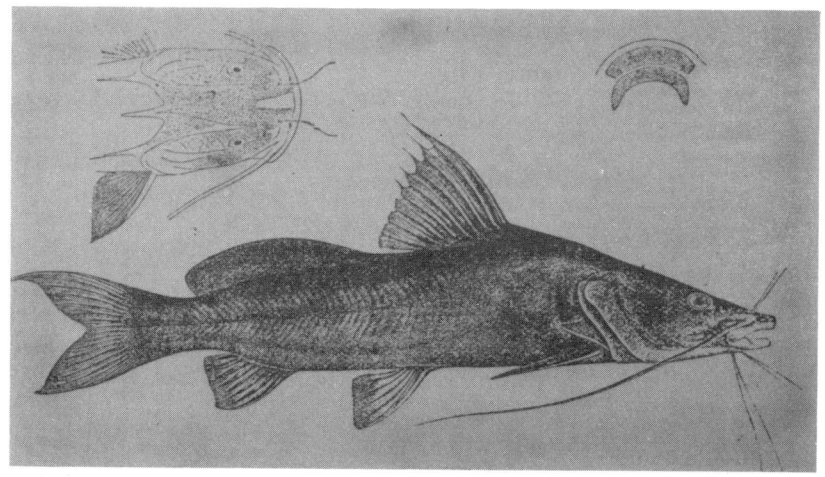

Bagrus docmac, dorsal view of head and roof of mouth, (from Boulenger, 1911).

mountain slopes. The fish are endowed with short and wide barbels and a mouth which enables them to get a hold on slippery pebbles in the fast-flowing water.

Key to the Identification of the Genera of Bagridae of the Lake Tanganyika Basin

1. Nasal barbels present 2
   Nasal barbels absent 4
2. Dorsal rays 8-11; adipose long .... *Bagrus*
   Dorsal rays 5-6; adipose short 3
3. Caudal rounded; maximum size about 100 mm; lips dark from below .... *Lophiobagrus*
   Caudal notched or forked; maximum size 200-770 mm; lips usually light from below .... *Chrysichthys*
4. Palatine teeth present; maxillary barbels often widened at anterior end by membrane, very long .... *Phyllonemus*
   Palatine teeth absent; maxillary barbels normal 5
5. Anterior nostrils dorsal; size small, 45 mm maximum ....
   .... *Leptoglanis*
   Anterior nostril on upper lip; size large, to over 1000 mm .....
   .... *Auchenoglanis*

Bagrus docmac (Forsskal)

Head 1.3 to 1.6 times as long as high. Maxillary barbels much longer than head, reaching the ventrals. Occipital bony plates narrow and long. First dorsal ray well in front of ventral. Distance between dorsal and adipose fins at least the length of the dorsal. Caudal with filamentous tip on upper lobe. Nile and Congo River basins, Lukuga and Ruzizi Rivers. 600 mm.

Table for the Identification of the Species of *Chrysichthys* in the Lake Basin

Head 1.3 to 1.7 times longer than wide; gill rakers 17-20; interorbital space 0.33 to 1.0 in eye; upper and lower lips seen from underneath pale .... *C. sianenna*

Head 1.1 to 1.5 times longer than wide; gill rakers 13-16; interorbital space 0.75 to 1.8 times wider than eye; upper and lower lips seen from underneath pale .... *C. brachynema*

Head 1.1 to 1.2 times as long as wide; 10 to 12 gill rakers; interorbital space 2.1 to 2.8 times wider than eye; upper and lower lips seen from underneath pigmented .... *C. grandis*

Head 1.4 to 1.6 times as long as wide; 9 to 10 + 1 gill rakers; interorbital space 1.3 times wider than eye; upper and lower lips seen from underneath pale .... *C. stappersii*

Chrysichthys stappersi, from Poll, 1946.

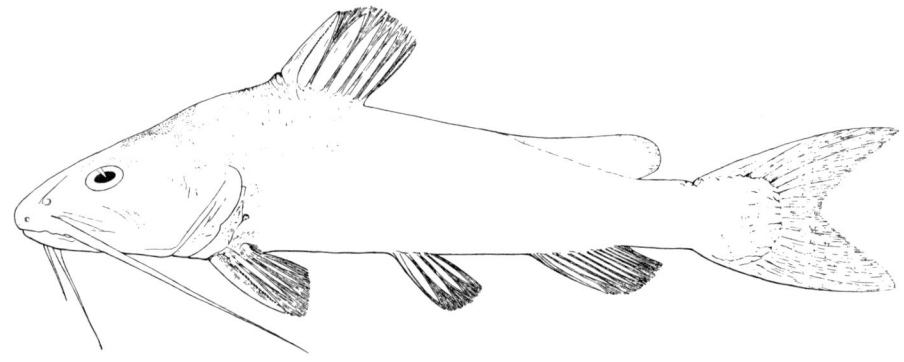

Head 1.2 to 1.5 times longer than broad; 8 to 10, sometimes 11, gill rakers; interorbital space 1.0 to 1.8 times wider than eye; upper and lower lips seen from underneath pale .... *C. graueri*

Head 1.0 to 1.25 times longer than wide; 5 to 8 gill rakers; interorbital 1.5 to 2.0 times wider than eye; upper and lower lips seen from underneath pale .... *C. platycephalus*

Lophiobagrus cyclurus (Worth and Ricardo)

Head 1.0 to 1.1 times longer than wide, included 3.0 to 3.6 times in standard length; body depth included 4.0 to 4.9 times in standard length; narrow occipital bony plate extending close to the interneural shield; interorbital space 3.6 to 5.3 times in head length; eye 1.0 to 1.5 times in snout, 4.0 to 6.6 times in head, and 1.0 to 1.6 times in interorbital space; mouth 1.4 to 1.6 times in head length; 16 to 19 gill rakers; D.I, 6, A. 11-12.

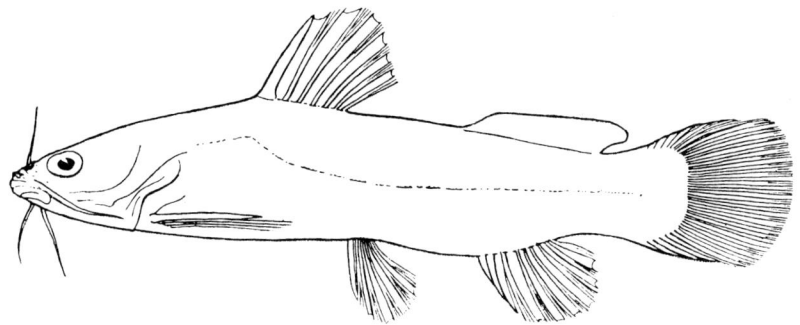

Lophiobagrus cyclurus, from Poll, 1957.

Key to the Identification of the Species of *Phyllonemus*

Maxillary barbel very long, 1.2 to 1.5 times longer than head, ending in broad black feather-like membrane; head 1.6 to 1.75 times longer than broad; snout 1.3 to 1.4 times broader than long; maximum size 100 mm .... *P. typus*

Maxillary barbel very long, 1.4 to 1.65 times head length, without a feather-shaped membrane; head 1.5 to 1.75 times longer than broad, the sides appearing concave; snout 1.4 to 1.55 times broader than long; maximum size 100 mm ....
....*P. filinemus*

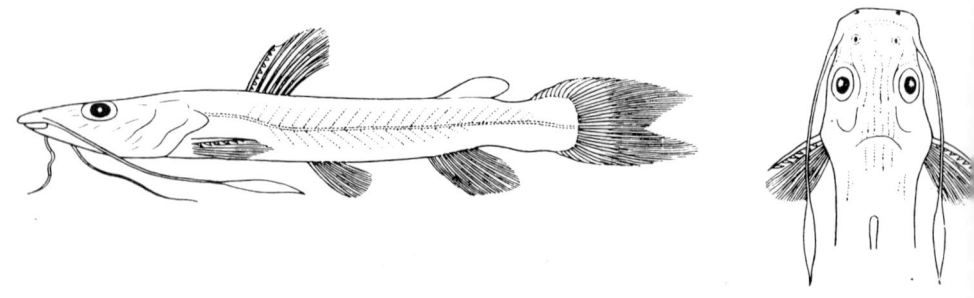

Phyllonemus and top view of head, from Poll, 1957.

Auchenoglanis occidentalis (Cuvier and Valenciennes)

Body depth 3.6 to 4.8 times in standard length; head length 2.8 to 3.8 times in standard length; head width 1.1 to 1.7 times in head length; snout a little more than two times longer than postorbital area; occipital bony plate in contact with interneural shield; premaxillary teeth in two groups, each twice as broad as long; mandibular teeth in two small and well separated groups; maxillary barbel 1.6 to 2.7 times, outer mandibular barbel 1.1 to 2.0 times, inner mandibular barbel 2.8 to 4.5 times in head length; dorsal fin I, 7; A. III-IV, 7-8; adipose fin height 4 to 6 times in fin length; marbled or spotted grey, with a few black spots arranged in rows; in excess of 1000 mm.

Auchenoglanis occidentalis, from Poll, 1957.

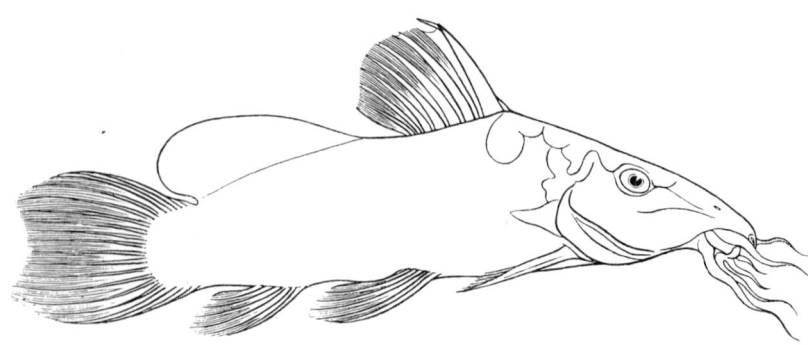

Leptoglanis brevis Boulenger

Body depth 5.5 to 5.8 times in standard length; head length 4.5 to 5.0 times in standard length; head flat, barely longer than broad (1.0 to 1.15 times); snout well rounded, 1.2 to 1.3 times longer than postorbital area; 1.7 to 2.0 times in head length; eye medium, 3.75 to 5.0 times in head length; maxillary barbel broad and as long as head; 6-7 gill rakers; D. I, 6, with a short but strong spine, much closer to head than to the tail and well in front of ventrals; adipose fin long and low; anal fin 10-11; caudal concave; maximum size 45 mm; mountain torrents.

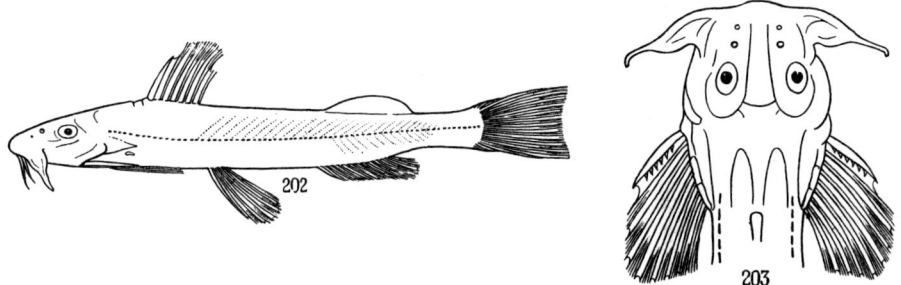

Leptoglanis brevis and top view of head, from Poll, 1957.

Family MOCHOKIDAE

In the lake basin this family is divided between the lake *Synodontis* and the *Chiloglanis* from the Lukuga outlet and its mountain affluents.

The lake *Synodontis* are divided into seven species, but most probably some of them have not speciated from a common original species. *S. melanostictus*, for one, is said to be found also in other parts of Africa south of the lake, but it is possible that the lake *S. melanostictus* is not really the same fish as the more southern one. Its habitat is much more coastal and nearer river estuaries than the habitat of the other *Synodontis* in the lake. *S. granulosus* has a very special type of skin, very rough, in strong contrast to the silk-smooth skin of most species of *Synodontis*. But *S. granulosus* shares with several of the lake *Synodontis* a typical unpaired fin pattern. This pattern consists of a very striking white or yellow-white edge (sometimes the pectoral fins as well), the main part of the fin being much darker, sometimes jet-black. When swimming deep in the twilight zone, it is by these striking white edges that one first discovers the *Synodontis*.

Here again we have an example of the help the study of the fish in the lake biotopes can provide for the understanding of fish in habitats, like murky rivers or swamps, where underwater study is impossible. It is common to hear people say that African *Synodontis* are nocturnal and that they spend the daylight hours hidden and at rest, coming out only at night to feed. When collecting in the Congo River basin the author had of course accepted this theory and knew, for example, that to collect *S. nigriventris* in the swamps one has to go on a pitch black night. In moonlight it was useless, for very few fish would be seen and collected. On the other hand, if the *Synodontis* were asleep by day, how did it happen that many of them would be caught on hook and line on sand ripples in open daylight. The Congo River, of course, is murky and at one meter depth it is already very dark.

In Lake Tanganyika, with its crystal clear water, one does not discover *Synodontis* in the open over shallows, but always hidden under rock shelves or in labyrinths. They come out of their shelters at night. But as soon as one goes deeper, a few *Synodontis* are seen wandering about over the rubble in the permanent twilight which prevails deeper than 15 meters. This holds true at least for *S. petricola, S. eurystomus, S. granulosus* and *S. multipunctatus*.

In deeper water yet, around the 30 meter level, the *Synodontis multipunctatus* assemble, sometimes in large flocks numbering as many as 300 to 400 fish, and wander slowly in the open over bare sand at the foot of the rock slopes. At this level the light has become very poor, the underwater scenery is bathed in an eerie grayish twilight and the fish's light-sensitive eyes are not hurt. These few examples show that *Synodontis* most probably are not nocturnal as was thought, but simply light-shy fishes. Given a reduced level of lighting they are as active by day as they would be at night.

The *Chiloglanis* are adapted to the extremely fast-flowing waters of torrential rivers tumbling down the mountains or to big river rapids like those of the Congo River. Their mouths show a remarkable adaptation to these unusual conditions—the lower lip, much broadened, has been shaped into a powerful suction disk. This disk, when applied on a rock, will help the fish withstand the strongest current. It is impossible to pry a *Chiloglanis* loose from its hold without severely hurting it.

The *Chiloglanis* are fantastic algae scrapers, and the strongest algae cover is scraped bare in a matter of time. As such, along with their small size and funny looks, they would be ideal for an

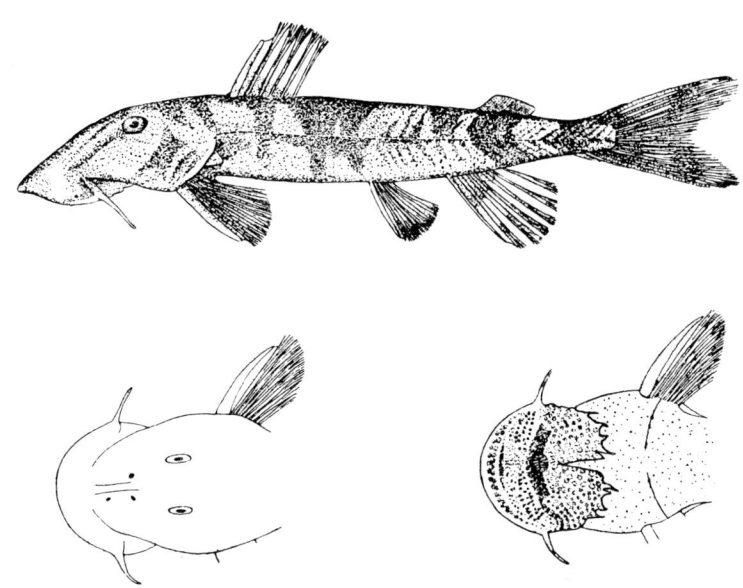

Chiloglanis lukugae, dorsal and ventral views of head, from Poll, 1946.

aquarium one wants to keep clean were it not for the fact that after a few days the *Chiloglanis* would begin to starve to death. Their mouth is so well shaped, so well specialized for the work it does, that the fish cannot easily get its food from loose vegetable matter or plants.

Key to the Identification of the Species of *Synodontis* From the Lake Basin (from Matthes)

1. Mandibular teeth 27-55 3
   Mandibular teeth 14-25 2
2. Eye large and protruding, on side of head, 2.55 to 5.25 times in head length; maxillary barbel 0.75 to 1.5 times as long as head; maximum size 60 mm .... *S. multipunctatus*
   Eye small, supralateral, 4.8 to 9.3 times in head length; maxillary barbel 0.55 to 0.75 as long as head; maximum size size 360 mm .... *S. dhonti*
3. Adipose fin high; maxillary barbel 0.9 to 1.35 times as long as head; top of head and occipital-nuchal shield rough and not covered by skin; adult size in excess of 200 mm 5

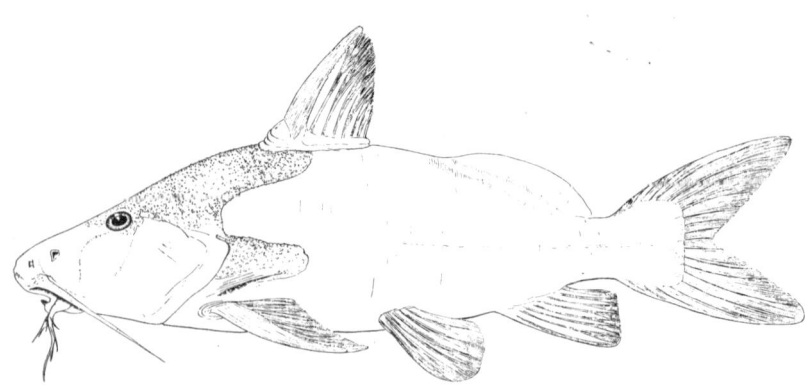

Synodontis dhonti, holotype, 400 mm long, from Poll, 1946.

    Adipose fin low; maxillary barbel short (0.5 to 0.8 times as long as head); top of head and occipital-nuchal shield covered by skin; adult size less than 200 mm 4

4. 40 to 55 mandibular teeth; snout 1.5 to 1.9 times longer than postorbital area; body depth 3.6 to 4.0 times in standard length; maximum size 150 mm .... *S. eurystomus*

    27 to 40 mandibular teeth; snout 1.35 to 1.6 times longer than postorbital area; body depth 4.0 to 5.2 times in standard length; maximum size 150 mm .... *S. petricola*

5 (triplet). 35 to 50 mandibular teeth; humeral bone narrow, pointed and keeled, 2.35 to 2.85 times longer than high; snout 1.0 to 1.4 times longer than postorbital area; maxillary barbel without a membrane; body gray to steel blue, without spots; maximum size 430 mm .... *S. granulosus*

    27 to 40 mandibular teeth; humeral bone broadly triangular and pointed, 1.2 to 2.4 times longer than high; snout 1.25 to 1.45 times longer than postorbital area; maxillary barbel with a narrow membrane at its base; caudal peduncle 0.87 to 1.15 times longer than high; body gray with countless small spots even on fins; all fins without white edge present on all other *Synodontis* from the lake; maximum size 320 mm .... *S. melanostictus*

    39 to 48 mandibular teeth; humeral bone broad, triangular and blunt, 1.7 to 2.4 times longer than high; snout 1.4 to 1.85 times longer than postorbital area; maxillary barbel with a rather broad membrane; caudal peduncle 1.25 to 1.48 times longer than high; maximum size 600 mm .... *S. lacustricolis*

Key to the Identification of the Species of *Chiloglanis* of the Lake Tanganyika Basin (from M. Poll)

Body height more than 5.5 times in standard length; eye included 7.5 to 9.0 times in head length; 12 to 14 mandibular teeth in a bunch; base of adipose fin twice in distance between this fin and dorsal fin . . . . *C. lukugae*

Body height less than 5.5 times in standard length; eye included 6.5 times in head length; 10 mandibular teeth set in a transverse row; base of adipose fin only 1.65 in distance between this fin and dorsal . . . . *C. pojeri*

Family AMPHILIIDAE

The Amphiliidae are again one of those specialized and very unusual catfishes which characterize the rich African fauna. *Amphilius* are found in mountain torrents as well as in the Central Congo River rain forest in fast-flowing brooks coming down low hill ridges. To get a good hold the fish don't rely, like *Chiloglanis*, on a suction type mouth, but on thick, rubbery pectoral and ventral rays. The pectoral fins themselves are low and flat and embrace the substrate on which the fish wants to settle.

Moreover, and this is really peculiar, *Amphilius* might be called a "walking catfish;" not that they will or even can walk much

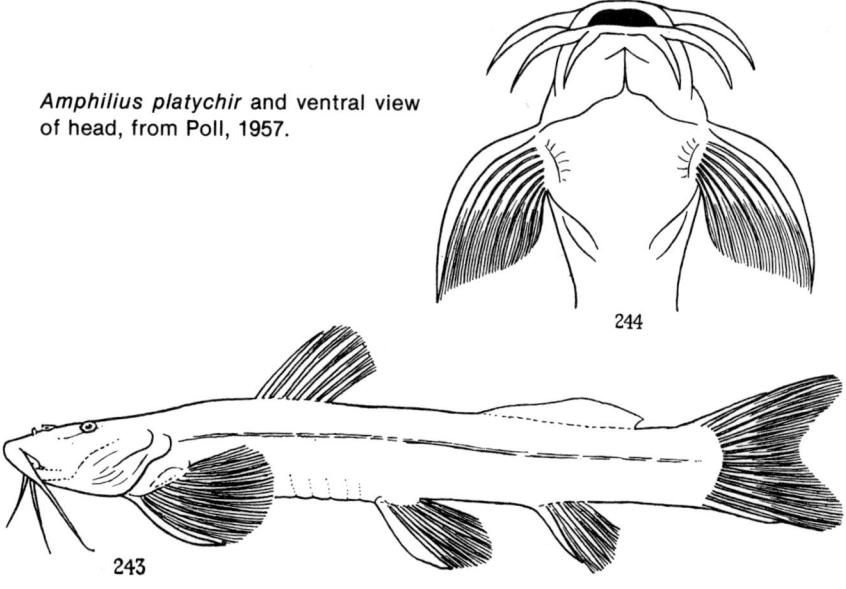

Amphilius platychir and ventral view of head, from Poll, 1957.

244

243

425

out of the water, but because the body bends sideways, alternately on one side and the other, using the ventral and pectoral fins as the anchors for their walk on or between the pebbles or the coarse sand of the substrate. Taken out of the water and put on the ground, the fish will wiggle their way forward over short distances. They are certainly not capable of covering more than short distances, probably just a few yards, in this way, but this capability very probably helps them climb up small springs or get out of the water and over a rock to the next pool, in dried out patches of mountain brooks.

They don't grow large and are perfect aquarium fishes, provided the water is properly aerated.

On the other hand, *Phractura* and *Paraphractura* are mostly found on plants, to which they attach themselves by embracing the stems with their pectoral and ventral fins. They live on tiny insect larvae, and microorganisms. Although they feed from the plant biocover for the most part, they are not found in swamps, but always on the stems and leaves of submerged plants washed by fast flowing water. They also have a very high oxygen requirement.

Phractura lindica might eventually be discovered in some of the lake affluents, although it has not yet, and very probably in those which, between the Congo River and the lake, flow into the 400 km long Lukuga outlet. *Paraphractura* has never been found in the basin, and probably will not, but has the typical ethology of the two genera. *Phractura* has the body and caudal peduncle covered with bony plates absent in *Amphilius*.

Key to the Identification of the Species of *Amphilius* of the Lake Tanganyika Basin

Body very compressed and long (7 times longer than high), with upper profile nearly straight; snout equal to postorbital area; caudal deeply notched; maxillary barbel much shorter than head; caudal peduncle as long as high; maximum size 130 mm; mountain torrents ....*A. platychir*

Body relatively compressed and long (6.2 times longer than high) with a slightly convex profile; snout longer (1.1 to 1.2) than postorbital area; caudal straight or lightly concave; maxillary barbel about as long as head; caudal peduncle longer than high (1.1 to 1.5); maximum size 90 mm; Lukuga affluents......*A. kivuensis*

Family CLARIIDAE

This family of catfishes has a very large distribution all over Africa and is found from the Sahara Desert to South Africa. In the

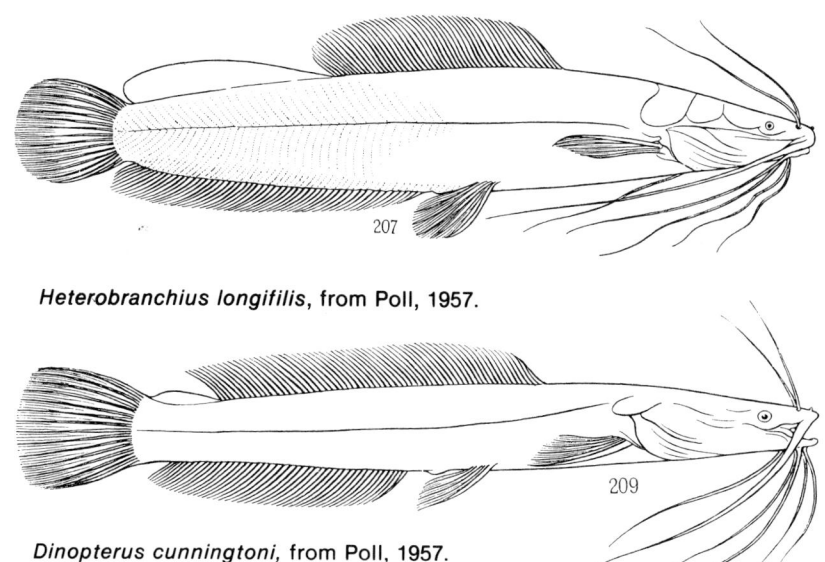

Heterobranchius longifilis, from Poll, 1957.

Dinopterus cunningtoni, from Poll, 1957.

lake basin it is represented both with very ubiquitous species, like *Clarias mossambicus* and *Heterobranchus longifilis*, as well as with endemic genera such as *Tanganikallabes* and *Dinotopterus*.

Heterobranchus is one of the giant catfishes of Africa, often exceeding 1.50 meters and 70 to 80 kg. It is also one of the most beautiful species of the family, with its long adipose fin, streamlined pale gray body and milk white belly, but it is by no means suited for the common aquarium.

To give some information on the rate of growth of *H. longifilis*, let us say that a specimen was caught in the swamp when it was about 30 mm long. Six months later, after having been fed on raw meat, it was 100 mm long; at one year of age it was more than 200 mm long. When 5 years old it was nearly one meter long and weighed more than 4 kg, even though its ravenous appetite could never be satisfied as well as it would have been in its natural habitat. It was fed on live fish. At first it would not take any dead ones but accepted raw hamburger very eagerly.

This fish had an incredible resistance. One day it escaped from its 60 gallon drum, spent the rest of the night and the next day scratching its belly on the ground in 85°C heat, was rescued in the evening, cleaned up, painted liberally with mercurochrome and was back to health in less than 15 days.

Clarias, which are a feature of many African river basins, as in the Congo River *Gymnallabes*, are also represented in the lake by

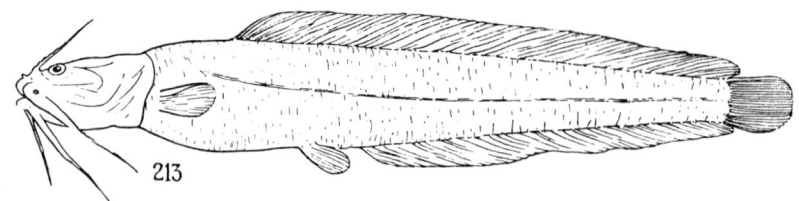

Tanganikallabes mortiauxi, from Poll, 1957.

Tanganikallabes which, along with *Dinotopterus*, is occasionally found in the crevices of the rock slopes.

While *Heterobranchus* might also be found under rock shelves, the author (nor apparently anybody else) has never discovered any of the four *Clarias* species (*C. liocephalus, C. mossambicus, C. ornatus* or *C. theodorae*) in such a habitat. This genus seems to be restricted to river affluents (or their estuaries at best).

Key to the Identification of the Genera of Clariidae of the Lake Tanganyika Basin (from M. Poll)

1. A rayed dorsal fin and an adipose fin present 2
   Only the rayed dorsal fin present; no adipose fin 3
2. Adipose fin large; sides of head protected by bony shields . . . .
   . . . . *Heterobranchus*
   Adipose fin short; sides of head not protected by bony shields; cranial roof shield reduced . . . . *Dinotopterus*
3. Head, at least in part, protected on sides by bony shields; cranial arch roof-shaped; head devoid of longitudinal median groove
   . . . . *Clarias*
   Sides of head not protected by bony shields; cranial arch not roof-shaped; strong longitudinal median groove . . . .
   . . . . *Tanganikallabes*

Clarias theodorae and dorsal view of head.

Key to the Identification of the Species of *Clarias* From the Lake Tanganyika Basin

1. Length of head less than 4 times in standard length; ventral fins equally distant from snout and tail.........*C. mossambicus*
   Length of head more than 4 times in standard length; ventrals closer to snout than to tail 2
2. Dorsal and anal fins joining with caudal base ......*C. theodorae*
   Dorsal and anal fins separate from caudal base 3
3. First ray of dorsal fin distant from head by half head length ....*C. ornatus*
   First ray of dorsal fin distant from head by head length ....*C. liocephalus*

Family MALAPTERURIDAE

The famous African electric catfish has apparently colonized the lake for a very long time, as it is found in all habitats and along the whole length of the lake. On rocky slopes, and even more on rocky outcrops isolated in the midst of huge sand plains when they offer appropriate shelters, they are quite common.

Malapterurus electricus. Photo courtesy of the New York Zoological Society.

The author knows of such an isolated place in a shallow area, where the concentration of electric cats and their average size reach an incredible level. In this area, one might say that there is one electric catfish at least 300 mm long (sometimes one meter long) every two or three meters along the rocky shelters. Squeezing a hand into these holes often results in a very jolting experience—but not dangerous for the diver who stays calm. The electric jolts appear to be less powerful than with specimens of an identical size in the Congo River. It is not at all impossible that the lake electric catfishes living in very conductive water (because of the high mineral salt content) need less power, with the result that direct contact provokes a less powerful electrical impulse. In the Congo River, on the contrary, the jolts are extremely powerful, and direct contact might be dangerous when wading chest-deep in the river. This might be due to the fact that the Congo *Malapterurus* needs more power to achieve the same protective or hunting jolt in poorly mineralized water. Anyway, it would be interesting to look into this problem and find an answer to the question.

What is rather difficult to explain is the low number of *Malapterurus* fry found in the places where the concentration of the large adults is highest. It appears from this observation that either they have special spawning grounds where they migrate for the spawn or that the losses are very high. Never, among the hundreds of *Malapterurus* discovered by the author and his team during five years of underwater fishing, was there one batch of babies discovered. Even when they are about 30 mm long, the baby electric catfishes are living on their own among the rubble.

Family CYPRINODONTIDAE

Eastern Africa is the poorest part of the continent for many species of fish mainly because it is poor in large and small river basins. In the case of the cyprinodonts, this holds especially true because the family seems to have proliferated much more in dense forest areas with high acidity and low mineralization of the water. The only three genera which are represented in East Africa are *Nothobranchius*, of which none have been found in the lake basin, *Aplocheilichthys* and the endemic lake genus and species, *Lamprichthys tanganicanus*.

Aplocheilichthys, represented by *A. pumilus*, lives in swamps and lagoons near the lake edge and is not found in the lake itself but all along the lake perimeter. The eggs seem to have a fantastic resis-

Aplocheilichthys pumilus. Photo by Dr. Herbert R. Axelrod.

tance to drought and to outside factors, if one might judge from the author's personal experience with these fish. Having to put wild caught plants in an outside artificially made breeding pool, the author's team collected *Ceratophyllum* in nearby swamps. To disinfect them from any snail or insect eggs, the plants were put into a strong solution of copper sulfate, knowing that most of the plants would rot away but that some stems would sprout anew and start growing. The plants remained in the solution for several hours and then were put into a freshly dug pool lined with new polyethylene sheeting. Fifteen days later there were young *Aplocheilichthys pumilus* fry swimming in the pool. The resistance of the eggs to unfavorable outside conditions might very well explain the very large area in which this species is found.

These tiny *Aplocheilichthys* are hardy and have fewer requirements as to their water conditions and diet than any other cyprinodont. They thrive in neutral or slightly acid water and are also at ease in a DH of 5 German degrees or more. They will take dried food without trouble and retain their original bronze-green metallic sheen. They are always active and not a bother to the other fish. What's more, they are very active, always on the move, and for the beginner have the added charm of easy spawning.

Lamprichthys tanganicanus is quite another matter. The only endemic cyprinodont in the lake, it is the giant of the family, reaching about 150 mm (a little less for the less colorful female). Far from being a swamp or an acid brook inhabitant like the other genera, it roams at will far from the shoreline, often in large schools, but sometimes all by itself. As such it is one of the fishes collected with the clupeids by the traditional native collecting methods or by the big commercial trawlers.

They are sometimes a nuisance for the diver when they follow him in his search for fishes. Always in search of food and inquisitive, they follow the diver everywhere, and whenever small fry try to escape the man's hands or nets and rush into the open, the *Lamprichthys* set upon it and the diver's victim is at once done with.

At other times when two divers haul a big net to catch some of the bigger lake fishes, hundreds of *Lamprichthys* follow the divers and get entangled in the nets. It's a nuisance to remove them afterwards from the net, and there is a considerable loss of time.

The spawning of *Lamprichthys* in the lake has been observed very often. In typical roamer fashion a pair meets in midwater, both partners descend to the rock substrate on the lake slopes, find at random a small corner (for example where two flat slabs join) and, swimming very slowly, lay and at the same time fertilize the eggs. The female is closest to the rock, the male a little behind (his mouth about at the female's ventrals) and in the open water both lean on their sides a little. The eggs and the male's sperm are totally clear and invisible. The author or members of his team have never seen a *Lamprichthys* egg, as it is invisible. The shape of the egg could only be guessed at in the lake by its apparently different refraction than the surrounding water. This phenomenon, or the smell of the eggs, might attract the predators living on or around the nearby rocks, since they rush to the spawning site as soon as the *Lamprichthys* descend to spawn. They lay in wait a few centimeters away and, as soon as the cyprinodonts depart, jump on the place where the eggs have been laid, apparently not missing many of them. Thus not many of the eggs stand a chance to survive, laid as they are on bare slabs amid countless predators.

But some do survive, enough of them to insure the survival of many young *Lamprichthys*. Two facts are noteworthy: first, this pelagic fish lays its eggs on unprotected grounds against great odds and has fully transparent eggs—which is the best protection it could afford its spawns under the circumstances; second, several rock-dwelling cichlids, especially *Telmatochromis caninus* and *T. temporalis*, know what it means when they see two *Lamprichthys* descending along the rock slabs. They stop at once what they are doing at the time, come near and several of them stand watch and wait until the spawning is finished. As soon as the *Lamprichthys* start to leave, they rush toward the eggs. The pairs are not a foot away before the eggs have already been gobbled up. Many times we have seen this scenario happen with a growing feeling of the apparent waste. But then, there are so many *Lamprichthys* around that it doesn't matter, and it feeds the other fishes.

The *Lamprichthys* fry, as might be expected from schooling pelagic fishes, bunch together apparently as soon as they are born, and it is not rare to swim across a school several hundreds or even thousands strong. Like their parents, the young *Lamprichthys* wander around endlessly, falling prey, like the clupeids, to the big roaming predators.

To catch and acclimatize these cyprinodonts is quite a problem, in fact just the reverse of the problem with cyprinodonts from the acid forest brooks. *Lamprichthys* is hard to acclimatize to another type of water when the mineral salts it is used to are missing. The fish develop sores and fungus on the body and die in a matter of days. Once acclimatized, they are one of the most gorgeous freshwater fishes ever. The body is an iridescent aquamarine, sparkling with each move of the fish. Even the tail flashes subtle green-blue because of the presence of minute scales well into the rayed fin. The male's body is still more enhanced by half a dozen horizontal rows of bright aquamarine spots, the long anal fin, the dorsal fin loosely hanging over the side of the body and both fins being an overall pale orange color. The fish is incredibly beautiful—there is no better word.

Lamprichthys can be kept in a tank provided much attention is given to a few rules. The DH should be around 10° to 14°; the temperature should be about the lake average (26-26.5°C); a little salt should be added to the water (perhaps even magnesium sulfate); and lots of room should be provided as the rather large fish are moving around most of the time. Feeding is easy. The fish will rush toward any type of food dropped on the surface of the water and eat it. But, as it is endowed with a ravenous appetite, it should be fed several times a day to compensate for an apparently rapid metabolism.

Key to the Identification of the Genera Cyprinodontidae of the Lake Tanganyika Basin

Dorsal fin with 10 to 12 rays, anal fin with 14 to 16 ....*Aplocheilichthys*
Dorsal fin with 13 to 16 rays; anal fin with 24 to 30 ..*Lamprichthys*

The genus *Lamprichthys* includes, at the moment, only one valid species, *L. tanganicanus*. At one time another species, *L. curtianalis* David 1936, had been described. This was later placed in synonymy with *L. tanganicanus*. The author believes that there are probably two different species of *Lamprichthys* in the lake, one with a long anal fin, the other with a much shorter one. For this reason, until the matter is settled the key to the identification of both species of *Lamprichthys* is given.

Key to the Species of *Lamprichthys* of the Lake Tanganyika Basin

Anal fin 2.6 to 3.2 in standard length; posterior rays of anal fin longer than anterior rays; eye 3.0 to 3.6 times in head ....*L. tanganicanus*
Anal fin 3.5 to 4 in standard length; anterior rays of anal fin longer than posterior rays; eye 2.75 to 3.0 in head length .*L. curtianalis*

Family CENTROPOMIDAE

The *Lates*, or Nile perches as they are called, are represented in most of central Africa, aside from Lake Tanganyika, by the species *Lates niloticus*. This common fish is found in lakes, large rivers and streams from the Nile to the Niger and often reaches enormous proportions. The few other known *Lates* species are restricted to large lakes. Fossil *Lates* remains have been discovered, especially around Lake Rudolph, of which some belong to a now extinct species. It is thus rather queer that Lake Tanganyika, which lacks *L. niloticus*, has been the birthplace of as many as five other species, separated into two genera, one of which is a dwarf form. It is probable that the five lake species have evolved from one or several forms of now extinct fishes and that *Lates niloticus* never entered the lake basin area before the lake was formed. One argument, in addition to the others, is to think that the lake area never was part of the Nile basin. Although the Congo River harbors *Lates niloticus*, it is possible that the fish couldn't (or wouldn't) climb the successive steps from the Lukuga outlet cascading down from the lake toward the Congo River.

The Nile perch is one of the giants among the African fish fauna; many specimens have been caught with a weight well in excess of 150 kg, and the record is over 200 kg. Not one of the three Tanganyika *Lates* reaches such a tremendous size, but they are very important as food fish for the people living on the lake shores and even farther inland. The lake perches live in schools, prey on the clupeids roaming in the lake and make up a very significant portion, if not the most important part, of all the non-clupeid commercial catch.

They are caught at night when the powerful lamps used for fishing have attracted the clupeids toward the nets. All the predators, *Lates, Luciolates, Bathybates, Haplotaxodon, Hemibates*, etc., follow this growing concentration of their prey and gorge themselves to the limit. While the splashing fight goes on they are getting trapped in the net. This is how the predators of the lake are caught (along with their victims). The catch is so important that at

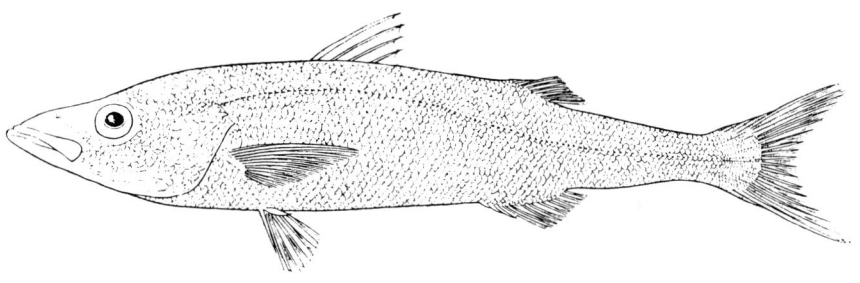

Luciolates stappersii, from Poll, 1957.

least two countries bordering the lake, Burundi and Zambia, are now planning to export to foreign markets frozen or smoked lake perches.

Needless to say, centropomids are not aquarium fishes, but research into the possibility of their being introduced into foreign waters might prove valuable. All over Africa, *Lates* flesh is considered as the very best and fetches very high prices.

Lates apparently breed close to the shores, although spawning has never been observed, since many young *Lates*, often in schools, are discovered along the rocky shoreline hidden in small patches of reed stems. The size of the fry increases with depth and it is not rare to find several dozen fish 25 to 30 cm in a small school 10 meters or a little more deep. The density of the schools and the size of the fish might vary considerably, but it appears probable from the data available that the schools are made up from specimens of a rather uniform size.

Key to the Identification of the Genera of Centropomidae of the Lake Tanganyika Basin (from M. Poll)

Body depth less than 4.0 in standard length; the two dorsal fins contiguous .... *Lates*

Body depth 4 or more times in standard length; the two dorsal fins well separated................................. *Luciolates*

Key to the Identification of the Species of *Lates* (from M. Poll)

1. Anal fin truncated; caudal fin crescent-shaped or at least concave; eye small, 3.6 to 6.4 (adult) in head; interorbital space 5.5 to 7.5 in head; gill rakers 12 to 15 .... *L. microlepis*

   Anal fin rounded; caudal fin rounded or straight; interorbital space 7 to 10 times in head; not more than 10 gill rakers....2

2. Eye very large, 3.1 to 4.8 in head, D. VII+I+I, 11-13; in specimens over 25 cm the 8th spine is between the two dorsals; 95 to 120 scales in lateral line; caudal rounded or straight; 9 or 10 gill rakers .... *L. mariae*

   Eye medium, 2.2 to 6.8 (adult) times in head; D. VII+I, 12 or 13; 88-99 scales in lateral line; caudal rounded; 5 to 8 gill rakers .... *L. angustifrons*

Key to the Identification of the Species of *Luciolates* (from M. Poll)

Body depth 4 in standard length .... *L. brevior*

Body depth 4.5-5.0 in standard length .... *L. stappersii*

Family ANABANTIDAE

The only anabantid in the lake area is *Ctenopoma muriei*, one of the more elongate forms of the genus. It is apparent that the many *Ctenopoma* from the Congo basin virgin forests and savannahs, all of them swamp or slow brooks dwellers and rather sluggish, could not climb the fast currents of the Lukuga outlet toward a habitat which is not to their liking. *Ctenopoma* are basically soft and acid water fish. The lake doesn't offer them this type of water. One might thus say that the only species of *Ctenopoma* to live in the lake basin is not a recent invader but was one of the few species which have spread eastward from the main grounds of the genus in central West Africa.

C. muriei, which is not one of the most striking species of the genus, is a dull fish with a brown body and a few black specks scattered at random. It is a typical swamp inhabitant and has never been collected, or even seen, in the lake itself.

Family MASTACEMBELIDAE
Key to the Identification of the Species of *Mastacembelus* of the Lake Tanganyika Basin (from H. Matthes)

I. *Anus more or less halfway between snout and tail*
   A. Strong preorbital and preopercular spines; D. XXVI-XXIX; 26-28 scales in a transverse line; pectoral fin 2.25 to 3.3 in head; body plain copper, belly white......*M. cunningtoni*
   B. Head spines in young, but tiny or absent (hidden under skin) in adults; D. XXV-XXIX; 32-35 transverse scales; pectoral 3.3 to 4.7 in head..................*M. moorii*
   C. Head spines absent (seldom a small preopercular spine in young)
      1) D. XXIX-XXXIV; pectoral fin 6.5-14.75 times in head; body plain purple.................*M. micropectus*
      2) D. XXX-XXXV; pectoral fin 2.7-4.75 in head; rostral appendix 1.0 to 1.9 times longer than eye; body dark and marbled........................*M. frenatus*
      3) D. XXXIV-XXXV; pectoral fin 3.5 to 4.3 in head; rostral appendix 0.6 to 1.05 times longer than eye; body pale yellowish with darker spots.............*M. flavidus*

II. *Anus much closer to tail than to snout*
   A. Preorbital spine present
      1) D. XXIII-XXV; body 6.6 to 7.5 times longer than high; flat, plain colored body..............*M. platysoma*
      2) XXIX-XXXII; body 10.5 to 11.5 times longer than high; crescent-shaped stripes present...........*M. ellipsifer*
   B. No preorbital spine
      1) D. XXIII-XXV; mouth low; body 8.9-10.5 times longer than high; body with dark stripes on pale brown background.............................*M. zebratus*
      2) D. XXX-XXXII; mouth low; body 10.6-12.1 times longer than high; saddle-like bars on back, body pale beige..........................*M. plagiostomus*
      3) D. XXXIII-XXXVI; mouth terminal; head 5.75 to 6.9 times in standard length; 25 to 30 transverse scales; countless whitish dots on a brown body.............
         ....*M. albomaculatus*
      4) D. XXXVI-XLII; head 7.0-8.8 in standard length; 17-21 transverse scales; many vermiculated stripes on a thin, light brown body...................*M. tanganicae*

Mastacembelus moorii. Photo by Glen S. Axelrod.

III. *Anus much closer to snout than to tail*
    D. XXII (young)—XXXIII; body pale beige; unmistakable viper-like head with eyes very much in front of head ......
....*M. ophidium*

All the mastacembelid eels inhabit the lake proper but occupy different habitats. *M. cunningtoni*, with its light and rather metallic copper color, a pure white belly, and the tail edged in black and white, is a typical sand-dweller in front of sand beaches and even around river estuaries. *M. moorii* is at ease in any type of water, be it crystal clear or murky, but as with all other spiny eels, always on rock. It is also the largest of all species of *Mastacembelus* the author has seen in Africa. Two large specimens caught recently measured, respectively, 75 cm and 1050 grams for the male, and 70 cm and 950 grams for the female. Some specimens seen under water were even larger than that.

Although some Congo River species of *Mastacembelus* are known to bury themselves in the sand, the lake rock-dwelling eels prefer to hide in rock crevices and holes, from which their head juts

Holotypes of four species of *Mastacembelus:* (a) *M. micropectus* (b) *M. flavidus* (c) *M. plagiostomus* (d) *M. zebratus*, from Poll, 1962.

out waiting for prey to pass by. Their ethology and habitat is thus very similar to the ecological niche of the moray eel in the ocean. Spawning has never been observed but should take place near the shoreline, as periodically huge quantities of baby eels are collected by the thousands. *M. ophidium*, with its vicious looking snake-like head, seems to choose particular bays in which to spawn. It is entirely possible, at least in view of the tremendous amounts of fry caught by native fishermen at the same time and the same place, that spawning occurs at the same time for all the *M. ophidium* eels in the neighborhood. The losses among these 7 to 10 cm fry must be tremendous, as the species is not as common as many others.

Several of these eels are well suited for aquarium life and match the best looking species of *Mastacembelus* from the Far East with contrasting colors. Among them are *M. ellipsifer*, *M. zebratus* and *M. plagiostomus*. But all three are rare fishes, as is *M. platysoma* with its laterally compressed body and funny, sea-horse like way of moving around with the body upright and bend into an "S".

No species of *Mastacembelus* should be trusted with fish small enough to be swallowed as all of them are carnivorous and fish eaters. The smallest specimens of the different eels can be kept without trouble if provided with enough crevices to hide in and proper food. Although they will thrive on shrimps and worms, they will also take to dried food.

The most common species, and fortunately also one of the smallest and most harmless, is *M. tanganicae*. With its slender, well patterned body, it is probably the best of all eels from the lake for the aquarium.

Family **TETRAODONTIDAE**

The puffer fish are poorly represented in the lake basin. Only a single species, *Tetraodon mbu*, has been discovered in the Malagarazi delta, and it is found nowhere else around the lake. This species, probably the largest among the African puffer fish, reaches close to a meter in length. The widest variety of African puffers is found in the Congo River basin—four species (*T. mbu*, *M. schoutedeni*, *M. miurus* and *M. duboiso*).

It is a well known fact that the puffers bury themselves in sand and mud and lie there in wait for an eventual prey animal to pass by, although basically they are shell-eaters or at most scavengers of dead fish. Big specimens of *T. mbu* can easily crush the thickest oyster or mussel shell with their parrotbeak-shaped teeth and are to be handled with care.

Tetrodon mbu. Photo by Hilmar Hansen.

About ten years ago, when collecting in the Stanley Pool, the author discovered hundreds of *T. mbu* carcasses rotting in the sun. There were no other dead fish around and, as the bodies were lined up along a huge sandbar on the main river channel, they could not have died from suffocation or lack of oxygen. This species had probably suffered either from a very specific disease or from feeding on poisoned or sick shells. It was the only such mass casualty ever observed for a single species.

In the lake, puffers, except perhaps *T. mbu*, would stand little chance of settling down. It is quite impossible for these sluggish and bulky fishes, which are definitely poor swimmers, to come up through the Lukuga rapids from the Congo River.

The lake puffer fish population might thus be considered as closed to any newcomers of the family.

Bibliography

BOULENGER, G.A. 1915. *Catalogue of the fresh-water fishes of Africa in the British Museum (Nat. Hist.).* 3 vol. Brit. Mus. (Nat. Hist.), London.

BREDER, C.M. 1959. "Studies on Social Grouping of Fishes," *Bull. Am. Mus. Natur. Hist.*, 171: 393-482.

CAPART, A. 1955. "L'echosondage dans les lacs du Congo Belge, Techniques et resultats acquis," *Bull. Agric. Congo Belge:* 1075-1104.

COULTER, G.W. 1967a. Unpub. thesis. Queen's Univ., Belfast.

―――――. 1967b. "Low apparent oxygen requirements of deep-water fishes in Lake Tanganyka," *Nature, Lond.*, 215: 317-318.

EIBL-EIBESFELDT, I. 1962. "Freiwasser beobachtungen zur Deutung des Schwarm verhaltens verschiedenen Fishe," *Z. Tierpsychol.*, 19: 165-182.

FRYER, G. and ILES, T.D. 1972. *The Cichlid Fishes of the Great Lakes of Africa.* T.F.H. Publications, New Jersey.

GOSSE, J.P. 1956. "Dispositions speciales de l'appareil branchial des *Tilapia* et *Citharinus*," *Annls. Soc. r. zool. Belg.*, 86: 303-308.

―――――. 1963. "Le milieu aquatique et l'ecologie des poissons dans la region de Yangambi," *Annales Mus Afr. Cen.*, 116: 113-270.

GREENWOOD, P.H. 1964. "Explosive speciation in African Lakes," *Proc. R. Instn. Gt. Br.*, 40: 256-269.

―――――, and TREWAVAS, E. 1955. "Scale-eating habits of African cichlid fishes," *Nature, Lond.*, 175: 1089-1090.

HULOT, A. 1956. "Apercu sur la question de la peche industrielle aux lacs Kivu, Edouard et Albert," *Bull. Agric. Congo Belge,* 47: 3-68.

KENLEYSIDE, M.H.A. 1955. "Some aspects of the Schooling behaviour of Fish," *Behav.*, 8: 183-248.

KUFFERATH, J. 1952. "Le milieu biochimique," *Result. scient. Explor. hydrobiol. Tanganyka* (1946-1947):31-47.

LORENZ, K. 1966. *On aggression.* Methuen, London.
MARLIER, G. 1959. "Observations sur la biologie littorale du lac Tanganyka," *Revue Zool. Bot. Afr.*, 59:164-183.
─────── and LELEUP, N. 1954. "A curious ecological "niche" among the fishes of Lake Tanganyka," *Nature,* Lond., 174: 935-936.
MATTHES, H. 1959a. "Un cichlide nouveau du lac Tanganyka, *Julidochromis transcriptus,*" *Revue Zool. Bot. Afr.*, 60:1-2.
─────── . 1959b. "Un cichlide nouveau du lac Tanganyika, *Petrochromis orthognathus,*" *Revue Zool. Bot. Afr.*, 60:3-4.
─────── . 1960. "Note sur la reproduction des poissons au lac Tanganyika," *C.S.A. 3rd Symp. Hydrobiol. Major Lakes:* 107-112.
─────── . 1961. "*Boulengerochromis microlepis,* a Lake Tanganyika fish of economical importance," *Bull. Aquat. Biol.*, 3: 1-15.
─────── . 1962a. "Poissons nouveaux ou interessants du lac Tanganyika et du Ruanda," *Annales Musee Afr. Cent.* 111: 27-88.
─────── . 1962b. "L'exploration sous-lacustre du lac Tanganyika," Africa-Tervuren, 8: 1-11.
─────── . 1964. "Les poissons du lac Tumba et de la region d'Ikela," *Annales Musee Afr. Centr.*, 126: 1-204.
MORROW, J.E. 1948. "Schooling behaviour in fishes," *Quart. Rev. Biol.*, 23: 27-38.
NELISSEN, M. 1975. "Sound production by *Simochromis diagramma* (Gunther), Pisces Cichlidae," *Acta Zoolog & Pathol. Antverpiensia,* 61/75: 19-24.
─────── . 1975. "Contribution to the ethology of *Simochromis diagramma* (Gunther), Pisces Cichlidae," *Acta Zool. & Pathol. Antverpiensia,* 61/75: 31-46.
POLL, M. 1939. "Poissons," *Explor. Parc National Albert. Miss. H. Damas. (1935-1936),* Fasc. 6: 1-73.
─────── . 1939. "Poissons," *Explor. Parc National Albert. Miss G.E. De Witte (1933-1935),* Fasc. 24: 1-81.
─────── . 1950. "Histoire du peuplement et origine des especes de la faune ichtyologique du lac Tanganyika," *Annales Soc. Revue Zool. Belge,* 81: 111-140.
─────── . 1953. "Poissons non-cichlidae," *Resultats scientifiques Exploration Hydrobiologique du Lac Tanganyika* (1946-1947), III, Fasc. 5a: 1-251.
─────── . 1956. "Poissons cichlidae," *Resultats Scientifiques Exploration Hydrobiologique du Lac Tanganyika* (1946-1947), III, Fasc 5b: 1-619.

———. 1974. "Contribution a la faune Ichthyologique du lac Tanganyika d'apres les recoltes de P. Brichard," *Rev. Zool. Afr.*, 88(1).

——— and H. MATTHES. 1962. "Trois poissons remarquables du lac Tanganyika," *Annales Musee Afr. Centr.*, 111: 1-126.

——— and THYS VAN DEN AUDENAERDE. 1974. "Genre nouveau *Triglachromis* propose pour *Limnochromis otostigma* (Regan), Cichlidae du lac Tanganyika," *Rev. Zool. Afr.*, 88(1).

THYS VAN DEN AUDENAERDE, D.F.E. 1964. "Revision systematique des especes Congolaises du genre *Tilapia* (Pisces Cichlidae)," *Annales Mus. Afr. Centr.*, 124: 1-155.

WICKLER, W. 1902 "Ei-Attrappen und Maulbruten bei Afrikanischen Cichliden," *Z. Tierpsychol.*, 19(2): 129-164.

———. 1963. "Zur klassifikation der Cichlidae, am Beispiel der Gattungen *Tropheus, Petrochromis, Haplochromis, Hemihaplochromis*, n. gen.," *Senckenbergiana biologica*, 44(2): 83-96.

INDEX

(Page numbers printed in bold refer to illustrations and photographs.)

Algae, 44, 45
Amphilidae, 425-6
Amphilius platychir, 364, 425
Aplocheilichthys, 430-1
   pumilus, 372, 431
Anabantidae 436
Aquatic plants, 22
Argulus, 28
Asprotilapia, 158
   leptura, 132, 159
Astatoreochromis, 159, 162
   alluaudi, 159
   straelini, 133, 159, 162
Auchenoglanis occidentalis, 420, **420**
Aulonocranus, 162-3
   dewindti, 133, 162-3, **163**
Azolla, 22

Bagridae, 416
Bagrus docmac, 417, 418-9
Barbus, 411
   nicholsi, 411
Barilius, 415
   ubangensis, 352, 415
Bathybates, 163, 166-7, 170
   ferox, **136**
   leo, 166
Behavior of sand-dwellers, 111
Behavior of rock-dwellers, 111-2
Bonds to light, depth, 65
Boulengerochromis, 61, 170-1
   microlepis, 55, **136**, 170-1, **171**
Boulengerina annulata, 29
Bridges and fords, 83-6
Bryconaethiops boulengeri, 404, **405**
Buccal incubation, 107

Calcite deposit, 52
Callochromis, 171, 172, 184-5, 178
   macrops melanostigma, **137**, 174, **175**, 178
   pleurospilus, **140**, 175
Cardiopharynx, 178-9
   schoutedeni, **141**, 178, **179**
Centropomidae, 434-5
Ceratophyllum, 22
Ceratopteris, 22
Chalinochromis, 129, 179, 182-3
   brichardi, 44, 114, 115, 118, 182-3, **183**
Chara, 22
Characidae, 402-4

Chemical analysis (lake water), 17
Chiloglanis, 364
   lukugae, 423
Chrysichthys, 418
   species, 356
Citharinidae, 405-7
Citharinus gibbosus, 345, **406**
Clarias, 427
Clupeidae, 398-400
Crocodiles, 29-31, 53
Crocodilus niloticus, 29
Crustacea, 27-9
Ctenopoma muriei, 377, 436
Cunningtonia, 186-7
   longiventralis, **186**
Cyathopharynx, 187, 190-1
   furcifer, **148**, **149**, **152**, 187, 190
Cyphotilapia, 191
   frontosa, **153**, **156**, **157**, 191, **195**, 195, 198-9, **199**
Cyprinidae, 407-15
Cyprinodontidae, 430-3

Dinopterus cunningtoni, 427
Direct buccal incubation, 109
Distichodus
   fasciolatus, 348
   sexfasciatus, 348, **406**
Dynamic form, 88

Ecology
   Coastal rock habitats, 50
   River estuaries & swamps, 51
   Rocky shores, 59, 62
   Sand floors & slopes, 54-5
Ectodus, 202-3
   descampsii, 202-3, **203**
Egg ocelli, **139**
Endemism, 76-82
   Cichlids, 76
   Non-cichlids, 78
Engraulicypris minutus, 415
Eretmodus, 52, 203, **203**
   cyanostictus, **160**, **161**, 206, 210
   teeth, 207

Feeding and teeth, 63
Fishes in river estuaries, swamps, 51, 54-5, 58-9

Genetic dynamism, 87-94
Grammatotria, 210-11
   lemairei, **161**, 211, **211**
Gymnallabes, 427

445

Habitat in substratum, 63
Habitat off slopes, 63
Haplochromis, 211, 114
  benthicola, 165, 215
  burtoni, 139, 164
  horei, 168, 218
  cf. *pallidus*, 90
  pfefferi, 165, 218-9
  species, 169
Haplotaxodon, 219, 222
  microlepis, 219
Hemibates, 222-3
  stenosoma, 222
Heterobranchus, 27
  longifilis, 365, 427
Hippos, 31, 31
Hippopotamyrus discorhynchus, 400
Hydrocynus, 402
  goliath, 403

Iridina, 27
IRSAC, 34

Jellyfish, 23
Julidochromis, 180, 223
  dickfeldi, 172, 173, 239
  marlieri, 52, 85, 177, 227, 230, 230
  ornatus, 99, 100, 130, 131, 172, 176, 234-5, 235, 238
  regani, 181, 185, 231, 234
    regani affinis, 184, 185
    transcriptus, 176, 180, 181, 238,

Julidochromis, distribution of, 101
Julidochromis, races of, 102

Key to the genera of the family
  Bagridae, 417
  Centropomidae, 436
  Characidae, 402
  Citharinidae, 405
  Clariidae, 428
  Cyprinidae, 407-11
  Cyprinodontidae, 433
  Mastacembelidae, 437
  Mormyridae, 400
  Polypteridae, 397
Key to the genera of Lake Tanganyika fishes, 143, 146-7, 144-5, 158
Key to the species of genus
  Alestes, 404
  Amphilius, 426
  Barbus, 404
  Barilius, 414-5

Bathybates, 166-7, 170
Callochromis, 174
Chiloglanis, 425
Chrysichthys, 418-9
Clarias, 429
Engraulicypris, 415-6
Haplochromis, 214-5
Haplotaxodon, 222
Hydrocynus, 402
Labeo, 412
Lamprichthys, 434
Lamprologus, 247, 250-1, 258-9, 262
Lates, 436
Limnochromis, 303, 306
Limnotilapia, 314
Luciolates, 436
Mastacembelus, 437-8
Petrochromis, 33
Phyllonemus, 419
Plecodus, 343
Sarotherodon/Tilapia, 350
Simochromis, 355
Synodontis, 423-4
Telmatochromis, 370
Trematocara, 378-9
Varicorhinus, 411
Xenotilapia, 391-2
Kneria wittei, 402
Kneridae, 401

Labeo, 412
  cylindricus, 349
  lineatus, 349
  velifer, 413
Lake Tanganika, 12, 15, 32, 36, 37, 39, 42, 60, 61, 110, 81, 135
  Chemistry, 16
  Fauna (history), 19-20
  Geological history, 11-2
  Physical properties, 15-6
  Shores and floors, 19
  Turbidity, 16
Lake Tanganyika, List of fishes of, 67-76
Lake Tanganyika, Phases of evolution of, 13
Lamprichthys, 431, 434
  tanganicanus, 62, 369, 431
Lamprologus, 114, 132, 239, 242-3, 246-7, 250-1, 254-5, 258-9, 262
  attenuatus, 188, 262, 263
  brevis, 263
  brichardi, 1, 38, 43, 60, 122, 123, 189, 263, 266
  callipterus, 188, 266, 267
  christyi, 267
  compressiceps, 134, 192, 193, 267

cunningtonia, 196, 267, 270
elongatus, 51, 197, 270
fasciatus, 200, 270
furcifer, 200, 270, 271
hecqui, 271
kungweensis, 271
leleupi, 204, 205, 274-5, 275
leloupi, 275, 276
lemairei, 116, 201, 278
meeli, 278
modestus, 208, 278
moori, 208, 279
multifasciatus, 279
niger, 196, 121, 279
ocellatus, 213, 282
ornatipinnis, 213, 282
petricola, 282-3
pleuromaculatus, 217, 282, 283
profundicola, 286
pulcher, 286
savoryi, 220, 286-7
schreyeni, 287
sexfasciatus, 221, 290
signatus, 291
staecki, 224
stappersi, 291
toae, 224, 225, 291, 294
tetracanthus, 229, 254, 291
tretocephalus, 221, 228, 294
wauthioni, 294-5
    species, 118, 201, 204, 209, 216, 220, 229
Lates, 436
    mariae, 373
    microlepis, 79, 376
Leeches, 26
Lepidosirenidae, 396-7
Leptochromis, 295
    calliurum, 236, 295, 298
Leptoglanis, 416
    brevis, 421, 421
Leptotilapia tinanti, 92
Lernaea, 28
Lestradea, 299
    perspicax perspicax, 298
    perspicax stappersii, 299
Limnochromis, 302
    auritus, 241, 307, 306-7, 310
    leptosoma, 240
    microlepidotus, 237
    nigricans, 60
    nigripinnis, 236, 237, 240, 311
    permaxillaris, 302
Limnococnida cognoensis, 23
    tanganycanae, 23
Limnothrissa, 398
Limnotilapia, 129, 311, 314
    dardennei, 255, 314, 315

Lobochilotes, 315-6
    labiatus, 64, 126, 244, 248, 318, 318-9, 319
Lophiobagrus cyclurus, 353, 416, 419, 419
Luciolates stappersii, 435

Malapteruridae 429-430
Malapterurus electricus 368, 429
Marcusenius discorhynchus 401
Mastacembelidae 437-440
Mastacembelus 384
    ellipsifer 380, 440
    flavidus 377, 439
    micropterus 439
    moori 381, 438
    ophidium 381, 440
    plagiostomus 380, 439, 440
    tanganicae 384
    zebratus 439, 440
Micralestes stormsi 345
Mochokidae, 421
Mollusks 26-7
Mormyridae 400-1
Mud-dwellers 138
Myriophyllum 22

Najas 22
Neothauma 27
Nest-spawning 107
Nile crocodile 30
Non-cichlids 396
Nymphaea 22

Ophthalmochromis 129, 322
    nasutus 322-
    ventralis 248-9, 323, 323, 326
Opthalmotilapia 326-7
    boops 327
Orthochromis 327, 330
    malagaraziensis 330

Paraphractura 426
Pelmatochromis thomasi 91
Perissodus 330-1
    microlepis 252-3, 256, 331, 331, 334, 334
    straelini 347
Petrocephalus bovei 89
Petrochromis 129, 257, 354-5
    fasciolatus 256-7, 339
    polydon 64, 260, 335
    species 261, 265
Phyllonemus 416, 420
    typus 352
Phractura lindica 426
Plankton 21-2
Planorbis 20

447

Platythelphusa 26, 27
Plecodus 341-346-7
   paradoxus 272, 346
   straelini 268-9
Polygamous spawning 108
Polypteridae, Family 397
Polypterus 397
   endlicheri 344
   endlicheri congicus 397
   ornatipinnis 54, 397, 398
Populations (category) 35
Potamogeton 22
Potamon 27
Protopterus 396-7

Red tide (plankton) 49
Reganochromis 295
Relic forms 87
Reproductive modes of lake fishes 105
   Non-Cichlids 105
   Cichlids 107
   Rock-dwellers 118
   Sand-dwellers 112
   Mud-dwellers 138
Rift Valley 33
Rock-dwellers 118
Rubble floor 56
Ruzizi River 37

Sand-dwellers 112-114
Sandy habitat 51
Sarotherodon/Tilapia 350
   nilotica 350, 351
   tanganicae 272
Simochromis 354-5
   babaulti 277, 358, 359
   diagramma 280, 358
   marginatus 280
   species 273, 281
Spathodus 359, 362
   erythrodon 284, 362, 362
   marlieri 285, 362-3
Speciation problem in the lake 94
Sponges 24-26, 25, 46, 48, 69
Static forms 88
Stolothrissa 398
   tanganicae 399
Synodontis 423
   dhonti 424
   eurystomus 357
   multipunctatus 361

   petricola 360
   species 364

Tanganicodus 363, 366
   irsacae 285, 366, 366-7
Tanganikallabes mortiauxi 428
Telmatochromis 367, 370
   bifrenatus 288-9, 371, 374, 374
   caninus 292, 293, 371
   temporalis 293, 370
   vittatus 288
Tetraodontidae 440, 441
Tetraodon mbu 441
Tilapia rendalli 350, 351
Trematocara 374-375
   marginatum 375
   nigriforms 375
   stigmatum 375
   unimaculatum 375
Triglachromis 379
   otostigma 297, 382, 382-3
Tropheus 129, 132, 383, 386-8
   brichardi 308
   duboisi 98, 297, 300-1, 304, 385
   moorii 97, 125, 305, 308-9, 312-3, 316-7, 320-1, 324, 387
Tropheus, races of 96
Tropheus, "types" of 95
Tropheus, varieties 312, 324-5, 328-9
Tylochromis, 388-9
   polylepis 388

Utricularia 22

Vallisneria 22, 23
Varanus niloticus 32
Varicorhinus leleupanus 412

Water snakes 29

Xenochromis 389-90
   hecqui 389
Xenotilapia 129, 390-5
   boulengeri 352
   longispinnis 340
   longispinnis longispinnis 341
   melanogenys 341, 395
   ochrogenys 336, 394
   ochrogenys ochrogenys 336
Xenotilapia sima 113, 337, 394, 395
   spilopterus 352
   species 353